**H.C.P. Bell
Archaeologist of Ceylon and the Maldives**

H.C.P. Bell, C.C.S. (1851-1937),
Archaeological Commissioner of Ceylon, 1890-1912

H. C. P. BELL

Archaeologist of Ceylon and the Maldives

Bethia N. Bell and **Heather M. Bell**

1993
Archetype Publications

Published for the authors by Archetype Publications Ltd., 12-14 Hall Square, Denbigh, Clwyd, Wales LL16 3NU

© 1993 Archetype Publications and the Authors

British Library Cataloguing in Publication Data

Bell, Bethia N.

   H.C.P.Bell : Archaeologist of Ceylon and the Maldives
   I. Title II. Bell, Heather M.
   930.1092

   ISBN 1-873132-45-x

All rights reserved. No part of this publication may be reproduced, stored in a retrieval system, or transmitted in any form or by any means, electronic, mechanical, photocopying, recording or otherwise, without prior written permission of the publishers.

Distribution by
Archetype Publications
and the authors

Distribution in Sri Lanka
Lake House Bookshop
Colombo 2

Typeset by Archetype Publications Ltd.

Printed in Great Britain by Henry Ling Ltd., at the Dorset Press, Dorchester, Dorset

Contents

List of Illustrations and Maps		i - iii
List of Abbreviations		iv
Foreword		v - vi
Acknowledgements		vii
1	Forebears	1
2	Early Career	7
3	The Maldives : Pyrard and Other Visitors	16
4	Archaeology before 1890 : The Collecting of Records	26
5	Archaeology before 1890 : Epigraphy and Monuments	33
6	Kegalla	42
7	The Anuradhapura Establishment	49
8	From Exploration to Excavation	58
9	Jungle Trails	69
10	Jungle Dwellers	77
11	Sigiriya : The Ascents	83
12	Sigiriya : Glories Revealed	91
13	Protection of the Heritage	102
14	Restoration : The Great Dagabas	109
15	Delay : Reasons and Remedies	118
16	Anuradhapura and Mihintale	126
17	Outlying Sites	134

18	The Lithic Quest	141
19	Epigraphia Zeylanica	151
20	Monks and Monarchs	158
21	Bell and his Family	167
22	Polonnaruwa : Promontory, Quadrangle and Citadel	173
23	Polonnaruwa : Hindu and Buddhist Shrines	182
24	Polonnaruwa : The Brick 'Image Houses'	189
25	Successors	195
26	Active Retirement	205
27	The Maldives : Return	214
28	The Maldives : Dream Fulfilled	222
29	Maldive Studies : Anthropology, History and Archaeology	229
30	Maldive Studies : Language and Epigraphy	239
31	The Old Man	247
32	Bell as a Collector	257
33	The Man and his Work	266
Notes		276

APPENDICES

H.C.P. Bell Bibliography	297
Bell Genealogy	306
The Anuradhapura Anthem	309
Trees of Sri Lanka by Bethia N. Bell	312

INDEX   314

MAPS   I - V

List of Illustrations and Maps

H.C.P.Bell, C.C.S. (1851-1937),
    Archaeological Commissioner of Ceylon, 1890-1912   Frontispiece

General Robert Bell, Madras Artillery (1759-1844).   Betweeen pages
    Fought in the capture of Seringapatam, 1799   48 and 49
Colonel Amelius Beauclerk Fyers, R.E. (1829-1882),
    Surveyor General of Ceylon. Father-in-law of H.C.P.Bell
    (By courtesy of Dr. N.Seeley)
The Archaeological Commissioner's bungalow at Anuradhapura,
    after 1911 when portico was added. In the garden, Mrs. Bell and
    Zoë, Harry Amelius and his wife Ethel (née Howard)
Zoë, Malcolm and Cyril Bell with donkey at Anuradhapura
Cyril Bell with pet pelican at Anuradhapura
Zoë Bell at Anuradhapura with pet deer
H.C.P.Bell as Acting District Judge, when
    seconded to Kalutara (1894-1895)
H.C.P.Bell at Anuradhapura with his wife Renée Sabine (née Fyers)
    and children, Eva Laura (seated), Renée Isabel,
    Cyril Francis, Zoë Iris and Malcolm Fyers

Sigiri-gala, view from North, showing entry to   Between pages
    Lion Staircase in foreground   90 and 91
D.A.L.Perera at Sigirya, photographing the frescoes from mid-air
Bell with his children, Renée and Malcolm, viewing the
    frescoes in Pocket 'B' from raft slung from pocket 'A'
Bell and the children, with Perera copying the frescoes.
    'The troupe resting in Pocket 'B' after their "turn"'
Sigiri Lady with elaborate headdress, scattering flowers
    from her right hand
Bell climbing jungle-stick ladder up to the frescoes,
    carrying his son, Malcolm, with Renée following.
    'The troupe in their swinging-ladder act'

Rock ledge on north-west slope of summit of Sigiri-gala,
    above Watch-Cave. The drop below is some 300 feet.
    'The A.C. resting on the brink of the precipice'
Labour force, Sigirya, 1896. D.A.Perera beside Bell.
    'Note the graceful pose of the "Chief" at the back'
Bell with Renée and Malcolm posing on Kasyapa's Throne
    on top of Sigiri-gala
Sigiri-gala : Lion's right claws at entrance to Lion Staircase, 1898

Yapahuwa : sculptures on Third Staircase, leading to the   Between pages
    'Raja Maligawa'   188 and 189
The Kuttam Pokunas (Twin Ponds) at Anuradhapura,
    in course of restoration
Sedent Buddha at Vihare No.2, Pankuliya, Anuradhapura,
    raised and restored
Bell at a ruined monastery in the forest, Ritigala
The Archaeological Commissioner's camp at Sigirya.
    'Excellent 12 feet square Cawnpore tent, with straw- roofed
    maduwa or dining and sitting room shed'
Bear shot by Bell with aid of decoy buffalo, Sept. 11, 1897,
    near Veragoda rock on circuit in Tamankaduwa
Polonnaruwa : 'The Wata-Dage or Round Treasure-House',
    sketched by C.F.Gordon-Cumming in *Two Happy*
    Years in Ceylon
Polonnaruwa : Wata-da-ge, South stairs restored in 1907
Polonnaruwa : Rankot Vehera, uncleared
Cyril Bell and Phyllis (née Aitken) with children,
    Bethia Nancy and Heather Margaret, and the Forest Staff
    at Hoshangabad, C.P., India, circa 1923
John Still (1880-1941), Assistant to Archaeological
    Commissioner, 1902-1907. Author of *The Jungle Tide*
    (By courtesy of his daughter, Mrs. E.A.Thesiger)
Edward Russell Ayrton (1882-1914), Egyptologist, Archaeological
    Commissioner 1912-1914, drowned near Tissamaharama
    (By courtesy of the Committee of the Egypt Exploration Society)
H.C.P. Bell, with daughter Zoë, son Malcolm, his wife
    Dorris (née Murray-Clarke) and children Ira Daphne
    and Kenneth Murray at Dorwin, Kandy, 1935

John Bell with Lourdette Lambert and four of her five children :
    Tony, Marie, Christabel and Joe, circa 1946
H.C.P.Bell between Ahmad Didi, Secretary to the Sultan of the Maldives,
    and Abdul Majid Didi, Treasurer, 1922
    (By courtesy of Hassan Ahmad Maniku)
Dorris and Malcolm Bell in costumes from the Maldives.
    Dorris wears her hair in Maldive style, a flat chignon on
    the right side of the head
    (By courtesy of Daphne Bell)

Sketch map of Ceylon with Archaeological Sites	I
Anuradhapura, showing areas to be explored	II
Sigirya, the Rock and surroundings	III
Polonnaruwa	IV
Southern India and Ceylon with the Lakkadive and Maldive Islands	V

LIST OF ABBREVIATIONS

ASCAR	Archaeological Survey of Ceylon Annual Report
CALR	Ceylon Antiquary and Literary Register
CLR	Ceylon Literary Register
CO	Records of the Colonial Office, London
EZ	Epigraphia Zeylanica
JRAS	Journal of the Royal Asiatic Society of Great Britain and Ireland
JRASCB	Journal of the Royal Asiatic Society, Ceylon Branch
JRIBA	Journal of the Royal Institute of British Architects
MLRC	Monthly Literary Register and Notes and Queries for Ceylon
RAS	Royal Asiatic Society of Great Britain and Ireland
RASCB	Royal Asiatic Society, Ceylon Branch
SLNA	Sri Lanka National Archives
SP	Sessional Papers, Papers laid before the Legislative Council of Ceylon
TA(LR Suppl)	Tropical Agriculturalist (Literary Register Supplement)

Foreword

The career of H.C.P.Bell, first head of the Archaeological Department of Ceylon, has not been widely known outside the Island where he spent his life. When we were preparing to visit the country in 1981, Dr. Roland Silva, the then Archaeological Commissioner, invited us to give a lecture about our grandfather to the Sri Lankan Branch of the Royal Asiatic Society. This we delivered, drawing on a few family memories and his published work. We had no personal knowledge of him - having met him only once when very young children - and had none of his private papers in our possession. However, the still vivid memory of his work which we found in the country of his adoption led to the idea that we should write a full life of H.C.P.Bell.

This was the beginning of a voyage of discovery. Our work started in libraries and archives. The resources of the British Library and the London Library naturally proved invaluable. Particular mention should also be made of material found and help received in the library of the Royal Commonwealth Society, and in those of the India Office, the Foreign and Commonwealth Office (old Colonial Office), the School of African and Oriental Studies, and the Royal Asiatic Society in London. When working in Colombo we were kindly helped by Miss Srimathie De Soysa and her staff. She was then the Librarian of the Colombo Museum Library, which holds Bell's personal library and other material unobtainable in England.

In compiling our bibliography of Bell's own writings, in checking the writings of his time for references to his work, and in general research on the period, we had the priceless resource of H.A.I.Goonetileke's extensive bibliography of Ceylon. Much of the history of Bell's career is recorded in the pages of the Journal of the Royal Asiatic Society (Ceylon Branch), of which he was for so many years the Editor. Yet above all we have relied on Bell's own writings, for even his official reports are redolent of his personality and revelatory of his life. This is still more true of his official letters. We gratefully acknowledge permission to use Crown-copyright material from the Public Record Office in London, and archival material from the Records in Colombo and Kandy. We have drawn from the Stanmore Papers in the Manuscript Department of the British Library.

While conducting our researches in Sri Lanka in October 1987, we received unstinting hospitality from Dr. Roland Silva and his wife Neela in Colombo, and in Kandy from Professor P.L.Prematilleke of Peradeniya University. There, too, we were shown round by Dr. Nihal Karunaratne, who helped us to find some of the houses where Bell spent his retirement. Dr. A.C.Clarke helped us to obtain publicity through an article by Nalaka Gunawardena in *The Island*, which brought in useful information. One of the interesting contacts that we made was with Miss Nira Samarasinghe, descended from Bell's assistant D.A.L.Perera, and her family. Moreover, we became acquainted with members of our own family of whose existence we had been unaware. We met many of our cousins again in 1990, when we were being royally entertained by the Archaeological Department at the celebrations of its Centenary.

Acknowledgement is made in the Notes to each chapter to the sources upon which we have drawn. Special thanks must be given to Chris de Saram, who allowed us to make use of his thesis in the chapter on 'Bell as a Collector', and to Mrs. Thesiger, daughter of John Still, at one time Assistant to Bell, for permitting us to make long quotations from his famous book *The Jungle Tide*, to illustrate aspects of life at that period.

Others in Sri Lanka have helped us with their memories, or by drawing our attention to newspaper articles and other sources.

A.T.G.A.Wickramasuriya, grandson of W.M.Fernando who worked with Bell, and son of P.Don Ambrose of the next generation of archaeologists, let us use one of his historical articles, and family recollections. The Curator of the Kandy National Museum, Senarath Panawatta, gave us information from his collection of cuttings. Peter Jayasuriya helped us by sending photostats of interesting documents; and we have used an article by Raja de Silva, himself formerly Archaeological Commissioner, written in defence of Bell. Manel Fonseka drew our attention to information to be found in Archaeological Survey Reports written after Bell's death.

Dr. Urmila Phadnis, of Delhi University, whom we met when she was reading Bell's works on the Maldive Islands in the British Library, permitted us to quote her appreciation of Bell. In 1990 we were in the Republic of the Maldives, as honoured guests of President Maumoon Abdul Gayoom, for the celebration of 25 years of Independence. We met members of the National Centre for Linguistic and Historical Research; also descendants of those who had worked with Bell. We found that his Monograph, which had been recently reprinted, was still valued by scholars. The pioneering work of Bell is fully recognised in the 1980 study by Andrew D.W.Forbes 'Archives and resources for Maldivian history', published in *South Asia* n.s. 3.

We have said that we knew nothing personally of our grandfather; but other members of our family in England, Canada and Sri Lanka have provided insights and anecdotes, both from recollections and from written memoirs. To all of these, and to any others whose names are not formally recorded, we tender our thanks. We received invaluable support from Dr. Nigel Seeley, once a colleague at the Institute of Archaeology in London, who provided technical advice and a photograph from his collection, and gave us one of Bell's original letters. We are especially grateful to our friends Professor Prematilleke and Dr. Nanda Prematilleke, who encouraged us throughout our enterprise. Publication has been achieved through the good advice and efficiency of James Black of Archetype Publications, and we also thank the editor, Jenny Oates, for suggestions towards the reshaping of the book and for her meticulous corrections, and Mic and Aubrey Claridge for the art work.

We are responsible for the emphases and for any errors in the final version. For Sri Lankan and Maldive names we have, in quotations, reproduced their authors' own transliterations; hence variants occur, e.g. for *Mahawansa* and *Qazi*. In our text we have adhered to Bell's spellings and his identifications of monuments. In particular we have retained the names of Abhayagirya for the Eastern Dagaba at Anuradhapura, and Jetawanarama for the Northern Dagaba, since Bell long maintained these incorrect attributions.

Bethia N. Bell
Heather M. Bell

Acknowledgements

All sources of quoted passages are indicated in the Notes to the chapters where they occur. We wish to acknowledge with thanks permission to quote from the following sources:

To Lake House Investments Ltd., Colombo, for two passages from S.Paranavitana *Glimpses of Ceylon's Past* (1972). To UNESCO for an extract from *Ceylon Paintings from Temple, Shrine and Rock*, UNESCO World Art Series (1957). To Associated Newspapers of Ceylon Ltd., Colombo, for three passages from A.C.G.Wijeyekoon *Recollections* (1951). To Oxford University Press for a passage from S.Paranavitana *Sigiri Graffiti* 2 Vols. published for the Government of Ceylon (1951); to the same publishers for a passage from *Epigraphia Zeylanica*, Vol. IV, published for the Government of Ceylon (1943). To Random House U.K. Ltd., and the Estate of Leonard Woolf, for permission to quote a passage from L.Woolf *Growing : an Autobiography of the Years 1904-1911*, published by the Hogarth Press in 1961. To the journal ARTIBUS ASIAE, Museum Rietburg Zurich for a passage from an article by D.T.Devendra 'Seventy years of Ceylon archaeology' in *Artibus Asiae* (1959). To Tisara Prakasakayo Ltd., Dehiwala, for a passage from an article by H.A.I.Goonetileke 'Writings on Ceylon Epigraphy' *Ceylon Historical Journal* (1960). To the Committee of the Egypt Exploration Society for an extract from H.A.Hall's obituary article on Edward Ayrton in the J*ournal of Egyptian Archaeology* (1915); and also for an accompanying photograph of Ayrton. To the British Library for permission to reproduce a map of Anuradhapura in the copy held by the Library in H.C.P.Bell *First Report on the Archaeological Survey of Anuradhapura*.

To our ancestors in 'the dark backward and abysm of time', to each other, patient collaborators, and to the ever-spreading branches of the family tree

1

Forebears

Harry Charles Purvis Bell, the first head of the Archaeological Survey of Ceylon, arrived in the island in 1873, having been appointed Writer in the Ceylon Civil Service on July 10. He remained there for the rest of his long life, apart from three brief visits to the Maldive Islands, and one cricketing tour in Madras. He was one of the many Englishmen who found not only a career but a raison d'être in a country and culture of another people. Although he sent his children back to England to school, he never at any time seems to have considered returning there himself. He lived out his retirement in the beautiful town of Kandy, complaining bitterly of the cold. In 1934 he wrote to Father Vossen of the Papal Seminary:

> Kandy nights are most treacherous (70,68,66,60(!),63,61(!),68) to one who became a 'salamander' after 23 continuous years of Anuradhapura's (to me) delightful dry heat.[1]

He came of a family with a long tradition of life in the East, although his forebears had served in India, not Ceylon. It started with his great-grandfather Robert Bell, an ebullient Irishman of Scottish extraction who has left an entertaining, though incomplete, memoir of his life as a soldier in the Madras Artillery in the days of the East India Company.

Robert Bell was born in Dublin in 1761 and was placed by his parents under the guardianship of a relation, John Bell. When he was seventeen his guardian died, and he found himself without occupation or visible means of support. He decided to enlist as a private in the service of the East India Company, and his memoir gives his reasons with disarming frankness:

> I was like many youths of similar age at that period in Dublin, exposed to, and anxious to participate in, many pursuits beyond my very limited means, or in fact without any means whatever. Such pursuits cannot be followed without expense, and such in my case being incompatible, I felt the propriety and indeed the necessity, of detaching myself from such habits as I had inconsiderately been led into.

> At this time - 1778 - Captain Brooke of the East India Service was employed in Ireland to recruit for that service, and his Placards and highly coloured descriptions of Honor and Glory were liberally distributed thro' the Capital. This appeared to afford me a good opportunity of flying from the danger that threatened disgrace by a continuance of idleness and unwarrantable expenses.

> Accordingly I paid a visit to the source of Honor and Glory - where, without any previous acquaintance or communication with, I met 3 or 4 lads about my own age who were Commoners of Trinity College and who I believe had recently been concerned in some irregularity or breach of College Orders. The Captain's levée that day was rather unusual - and in justice to the memory of that Officer I bear testimony to his Gentlemanly and Liberal conduct in our reception. He forcibly pointed out the

impropriety of Gentlemen engaging on the terms he was authorized to offer - and strenuously recommended the party to relinquish the intention or at all events to reconsider it.

At a subsequent interview some of the Party, feeling the justice of the Captain's observations, retracted - but two of the aforementioned lads, and some others with myself, unequivocally engaged to serve in the East India Company as private Soldiers.

On the arrival of the volunteers in Madras in January 1779 they found that war had broken out with the French and they were welcomed and immediately promoted as cadets in the Madras Artillery.

Robert, in his memoir, specifically disclaims the 'character of Historiographer of Indian Warfare'; his object was personal recollection. A complete account of the military affairs of the period would indeed have taxed his pen, as they were of considerable complexity. During his time of service the East India Company was moving from its original position as a trading company with fortified posts to becoming a dominant power, with much territory under direct control and further large areas under general 'protection'. This change of policy was accepted with considerable reluctance by the Directors of the Company, who were primarily interested in making money by trading; its gradual evolution had much to do with the continual efforts of the French to regain the position which they had lost by their defeat in the Seven Years War. They stirred up war, but the wars led to further conquests by the English.

The French encouraged the Indian rulers who opposed the English, or who opposed other Indian rulers temporarily allied to the English, and when at war with England in other parts of the world sent out military or naval expeditions of their own. This policy was intermittently pursued by all French governments, those of the Ancien Régime and that of Revolutionary France, and it culminated in Napoleon's expedition to Egypt in 1798.

As far as the Madras Government was concerned their chief enemy in India was the Sultan of Mysore, a Mohammedan ruler of a Hindu state on the opposite side of South India, and so Robert, as an artillery officer, was involved in the 2nd, 3rd, and 4th Mysore wars. He gives some details of his own adventures in all these campaigns, but of greatest interest are his accounts of his participation in the last of these, which ended in the siege of Seringapatam and the death of Tippoo Sultan, and his part in the expedition from India to join in the battle in Egypt.

In an article by May Poynter, a grand-daughter of Robert through his second wife, in the *Journal of the Royal Artillery*, we read:

There is a well-known picture by a Scottish artist, Sir Robert Porter, of the taking of Seringapatam, copies and engravings of which are often found in old Scottish families and houses. In it the subject of this memoir is depicted as a Major of the Madras Artillery on the left of the picture, facing the spectator, brandishing his sword as he rushes across the bridge to enter the city, within the walls of which, strewn with dead and wounded, the corpse of Tippoo Sahib was then lying. On the right hand stands a group of superior officers: Lord Wellesley, Lieutenant-General Harris - soon after to become Major Bell's uncle by marriage - and others, who looted Tippoo's body of clothing and jewellery so effectually that by the time their subaltern could reach it, there was nothing left for his share but the

Forebears

dark blue cotton pyjamas of this fallen foe, which he carried off as a trophy, and they are in the possession of his descendants to this day.[2]

Robert's own account reads as follows:

> The operations of the siege of Seringapatam I do not attempt to detail, my observations are merely personal. In the 4 Gun Battery which I commanded I received a slight but dirty wound from the head of an Artilleryman just knocked off, the whole of the brains, I conclude, from the quantity having lodged between the collar of my jacket and my neck. At this instant Tom Sydenham entered the Battery and partook of the curry just brought from Camp for my dinner.
>
> On May 4th I commanded in the breaching Batteries and with 100 Artillery men and proportion of Officers joined the storming party. In ascending the Breach I was twice struck by nearly spent balls, one wounding my empty sword scabbard which otherwise might have entered my thigh.
>
> I was present when Major Allen brought Tippoo's sons to Gen. Baird, indeed saw them brought from the Palace where a Guard was posted by Major Allen for its protection. Some short time after a person of rank attached to Tippoo's person assured Gen. Baird that Tippoo's body was amongst the slain in the Gateway of the inner Fort and so it proved to be, having been taken from a large heap of dead where this person pointed it out. The body was placed on an army dooly and put down in the Palace yard close to the Treasury.
>
> My detachment took possession of a principal Bastion during the night, where some of the Officers slept soundly - but not so the party of men, as was evident at daybreak, when the Bastion was strewn with plunder of various kinds, too extensive to be enumerated - amongst which were silks, jewels, shawls, brass vessels, grain, swords and firearms in great variety... A distribution of the Artillery took place as nearly as possible to the different Bastions and at 4 o'clock, the interment of Tippoo took place in the Bagh. During the funeral procession from the Fort, my party fired from the walls of his own capital, 53 minute guns. So ended my troubles with Tippoo Sultan who from the time of my joining the army was the cause of much harassing fatigue to me.

The expedition from India to Egypt is a little known sideline of the war with Revolutionary France. As part of their plan to regain power in India the French had often considered the possibility of wresting Egypt from the overlordship of Turkey, but it was Napoleon who put this into effect. He arrived in Egypt early in 1798 and defeated the Mamluks, the ruling and fighting race of Egypt, at the battle of the Pyramids. His plans for further advances towards India were frustrated by Nelson's destruction of the French fleet at the Battle of the Nile, and Napoleon eventually left his army in Egypt and returned to France. His army remained a threat, however, and early in 1800 the English Government sent out an expedition under General Abercrombie and requested the assistance of a force from India.

Robert took part in this, and May Poynter gives the following summary of the march through the desert from the coast to the Nile:

From the length of time that the musacks, or leathern water bags carried on camels, had been on board the transports they were in general unfit to hold water. The water found by digging was scarce and bad, sour, bitter and stinking. For three or four days all who tasted it, and there was none other, were affected by dysentery. Bad as the water was it was necessary to husband it with care, for, with the exception of a small spring 40 miles in the desert called the New Well, no water could be procured before reaching Logatta within two marches of the Nile. My detachment manned 8 guns, 6-pounders, drawn by well-trained bullocks from Bombay and Surat, and crossed from Cosseir to Genna in eight marches, at the rate of nearly 16 miles per day. I obtained permission for my detachment to precede the regiment the latter part of the march, and sent back a supply of water in my own bags, which the Corps gratefully acknowledged was most timely. I had advantages for preserving my musacks by placing them when taken off the camels on trusses of hay, the provender for the bullocks, by which means the leakage was trifling and the bags preserved. My detachment crossed without any anxiety, although night marching in the desert is in my opinion dangerous. Europeans will not sleep in the day, are very drowsy in a slow night march, apt to lie down during a momentary halt a few paces from the line, and on awaking know not how to follow the line, there being no track to guide them.

After a pleasant voyage down the Nile my detachment joined the headquarters of the Indian Army on the island of Rhoda, and I was appointed commandant of a very efficient Artillery Corps. On the arrival of the Indian Army at Rosetta we learned that the French army had capitulated and was then embarking for France...[3]

Robert returned to India and from 1805 was commandant of the artillery at St. Thomas Mount, eight miles outside Madras. By 1819 he had been promoted to the rank of Lieutenant-General.

He records his participation in the social life of the time: the amateur theatricals during the long voyages to and from the East, the dinners and the race meetings. He mentions that he was known as the 'Handsome Cadet' but adds that 'these distinguishing charateristics have long since been obliterated', and the miniature painted on his return to England shows a plain, though cheerful, gentleman with a bald head fringed with scanty grey hair, a long nose and clear blue eyes.

Handsome or not, Robert seems always to have been most friendly with the ladies; he was married three times and sired six sons and eight daughters, four of whom, however, died young. He particularly mentions one of these, little Jemima, 'as a most interesting and amiable infant'.

His first two wives came from among the families of his military friends. Sarah Sydenham was aunt to the Thomas Sydenham who took curry with him during the siege of Seringapatam; and Jemima Scott was niece of Lieutenant-General Harris, later 1st Lord Harris of Seringapatam and Mysore. He had met and flirted with her on board ship when returning from his only leave home in 1798. His last wife, Margaret Bell, a cousin, was, curiously but legally, sister of the wife of his own eldest son. Her one child, Charles, only lived for seven years and was known in the family as 'Charles the Prodigy, Pet Lamb' as he was extremely precocious and was said to possess a remarkable vocabulary for one so young.

When Robert returned to England in 1820 he found himself comfortably off. By his own account he 'had shaken the Pagoda tree' to good effect, and he enjoyed a retirement of twenty-four years. His grand-daughter, May Poynter, writes:

Forebears

He settled in Bloomsbury, where he found congenial society in many retired Anglo-Indian officials, military and civilian, the prototypes of Colonel Newcome and Jos. Sedley; first in Great Ormonde Street, in Lord Chancellor Thurlow's house from whence the great seal was stolen, and then in the new, fashionable quarter of Russell Square. Here he furnished his house in the solid style of that day, and much of the plenishing still survives. Massive silver and Sheffield plate; Copeland and Spode china; English rosewood, and Indian ebony and ivory furniture; lacquer figures, inlaid boxes of all shapes and sizes, antique Indian jewellery, native pictures on talc and metal, all the valuable knick-knacks then brought home from the East, including the carved black and white ivory chessmen with which he played a game with one of his daughters every day. Books were not omitted, and there still remains of his library a complete set of the British Novelists edited by Mrs. Barbauld, a 1788 edition of the *Spectator* in 8 vols., Johnson's *Lives of the Poets*, and other such books indispensable to a collection of polite literature in those days. In these surroundings he fulfilled his hopes of spending 'the fag end of my life in great domestic comfort', dying at the ripe age of 83 of gout, in spite of his annual visits to Bath and Cheltenham to control the malady.[4]

Two of General Robert's sons entered the service of the East India Company. One, Alexander, born in 1794, entered as a Writer in the Bombay Presidency in 1815. By this time the Company had established a College for the training of its Civil Servants. This was the East India College, started in 1806 at Haileybury, Hertfordshire, which came to be known simply as Haileybury. The aims of the college, which reflect the changing situation in India, were laid down as follows:

Within the last thirty or forty years, a great change has taken place in the state of the Company's officers in that country: the extension of empire has been followed by a great increase of power and authority, and persons of the same description who before had acted in the capacity of Factors and Merchants are now called upon to administer, throughout their respective districts, an extensive system of Finance, and to fill the important offices of Magistrates, Ambassadors and Provincial Governors...the education of those destined to fill these important posts should certainly be founded on a firm basis of learning and science, on a knowledge of the principles of ethics and civil jurisprudence, of general history and the law of nations. To this should be added a more particular acquaintance with the language, history and manners of those nations among whom they are to exercise their respective functions. The cultivation and improvement of their intellectual powers should be accompanied by such a course of moral discipline as may tend to excite and confirm their habits of application, prudence, integrity and justice and to render this system of justice fully efficient it is essential that it be inculcated and enforced with the sanction and influence of the Christian religion.[5]

This is all rather different from the light-hearted way in which General Robert started on his career. However, despite the elevated aims of the founders of the College, the boys that they had to deal with were a pretty unruly lot, and had to be kept within bounds by strict rules. In the *Directions for the Guidance of Students at the East India College* published in 1814 a comprehensive set of prohibitions were set out: against the playing of games before 1 p.m., against riding, driving, keeping dogs or other animals, against playing cards, billiards or other games of chance. Students were particularly forbidden to bring fire-arms or fireworks into the college and severe penalties were laid down against those who discharged the same. There were rules against bringing in wine, and the students were enjoined to abstain from all immoral and irregular pursuits and to behave with the propriety and decorum of a gentleman. In a final desperate attempt to block outbursts of high spirits the students were warned against 'concluding that everything is permitted which is not positively forbidden'. [6]

We do not know how Alexander behaved himself at this school, which he entered on July 14, 1813 and left in 1815, but he must have passed through successfully for, on completing his terms, he was sent to India where his first post was as Assistant Registrar in Surat. In November 1817 he married Catherine Baynes, daughter of the chaplain, the Rev. Robert Baynes, at Tannah, by whom he had three sons. Two of these died young and the survivor, Harry Wainwright Bax Bell, was the father of H.C.P.Bell. Alexander married a second time, a Maria Ramsay, and had numerous further progeny. He proceeded up the ladder of his service and ended as a Member of Council and Chief Justice. He resigned, in India, on June 29, 1853, presumably because of ill-health, as he died at Poona on July 6 of that year.

Harry Wainwright Bax Bell, son of Alexander and father of H.C.P.Bell, was born in India on August 9, 1821. He took up a military career and in 1837 he was entered at the Military Seminary run by the East India Company at Addiscombe House, near Croydon in Surrey.

Harry's friends at Addiscombe included one Charles Alexander Purvis, later of the Madras Artillery, who was godfather to Harry Charles Purvis Bell, and from whom he was named. When the two boys left Addiscombe Charles Alexander Purvis gave Harry Wainwright Bax Bell a finger ring, gold set with a carbuncle, which he, in turn, passed to his son in the Memoranda attached to his Will in 1875. Another cadet at Addiscombe was Henry Yule, famous as traveller and writer, and Harry also kept in touch with him.

In 1839 Harry was appointed as a temporary ensign, attached to the Engineer corps, in the establishment for field instruction at Chatham, and in 1841 he began his service in India with the Bombay Engineers. From 1843 to 1846 he was stationed at Aden, and there he married his wife, Harriet Eliza Isabella Croker, eldest daughter of Lieutenant-General Croker of the 17th regiment, who was commanding troops at Aden. The marriage took place on February 10, 1845, and there were four children, two girls and two boys.

For most of his career Harry was seconded to the Public Works Department as a civil engineer, although he continued to rise in the military ranks and ended up as a Major General. He retired on March 30, 1876, and lived in London for the rest of his life, dying in 1888.

2

Early Career

The two sons of Major-General H.W.B.Bell, Alexander William Croker Bell, and Harry Charles Purvis Bell, born in 1849 and 1851 respectively, were sent home from India to school at Cheltenham College, entering in August 1863 and August 1864. The period note is struck by a water colour sketch in the possession of the family which shows Alexander leaning negligently on the back of a chair with Harry standing stiffly beside him. They are dressed in grey suits with long trousers, waistcoats and cut-away jackets; Alexander has a loose grey bow, Harry a blue, and while Alexander carries neat white gloves, Harry carries a cap in his left hand, which rests on his hip.

Cheltenham College, founded in 1841, was the first of a new type of school which came into being in the nineteenth century to meet the growing demand for education among the professional classes, a demand for a type of education which would give the same results, both scholarly and socially, as that provided by the older 'public schools'. The proprietary schools were created by groups of private individuals, who put up the money for the purchase or building of the school houses and the initial hiring of masters. They retained shares in the school and the right to nominate boys as collegians. At the original meeting of Cheltenham residents on November 9, 1840, a committee was elected and thirty-six shares immediately taken up. At the first meeting of the committee it was resolved that no one should be eligible to become a shareholder 'who should not be moving in the circle of gentlemen, no retail trader being under any circumstances to be considered'.

Cheltenham had long been a place to which military men retired and, from the first, many of the boys were soldiers' sons, and many went on to make their career in the army. The tone of the school was military; it was also strongly evangelical. When the first meeting of directors was called it was stated that their aim was 'by public and united prayer to endeavour to secure for the school and the children in it, the blessing of Almighty God, and by a public and unanimous act decidedly and openly to avow the Christian basis on which the school is established'.

The elder brother, Alexander, or Alec as he was always known, conformed to the school type. He left school in 1857, went to Sandhurst Military College, from which he passed out fourth in 1869, thus obtaining a commission without payment. He entered the Indian Army, the 58th Foot, joined the Bombay Staff Corps in 1872, and rose to become Brevet Colonel in 1899. He retired in 1906 and spent the rest of his life in Tunbridge Wells, supporting numerous missionary societies, attending an austere evangelical church and playing croquet. He died in 1938.

Harry's reaction to the school ethos was more unpredictable. He was not a docile sheep in the Christian flock. His daughter-in-law, Dorris Bell, in an unpublished autobiography, tells how, when she first went to stay with the family in Kandy in the early 1920s, she was told a story about 'the Old Man', as his children always called him:

Apparently last Christmas he had decided to accompany the family to church, but thought he would write a sermon for the Vicar to deliver, of what he considered the right length. Needless to say the Vicar disregarded this and preached his own sermon, and Mr. Bell was furious, said he had been insulted and would never go to church again. [1]

Perhaps he felt that there was precedent for an assumption of clerical duties in the life of his great-grandfather, General Robert, who wrote in his memoir of the situation in Madras in the 1780s:

At this period the Church Establishment was very small - two chaplains only belonging to the Madras Presidency - the clerical duties therefore at the stations devolved on the Staff Officer and, on a allowance of 5 pagodas per mensem, I performed several ceremonies, Marriages, Christenings and Burials, and in some instances of Divorce. On one occasion I christened 6 infants before breakfast. [2]

Harry was certainly no bigot. His work entailed some clashes with Buddhist feelings over the excavations of dagabas, but his relations with Buddhist scholars were normally both friendly and respectful. He made close friends with the Moslem Maldivians, and firmly advised missionary societies in England against attempts at proselytising in the islands. He conducted a long and friendly correspondence with Father Vossen of the Papal Seminary in Kandy.

At school Alec was in the Modern side, or department, Harry in the Classical. The Modern side prepared boys for entry into military and technical careers, and the Classical mainly for the universities, with a special class in which preparation was made for the Indian Civil Service entry examination, and in which Sanskrit, Hindi and Persian were optional extras. Each side had roughly the same curriculum, but Greek was only taught on the Classical, and stress was laid on Mathematics, Chemistry and Drawing on the Modern. Cheltenham was unusual in that English was taught as a regular subject, and thus the foundation was laid for Harry's wide acquaintance with the English classics, and his facility in quoting from them to enliven his archaeological reports and articles.

There is no record of Harry's excelling in any subject and he won no prizes for hard work. On the other hand his passion for the outdoor life and interest in various kinds of sport may be traced to early days at school. Considerable freedom was allowed to the boys to wander about the countryside, up to the gorse-covered tops of the Cotswolds by lanes which were ideal haunts for birds. Games were of great importance in the development of public schools in the nineteenth century, both in fostering the idea of the 'team spirit' and in establishing the status of the school itself, which was partly judged by that of the other schools with which it competed in matches.

Neither Harry nor his brother was sent to one of the regular boarding houses. Instead they were placed in the care of one of those masters who were permitted to supplement their earnings by lodging a small number of boys. Harry lodged with Charles Dallinger Chenery, a classical form master. As most of the in-school matches were between the major boarding houses this may be the reason why, although he was devoted to various sports, and claimed tennis and cricket as his recreations in the entry he sent to *Who's Who*, his name does not appear in any of the teams except the shooting team.

Early Career

In this more individual sport he seems to have excelled; he belonged to the Rifle Corps, and was in the shooting XI as a private in 1869 and a sergeant in 1870. He shot at the public schools' rifle competition which at that time was held at Wimbledon. In 1869 his captain, L.Neville, remarked on him as 'a persevering but unfortunate shot. Does best in the long range'. But in 1870 it was reported that 'Bell made a splendid score shooting for the Ashburton Shield', although he did not come up to the record of one C.W.H.Sims, who had won the Spencer Cup in the preceding year. The Spencer Cup was for individual marksmanship, and had been given by Lord Spencer, Lord of the Manor of Wimbledon, in 1861. The Ashburton Shield had been first presented by Lord Ashburton, also in 1861, for any team from a public school with a volunteer corps.

The following vivid account of the school camp on Wimbledon Common during the competition was printed in *The Cheltenham College Magazine* in June 1872:

In recalling my camp life at Wimbledon it always appears to me one of the happiest times of my life. With that recollection come thronging on my mind reminiscences of those jovial days of 'camping out'; - not such playing at soldiers either, as you would confess could you have seen our saturated tents last meeting, and the water standing in them a foot deep. Terrible times these for the improvident ones who had omitted to dig their trenches, and who saw their 'little all' literally floating away. Terrible times, too, for those inexperienced in tents, for the tent ropes get so tightened by rain that they eventually pull the pole down, and bring the tent about your ears, if you do not slacken them in time. But, upon the whole, the enjoyments triumph over the hardships; and although it may seem unpleasant at first to sleep between coarse hair blankets, not a foot from mother Earth, and with nothing but the canvas between you and the air of heaven, still after the first night you will sleep sounder there than on the softest bed of roses. Early in the morning you are awakened by the clear echoing notes of the bugle; after turning out (the feeling of putting one's feet on to the grass is rather surprising at first) comes your bath, which takes place on the green-sward in front of your tent. Breakfast over, you generally adjourn to the ranges, where, however, not a shot can be fired till the boom of 'gun-fire' startles those unaccustomed, and at the same time announces that shooting for the day has commenced. At the ranges there is always some interesting match going on, as the Elcho Challenge Shield, for which England, Scotland, and Ireland yearly compete; or the Queen's Prize; or the Oxford and Cambridge match; or the School's Competition for the Ashburton Shield. This last, with the 'Lords and Commons', draw [sic] larger and more fashionable crowds than any others. [3]

The only other records which appear of Harry's life at school concern shooting competitions within the school, in which he generally seems to have come second to a certain Ensign Oaks; but on May 28th of 1870 he won a cup presented by W.Godfrey with a score of 32.

That he was happy enough at school we know from a letter to one of his Maldive friends, Muhammad Amin, a boy at Aligarh University, who was longing to be at home:

As a schoolboy in the sixties of the last century I used to 'count the days' as they lessened steadily towards the holidays, though I was lucky in being at a very happy school, with plenty of recreation to balance hard study, viz. *Cheltenham College* in England (730) boys. I left school in 1870 and did not come out till 1873. [4]

We do not know exactly how those three years were spent, but it is probable that some part of them will have been devoted to preparation for the competitive examination which gave entry to the Ceylon Civil Service. This examination, which was instituted in 1863, was held whenever there was a vacancy for a Writer in Ceylon, and candidates were required to be between the ages of 21 and 24. This age range was intended to attract University graduates, and many of the entrants held degrees. Bell, however, never went to the University, though he may have attended one of the special 'crammers' which existed to prepare candidates for entrance to the Indian Civil Service, and to the colonial services, which included those of the Federated Malay States and Hong Kong. Those passing this examination were all known as the Eastern Cadets.

Bell took the examination in June 1873, passing second in a field of nine candidates and was appointed as a Writer to the Ceylon Civil Service by the Secretary of State on July 10, 1873. [5]

His first post was in the Kandy Kachcheri, where he was sent on October 6 in that year, but he was transferred on November 28 to the Colombo Kachcheri, and attached to the Colonial Secretary's office. Among his colleagues there were two whom he later came to know much better. These were Albert Gray, who was in Ceylon only from 1871 to 1873, but with whom he was to have a long correspondence concerning the Maldive Islands and a fruitful collaboration in the editing of the voyages of François Pyrard, and the young R.W.Ievers, later Government Agent at Anuradhapura at the beginning of Bell's archaeological work there, and a very good friend.

It was the usual practice to attach the young cadet, or Writer, to one of the Head Offices to learn the rudiments of the service, and then to try him out in an acting post in the various branches, either in administration in the office of a Government Agent in one of the provinces, as acting police magistrate, or in the customs department. Each of these jobs covered a wide range of activities. When Acting Police Magistrate at Balapitimodera, for instance, Bell was also acting justice of the peace, acting coroner, acting commissioner of requests and deputy fiscal. The duties of the Principal Collector of Customs were said, in the *Ceylon Blue Book* 'to consist in the collecting of duties and imports under the regulations of Government, in suggesting improvements in the methods of collecting and granting port clearance and preventing smuggling'. [6]

Later in life, when writing of the sad story of a young officer in the service of the Dutch administration, he recalled:

> The writer has still a lively recollection of a fortnight's misery, when in 1873-4, as a raw Writer but lately appointed to the Ceylon Civil Service, ignorant of the country and its languages, he had to proceed from the Colombo Kachcheri, during the most inclement of weather, to weigh up confiscated plumbago at the jungle-buried pits of Pelawatta, on the *oya* of that name, not very far from Pitigala, in the Pasdum Korale, Kalutara district. [7]

Young Writers had everything to learn about the job they were to do, and this was provided for in government regulations. Some time in the first eighteen months of their service they were required to take an examination, and no promotion could be granted until this was passed. The subjects prescribed were: 1) Precis-writing and the conduct of official business. 2) The system of accounts employed in government offices. 3) Government regulations and minutes in force in the Colony relating to police courts and courts of request and fiscal duties, customs acts and those relating to tolls, stamps and licenses, the laws of evidence. 4) A native language, with exercises in reading, writing and translating and with a *viva voce* test.

A further examination had to be passed at a subsequent time in which two native languages were tested and more detailed papers were set on government regulations, minutes and ordinances, on forms of court and judicial procedures and on Roman Dutch Law, Kandyan Customs and Mercantile Law. A list of text-books was provided and time was allowed for study. During the first eighteen months of service Writers were not required to attend at Public Offices for more than two hours daily, 'a period which is considered sufficient to give them an opportunity of learning the details of public business without interfering with their reading'. They were also given a pundit allowance of £3 a month to enable them to pay a teacher of Tamil and Sinhalese. [8]

Bell passed the first examination on 19 October 1874 and thereafter held a number of varied appointments. He was attached as office assistant to the G.A. of the Western Province in 1874, and returned there and to the Colombo Kachcheri at different periods up to 1879. He was briefly Police Magistrate at Matale, Harispattu and Balapitimodera. In July 1879 he became Acting Landing Surveyor in the Customs in Colombo, and in May 1883 he was confirmed in this post. In April 1884 he became Assistant Collector of Customs and Landing Surveyor in Galle. For brief periods in 1878 and 1879 he was Acting Assistant Government Agent in Kalutara. He was disappointed at not being confirmed in this post, for it was in administrative posts that careers were made.

At the beginning of his service he attracted the favourable notice of the Governor, Sir William Gregory, who wrote to him soon after his own retirement on May 19, 1881:

> I hope you are getting on well and distinguishing yourself. There were several young officers in whose careers I took much interest and from whom I expected much, and you were in the van of that small band. [9]

Bell in his reply, on June 6, clearly felt that his career had not yet taken off, and complained that promotion was slow. He was glad, though, of his appointment as Landing Surveyor in Colombo, for the rise in pay was a godsend to him, as by that time he was married with three young children.

His marriage to Renée Sabine Fyers took place on June 6, 1876 in Colombo and, as we have seen, for the first ten years of his service he spent much of his time in that city. While not engaged in official duties or in his studies, he would have taken a full part in the pleasant social life which is described as follows by M. Bremer in his memoirs:

> The social life in Colombo in those days was a quiet but pleasant one; rowing on the lake in the evening and whist after dinner, with an occasional sing-song, were the chief amusements. There was no theatre, of course, and fortunately no cinema. There were no late hours, because everybody got up at daybreak. [10]

H. C. P. Bell

Sport was always an important ingredient of social life in the East and a means of keeping fit in an enervating climate. Bell continued to play cricket and tennis, the usual relaxations of young Civil Servants. He played for Colombo against the up-country team in 1875, when Colombo won by 99 runs to 43.[11] He became known, indeed, as one of the best of Ceylon's cricket players, and was selected in October 1883 to form one of the team which played the touring MCC team on its way to Australia to attempt to regain the 'Ashes'. He was also one of the team selected by A.S.Tabor, a leading planter cricketer, to tour Madras during the Christmas vacation of 1885. On January 1, 1886 he wrote to Albert Gray proudly relating their success:

> Only just returned from 3 weeks cricketing tour in the Madras Presidency. Last year Ceylon ventured to Calcutta and held her own there. This Xmas we essayed to vanquish the benighted Presidency and again returned victorious on the whole. The Madras CC beat us by 45 runs (sheer bad luck), and we played a stubborn draw with the combined Presidency and 'took tea' with Bangalore, winning by 274 runs. As we 'walked around' both Madras and Bangalore at tennis I think we may congratulate ourselves on the results of the tour. People in Madras are beginning to think that Ceylon is not such a 'one-horse' place after all. You will appreciate this as a quondam cricketer, I know.[12]

Bell's opportunities for playing cricket were naturally less frequent as time went on. It would have been difficult to collect one team, let alone two, at Anuradhapura, but his interest in the game did not diminish. Even as late as in May 1931 he wrote to Muhammad Amin Didi in Male, when the crew of H.M.S. *Enterprise* had played a local team, winning lavishly:

> How as an old and keen cricketer of yore, I should have enjoyed watching the Cricket match, the first time, I take it, that a Maldivian Eleven has faced British bowling. *Macte virtute esto!*[13]

Riding was a necessary accomplishment, although most of his tours through the jungle would have to be taken on foot or by bullock cart, and there is one record of his taking part in a jump race at Galle in 1886. He wrote to Gray: 'Galle is in the throes of a spring meet and we are all boiling over with excitement. Even I have arranged to run a jump, after 20 years farewell to such things'. He did not win, however, for Gray replied: 'I see by the *Observer* that you did not succeed in your race at the Spring Meeting - probably some lusty soldier was too much for you. I was glad, however, to see that Mrs. Bell came off victorious in lawn tennis'.[14]

English officials in the East were not exclusively occupied with administrative work and a social life. Many engaged in a study of the cultures of the countries in which they served, and at this time Bell was already turning his mind to more scholarly pursuits.

One of the first requirements of the service was for the young Civil Servant to learn the languages of the country. For Bell this was the beginning of a life-long interest in oriental languages. J.R.Toussaint, in *Annals of the Ceylon Civil Service* noted that in the opinion of J.P.Lewis 'the best speakers of Sinhalese in the Civil Service in his day were M.S.Crawford, R.W.Ievers, F.R.Ellis, H.C.P.Bell, E.M.Byrde and Herbert White'.[15]

It was not only the Sinhalese and Tamil languages that Bell set himself to learn. On September 26, 1877, when he was stationed at Balapitiya, he wrote to Louis de Zoysa, Chief Translator to

Early Career

the Government and Librarian of the Government Oriental Library, asking for information on the Maldives and saying:

> If I am stationed in Galle I shall endeavour to study that little known though interesting language regularly.[16]

Sir William Gregory encouraged him and on July 7, 1881 wrote to suggest:

> I think that there is an opening for a man to make himself a name as a scholar in Ceylon and as you seem to like Oriental Studies I should almost advise you to devote your spare time to this branch of literature.[17]

By this time Bell was also committed to work for the Royal Asiatic Society, Ceylon Branch. On September 18, 1880 he had been proposed as a member by Colonel A.B.Fyers, President of the Society, and Bell's father-in-law, and seconded by A.Murray, the engineer who was concerned in the restoration of the dagabas of Anuradhapura, and was one of those who climbed Sigiriya before Bell. On December 16, 1880, the next meeting of the Society, Bell was elected Honorary Secretary. It is tempting to assume that Colonel Fyers may have been instrumental in opening up before Bell the prospects of a career in archaeological exploration in Ceylon; certainly it was one of his own great interests.

Colonel Amelius Beauclerk Fyers was a regular soldier in the Royal Engineers who, after serving in Mauritius, had been appointed Surveyor General of Ceylon in 1866. In 1870 he was elected a member, and at the same meeting elected President, of the Royal Asiatic Society, Ceylon Branch. On January 16, 1871 he gave his first Annual Address to the Society, which included an eloquent passage on the need for concern for the monuments of Ceylon:

> Any one who has travelled much in this Island, must have been struck by the remains of ancient Cities, Temples and Irrigation works which he meets with in all parts. I know of nothing more touching than to wander amongst the ruins of some of these cities. The silence is so marked, the utter desolation so apparent, and the contemplation of the great changes that have taken place in what was formerly a populous city inhabited by thousands of human beings, but now taken possession of by the wild beasts of the forest, engenders feelings of sadness and deep thoughtfulness. I know of no place in which this feeling is so strongly developed as at Pollonnaruwa, where [there] are still buildings in a wonderful state of preservation, testifying not only to the Architectural taste of those who designed them, but to the excellence of the skilled workmen who carried out the designs. Bold cornices and handsome plinths, wonderfully cut landings and janitors and steps, colossal figures cut out of solid rock, columns with their capitals, dagobas, temples, etc., are met with everywhere, and the thoughts are at once turned into the channel of conjecture as to what became of the large population which must have resided there, and how it is that the city has remained so utterly deserted ever since its inhabitants were driven out. This is only referring to Pollonnaruwa, but there is the more ancient city of Anuradhapura, abounding in objects of Archaeological interest, and many other cities in every part of the Island, and singularly shaped rock temples, with inscriptions on them in ancient characters, are scattered all over the jungle.[18]

H. C. P. Bell

Fyers also spoke of the 'tanks', the remains of the great hydrological civilisation of ancient Ceylon, and urged his hearers to study the antiquities of the Island and contribute papers to their own Society rather than sending them to learned journals at home. Fyers died in 1883, but two of his sons made their careers in Ceylon; Charles Cornwallis Meadows Fyers, who retired as Superintendent of Survey in 1907, and Henry Francis Clifton Fyers, who was in the Forest Department; while a daughter, Laura Isabella Fyers, married Charles Morant Lushington who was in the Civil Service. Bell remained on very friendly terms with all his in-laws, and his children were sent to stay with Colonel Fyers' widow, his second wife, in Scotland. Bell's eldest and youngest sons, Harry Amelius, born 1879, and Malcolm Fyers, born 1889, were both given 'Fyers' family names.

Meanwhile Bell had entered upon his duties as Secretary with enthusiasm. At the Annual Meeting on December 16, 1881 a report was submitted by the Committee and read by the Secretary, detailing some of the achievements of the past year, thus reviving a custom which had been allowed to fall into abeyance. The style is characteristic of Bell, and the report was probably largely compiled by him. It opened as follows:

> As in 1871, when the last Report was issued, so now your Committee is able to congratulate the Society on 'the new era which has dawned upon it'. It is highly satisfactory to believe that the efforts made to resuscitate the 'dry bones' from the apparently hopeless sleep of at least five years (1874-1879) have met with success, and that the Ceylon Branch of the Royal Asiatic Society is once more in a fair way to re-assume the creditable position it formerly held among learned sister Societies.[19]

Bell reorganised the Library of the Society, for which he and W.E.Davidson prepared a new catalogue, completed in 1882. He caught up with the publication of the Proceedings of the Society and encouraged members to submit articles for the Journal. Then and thereafter Bell's primary interest in the affairs of the Society was in the editing of the Journal. The subject range covered has always been wide. In the Journal, on the occasion of the 125th Anniversary of the Society, P.R.S.Sittampalam wrote:

> A brief analysis shows that the Society justified its aims by presenting the variegated scenes of cultural life wholly unaffected by bias towards any particular ethos or religious group in the Island. Zoology and Botany figured prominently in the early years of the Journal and antiquarian subjects such as History, Numismatics, Epigraphy and its parent Archaeology rather less. With the passage of years the position was reversed, antiquarian subjects quickly pushing themselves through to the forefront. This may have been due to the circumstance that Mr. H.C.P.Bell bestrode the Society like a colossus - he was Honorary Secretary-cum-Editor for 34 years, indeed a unique record.[20]

During the first ten years of Bell's editorship the Journal contained a number of important articles on inscriptions, including two by Edward Muller, who had been appointed by Government to collect these. There were also contributions from B.Gunasekera and D.M.de Zilva Wickremasinghe, who both worked later on the epigraphical side of the Archaeological Survey. A whole issue was devoted to H.Parker's detailed report on the archaeological discoveries he had made at Tissamaharama; S.M.Burrows contributed accounts of his work at Anuradhapura and Polonnaruwa, and there were other archaeological reports by W.J.S.Boake, J.H.F.Hamilton and R.W.Ievers. There were also a number of articles on more purely historical themes, and many ethnographical and literary items, as well as those which were strictly scientific. Bell himself, in his publications at this period, illustrated the wide range of interests of the scholarly Civil Servant. He wrote three articles on customs connected with paddy cultivation, two of which were published in the JRASCB and one in the *Orientalist*; he contributed a list of Sinhalese, Pali and Sanskrit books held in the Oriental Library at Kandy to the *Journal of the Pali Text Society* and the beginnings of a Sinhalese glossary to the JRASCB. He also completed three purely historical articles, one for the *Orientalist* and two for the *Ceylon Literary Register*. He also edited for the JRASCB his father-in-law's article on the attack on Colombo in 1796.

Bell's connection with the Society was not entirely uninterrupted. In the early years he sometimes shared the job of Secretary with W.E.Davidson and F.M.Corbet. Nor were relations between himself and the Council always smooth. He exhibited a marked tendency to take umbrage when any of his proposals were not meekly accepted, and had to be tactfully persuaded to reconsider offered resignations. The Society seems to have thought that his work for the archaeology of Ceylon made up for a prickly manner. They elected him as an Honorary Member in 1898, and when he finally resigned in 1914 passed a formal vote to place on record the Council's appreciation of the 'very valuable services rendered by Mr. H.C.P.Bell as Honorary Secretary during the last 34 years'. [21]

3

The Maldives : Pyrard and Other Visitors

The Introduction to Bell's final report on the Maldive Islands, published in 1940, begins with a brief summary of his first visit to them in November 1879:

> The wreck of the ss. 'Sea Gull' on Gafaru Reef in 1879, afforded Mr. H.C.P.Bell, of the Ceylon Civil Service, stationed at Colombo, an opportunity of visiting the Maldives. A native boat conveyed him Southwards from Gafaru Island, through North Male Atol, to Male or 'Sultan's Island'; where he spent two or three days before returning to the wreck, and thence to Ceylon.
>
> At Male 'sports' were being held in honour of the birth of a first son (the present Sultan Muhammad Shams-ud-din III) to the Heir Apparent, afterwards Sultan Ibrahim Nur-ud-din (A.C. 1882-6; 1888-92), younger son of the reigning Sultan Muhammad Imad-ud-din IV (A.C. 1835-1882).
>
> After his trip Mr. Bell submitted a Report to the Ceylon Government.[1]

Bell was not the first traveller to what is now the Republic of the Maldives to chronicle his visit. Albert Gray, in his review for *The Athenaeum* of Bell's first report wrote:

> The Maldive Kingdom 'of the 12,000 Isles', although since the English conquest of Ceylon it has been (to use a fine distinction lately in vogue) under the 'suzerainty' of England, yet enjoys a virtual independence; and the sultan, though he rules over probably no more than twenty or thirty thousand subjects, occupies one of the most ancient existing thrones in the East. When the islands were first colonized is uncertain; there is no doubt, however, that the inhabitants are of the same race as the Sinhalese, though it is curious that the diligence of the Ceylon pandits has not discovered any reference to the Maldives in the Sinhalese chronicles. The language is largely Sinhalese in vocabulary, showing affinities with the ancient 'Elu'. The written alphabet resembles that of the early Sinhalese inscriptions, and more closely, perhaps, the Vatteluttu of Southern India. The form of writing was formerly from left to right, but since the Mohammedan conversion at the beginning of the thirteenth century the mode has been reversed - a change similar to that made by the Tagals of the Philippines after the Spanish conquest.
>
> The history of the Maldives, as often as light is thrown upon it, is interesting enough. Unfortunately the archives formerly kept by the sultans are either lost or not yet disclosed to European eyes, and we are thus dependent upon the writings of Western travellers and historians. Passing over the uncertain notices of the early geographers, the first full account we have of Maldive life is from the pen of Ibn Batuta of Tangier, who in 1343-4, in the course of his grand tour of 'Greater Arabia' passed eighteen months at the Atols. The natives welcomed him in Maori fashion as a 'pakeha', and pressed him into their service as cadi. Their simplicity and humanity are well illustrated by the following quotation from

the French version of this traveller: - 'Leurs corps sont faibles; ils n'ont pas l'habitude des combats ni de la guerre, et leurs armes, c'est la prière. J'ordonnai un jour en ce pays de couper la main d'un voleur; plusieurs des indigènes qui se trouvaient dans la salle d'audience s'évanouirent'.[2]

The proper name of Ibn Batuta, the Maghrebin traveller, was Abu Abd-Allah Muhammed. Between the years 1324 and 1354 he visited Spain and North Africa, Egypt, East Africa and the Niger Basin, all the Middle East, Central Asia, China, the East Indies, India and Ceylon. In the Maldives he acquired four wives from the nobility (in spite of his disapproval of the topless female costume) and ventured to ride one of the only two horses in Male, reserved for the Sultan. Ibn Batuta related a romantic legend of the Mohammedan conversion of the Islands, in which a young Berber missionary saved a virgin victim from a demon by reciting the Koran, so that 'God disposed the heart of the king to receive the true faith'. In 1882 the RASCB issued as an extra number to volume VII, 'Ibn Batuta in the Maldives and Ceylon, translated from the French of M.M. Défremery and Sanguinetti, by Albert Gray, M.R.A.S.'. Gray also recorded Ibn Batuta's travels in the third volume of *The Voyage of François Pyrard of Laval to the East Indies, the Maldives, the Moluccas and Brazil*. The review for *The Athenaeum* went on to introduce this next important visitor to the Maldives:

> The interval between Ibn Batuta and the arrival of the Portuguese in the Indian seas is a blank page in Maldive history; but during the following century the islands had to suffer their full share of the evils attending that event. Driven from the trading towns of the Malabar coast, the merchants of Arabia, Cambay, Acheen, and China, in endeavouring to evade the Portuguese monopoly, used the Maldives as a refuge and emporium. The Portuguese set themselves to reduce the sultan to subjection. Male, the 'King's Island', was for a period garrisoned by a Portuguese force, who, according to their own national historian, 'behaved themselves with so much pride' that the natives, falling upon them unawares, slew them to a man, and so regained their freedom. Subsequent invasions resulted in disaster, or at best in treaties favourable to Portuguese commerce. As Ibn Batuta gives a glimpse of the islands in the halcyon days of Arabian commerce, so Pyrard de Laval is our authority for the period when the Portuguese dominion was first challenged by the Dutch. This traveller went out to seek his fortune in the first French voyage of 1601, and, being wrecked on the Maldives, was kept a captive there for five years. Endued with the unaffected piety and simplicity characteristic of the best old travellers, he was also a man of keen observation and natural intelligence, and his book, like Knox's 'Ceylon', is remarkable among captives' tales for its approved veracity, and for the kindly interest he took in the race among whom his lot was cast. Mr. Bell makes frequent reference to this invaluable text-book; he has also good store of material from the Portuguese histories and from the Dutch records at Colombo. Only one Englishman before Mr. Bell himself seems to have had a local knowledge of these islands. This was Mr. Christopher, of the Indian navy, who was engaged in the survey of the Maldives under Capt. Moresby in 1834-5, and afterwards published a vocabulary and an excellent report upon the social economy of the people.[3]

Bell drew largely on Pyrard de Laval's book in his report, and he was to be associated with Gray in the latter's translation of it. He also showed considerable interest in Willmott Christopher. In his report of his own visit he chronicles the stay in Male from November 1834 to 1835 of

Lt. Young and Mr. Christopher. He used the latter's report for historical and commercial detail and for his confirmation of the peaceable character of the Maldivians. Christopher's eyewitness experiences also appeared. He had seen coins scrambled for by the poor at a noble funeral, and the ceremonial elevation in a procession of the umbrella over the heir-apparent. A particular interest attaches to Willmott Christopher's connection with Bell's father. On the back of a letter from The Grange, Kandy, on January 8, 1925, Bell wrote:

> It is a strange coincidence that I should have succeeded Willmott Christopher of the Indian Navy as *pro tanto* 'authority' on the Maldives. No account intervened between his 'Memoir' (very full and interesting) of 1836-8 and my report of 1881. When I wrote the report I was not aware that Christopher had been a close friend of my father, General H.W.B.Bell, R.E., who served 35 years in India after leaving Addiscombe. Subsequently my father wrote from England, 'Col. H.Yule and Capt. Christopher were both friends of mine when in India. The latter was my *best man*. He was an earnest Christian and anything he wrote you can rely on thoroughly. Christopher died a heroic death before Multan, volunteering to guide the attacking force (once repulsed) at night. In the second attack he fell: *multis ille bonis flebilis occidet*'.

General Bell, when writing on January 1, 1880 had said: 'You can trust Christopher's account. I was best man at his wedding in, I think, 1844.' This friendly service seems therefore to have been reciprocal.[4]

Bell's own interest in the Maldives began with the language. However, it was his position as Acting Landing Surveyor, Customs, Colombo, from July 3, 1879, which led to his visit to the Islands. The Maldives consist of a chain of about 2,000 low-lying coral islands grouped in a number of clusters or atols. They were at that time unofficially under the protection of the Ceylon Government, but the agreement was not formally ratified until 1887. Bell was sent to investigate the wreck of the ss. Sea Gull which, while sailing from Calcutta to London had been wrecked on August 31, 1879 on Gafaru Island, becoming a total loss but without loss of life.[5]

A map of the Male Atol, of which Bell sent a copy to Albert Gray in 1881, shows the wreck of the 'Sea Gull' as 404 miles south-east of Colombo. Bell's journey to and from Male itself is traced in red, and dots mark a possible short course if the wind is favourable.[6]

One aspect of Bell's visit is indicated in an undated semi-official letter to him which read:

> Pleasant voyage and safe return. I'm sorry you cannot have a passport and you will have to depend on your diplomacy to get on. Have you thought of taking presents for the Sultan ?

In fact, Bell did so, for he presented the Sultan with forty yards of red silk which was highly appreciated, and could not be touched by any inferior person with impunity; and in return received a kid to eat.[7]

The 'Sports' Bell witnessed at Male, to judge from the section 'Recreations' in his report, may not have been very entertaining. He describes them as 'mimic hand to hand combats' with sword and targe, lance or quarter-staff. Little skill was shown, and the spectators, including the Sultan and ladies of the harem, 'appeared to evince no real interest in the proceedings, which are conducted from first to last in gravity and silence'. In Male Bell himself was induced to fire some obsolete guns, but avoided trying the rusty iron cannon.

Bell's report praised the Maldive mats, made only in Suvadiva Atol from a rush which best thrives there, for their delicacy of pattern in three colours, black, yellow-brown and white, and their permanency of dye. On his return to Ceylon he began a practice of sending these mats as gifts: immediately to General Bell and to Sir John Douglas, the Colonial Secretary in Ceylon; and two years later to Albert Gray. The General, in thanking his son, admired the mats greatly and proposed to 'try the King's Mat in the Dining Room in front of a cabinet of Indian curiosities' which would now contain as well a Maldive fan and a Moorman's cap. In a letter from their home at 31 Fopstone Road, London, Bell's mother showed interest in his descriptions of Maldive dress, which she would like to wear as fancy dress. She wrote, 'I will look very nice indeed in it'. On this, or another occasion, Bell certainly brought back Maldive costumes, for a photograph exists of his son and daughter-in-law wearing them.

Much of the correspondence of the next few years is concerned with Bell's efforts to publicise his visit. The General had received his son's photographs by April 1880. They were eventually accepted by *The Graphic* which tried to pay only three guineas but finally sent twice that amount, possibly the only sum Bell actually earned from publications throughout his life. He received the issue with his photographs reproduced as engravings by the end of June, 1881 and wrote to Gray, 'My comely maiden looks for all the world like a broad-faced Malay!' Certain of the pictures (a street, a mat, other artefacts, a fishing boat and the nobleman Ibrahim Didi) were never reproduced elsewhere, but others did reappear.

The General encouraged his son to produce his written report, and advised him to be exact in measurements and to write clearly on thin paper. For the first but not the last time, Bell's wish for completeness rather than immediacy in his publications made itself apparent; he did not want merely to write notes for a paper for the Intelligence Department of the War Office. By November 1880 the General was pleased that the manuscript of an extended report was at last ready.

In December Colonel Fyers in his Presidential Address to the RASCB gave a short account of the Maldive Islands based on information provided by Bell. He said, 'In November of last year (1879) Bell paid a short visit to Male Atol and Sultan's Island, and since his return has presented the Museum with a varied collection of articles of produce and manufacture gathered during his trip and has embodied the results of his investigations into the history and conditions of the Islands in a report lately submitted to Government'. Turning to Sir James Longden, the Governor, who was present as patron of the Society, he added, 'The report, I hope will either be published by Government or your Excellency will allow it to be handed over to this Society when it will be published in our Journal'.[8]

Bell, sending his manuscript to Sir John Douglas, who shared his interest in Eastern culture, hoped that it would be 'of service to this colony should a closer intercourse with her chief dependency be projected'. The report was appreciated and in February 1881 the Governor, Sir James Longden, had sent a copy to the Colonial Office in London. On April 7 Albert Gray suggested to the Under Secretary of State for the Colonies that it should be published as a Council Paper, and the Colonial Office shortly encouraged Longden to arrange this in Colombo.[9]

H. C. P. Bell

Over the next two years letters indicate delays in the printing of the report as Sessional Paper XLIII, 1881; it did not come out until 1883. In several places it had dealt with the defensibility of the Islands and their possible use for coaling stations. It was later used by Naval Officers visiting the Maldives, one of whom commented that 'it would be useful for reference on the East India station or by the Intelligence Department at home'. [10]

From soon after the voyage Bell found some honours, whether or not agreeable ones, accruing to him. He was repeatedly invited to attend in morning dress at receptions for the Maldive Ambassador who came yearly with gifts from the Sultan. The practice soon began of making requests to Bell for advice about the islands; for example from Trinity House, which wanted to build a lighthouse on Minicoy, which lies between the Maldives and the Laccadive Islands.

The practical value of a work and its general interest are not identical. In February 1881 Bell suggested to Gray that he should read extracts from the report at a London Royal Asiatic Society meeting at which would be discussed a possible archaeological survey of the Maldive Islands. The reading did occur at the meeting of June 20, 1881, and Gray wrote to Bell that the attenders included General Bell, Colonel Fyers, Sir W.Robinson (who later wrote on the Laccadives) and Sir William Gregory, who subsequently pressed for Bell to be sent again to the Maldives to investigate the language. In the account of this meeting in the proceedings of the Society, it appears that it was this aspect of Bell's visit which especially interested the Society, in particular the tracing of the link between Maldivian and Sinhalese in its earlier form, Elu. [11]

Gray's estimate of the report appeared in his review for *The Athenaeum* which began as follows:

So little is known of the Maldive Islands by the world at large that Mr. Bell is to be thanked for not confining his report to the new information acquired by himself, valuable as that is. Begun as a report to the Ceylon Government of a visit made by the author to the Maldives in 1879, the subject has subsequently grown in his hands. All the known authorities have been laid under contribution, and the result is a pamphlet of 133 folio pages, illustrated with useful maps, a lithographed specimen of a Maldive letter, and a photograph of coins, besides some tables of statistics.

Gray then gave his summary of the visitors to the Maldives before Bell and concluded with this appreciation:

Mr. Bell now comes forward to gather all these loaves and crumbs into one basket and to add his own contribution. He is probably the only living European acquainted with the Maldive language, the value of which for the study of Sinhalese and the Indian *prakrits* has already been recognised by Dr. E.Muller and Prof. Kuhn, and he garnishes his report with much valuable information on this head, but he reserves for the learned societies his examination of the Maldive grammar and vocabulary. He has obtained a collection of Maldive coins, none of which, we believe, is yet known to European numismatists; and it may be noted that he has acquired a single specimen of the old silver *larin*, the so-called 'fish-hook' coin, which was adopted from Persian use and minted at Male. On the subject of Maldive trade Mr. Bell had much to say, showing that it is not inconsiderable in amount and that it is capable of improvement. By far the largest export traffic is in dried fish, which finds its way into all the bazaars of the East, while that in coir and cowries, formerly so extensive, is nowadays reduced as well in bulk as in value.

If, as may be hoped, Mr. Bell is enabled to make another and a more lengthened visit to the Maldives, he may be successful in following up the faint traces of Buddhism which are said to exist, in obtaining copies of the numerous ancient inscriptions on the walls and tombstones spoken of by more than one visitor, and in retailing for European use other desirable information, of which he is at present the only possible exponent. [12]

Bell's continued interest in the Maldives was to be displayed in his collaboration with Gray in the latter's translation of Pyrard's Travels. This had been first suggested by Colonel Sir Henry Yule immediately after Bell's return from Male, about which he had heard from his friend General Bell.

Colonel Sir Henry Yule, R.E., C.B., K.C.S.I., Corr.Inst.France, was a Scot, born May 1, 1820. Yule passed out of the East India Company's Military College at Addiscombe (where his time coincided with that of H.W.B.Bell) with the top cadet's prize sword in December 1838. After he reached Calcutta, in 1840, Yule's career was concerned with railways, irrigation canals, and bridges, sometimes connected with military campaigns. Notably during the Mutiny in 1857 he was concerned with accommodation for troops and the defences of Allahabad. On a long furlough in 1843 Yule had married his cousin Annie White, but her precarious health precluded much residence in India. Their only child, Amy Frances Yule, contributed a full memoir of her father to the 1903 edition of *The Book of Ser Marco Polo* which he had translated and edited. Yule liked to sign himself M.P.V. after the great Venetian. Yule's special interest was in mediaeval travellers to the East, of which he wrote in *Cathay, and the Road Thither*, and he was an acknowledged authority on Central Asian geography.

He was a prolific writer on allied subjects - hence his L.L.D. from Edinburgh - and was President of the Hakluyt Society, and of the Royal Asiatic Society from 1885. Just before his own death on December 30, 1889, in his message of thanks for his honour from France, he telegraphed 'Moriturus vos saluto', and his old friend, Field Marshal Lord Napier of Magdala, told Miss Yule of her dead father, 'he looks as if he had just settled to some great work'.[13]

Albert Gray (1850-1928) entered the Ceylon Civil Service in 1871 but resigned four years later, having served in Colombo, Kandy and Anuradhapura. Back in England he was called to the Bar and took silk in 1905. He succeeded Yule as President of the Hakluyt Society. On March 26, 1880, Gray wrote to Bell expressing interest in his Maldive visit and his photographs; also in Maldive coins and especially in the Maldivian language. Gray had already contributed to the JRAS, Vol.6, an account of Lt. Christopher's vocabulary of the language, given to Dr. John Wilson of the Bombay Branch of the Society; and had written for the JRAS, Vol.10, 1878 an introduction to the Maldivian vocabulary of Pyrard.

Writing to Bell he suggested the latter should publish notes on Maldivian grammar, called his own vocabulary 'a very crude performance' and asked for a revision. He referred in October 1884 to the Maldive vocabulary of De Zoysa, and inquired earlier on behalf of Colonel Yule about the derivation of 'tava karhi'. Bell's information - 'the so-called sea-cocoanut, rated at so high a value in the estimation of the Maldive Sultans as to be retained as part of their royalties' - was incorporated in *Hobson-Jobson*, the monumental glossary of Anglo-Indian colloquial words and phrases compiled by Yule and A.C.Burnell and published in 1886. Bell gratefully received a copy of this from Gray. [14]

In January 1881 Bell had received from Gray a copy of Pyrard's French text for the collaboration. In the event it was Gray only who did the translation, Bell contributing some notes. Colonel Yule in 1882 described the projected first volume as a venture of equals, 'the bower that was biggit by Bessie Bell and Mary Gray' (as in the *Oxford Book of Ballads*). He had been sufficiently impressed by Bell's Maldive report to consider using it for his article on the Maldives for the *Encyclopaedia Britannica* - he wrote also that on Ibn Batuta - but actually he turned for help to Gray, for on their meeting he took to him greatly. Bell commented that 'they preferred the Triton to the Minnow'.

In respect of *Pyrard*, in October, Bell was realising that as merely a contributor of notes he should only be ranked as co-editor. Indeed, his contribution was continually delayed, partly by his work for the RASCB, and Gray began to complain. In May 1884 he wrote, 'Unless you can begin to send me some material our publication of *Pyrard* must be put off till the Greek Kalends'. 'I deserve your just rebuke', said Bell, 'I will send you matter shortly or relieve you of a useless encumbrance'.

Yet on October 14 Gray had to write, 'It is a pity that I relied on you', and Bell replied, 'I have forfeited the claim to be considered your collaborator'. He was hindered by his official duties. In 1884 he had acted for men on leave nearly half the year, and in 1885 wrote that he had been doing double duty for three months.

Gray, in his Preface and on the title page, acknowledged Bell's assistance, and Bell accepted that it would have been absurd for him to claim the right to joint editorship, though he was greatly disappointed. If Gray had hurt him once by what he called a 'crusty' letter, his excellent concise review for *The Athenaeum* of Bell's own report made up for it. In thanking him Bell said, 'I have done little to deserve your taking so much trouble'.

Some of Bell's contributions had in fact brightened the production. He had pressed for more illustrations and seven of those in the first volume reproduced his own, previously published in *The Graphic*. These were a view of Male Harbour, showing the artificial coral breakwater; the minaret of a Mosque; the street arena for Male Sports; a young girl carrying water together with an old man, Mahamadu Didi, son of the late fourth vizier; the entrance to the palace; a Maldive *larin* or long silver coin and some copper coins; and the wall at Male of the Old Fort with many derelict cannon, probably Portuguese. Bell also supplied a ground plan of the interior arrangement of the Chief Mosque (Hukuru Miskita) at Male, indicating the places for the Sultan, his Ministers, and priests.

Colonel Yule felt that the *Pyrard* publication would redeem the character of the Hakluyt Society, though an anxiety surfaced in March 1886; he felt it would be better to leave out the indecent poetry on page 195, for 'books are read in families'. Many years later, after sending a copy of *Pyrard* to his Maldive friend Ahmad Didi, who found the book vivid, Bell commented:

Mr. Gray and I had to 'soften down' his descriptions once at least into Latin. [15]

The Maldives: Pyrard and other visitors

Consideration for Colonel Yule had fuelled the impatience of Gray for Bell to hasten his contributions to *Pyrard*. In May 1884 Gray wrote, 'Our kind old friend Colonel Yule is in very precarious health and I fear he will never see *Pyrard* in his English dress'. Still living in October 1889, he was described as 'very frail and emaciated'. Bell himself had written sadly from Kegalla in May, 'My father passed away, you may know, during the last few months. Colonel Yule seems likely to follow. What a loss his death will be to the many who have learned to respect and love him'.

The first volume of *Pyrard* contained the Frenchman's shipwreck, his residence at Male, and some chapters of his journey to India. Bell's contribution to the Notes of this volume was confined to the Maldive chapters and frequently dealt with points of vocabulary, though he also supplied directly, or through Gray's quoting of his report, details of the channels between the atols, the boats and fish, the appearance of the inhabitants, their dress and hairdressing, food and drink. He brought up to date the list of court officials, gave the names of ten demons venerated in the southern atols, and contributed from the mouth of his Maldive pandit an account of the murder of Sultan Ali during the national struggle against the Portuguese. Bell also gave notes on rulers and their bodyguards, on titles, punishment (the most severe being banishment to remote islands), on taxation and debt slavery and how cowrie shells were exported for use as coinage.

In 1885 and 1886 proofs were passing to and fro, once sent on by Mrs. Bell to her husband in Madras, on his cricketing tour, and the first volume appeared in 1887. Bell and his father received copies in the summer.

Bell contributed no notes to Vol.II, Part I, about Pyrard's stay in Goa, which came out in 1888. Vol.II, Part II chronicled Pyrard's return to France, and to an Appendix on 'Early Notices of the Maldives' Bell contributed a list of the Maldive Sultans, extracting it from the *Tarikh*, the Maldivian chronicle, supplemented by Ibn Batuta. Bell also supplied notes on Maldivian natural history, and on a ruined dagaba on Fua Malaku.

Bell's main preoccupation was with Gray's Appendix on Pyrard's 'Dictionary of Some Words of the Maldive Language'. In Vol.II, Part II the 'Dictionary' appears in four columns of English, Old Maldivian, Modern Maldivian and Notes (mainly supplied by Bell). Gray pays tribute also to B.Gunasekera, Chief Government Translator at Colombo, and to D.M. de Zilva Wickremasinghe, Assistant Librarian, Colombo Museum. Bell in April 1888 had acknowledged the help of these two in compiling the vocabulary with his own and Christopher's translations in parallel columns.

As volumes of *Pyrard* became available, copies were in demand, but Gray deprecated giving them away too freely, saying, 'There is no reason why we should not recoup ourselves for our costs'. Bell had few hopes of sales, 'as the Ceylon reading public fancy lighter pabulum'. Some further readers, however, were pleased. St. George of the Colombo Library wrote, 'The Maldive ladies must be a charming lot if they are like what Pyrard describes them to be', and in 1892 the new Governor was said to have been deep in the volumes ever since his arrival.

François Pyrard's accounts are indeed of absorbing interest: his first impressions of the tropics, his delight in the flying fish and his first monkeys, his graphic accounts of the storm and of the shipwreck of the 'Corbin'. He survived most of his companions because he troubled to learn the Maldivian language, and because of his tactful behaviour to a noble patron and to the Sultan. He grieved deeply for the death of a friend, and was indignant at the mismanagement of the French expedition in which he had sailed. His account of the islands covers a wide field of geography, ceremonial, government and social customs. The climax is the sack of Male in the Bengal invasion which gave him his liberty.

Interest in aspects of the Maldives continues to be shown in the letters, especially interest in their products. Bell himself contributed an article on 'Fish curing at the Maldives' to the *Indian Antiquary* in 1882. In August 1885 an intended visitor to the Islands was a Swiss collector, C.R.Rosset who was not, said Bell, interested in their language or archaeology, but might amass specimens. He remarked, 'If he does not die of fever he may turn his trip to some use'. In January 1886 Rosset brought back some plants and a fine collection of Maldive artefacts for the 'Exhibition'. This was the Indian and Colonial Exhibition to be held in London, and Bell had been asked to collect a good show of products for 'the munificent sum of Rs. 150'. On August 17, 1885 Bell wrote:

> My Maldive friend has promised to aid me and you may yet see the 'Thousand Isles' fairly represented in London for the first time.

In July 1886 Bell asked Davidson, joint Secretary with him of the RASCB, who was on leave in London, for a list of the items contributed by Ibrahim Didi, and urged that he be awarded a gold medal. In fact Ibrahim, a year later, received a silver medal.

Often in the early letters appears Bell's wish to revisit the Islands. Already in June 1881 he had written to Gray, 'Oh that it may come about sooner or later that I may be sent to the Maldives with some authority!' However, efforts by Gregory and Fyers to win permission for this from the Colonial Office and the Government of Ceylon came to nothing.

Bell's curiosity about the Islands had to find vent in inquiries to other people. Enquiries for books on the Maldives went from the first to General Bell and to his friend Robert Cust of the Royal Geographical and Royal Asiatic Societies. Bell also wrote, 'I want to add as many books on Ceylon to my library as possible'. He studied a book by O.Bartholomeus on the northern island of Minicoy and corresponded with Winterbottom, Collector of Malabar, on the difference between the Laccadive and Maldive archipelagoes. He was glad that Winterbottom favoured his idea that Minicoy should be transferred from Indian administration to that of Ceylon, for as he wrote on September 30, 1889:

> It is Maldivian in everything, originally (two or three centuries back) was included in the group and more or less subject to the Sultan at Male (or where there were two or three 'Richards in the field' to the most northern) and but for the greed of one of the four Canarese Adi Rayas would belong to the Sultan of the 12,000 Islands at this day. [16]

Bell had drawn on Portuguese records for his report; as early as 1880 his father was looking at some for him in the Record Office. In 1889 Bell wrote from Kegalla to A.C.Teixera de Aragoa, sending a lithogram of Maldive writing and asking if any similar documents were to be found

The Maldives: Pyrard and other visitors

in Portuguese archives; and some months later wrote to Lisbon again. As for the important Dutch records, in 1887 A.E.Buultjens offered to search the Hague Archives for Bell. The Dutch records in Ceylon had not been well looked after. About 1880 Bell, in co-operation with the Assistant Colonial Secretary, J.A.Swettenham, abstracted from them nearly all the original Maldivian letters and translations and had them bound together. Bell used them in his report of 1881 and in his 'Excerpta Maldiviana' in the Journal of the RASCB, from 1922 to 1927.

Bell's scholarly interests could not have been missed by the authorities, but it was to be a few years more before these would have a determinative effect on his career. It will, though, appear that he was already informing himself on local topography and archaeology, and was becoming recognised as a person to be consulted about them. Consequently, when the Archaeological Survey came to be set up, he was to become a natural choice to conduct it.

4

Archaeology before 1890 : The Collecting of Records

Before moving on to the setting up of the Archaeological Survey in 1890 and the start of Bell's career as Archaeological Commissioner, it will be useful to give an account of the development in Ceylon of archaeological studies in the broadest sense, and the way in which the Government gradually involved itself in official support for archaeology. Archaeology in Ceylon, as elsewhere in this period, developed from antiquarianism. Indeed it may be said that, partly because of the wealth of 'historical' material available in the shape of chronicles and inscriptions, archaeology long remained merely the handmaid of history.

Ancient manuscripts had been preserved in Buddhist monasteries; ancient ruins were discovered in the jungle by exploring soldiers; records and inscriptions were studied by Sinhalese scholars and Civil Servants. Much useful information was collected, albeit in a haphazard way, either in the journal of the Royal Asiatic Society of Great Britain and Ireland, or in that of the Ceylon Branch of the Society which was founded in 1845. Both Societies endeavoured to bring to the notice of Government the importance of salvaging the historical heritage of the Island, its monuments and its records, literary or epigraphical.

Both in the initiation of action and the carrying through of government policy much depended on the enthusiasm or otherwise of individual Civil Servants; of primary importance was the attitude of the Governor. Outstanding were the contributions of Sir Hercules Robinson (1865-1872), Sir William Gregory (1872-1877) and Sir Arthur Gordon (1883-1890). Records of the initiatives of the first two are collected together in Sessional Paper I of 1878, entitled *Papers on the Subject of Literary and Scientific Work in Ceylon* which, according to R.W.Ievers, was compiled by Edward Muller. Information may also be found in the Administration Reports of Government Agents, and in the section on 'Archaeology' in R.W.Ievers' own *Manual of the North-Central Province* which lists some of the other important Sessional Papers of this period.In the collection of ancient manuscripts, as in the patronage of other aspects of antiquarian research, the Government of Ceylon followed the example of India, which had set up its own Archaeological Survey in 1861. On December 7, 1868 the Government Agent of Jaffna, H.S.O.Russell, wrote to the Colonial Secretary drawing his attention to the fact that in India steps were being taken to search out ancient Sanskrit manuscripts. He suggested that others might be found in the Pansalas (monks' dwellings) in Ceylon.[1]

The Chief Translator to the Government, Louis de Zoysa, was consulted and gave it as his opinion that most of the Sanskrit manuscripts to be found in Ceylon came originally from India, but that if a search was made for Pali and Sinhalese manuscripts, important discoveries might be made. In the Memorandum dated June 12, 1869 he wrote:

> Should the proposed inspection of the Buddhist libraries of Ceylon bring to light any works on history not known at present, the interest that may be excited by such discoveries, and the benefits to be derived

thereby, will not be confined to Ceylon, but will be shared by the learned in India and Europe. It is now generally believed that the ancient historical records of the Sinhalese are far more valuable and authentic than those of other Indian nations. The *Mahawanso*, (History of Ceylon) translated into English by the late Hon'ble George Turnour of Ceylon, has been pronounced by high authority to be 'the most valuable historical record we possess in relation to Ancient India'. [2]

The task of collecting manuscripts was first entrusted to James de Alwis, already known for his publications on Sinhalese literature and grammar. He proposed that a Library should be set up to contain the rare manuscripts obtained or copied. Established in 1870, it was called the Government Oriental Library and by 1897 De Alwis and his successor in the work, Louis de Zoysa, with the aid of Government Agents, had collected 209 olas. 'Olas', those ancient records, are well described by a lady travelling in Ceylon at this period as:

> ...quite unique manuscripts of very great antiquity, and all written, or rather scratched, with styles on long narrow strips of carefully prepared palm-leaf, generally about two and a half inches wide, and sometimes twenty inches long. Each leaf, when written, was smeared with dark oil, coloured with charred gum, which blackened the indented letters and has preserved the leaves (*olas* is the right word) from attacks of insects. All the leaves, forming a book, are placed between two neat wooden boards, some of which are elaborately painted, others embossed with precious metal, and even gems: the whole are pierced with two holes, and strung together by cords. [3]

The works placed in the Oriental Library were afterwards transferred to the Library attached to the Colombo Museum and staff of the Museum continued to add to the collection. In the diary of F.H.Price, A.G.A. at Kegalla on April 4, 1889 we read:

> Mr. Wickremasinghe, the assistant librarian of the Colombo Museum, came to me a few days ago and asked for assistance in collecting valuable manuscripts for copying.... he has already succeeded in obtaining the loan of five books which he wanted. [4]

Lists of the manuscripts, collected and copied, were published in the Administration Reports of the Colombo Museum. That of 1889 lists thirty-five manuscripts, including texts of the canonical scriptures of Buddhism, miscellaneous religious works, historical and philological works, poetry and scientific studies. Seven of them were copied from manuscripts lent by Bell, and after he became Archaeological Commissioner his Annual Reports from 1895 record the number of copies he had made of those he discovered while on tour and sent to the Museum.

Less satisfactory was the manner in which Government acted in the matter of the preservation and publication of the records of the Dutch Administration. These had been collected from the Colombo and Galle Kachcheris in the 1860s, roughly bound and stored in the Government Record Office. M.W.Jurriaanse, who produced a catalogue of these archives in 1943, complained that they were bound together in the order in which they were found, with no consideration of chronological order, and so inefficiently that in some cases it was impossible to open the volumes or read the contents. Jurriaanse went on to criticise Bell for the way in which he and Swettenham

27

had treated the records about 1880 when Bell was searching for Maldive material. According to Jurriaanse, Bell had raided the archives only for his own research purposes and had even removed the documents in which he was interested. [5]

Bell's own account of his raid on the records reads as follows:

Any 'explorer' who ventured into the semi-darkness of the then stuffy 'Black Hole', wherein these old-time volumes were left, year after year, to choke for want of light and air had - literally - to trample under foot a mass of loose documents that had been crowded, or fallen, out of the inadequate shelving made available, and lay higgledy-piggledy, almost disregarded, and partially blocking the very narrow passage-ways.

The sorting, and disposal (as far as practicable), of this heterogeneous jumble of dust-laden papers, and the taking down, examining, and re-shelving of some 3,000 heavy volumes, begrimed with dirt, of necessity involved considerable labour; but, though unpleasant enough physically, this greatly needed 'clean-up' was not without its reward to the antiquarian. For - independent of the timely relief thus afforded towards the better preservation of these hoary records, important historically and in other ways from detailing Dutch Administration in Ceylon throughout a period of more than a hundred and fifty years - the work proved not unprofitable collaterally.

Many valuable documents, which had been long lying *perdu*, came to light. Among these were found (i) original letters addressed to Dutch Governors by Raja Sinha II, King of Kandy, 1632-1679; (ii) missives, mostly annual, to, and from, Sultans of the Maldives in the 17th and 18th centuries; (iii) communications from Southern Indian Rulers; besides (iv) sporadic letters, some directly from, others relating to, the luckless European captives in Kandy during the latter half of the 17th century; and (v) many other papers of a miscellaneous nature - all of more or less interest and value. [6]

Efforts to interest Government in the preservation of these records were made by the RASCB. In 1880 Fyers had spoken of them in his Presidential Address and urged that they should be properly indexed, and on February 7, 1888 Bell wrote to the Colonial Secretary on behalf of the Society reiterating Fyers' remarks and further urging that at least the most important volumes should be translated. The Society offered to arrange for a translation of the Resolutions of the Galle Council 1641-1644 to be undertaken in Holland, and to pay something towards the cost. In response the Government agreed to transfer the Galle records to the Museum and in the Supply Bill of 1891 a vote of Rs. 200 was made towards the preservation and translation of the Dutch records.[7]

Sadly, the good work was not kept up. On November 10, 1892 Bell wrote to the Colonial Secretary asking that the unexpended balance from the 1891 grant should be given to the Society, but the request was refused, and he was told that it had not been the intention of Government to make an annual grant. It was not until 1900 that Mr. R.G.Anthonisz was appointed 'examiner of the Dutch records' and some progress began to be made towards the listing and translation of the records. In 1902 Anthonisz eventually published the translation made in The Hague of the two volumes of the Galle Records, stating that no time had been found before then for checking them with the original manuscript.[8]

Archaeology before 1890: The collecting of records

Several references have been already made to the establishment of the Colombo Museum, of which the Library formed an integral part. The Museum was the particular creation of Sir William Gregory. In his *Autobiography* he quoted with satisfaction his own speech to the Legislative Council in September 1872, introducing his project:

> The want of a museum, in which may be represented the natural history, antiquities, and industrial products of the island, has been forcibly urged on me. During the period when the revenue of the island did not suffice for its most imperative wants, it would have been inexpedient to have sanctioned an institution which it was better to leave untouched rather than establish on an inadequate and unsatisfactory footing. For a comparatively small sum, considering the object in view, a museum may be constructed which shall not be a mere random collection of miscellaneous objects, but a scientific, teaching exhibition, which, while ministering to the amusement of many, may convey instruction to all who seek it.
>
> I propose, in connection with this museum, to obtain reproductions of the inscriptions throughout the island, by means of photography, casts, and hand-copying. These inscriptions, varying in character and dialect, will be of deep interest to the philologist, and throw light on the ancient usages, religious customs and early history of Ceylon. [9]

The proposal was warmly welcomed by Fyers in his Presidential Address to the RASCB on November 7, 1872. At the same meeting Sir William Gregory accepted the office of Patron of the Society, and told a cautionary tale of the vandalising of ancient inscriptions:

> He was much struck some time ago when, visiting an irrigation work in the Eastern Province, he saw an annicut being constructed with massive stones some of which had ancient inscriptions on them; he told the officer who was in charge of the work, that he thought it was a great pity to take these for such a purpose. The reply he received was that the stones were found very near the work, and came in very handily, and it was a pity to go further for stone. He (the Governor) however, thought differently, and gave instructions that no more such stones should be so used. A museum would be the means of preserving and utilising many monuments of the past, and it and the Society might be of service to each other. The Society would find, close at hand, objects for reference to the student and the lecturer, whilst the general public would not only be gratified by an inspection of the collection, but many might be induced to take the opportunity thus afforded, of studying the works of God and man. [10]

Gregory gave a description of the Museum at its opening in his letter of August 1, 1877 to the Earl of Carnarvon, Secretary of State for the Colonies:

> Although this institution was only opened in January last, it already possesses many objects of interest to antiquarians. I have had sculptures sent in from various ruined cities; among them is a very fine stone lion weighing about eight tons from the city of Pollonaruwa; upon it there is an inscription to the effect that King Nisanka Mala (about A.D. 1180) sat on this lion and administered justice. The constant destruction of sculptural works of art and of inscriptions by Indian coolies, who are under the impression that they contain or are placed over treasure, and the careless manner with which they have

at times been treated by officers of the Public Works Department, render it advisable that all sculptures of value should be brought at once to Colombo, where they will be carefully preserved. But the present space of the Museum will not suffice for the various objects, some of them large, which are likely to be received; and I left with our very accomplished and able architect, Mr. Smither, my views as to the erection of an additional building to be attached to it, in which there will be ample space to exhibit all the antiquities which we possess at present, as well as all accessions which we are likely to obtain. I am indebted to Sir Joseph Hooker for the idea of a structure which will be of moderate cost, elegant in appearance, and well adapted for the exhibition of sculpture. It is to be a roofed oblong building on the same principle as, but of course of much less area and height than, the Campo Santo of Pisa, with a cloister running round it. To the outside wall of this cloister the inscriptions should be attached in chronological order, and smaller objects can also be exhibited on stands and brackets. In the centre should be placed the larger objects, such as the Pollonaruwa lion. Though the objects exhibited in this building will not have the attraction of the Indo-Greek remains now being collected by General Cunningham in India, still they have an interest as representing Buddhist art, and some of the early stone carvings are original and graceful. [11]

Gregory regarded the collection of inscriptions as one of the main purposes of the Museum. It was also one of the objects of the Archaeological Commission which had been set up by Sir Hercules Robinson in 1868. Fyers was appointed chairman of the Commission (or Committee as is was sometimes called) and in his Administration Report of 1868 he wrote:

I may also state that in the early part of the year I was appointed to a Committee of which the other members are the Director of Public Works, the Assistant Government Agent of Puttalam and the Architectural Assistant of the Director of Public Works. The object of the Committee is to obtain information respecting the different Ancient Architectural Works in the Island, to report on them generally and to state what steps we would recommend to have the most interesting of them preserved or photographed. The information required was as a preliminary step prepared in tabular form and copies were forwarded to Government Agents and Assistant Agents and we are awaiting their replies (none of which have been received) before proceeding to visit the different localities where there are known to be works of Ancient Architecture. [12]

Fyers, however, also considered the collection of inscriptions to be in the remit of the Commission. When on July 28, 1870, the committee of the RASCB wished to send a memorial to Government urging the consideration of this subject, Fyers 'informed the meeting that the matter had been fully laid before the Archaeological Commission and that he was sure that they would do all in their power to save these valuable relics from further destruction'. The committee therefore restricted itself to asking that they should be sent duplicates of any impressions that might be taken. [13]

It might be thought that the setting up of the Commission could be taken as the official recognition of the responsibility of Government for all aspects of archaeological activity. But it was, in fact, only one of the many tentative steps forward which led at last to the establishment of the Archaeological Survey in 1890. No official report of the work of the Commission seems to have been published, but at the Annual Meeting of the RASCB in 1871 Fyers gave the

Archaeology before 1890: The collecting of records

following outline of its activities to date:

> An Archaeological Committee has been appointed by Government to explore, take photographs, decipher inscriptions, and endeavour to trace the history of each work in various parts of the Island. Mr. Lawton of Kandy has been appointed Photographer to the Committee, and has already taken very good photographs of the principal buildings in Pollonaruwa; of Minniri, Giretella and Topare Tanks; of the ancient fortified rock of Bijeri and some of the most important objects of interest in Anuradhapura. The Committee are endeavouring to obtain from ancient works, and inscriptions, the date of construction and history of each building and work, and we hope shortly to have completed albums containing both views and descriptions. I hope that any gentleman who has a taste for investigations of this nature will co-operate with the Committee, and give us the benefit of his experience and knowledge. [14]

It is not clear how far the Commission succeeded in collecting details of archaeological remains from the Government Agents. The only published list is the *Return of Architectural and Archaeological Remains and other Antiquities existing in Ceylon on January 1, 1887*, published in Colombo in 1890. It is possible that the Government collected material but did not publish it.

However, the Commission was certainly active in arranging for the taking of photographs of ruins and inscriptions, and in organising survey work at Anuradhapura. From 1873 to 1875 George Capper of the Survey Department was busily at work there. According to his father, who edited the notes which he took during this period, 'The results of his labours were shown in upwards of thirty large sheets of tracings which have since been copied and forwarded to the Colonial Office in London'.[15]

Detailed plans and drawings of the major known monuments were also made by the Secretary of the Commission, J.G.Smither, and these were later published in the famous *Architectural Remains, Anuradhapura, Ceylon : Comprising the Dagabas and Certain Other Ancient Ruined Structures* published in London by the Ceylon Government in 1894.

In his Administration Report for 1871 Fyers stated that:

> Mr. Smither proceeded to Anuradhapura early in the year, accompanied by Mr. Lawton and Mudaliyar de Zoysa, the Government Interpreter in the Colonial Secretary's Office, and a most interesting set of photographs was taken. Two large volumes of plates of ruins, etc., in Pollonaruwa, Anuradhapura and Sigiri are now in my possession and available for inspection. Duplicate copies of these have been sent to England to the Secretary of State for the Colonies. [16]

Notes and comments on each plate were made by Mr. Liesching, the A.G.A. at Anuradhapura, himself very interested in the work. Sadly Mr. Lawton did not long survive. Fyers told of his death at a meeting of the RASCB on November 7, 1872, saying that his health had been seriously affected by his strenuous work. Not only did he take photographs but he supervised the clearing of the ruins. He added:

> Mr. Lawton was a thoroughly honest, upright man, very hard working, and desirous at all times of doing his work efficiently and to the satisfaction of those under whom he was employed. By diligence,

patience and strict integrity he had become a first class photographer, and he was justly respected by all with whom he was associated. Had the unsparing hand of death not visited him he would, I feel confident, have made a European name for himself by the excellence of his photographs, especially of those of ruins in this Island. [17]

Further photographs of inscriptions were taken by Captain Hogg of the Royal Engineers, and sent back to the Colonial Office with a request that they should be shown to Robert C.Childers and Dr. R.Rost of the India Office, and Professor Eggeling of the Royal Asiatic Society. Robert Childers submitted the following opinion of the value of the photographs of inscriptions:

> Three of the inscriptions have come out so well, that of the words they contain probably nine-tenths might be read from the photographs as they stand. The remaining tenth consists of words more or less uncertain. Now, if instead of a single photograph of each of these three inscriptions, we had several, taken at different times of the day, it is possible that doubtful words might be all, or nearly all, recovered, since lines which are invisible in a photograph taken at one hour of the day, often stand out clearly in a photograph taken three or four hours earlier or later. But the necessity of multiplying photographs of each of these inscriptions would be obviated, if the reader had the inscription before him, and was able to supplement the imperfect photographic representation by the eye and touch.
>
> By a curious coincidence the last mail from Ceylon brought me a manuscript in the Sinhalese character of one of these very inscriptions, made by a Buddhist priest from an ocular inspection of the inscribed slab. He has succeeded in making out the whole inscription, which could not I think be done from the single photograph taken by Captain Hogg....
>
> Among the photographs there are a number of inscriptions which from their high antiquity are probably of very great importance, but which it would not be possible to decipher and translate from the photographs alone. A few will require every available process: for instance, two or three photographs taken at different times of the day, long and careful ocular examination, and the collection of relief copies taken from the rock by squeezes. [18]

Many similar complaints came to be made by scholars in England who were asked to decipher inscriptions from copies made in Ceylon.

5

Archaeology before 1890 : Epigraphy and Monuments

The authorities were beginning to realise the wealth of epigraphical material which might be uncovered by systematic research, and the 1870s saw the appointment of two outside experts to examine inscriptions on the spot. The first was a Dr. Paul Goldschmidt, recommended to Sir William Gregory by Eggeling of the RAS as 'the best person for the task with whom he was acquainted'. Gregory wrote to the Earl of Carnarvon, Secretary of State for the Colonies, on August 17, 1874:

> I should be prepared, with Your Lordship's sanction, to offer Dr. Goldschmidt 4,000 rupees per annum for an engagement of three years, with power for either party to conclude the engagement at the expiry of the first or second year. He should have his travelling expenses, a tent when required, and a proper staff of coolies, also a free first class passage out and home.
>
> It might also be convenient for him to take out a competent photographer with his materials, but I do not consider that an expensive artist need be engaged, as the duties will be simply that of carefully reproducing the inscriptions, and artistic taste and education would not be a requisite.[1]

Goldschmidt's appointment was approved, and he accepted the post, but asked that a competent photographer should also be sent out. However, Government jibbed at the extra expense. It was therefore agreed that, as Captain Hogg had been posted away from Ceylon, another Royal Engineer should be found to do the work, and a Corporal Sharp who had been on detachment in New Zealand 'observing the transit of Venus' was suggested. The precedents of the employment of the military in the survey of the Sinai Peninsula and in Palestine were cited, but it is not clear from the correspondence whether Corporal Sharp actually arrived in Ceylon to help Dr. Goldschmidt.

At all events Goldschmidt began work in 1875. He naturally made Anuradhapura his headquarters, but also visited Mihintale and Polonnaruwa. He then turned to the east and the south and explored at Trincomalee, Batticaloa and Hambantota. He copied an inscription inside the great dagaba at Tissamaharama, which was temporarily visible as repair work was being undertaken. Some of the results of his researches were published in three Sessional Papers, two of which were reprinted in the *Indian Antiquary*.

In Goldschmidt's last official publication he grouped inscriptions chronologically into three periods, from the introduction of Buddhism to the beginning of the Christian era, up to the 4th century A.D. and up to the 11th century A.D. He was, however, primarily interested in the linguistic importance of the inscriptions, and in the light they threw on the Aryan origins of Sinhalese. He was working to the last on a paper for the JRASCB which analysed all the forms of words found during his researches.[2]

Goldschmidt never completed his three year engagement, for he died of malaria in Galle on May 7, 1877. His loss was deeply regretted by Sir William Gregory, who appreciated him for his personal qualities as well as for his scholarly attainments. He wrote on the very day of Goldschmidt's death:

> To the literary world his loss will be very great. He was a profound Oriental scholar, and he had devoted himself to a branch of Oriental literature hitherto but little cultivated, the Sinhalese and cognate dialects. It was his intention, had he lived, to have thoroughly worked out the Veddah and Maldive languages and the Rodiya dialect.
>
> When he first came here his health was so strong and the climate suited him so well, that he felt satisfied he could do out-door work by day as well as in Europe. I constantly remonstrated with him on his extraordinary imprudence; a severe attack of fever last year shewed him that he had no immunity from the diseases of the country, if he rashly courted them; and since then he has had other attacks, which, however, he seems to have disregarded.
>
> Two days ago I wrote to him privately, and also officially, requesting him to send in all the work he had completed to the Colonial Secretary's Office. He was very averse to this, solely on the ground of not being perfectly satisfied with the accuracy of his investigations. He expected next year to prepare the volume of *Ceylon Inscriptions* for publication. This must now be done by other hands, if a competent man can be selected.[3]

Gregory suggested that Dr. Rost of the India Office Library be asked to look over the work which Goldschmidt had left behind, and to recommend a successor. Unfortunately his papers were left in considerable confusion; he was extremely conscientious, and unwilling to commit himself to a final version of any transcription or translation until he had checked and rechecked his sources. The papers were roughly sorted in Ceylon and sent back to England, where they were looked over by Dr. Rost and Dr. Edward Muller. The latter had been appointed early in 1878 to succeed Goldschmidt. When Bell took over the work of the Archaeological Survey he was very anxious to obtain both the papers and any photographs of inscriptions left by Goldschmidt, and in 1899 he wrote to Wickremasinghe, Epigraphist to the Ceylon Government, who was in London, asking him to trace them. Dr. Muller, then long back in Europe, was consulted. He replied that he had taken all the papers out to Ceylon, worked over them and incorporated what was useful in his own publications. He had taken back to Europe those papers which he had not considered fit for publication, but they had been destroyed in a fire in his house in Berne in 1886 or 1887. He had no knowledge of what might have happened to the photographs.[4]

Muller, who called himself Government Archaeologist, or Archaeological Commissioner, also only worked in Ceylon for two years, from 1878 to 1880, but in that time he wrote a number of preliminary reports in the form of Sessional Papers, and also contributed articles to the JRASCB; he was elected to the Committee of the Society on September 11, 1879. He checked many of Goldschmidt's inscriptions and collected others, and returned to England in September 1880 to prepare a book on the subject which came out in 1883.[5]

Archaeology before 1890: Epigraphy and monuments

In Bell's reports we often meet with comments on the inadequacy of Muller's observations, and R.W.Ievers wrote that Dr. Muller's 'contributions to our knowledge of the inscriptions are most disappointing. The inscriptions have been copied in a most perfunctory and inaccurate fashion, and only those which are readily accessible are dealt with'.[6]

Senerath Paranavitana, a later Archaeological Commissioner, commented more kindly on the work of all his predecessors:

> That we can today discover glaring errors in many of the texts of the inscriptions and their interpretations...should by no means detract from the great credit due to these pioneers for their contributions to our knowledge of the ancient culture of the Island, which was often the result of work undertaken at great personal risk and sacrifice, and in circumstances of which the difficulties can hardly be imagined by those who pursue their studies of Ceylon history in well-equipped libraries in Europe.[7]

Digging up and transcribing inscriptions was one aspect of research, but many of the great architectural ruins, secular and religious, were still to be uncovered. Action by Government towards the unveiling and restoration of these monuments of the past was at first confined to the grudging provision of money for clearing the jungle that surrounded them. In 1840 the small sum of £40 was allotted for the clearing of areas round the main buildings then known at Anuradhapura and some further work was undertaken in 1845. In 1863 the Medical Officer complained that the overgrown state of the area round the Brazen Palace attracted large herds of deer, and that the unrestricted shooting of the deer was a danger to officers resident near by. On this, the magnificent sum of £2 was given for further clearing, but it cannot be said to have had an archaeological purpose.

However, individual efforts were made both to excavate and to restore - sometimes with less than happy results. The restoration of the Thuparama by a Buddhist bhikkhu in 1841, who collected money personally for this with the aim of restoring a sacred shrine, was not undertaken with the idea of recreating the original form of the dagaba, and the result has been severely criticised. This divergence between the preoccupations of those concerned with the religious significance of the monuments, and of those thinking only of their historical and archaeological importance, was to recur and cause conflict in the future.

The rebuilding of the Ruwanveli dagaba, which incurred Bell's disapproval, was an individual effort. It was undertaken by a Buddhist priest by the name of Naranwita Sumarasara Unnanse, with enthusiastic encouragement from Sir William Gregory. In a personal testimonial dated February 18, 1876 Sir William wrote:

> I have visited the Ruwanveli Dagaba and have been quite satisfied with the progress made by Naranwita Sumarasara Unnanse in the restoration of the work; only three years ago it was a mere pile of bricks. He has completely cleared it and has restored the greater part of the basement. The vigour displayed by Naranwita Sumarasara Unnanse deserves every encouragement, and I trust that it will be appreciated by his countrymen. I have myself contributed to this restoration, not looking on it as a religious work, but as the conservation of a great national monument characteristic of the best period of Sinhalese art and identified with one of the most powerful and enlightened kings who ever ruled this country.[8]

Ievers, Government Agent at Anuradhapura, later cast doubts on the viability of the restoration. He said:

> It is to be regretted that the rebuilding by this priest has not been carried out under skilled professional advice. The work done is worse than useless, as the new brickwork has not been properly bonded with the old structure. It bulges out in places, and falls in wet weather, with disastrous effect, on the ambulatories and objects of interest in the 'Maluwa'. [9]

Early restorations put in hand by the Public Works Department were later subjected to Bell's criticism. In 1886 the Provincial Engineer, A.E.Williams, on direct orders from Sir Arthur Gordon, undertook repairs at Yapahuwa. However, when S.M.Burrows, G.A. for the North-Western Province, wished in 1903 for a grant to continue operations, Bell wrote that 'the work appears to have been carried out most conscientiously by Mr. Williams, but from unfamiliarity with ancient Ceylon architecture, not without some errors'. In official correspondence of the previous year, however, his criticism was more strongly worded, and he wrote that Williams' work was haphazard and incorrect in places, softening his remarks somewhat by adding that he knew of some of the errors from Williams himself - 'from his own lips'.[10]

The work carried through by Williams had been commissioned by Government; it is not always easy to determine to what extent early forays into excavation were carried out by Civil Servants on their own initiative or in response to prodding from above. Not all would have shared the views of Ievers who remarked in his Administration Report for 1888 that 'the claims of archaeology and the excavation of some, and preservation of other, ruins afford a pleasing and useful change from the monotony of the Kachcheri and court routine'.[11]

After the setting up of the Archaeological Commission there was more direct activity organised by Government. A grant of £50 was made towards the clearing of ruins at Anuradhapura before the Commission paid its exploratory visit and, as we have seen, projects for the photographing and surveying of the ruins were initiated. Sir Hercules Robinson also arranged that an annual sum should be devoted to the clearing of the jungle, and Sir William Gregory in his letter of August 1, 1877 said:

> This undertaking was still further carried out by me and at present the station has the appearance of a fine spacious park studded with clumps and single trees, and a vote has been taken for the construction of a road, about six miles in length, which is by this time probably finished, and which enables visitors to drive to all the monuments of note known at present. [12]

Between 1869 and 1882 there were several government officers at Anuradhapura who took a keen interest in further exploration and excavation. L.Liesching, A.G.A. from 1869 to 1870, published a detailed account of the state of the ruins in his Administration Report of 1869 and supplemented it in that of 1870 with an account of further discoveries made during the work of the photographer Lawton. In the 1869 Report he made the following comments on the ruinous state of Anuradhapura:

It seems at first strange that works of such solidity as many of the ruins about Anuradhapura should have fallen into such complete decay, constructed as many of them are of solid masses of stone, while some of the structures of Rome of a date more ancient are still in such perfect repair. But apart from the effects of climate and those powerful wedges, the roots of trees, there was one very serious and radical defect in the architecture of Ceylon. No proper foundations appear to have been made, and consequently the mere weight of buildings has been fatal to their permanence. The stone pillars seem simply to have been buried a certain distance in the ground, and then it was required of them that they should support edifices of immense weight; and as a natural consequence they sank, and the buildings fell. [13]

In 1872 T.W.Rhys Davids, who had been appointed to the Archaeological Commission by Sir Hercules Robinson, was sent to Anuradhapura as Acting A.G.A. His short stay there is well documented by A.Wickremeratne, who quotes correspondence between Rhys Davids and the Colonial Secretary concerning special grants of money allocated to him for archaeological purposes. Sir William Gregory sent him very precise orders regarding the clearing of the areas round the dagobas, the making of plans and the collection of inscribed stones and other large objects which might be sent to his Museum. Rhys Davids, however, got into bad odour with the Government, and was required to resign the service. [14]

The Administration Report for 1872 was written, therefore, by his successor, H.H.Cameron. He described with enthusiasm the advantages to be gained from excavations:

A most interesting addition has this year been added to the curiosities of this ancient city, in the handsomely-moulded basement of a Maha-Datu-seya or some such building in close proximity to the Ruwanweli-seya. It is in the centre of this structure that the stone couch stands, on which it is said that the king Datugemunu was wont to recline and which has been so artistically portrayed by the camera of the late Mr. Lawton. The stone basement with its three carved porticoes was at its lowest point some three feet buried in the ground and it is of a consequence in the most perfect preservation; at one corner of the building lies an elaborately chiselled specimen of that domestic contrivance, the use of which has long been abandoned by the Sinhalese and which bears the name of Kesakuttiya. This stone is entirely unique, both with regard to the design and the preservation of its workmanship which, after perhaps 2,000 years of time, still seems fresh from the hands of the artist...The discovery of these remains has afforded a most valuable clue to the researches of the archaeologist, showing, as it does, that many objects of beauty and interest are lying not many cubits beneath our very feet. [15]

In 1873 the North-Central Province was detached from the Northern Province and Anuradhapura became its administrative centre. The new Government Agent, J.Dickson, later Sir John Dickson, who was also actively engaged in the restoration of ancient tanks, carried on with the work of clearing and preliminary excavation around the Thuparama and the two great dagabas, Abhayagiriya and Jetawanarama. His detailed report to Government is given in full in Ievers' *Manual*, and there are many references to his work in Bell's early reports on Anuradhapura.

In 1884 S.M.Burrows was commissioned by Sir Arthur Gordon to undertake exploration at both Anuradhapura and Polonnaruwa. He was engaged in work at both places up to August 1886 and wrote a full account in Sessional Paper X, 1886, entitled *Report on Archaeological Work at*

Anuradhapura and Polonnaruwa, as well as a number of articles contributed to the JRASCB and letters published in the proceedings of the Society.

Burrows cleared large areas of the Anuradhapura ruins and laid bare some interesting new buildings including that with a stone canopy near the great northern dagaba which has been termed 'Burrows' Pavilion', and a large vihare opposite the stone canoe with a fine stairway. Ievers, who was Government Agent at the time, joined in the work and discovered three large stone sannasas near by, and these were copied. A large sedent Buddha was found and set up in position and a square pokuna north-west of the Kuttampokuna cleared. Burrows strongly recommended that a detailed survey should be made, for he had no doubt that many more buildings awaited discovery.

Burrows also undertook excavations around the Mirisavetiya dagaba, excavations under the auspices of the RASCB. Dickson and Smither had together excavated the finely carved structure on the west side of the Mirisavetiya, at that time variously termed a 'frontispiece' or 'chapel'. It was believed that further excavation would reveal similar structures at the other cardinal points, and on February 9, 1884, at a meeting of the RASCB, Sir Arthur Gordon proposed the setting up of a subscription fund, the proceeds of which should be devoted to this project. Rs. 1,000 was raised, and Burrows was entrusted with the work. In the event the excavations on the east side of the dagaba were fruitless, and the work was suspended. In 1886 the north 'chapel' of the great northern dagaba was also cleared of debris and the copper plaques were found which were at that time believed to be coins.

Further excavations were carried out on the Mirisavetiya by Ievers in 1888, using money donated by a Siamese prince and employing prison labour. The plan for the restoration was made by the engineer A.Murray, who based his drawings on the measurements of the Rankot dagaba at Polonnaruwa.

At Polonnaruwa also many buildings were cleared of vegetation and debris, including the Thuparama, Heta-da-ge and Sat-Mahal-Prasadaya, the Rankot and Kiri dagabas and the Nayipena vihare. Inscriptions were revealed and copied, and some coins discovered and sent to Bell for identification. Burrows also tunnelled into the Demala-Maha-Seya and revealed wall paintings, some of which were copied by A.Murray. Burrows went on to become Director of Education in Ceylon, and his continued interest in the ruins he had explored found issue in his little guide, *The Buried Cities of Ceylon*. [16]

Sir Arthur Gordon, who had instigated the RASCB's Fund for excavations, also authorised considerable government expenditure on repairs to the great Abhayagiriya dagaba at Anuradhapura. A section of the square 'tee', the box or tower on its summit which supported the crowning pinnacle, had fallen down. In a letter to the Secretary of State for the Colonies, written from Anuradhapura on August 11, 1886 he applied for retrospective sanction for this work, which he had set in hand immediately in view of the precarious stability of the structure:

> It appeared to me that the preservation of a national monument of such historical and archaeological interest as this structure (only inferior to the pyramids in mass and elevation) was well worth the attention of this government, and seeing the danger to the pinnacle to be imminent and immediate

Archaeology before 1890: Epigraphy and monuments

action to be necessary, unless the dagoba was to be allowed to perish, or greatly increased expenditure incurred in undertaking repairs at a later period, I authorized the immediate commencement of such repairs to the base of the 'tee' (as it is called) as were necessary to ensure its continued support of the terminating pinnacle which rises to the height of nearly 300 feet. Of these repairs, which are satisfactorily progressing, I have now to ask for your Lordship's approval. They have been made on an estimate by the Provincial Engineer, Mr. A.Murray, amounting to Rs. 3,000; out of this sum Rs. 1,500 will be paid by the Buddhist Committee of this place, from the scanty funds in their hands. The remaining Rs. 1,500 is not, I think, an unreasonable contribution from the government towards the preservation of so remarkable and ancient a building, more especially when it is remembered that the estates once supporting it have passed into the hands of the Crown.[17]

The work was carried out by successive Provincial Engineers under the keen supervision of Ievers. As well as repairing the summit, they dug into the centre. A shaft was driven from 33 feet above the level of the surrounding courtyard or *maluwa*, continuing 54 yards to the centre and then dropping to the level of the maluwa. Tradition had asserted that valuable Buddhist books had been buried there, but in his diaries of February and March 1887 Ievers only recorded the finding of scattered objects which included beads and pottery, a small crystal dagaba and one coin which Reginald Lane Poole reported to be an Indian coin 'of some time before the seventh century'.[18]

The work carried out on the Abhayagiriya in these years called forth opposition from two different directions, illustrating most aptly the difficulty of the archaeologist concerning himself with the excavation of sacred places. The repairing of the dagaba was criticised on the grounds that the Government should not spend money on religious monuments, as this compromised its position of impartiality between all religious faiths; the tunnelling into the dagaba was attacked as being an outrage on the religious feelings of Buddhists.

Grants of money for the repair of the Abhayagiriya and also of the Maha Seya dagaba at Mihintale were strenuously opposed by H.Bois in the debate on the subject in the Legislative Council on Tuesday, December 21, 1886. He argued that these buildings were religious shrines, and should be kept in order by those for whom they were sacred. Furthermore, he said that any restoration of a dagaba was unwise from a strictly archaeological point of view, and he cited the criticism of the restoration of the Thuparama by James Fergusson, the architect, author of the *History of Indian and Eastern Architecture*. He concluded as follows:

In all I have said, sir, I wish most distinctly to disclaim any want of sympathy with your Excellency in the interest you have manifested in the archaeological remains that are scattered throughout this island, and more particularly in the ruined cities of the North-Central Province. I do not think any man of ordinary intelligence can fail to take a deep interest in the evidences of a civilization that existed 2,000 years ago, nor can the thoughtful mind view with absolute indifference the monuments of a religion that has dominated so large a proportion of the human race for over twenty centuries. But allowing full scope for all legitimate feeling, I think there is a point beyond which the indulgence of that feeling becomes blameworthy, and in my estimation that point has been distinctly passed when it is proposed to vote public money from the revenues of the colony for the repair of Buddhist relic shrines. As a member of this Council I am not prepared to depart in favour of the Buddhists from that position of complete neutrality which has been announced as the policy of this Government and concurred in by this Council, and as a Christian, I am not prepared to participate in an act which is in the estimation of many in the nature of a public sin.

The Governor refused to be drawn on the implication of Government support for Buddhism, but rested his case on the duty of Government to maintain important historical monuments irrespective of their purpose. He quoted the example of the secular Government of France which gave money for the upkeep of cathedrals, and of the Government of India which restored mosques. Mr. Bois did not press his opinion and the vote was passed without a division, but we will find some of his arguments echoed by Bell when proposals for the repair of dagabas were put forward at a later date. [19]

On the other hand, Mr. Ievers' tunnelling, although he had been careful to obtain the agreement of 'a leading and intelligent Buddhist Chief of the Central Province, of the High Priest of Adam's Peak and of the High Priest of the Bo Tree', was opposed by a number of individuals who constituted themselves as an Abhayagiriya Defence Committee and sent a Memorial of protest on May 16, 1888. This was addressed to Sir Edward Noel-Walker, the Lieutenant-Governor, as Sir Arthur Gordon was in England. The Memorial reads:

> The great Dagoba Abhayagiri, where the Vihara Abhayagiri was situated, is not only one of the greatest, but one of the oldest, one of the most revered and most important of the Buddhist Dagobas in Ceylon. It was planned and built by the great King Wattagamini Abhaya some 1,976 years ago, and ever since his time up to the act complained of below it had always been protected and preserved by that great king's successors.
>
> Your Honour may then imagine what the feelings of your Memorialists must have been when they heard that the Government Agent of the North-Central Province is excavating this Dagoba, your Memorialists were too much excited to remain quiet. A Committee was immediately appointed by them on April 3, 1888, to visit the said Dagoba, and find out if there was any truth in this rumoured excavation. That Committee repaired thither, and found out that the rumour was only too true, and that the said Dagoba has already been excavated. They surveyed the base of the Dagoba, and have made plans of the excavations, which plans are hereto annexed.
>
> To gain what object, to gratify what curiosity, the Government Agent of the North-Central Province is excavating a sacred place of worship, your Memorialists fail to see. Instead of repairing that sacred edifice and restoring it to its former condition, the Government Agent has bored right through its centre for a distance of 150 ft., and has despoiled that sacred building of its hidden treasures. Your Memorialists submit that this is not only an act of open irreverence offered to their religion, but it is an insult and indignity offered to all Buddhists in Ceylon.

The matter was treated seriously by the Colonial Office and by the Ceylon Government, although both Ievers and Noel-Walker were strongly of the opinion that the opposition was factitious. Noel-Walker said that it had been stirred up by a Mr. Leadbeater, 'lately a clergyman of the Church of England, who came to Ceylon as a Theosophist rather than as a Buddhist and is regarded with suspicion by the leading Buddhists. There are some ridiculous rumours current, I am informed, as to the discovery and appropriation of gems and other valuables, and this uninformed allegation may doubtless be ascribed to the like untrustworthy source'. [20]

However, Government decided that it would be better to discontinue the operation, and on November 8, 1888 issued an order to that effect. Ievers had, in any case, previously agreed that all finds should be replaced, and this was done under the supervision of the Annunayaka Unnanse, the High Priest of Adam's Peak.

In the years leading up to the establishment of the Archaeological Survey we have traced the ever rising degree of interest in the historical and archaeological records and remains of Ceylon shown by individuals, by the Royal Asiatic Society, Ceylon Branch, and by successive Governors. Sir Arthur Gordon was particularly active. His personal interest was great; wherever he went on tour he inspected ruins and took photographs. He was friendly with Ievers and Burrows, and authorised their explorations; he organised the RASCB Fund which contributed to the excavation round the Mirisavetiya dagaba. In the autumn of 1889 he determined that a regular Archaeological Survey should be established. In his message to Council regarding the Supply Bill on November 20, 1889 he stated that:

> In the vote for Miscellaneous Services that for Archaeological purposes has been increased. It is proposed to make some systematic examination of the interesting remains at Sigiri, and to commence, on a modest scale, before the rapidly disappearing monuments of the past have altogether perished, a species of Archaeological Survey resembling that carried on in India. Such an examination should have been completed in about three years, and the vote is proposed to cover the salary and travelling expenses for 1890 of the officer seconded for the purpose. [21]

This was not to be the last occasion that the length of time required to complete the Archaeological Survey was underestimated.

6

Kegalla

Although Gordon had proposed that Sigiriya was to be the first object for systematic examination, work was not started there until 1895. It was when Bell was stationed at Kegalla that he came to be seconded to undertake the Archaeological Survey. In April of 1888 his wife Renée had gone home to put his three eldest children, Eva Laura, Hal and the young Renée to school. On November 6 of the same year he had been appointed Acting District Judge at Kegalla, and took up the post with some reluctance. Albert Grey was not encouraging, writing in May 1889 that 'I never was there but fancy it is somewhat warm and not very exciting from a social point of view'. Bell had already reported the 'outlook gloomy', for he was not even an Assistant Government Agent:

> ...but no matter, it is hopeless to kick against the present Governmental pricks. The King can do no wrong. I lose Rs. 300 per mensem and am likely to keep wife and children at home and 'worm on' here...a bare existence. [1]

However, it was in unpromising Kegalla that he was to find the beginning of his life's work. Already, as was his habit, he was collecting material for research; for instance he followed up his earlier work on paddy cultivation ceremonies with an article in the JRASCB on those in the Kegalla district. He read up all previous accounts of the district, asking for, and obtaining, copies of the diaries of the Assistant Government Agents who had served there. When he came to write the Kegalla Report he was scrupulous in referring to the work of others before him. [2]

He was also engaged in some excavation work on his own account and in supervising that of others. In his Administration Report of 1889 the A.G.A of Kegalla, F.H.Price, printed his own diary extract for May 22:

> Arranged with Mr. Bell about clearing Beligala (where the tooth relic was kept in the 13th century) and about excavations there after the jungle has been cleared. Mr. Bell is good enough to undertake the superintendence of this in conjunction with the Wattegama Ratemahatmaya and we are fortunate in securing his assistance. I have also asked for his opinion with regard to the work of excavation which I requested Kubbekaduwa Ratemahatmaya to supervise at Dehinaduwa, now going on, and further Mr. Bell will let me know if he advises the undertaking of similar work at one or more of the following: Ganetenna, Keriyagama, Ambulagala, Wakirigala or Dedigama. [3]

Bell was known for his interest in historical and archaeological matters, both because of his published work on the Maldives and because of his position as Honorary Secretary of the RASCB. It seems also that he might have been chosen for his new job because he was not outstandingly successful in ordinary administrative work. There is a family tradition that he admitted to his children that he often got his official finances into a hopeless tangle, and he much preferred the practical side of archaeology to the writing of reports. But the following comment, based apparently on the reports of W.E.Davidson, once his co-Secretary at the RASCB, is possibly too harsh. It appears in the draft of a letter from G.V.Fiddes, Principal Clerk, to be sent from the Colonial Office in London on June 22, 1907 to Hugh Clifford, then Colonial Secretary. It was written during the long drawn out controversy between Bell and Wickremasinghe about the production of *Epigraphia Zeylanica*, and the Colonial Office staff were getting rather irritated with Bell. The draft reads:

> I have heard that the latter gentleman, after being tried in the Colonial Secretary's office and found a hopeless failure, and tried again in the Customs and proved again a failure (Mr. Davidson being my authority) has been dumped down in Anuradhapura as Archaeological Commissioner and left there for twenty years to dig among the ruins. [4]

It seems unlikely, though, that Gordon would choose someone he did not trust for his pet project, and the letters which passed between them at this period were cordial. Bell describes in the Preface to the Kegalla Report the reasons why the Survey began in that district:

> The commencement of the Archaeological Survey of Ceylon was entrusted to my charge in February, 1890. Being at that time stationed at Kegalla it was deemed convenient to select the Four and Three Korales and Lower Bulatgama as the first scene of work. These divisions, jointly known as the 'Kegalla District', formerly belonged to the Western Province, but since January, 1890, have been attached to the Province of Sabaragamuwa. Virtually an unworked field of antiquarian research, the Kegalla District was, not without reason, believed to contain several sites of considerable historical interest, with not a few temples originally founded at an early period and embellished both during and since 'the middle ages' of Ceylon history. [5]

On February 4 and February 21, Bell wrote to Gordon suggesting that he should spend six months completing this survey and then move on to Tissamaharama and Anuradhapura. Gordon agreed that Kegalla should be the first area of research, but decided that Bell should then proceed to Anuradhapura, which became the permanent centre for the Survey. [6]

Bell threw himself into the new work with enthusiasm. On April 9, 1890, F.H.Price noted in his diary:

> Mr. Bell showed me the excellent photographs which he has taken in conjunction with the archaeological work in the district. Knowing the country as well as I do, I was much struck with the great extent of Mr. Bell's achievements during the comparatively short time for which he has been on special duty. The report he is now compiling will be a very valuable one. [7]

The Kegalla Report, which has been termed a landmark in antiquarian studies in the Island, was not finally published until 1892. It was issued after the first four Progress Reports of the Archaeological Survey, although on May 23, 1890 Bell had read some extracts from his manuscript to the RASCB. They were referred to as the first fruits of the recently inaugurated

Archaeological Survey of Ceylon. In addition to the photographic illustrations in the Report there is an album of 150 photographs taken by Bell in the Kegalla District. A copy is in the Colombo Museum Library.

In the Preface to the Kegalla Report Bell outlines its scope as follows:

> The 'Introduction' deals with the historical geography of the Kegalla District. In Part I. (Historical) is recorded so much of its history as I have been able to glean from records, chiefly from the fifteenth century onwards. Part II. (Antiquarian) sums up briefly the characteristic forms of architecture and temple adornment in the District, and gives in some detail descriptions both of ancient sites, legendary and historical, and of the more important vihares, dewales and kovils of each Korale and Pattuwa. To Part III. (Epigraphical) has been left the treatment of all stone inscriptions and copper-plate or palm-leaf (ola) grants discovered in the course of research. Finally in the 'Appendices' will be found miscellaneous information bearing on the District which would have been out of place in the text.
>
> The Report does not claim to be exhaustive. Historical particulars furnished prior to 1400 A.D. are exceedingly scanty. Much information locked up in native works and tradition has yet to be brought to light; whilst to have described every temple in detail would have been to still further incur Falstaff's charge of 'damnable iteration' almost inseparable from much of a Report of this nature. [8]

In the 'Historical' section Bell endeavours to establish the chronology of the many internecine struggles in the area, and the wars against invaders, from the first reference to Devanampiya Tissa (306-266 B.C.) to the period of British rule in the 19th century. Although Bell says that 'the interest of the Kegalla Division is rather historical than archaeological' he devotes the largest part of the report to that section termed 'Antiquarian'. He introduces it as follows:

> Archaeologically - using the term of higher antiquity - the Kegalla District is somewhat barren. Though possessing a few of the older cave and rock inscriptions, and one or two ancient historical and legendary sites, it cannot be positively asserted, as of the Anuradhapura and Tissamaharama ruins, that many of its temples date from very early times. This may be, and, as regards some of the cave temples, doubtless is the case, but in the absence of rock-hewn shrines and free-standing structures of stone, data are wanting on which to base the conjectural age of vihares and dewales... Unless the original name be handed down by tradition, the *Mahavansa* and other annals may be searched in vain for the ancient denominations of existing fanes, of whose antiquity there can be no reasonable doubt.
>
> Nevertheless, apart from the historical view, the district has, if not an archaeological, at least a definite antiquarian interest. Some of its temples, as they stand ornamented to this day, are undoubtedly some centuries old, and afford ample material (not available in less secluded districts) for the comparative study of modern Sinhalese plastic art and painting with those of the past. We are thus enabled to trace to their prototypes forms and details otherwise difficult of comprehension. For instance, the makara of Kandyan temples is both more artistically modelled, and withal far closer in resemblance to its Indian brother than the ill-formed abortion, vilely bedaubed, commonly seen in low-country vihares.[9]

Bell goes on to define the types of buildings that he would be describing, broadly dividing temples into a) cave-temples, semi-natural, semi-structural and b) detached buildings, usually constructed of wood and clay and entirely structural. He says:

> Buddhist temples, properly so-called, consist of three separate buildings besides a pansala : the vihare, or image-house; a dagaba, or dome-shaped monument usually enshrining some sacred relics of Buddha or Buddhist saints; and a bodhi-maluva, a platform, with or without altars, surrounding the bo tree. The vihare and pansala are naturally essential, and rarely indeed is the sacred bo missing, be it only a sapling or shoot recently planted on a cramped makeshift maluva. Dagabas are less universal, but their absence does not necessarily imply lesser antiquity of the vihare, as Danagirigala, Lenagala, or Hakurugala are witness. [10]

Bell defines devales as follows:

> Devales, connected with the Buddhism of the Island, are temples consecrated to certain gods of the Hindu pantheon, whose characters and attributes, as adopted into the Ceylon Buddhist cult, entirely alter their nature and the worship paid to them. With the Hindus these gods are immortal, revengeful, licentious : here they are but mortal, well-behaved, guardian deities, and even candidates for Buddhahood. Shrines are erected to them, and offerings made solely to obtain temporary benefits - not by religious supplication to merit reward in a future world. This essential difference between the Hindu and Buddhist notion of the gods, common in name to both forms of worship, is rarely understood. [11]

Before going on to the description of the remains to be found in each place Bell gives a brief general account of the architecture, sculpture and painting characteristic of the district. He says that 'no claim to architectural merit can be put forward for the temples of the Four and Three Korales, Ganegoda and Berendi Kovil excepted'. There was little elaborate stone carving to be found, though he makes a special mention of the moonstone at the Beligala vihare and of another at the foot of the steps up to the modern verandah of the Alutnuwara Dewale. Wooden carving is described; also the general lay-out of vihares and the various positions of Buddha images.

After the long, detailed topographical section Bell turns to the 'Epigraphical' records, giving photographs, transcriptions and translations. He sums up his finds as follows:

> The Four and Three Korales are fairly rich in inscriptions, and those which have been discovered cover a wider period than perhaps any other district of its size.

> Here are found cave inscriptions in nearly, if not quite, the oldest form of cave character; an illegible slab, inscribed with characters of about the fifth century A.D.; the tantalising pillar fragment of Kassapa V (early tenth century); the weather-worn, sprawling inscription at Selawa on slab rock, of the same century; the pillars at Wattarama and fragments from other places, dating probably from the succeeding century, their age only determinable by the few words legible here and there; of the twelfth and thirteenth centuries, two rock inscriptions of Parakrama Bahu I, and his hardly less 'Great' namesake, the Pandit King, Parakrama Bahu III, the major part of both legible, besides the Evunugalla and Galatara slabs; two of Vikrama Bahu III, who reigned at Gangasripura towards the close of the

fourteenth century; a single inscription of Sri Parakrama Bahu VI, the pillar at Dedigama, granting an amnesty by Bhuvaneka Bahu VI; two inscriptions of Vijaya Bahu VII of Kotte; the second Dewanagala inscription, probably of the reign of Vimala Dharma Suryya I; then - skipping a century and a half - the short record at Pondape Vihare dated 2306 A.B. (1763 A.D.); and finally, the inscribed slab built into the wall of Selawa Vihare detailing at length its restoration by Moratota Unnanse and the re-endowment by Sri Vikrama Raja Sinha in 1806 A.D...

Of the later Sinhalese inscriptions, by far the most valuable is the gal-sannasa of Parakrama Bahu the Great on the Devanagala rock. This must take rank among the most important of rock records in the Island, from its definite allusion to contemporary history, - the protracted war with Gajabahu II, and the punitive Burmese expedition of Parakrama Bahu's 12th year.

With this exception the contents of the inscriptions are commonly bare recitals of lands gifted to vihares and pirivenas, closing often with an imprecation on any sacrilegious molester of the grantees in their peaceable possession. Almost all are introduced or closed by the sun and the moon as symbols of eternity, and some by figures of a dog and crow explanatory of the curse.

An unexpected 'find' at Kotagama Vihare in the Kinigoda Korale was a dressed stone slab bearing a short inscription in Tamil characters of about the fifteenth century. This occurrence of a Tamil inscription some four centuries old in the heart of a purely Sinhalese district is highly suggestive.

Hardly less important than stone inscriptions are the many genuine sannas held by vihares, dewales and private individuals in the district. The majority are engraved on copper plates, elongated and smoothed to receive the writing; a few are written on olas. Some are richly ornamented with sun, moon, and the sign manual 'Sri' inlaid in gold, and a fancy silver rim, presenting beautiful specimens of Sinhalese caligraphy. The oldest sannas brought to light belong to the reigns of Bhuvaneka Bahu V and Parakrama Bahu VI of Kotte, and Raja Sinha I of Sitawaka.

The value of these old grants in supplementing the lithic records cannot well be exaggerated. Many side lights of history may not infrequently be gleaned from them; epigraphically they exhibit with faithfulness the gradual development of the Sinhalese character from the period when writings on stone began to fail; of the philology of the language itself, they help to build up our knowledge.[12]

Bell then writes of treasure and boundary marks:

Scattered all over the Island, and plentifully throughout the Kegalla District, are found so-called 'treasure-marks'. Of a few this may be the true signification: the Wadula-pot, or 'treasure-books' (in which many of these signs, their locality, and the mantras essential for the successful discovery of the treasure concealed, are seriously specified), can hardly be altogether base forgeries. But in most instances - and almost certainly whenever the sun and moon appear engraved - these signs merely denote boundaries, and in some cases are accompanied by a few letters to that effect, as at Niyadandupola in Beligal Korale.[13]

Kegalla

Some interesting notes on treasure marks and treasure hunting appear in the diaries of F.H.Price in the Kandy Archive. On November 5, 1889 he wrote:

> Having heard that ancient treasure was supposed to be concealed in a slab rock in the village Kalagala about 4 metres out, I went there with Mr. Bell. A sword and a cock drawn in the rock were the indicators. The rock sounded hollow when struck and someone had already tried to split it by lighting a fire on the surface but without success. We tried the effect of a charge of blasting powder, but found to our chagrin but rather to the delight of the villagers that we only split off a horizontal layer from the rock a few inches thick, which was evidently cracked before, while beneath the rock was perfectly solid. [14]

On November 20 he recorded the following notes he had been given respecting the methods of native treasure hunters:

> First of all a book of notes of the hidden treasure called 'Nadu Wadula' is consulted, and after that a charmer called 'Anawan Karaye' is called in. He is made to charm and send the Anjananam light (Anjanan is a charmed medicine prepared by grinding different kinds of ingredients mixed with honey or gingelly oil). The charmer after performing some devil ceremonies puts the medicine on a plate or on a betel leaf or sometimes on a bo-leaf and makes a small circle two or three inches in breadth with the medicine on the plate or leaf. He then gets a boy or young man to hold the plate with both hands and to look at the Anjanan while he himself recites charms. This ceremony is always performed during the night. The man who looked at the Anjanan will see a deity called Anjanan Deio with a torchlight in her hand through the plate or leaf.

> When she appears the man holding it will enquire where she wishes to go. When the place mentioned in the Wadula Book is named she will go there and describe by signs the place where the treasure is buried and whether it can be taken, and if it can be taken what ceremonies should be performed before attempting to take it. One lucky day a charmer accompanied by three or four other men (Dousterswivel, Edie Ochiltree and Monkhouse) goes in the evening to the spot indicated by the deity and performs the ceremonies necessary to drive away the devils in charge of the treasure. He sacrifices a cock or some other animal at the spot mentioned in the Wadula Book, and burns a heap of firewood on the spot where the treasure is hidden in the rock. When the rock is heated he pours water mixed with limejuice on it, and when it splits the treasure is taken. If it is buried in the earth a charmed thread is spread on the ground and a square made and then they commence to dig. Unless these ceremonies are performed the devils in charge of the treasure will not allow it to be taken out. [15]

The Kegalla Report was reviewed at some length by William Simpson in the *Journal of the Royal Institute of British Architects*. He says that:

> The Report seems to give an exhaustive account of the archaeological remains including inscriptions, with historical notes and legends about each spot; the divisions of the district with the towns and villages are added, with details of their productions; the whole forming a complete guide to the region. This document, I am glad to say, has a glossary of Sinhalese words relating to archaeology, which is

of great use to those who are not acquainted with the language...If the whole of Ceylon is to be reported in a manner similar to this specimen, it will form a most comprehensive work of reference, and be of the utmost value to those who wish to study the archaeology of the Island. [16]

This review was reprinted in the *Monthly Literary Register and Notes and Queries for Ceylon* in April 1893, and in the May issue of this journal a further, unsigned, review appeared. It is largely made up of quotations from the Report itself, and ends as follows:

> We feel that the above hurried notice does not do adequate justice to Mr. Bell's interesting monograph (for so it practically is) on the Kegalla District; but we recommend our readers to purchase it (the price, Rs. 6, is a trifle) and enjoy it for themselves. [17]

Bell did not relinquish his interest in the Kegalla District when stationed at Anuradhapura. Sessional Paper XX, 1894 prints the correspondence which took place between him and the various Assistant Government Agents stationed there in 1893 and 1894 regarding further excavations carried out at his suggestion. These included the excavation of the Peradeni Nuwara in Beligal Korale and the clearing of the Beligala Rock. In the Annual Reports for 1894, 1895 and 1896 it is noted that other work was carried out at his request, in particular the restoration of the basement of the Berendi Kovil.

General Robert Bell (1759 -1844)

Colonel A.B. Fyers (1829 -1883)

The Archaeological Commissioner's bungalow at Anuradhapura

Zoë, Malcolm and Cyril Bell with donkey at Anuradhapura

Cyril Bell with pet pelican at Anuradhapura

Zoë Bell at Anuradhapura with pet deer

H.C.P. Bell in court at Kalutara

H.C.P. Bell with family at Anuradhapura

7

The Anuradhapura Establishment

In June 1890 Bell started work at Anuradhapura, and the following ten years were possibly the happiest and most interesting of his life. In them he produced the seven detailed Progress Reports on Anuradhapura and the three Interim Reports on Sigiriya, and he commenced work at Polonnaruwa. He also toured the whole of the North-Central Province visiting and recording all ancient sites and many of the great waterworks of the district.

Although he undertook his task with energy and enthusiasm it was only gradually that Bell realised that it was to be his life work. He complained that his pay as 'Special Commissioner detached for archaeological research' was less than that he had been getting as District Judge at Kegalla, and on July 24, 1890 wrote to Sir Arthur Gordon saying that he did not see how he could manage on it, speaking of 'my lonely work' and threatening to give up. This was unwise, for Gordon replied on August 18 virtually accepting the resignation and remarking that he was 'not surprised, in view of all your complaints'. Luckily for Bell his friend Ievers, Government Agent at Anuradhapura, took it upon himself to intervene and wrote to Gordon explaining away Bell's imprudent letter. On September 22 Bell wrote to the new Governor, Sir Arthur Havelock, saying that he was anxious to remain at his post, and, although the Government refused to raise his pay, he withdrew his resignation. Thereafter we find Bell gradually becoming more and more absorbed in his work and satisfied by it. He certainly enjoyed the independence that it gave him. On March 3, 1892 he wrote to Herbert Wace, a colleague from early days in Colombo and now Assistant to the Colonial Secretary, that 'after all it is good to be Head Man, even in Hell'. [1]

It was not the original intention of Government to make it a permanent appointment, but from the first Bell was insistent that his post should carry the title of 'Archaeological Commissioner'. He was told in 1892 that he was not yet officially seconded, and indeed in 1894 he was taken from Anuradhapura and for nearly eight months was stationed at Kalutara as Acting District Judge. Bell returned to the charge in 1895 and finally on February 15 Havelock wrote to tell him that he had been officially appointed as Archaeological Commissioner with a salary of Rs. 9,600. In 1897 the appointment was back-dated to February 1890, so that one may say that he was Archaeological Commissioner from the beginning of the Survey. On receiving news of the confirmation Bell wrote to Sir Edward Noel-Walker, the Colonial Secretary: 'The die is cast and I am to cling to my Archaeology dry bones. I am eccentric enough to sincerely rejoice'. [2] This did not prevent him from continuing to complain that his work was 'semi-banishment from civilization' and from asking for a rise in pay on the grounds of 'ad misericordium' because his work involved exploring 'backwoods in the wildest and most inaccessible nooks and corners of Ceylon'. [3]

By 1890 Bell had six children, three at school in England and three living with his wife at the hill-station Nuwara Eliya, for there was no suitable accommodation in Anuradhapura. However in 1891 Ievers reported that a 'portion of the old hospital standing on high ground will be utilised as a residence for the Archaeological Commissioner and subsequently as quarters for clerks and a registry office'. [4] There Bell made his headquarters when not on tour, directing operations at Sigiriya or exploring the possibilities of Polonnaruwa. His wife and the three younger children, Cyril, Zoë and Malcolm, joined him and made their home there. Zoë much later recalled her impressions of the building:

> This was a bungalow with three front rooms, one merely a passage to the back, with a verandah facing a small garden and two small back single rooms. Two separate blocks of a couple of small rooms were detached from the main building; one was my father's office. At the back of the main building was the dining-room which had low mud walls, wooden pillars, a roof of cadjan (dried coconut-palm leaves), and a floor of cow-dung (much in use in those days in native huts). The kitchen was beyond this room along an open passage. There was only a brick range and oven and it was wonderful how well the native cook managed excellent meals.

Zoë also described what a child saw of life at Anuradhapura:

> The few residents of Anuradhapura were, I think, mostly Government servants. There was plenty of entertaining, especially by way of dinner-parties, and these were most formal. Everyone wore evening dress, great care was taken to see that the right couples went in to dinner arm-in-arm, and sat at table according to seniority. The menu consisted of Hors-d'oêuvres, Soup, Fish, Entrée, Joint or Chicken, Puddings, Savory and plenty of Dessert. Sherry and Port were put before the host with dessert, and the ladies then left the table for coffee in the drawing-room. I used to peep from my bedroom as the guests went in to dinner.

So was the tradition of the niceties of social life kept up by 'dressing for dinner' in the heart of the jungle. The bland ignoring of its dangers is well illustrated by a family story. A bridge party was in progress at the Anuradhapura bungalow when Mrs. Bell pointed to a corner of the room and said to a servant, 'Boy! Take away that cobra'. She then calmly resumed her game with 'Three no trumps, partner'.

Zoë recalled with appreciation the surroundings of her childhood home:

> Anuradhapura was a fascinating place. The Buddhist Temple in the centre of the small town had a lovely Bo-tree, most sacred, and here on Full Moon nights the worshippers came dressed in white, carrying temple flowers and offerings. There were four dagabas (I went up those that could be climbed), and three huge irrigation tanks which were lovely to walk round. There was a native bazaar and one store shop; no clothes shops, of course. A nice Botanical Garden was well kept up. [5]

The three children had their own life. Pictures survive of the solemn, over-dressed trio, two boys and a girl, taking rides on their donkey or posing with pet pelican or tame gazelle. The family continued to live in the old hospital, for it was not until 1900 that the large two-storey house was built for the Archaeological Commissioner, and not until 1911-12 that the portico was added to its façade. There still stands in its grounds the large brick wall on which the estampages taken from cave inscriptions were hung to be studied and deciphered.

Bell was not only concerned with establishing his own official position; he was constantly striving to increase the size of his staff and coolie force and improve their working conditions. He wrote to Gordon on February 22, 1890 saying that he must have as staff a clerk, interpreter, draughtsman and one peon; and in fact was allocated a staff of native assistant and clerk combined, a draughtsman and twenty coolies. By 1900 this had been increased by a second clerk, two extra draughtsmen and a European Assistant, while the work-force, operating in two centres at once, had increased to one hundred men.

Bell fought to better their lot. He continually applied for further money to pay his labour force and in 1900 sent in a complaint about the inadequate housing provided for his assistants. He said that they were worse off than the humblest overseer on a tea estate, being supplied only with a wattle and daub thatched hut. In 1902 the staff themselves submitted a Memorandum asking for an incremental system of pay and better accommodation. Bell supported it, writing that 'they are disheartened at their prospects'. [6]

Bell never stinted appreciation of good work. D.A.L.Perera was appointed as draughtsman in September 1890, and from the first he became a valued member of staff. Many of the drawings and plans printed in the early Reports are by Bell himself, but increasingly the name of Perera appears, and on numerous occasions he was detailed to make drawings of ruins discovered on circuit. Another long-serving officer was W.M.Fernando, who joined in 1896. There are tributes to the work of both these men in the Memorandum submitted by Bell in 1908 when reorganisation of the staffing was proposed. Bell was suggesting that instead of engaging a new European Assistant these two should be promoted to act jointly as his Assistants on a higher salary. He wrote as follows:

Mr. D.A.L.Perera, 1st Draughtsman, has served in the Archaeological Survey Department for 18 years, Mr. W.M.Fernando, 2nd Draughtsman, for 11 years.

Mr. Perera is admitted to be almost without an equal in Ceylon as a Draughtsman. His copies of the Sigiriya frescoes, and architectural drawings of Polonnaruwa structures, are sufficient testimony to his exceptional talent.

Mr. Fernando (of whose skilled work His Excellency the Governor has recently had an opportunity of judging at Anuradhapura) is a Draughtsman much above the ordinary standard, and in architectural drawing is hardly inferior to Mr. Perera.

In general character and ability both these officers leave nothing to be desired. Their long experience in the Department, and the work they have done under my own eyes, have fully satisfied me that they are not only capable of properly performing their duties, but that they will prove most efficient Assistants.

To retain their services in the Department - for both can easily command remunerative employment in Colombo - when saddled with double duties (as Assistants and Draughtsmen) the inducement of an small annual increment should be offered. [7]

Another long-serving officer was A.P Siriwadhana, Head Overseer. A tribute to his work is given in an article written by Bell in 1917:

> This intelligent officer, A.P.Siriwadhana, now dead, did sterling work in the Archaeological Survey Department for many years. To a fair knowledge of Surveying, he coupled natural, though undeveloped talent for Drawing. In Epigraphical training he proved himself an apt pupil, and the very numerous 'eye-copies' and 'squeezes' of lithic inscriptions he made for the Department were executed for the most part with great care and success, to which some acquaintance with high Sinhalese, Elu, and Pali helped not a little. Virtually the whole extensive set of the estampages of Ceylon inscriptions secured for the Archaeological Survey and since forwarded to Professor Wickremasinghe at Oxford to be utilised for the *Epigraphia Zeylanica* was prepared by Siriwadhana.
>
> To his memory this slight tribute is offered by an ex-Archaeological Commissioner (with whom he served for nearly twenty years) mindful of the very efficient aid rendered, often under most trying conditions, which may have undermined his health from the frequently recurring attacks of malarial fever he suffered. [8]

In the 1908 Memorandum already mentioned Bell wrote further of the difficulty of retaining good staff:

> The real and constant difficulty of getting even Fixed Establishment Clerks to remain, *sua sponte*, for any length of time in Anuradhapura is well known to the Government. In the case of the Archaeological Survey Clerks and Draughtsmen the difficulty is accentuated from the fact that they are subject to special disabilities. Not entitled to pension, they are further debarred from subscribing to the Widows and Orphans Pension Fund; and, in addition, year in year out, they have to live in Anuradhapura and face its inevitable fever. There is not a member of the Archaeological Survey staff but has suffered badly at times from illness, due to the climate of the North-Central Province.
>
> I trust I may be absolved from the charge of egotism, when I venture to say that personal influence has induced an attachment to their Head, and *esprit de corps* among the officers, which has enabled the Archaeological Commissioner to keep his staff together so many years.

Bell plumed himself on the fact that his Head Clerk, Mr. E.R.Saranayaka had served him well for fourteen years, and the 2nd Clerk, Mr. L.F.Abeyakoon, for eight years. [9] However, he was not so fortunate in retaining the services of his more immediate subordinates. At the end of 1890 he obtained the assistance of the young Wickremasinghe, on detachment from Colombo Museum; he did not arrive until March 1891, but then stayed for nearly two years and took part both in excavations and in the collecting and deciphering of inscriptions. He accompanied Bell on circuit and his help is particularly noted in the Annual Report of 1891 when Bell was prostrated with fever in the jungle and Wickremasinghe made some of the explorations on his

The Anuadhapura establishment

own; he was also on his own from August 1892 to January 1893 while Bell was absent on sick leave. In February 1893, however, Wickremasinghe decided to leave the Survey and to take up a scholarship for study in Europe. Bell noted that 'his loss has been much felt by the Department to which he rendered very valuable service at the expense of his health'. [10]

In 1893, therefore, it was decided that Bell should have a European Assistant, and that the work of editing the inscriptions discovered in the course of the Survey should be entrusted to B.Gunasekera, Chief Translator to Government at Colombo. He continued to afford help in this field until his death in 1903, working at first on his own, and later in collaboration with Wickremasinghe in London.

The first European Assistants did not stay long, either finding the work uncongenial, or obtaining better-paid posts elsewhere. Mr. G.Hawkins served for eight months in 1893 and Mr. F.M.Maxfield from March to December of 1894. Mr. F.G.Bosanquet, who followed him, stayed only six months. There was then a long gap in which Bell worked single-handed. In 1898 a Committee was appointed to report on the progress of the Survey, and one of its recommendations was as follows:

> Efficiency has been hitherto needlessly limited by Mr. Bell's having to give much of his attention to the business of engaging, directing, and checking the working parties. To relieve him of this, and to enable him to employ a larger force of workmen, the Committee recommend the addition to the staff of a Labour Assistant (European), who would undertake the immediate direction, under Mr. Bell's orders, of the working parties. [11]

As a result Bell again obtained an Assistant, but we find from his Annual Report for 1899 that he still found himself overburdened with administrative detail. He wrote:

> The appointment of Mr. C.E.Dashwood as Labour Assistant from January 1, 1899 has at last afforded the Archaeological Commissioner some relief in the conduct of the Archaeological Survey. But, with work carried on simultaneously at two sites during nine months of the year, the Head of the Department cannot but be still unduly hampered by having to personally attend to the countless petty details, mechanical and other, essential to direct daily supervision of field work and immediate charge of the labour force. [12]

Moreover Dashwood suffered bouts of malaria and after going on leave to England in May 1901 resigned later in the year. It was not until the appointment of John Still in 1902 that Bell acquired an Assistant of calibre who combined enthusiasm with scholarship and stayed till 1908.

More staff, more coolies, more money for clearing operations, there was of course no end to the hopeful demands of Bell upon the Government. Expenditure on archaeology tended to be considered as a luxury, and it says much for persistence that the Annual Vote rose from Rs. 10,000 to Rs. 40,000 from 1890 to 1899. Over and above that was Bell's own salary, so that the total expenditure in 1900 was Rs. 52,641. [13]

There was always more that could be undertaken, and it is not surprising, therefore, that proposals were put forward from time to time to raise money from outside sources. Bell, writing in 1891 to Gregory, the retired Governor who continued to take a great interest in the progress of the work, put forward the suggestion that what was needed was money from a millionaire or from a Society devoted to archaeological research. [14]

In the same year the Annual Report of the RASCB noted 'that it would be well if an Antiquarian Society in Europe willing and pecuniarily able to carry out the work would take a practical interest in the Survey so that it might be conducted on a more extensive scale than is at present possible'. They could well have been thinking of the Egypt Exploration Fund, first organised in 1882, and the even longer established Palestine Exploration Fund, which dates back to 1865, both of which were financing excavations by that time. But Ceylon was further away and even the Royal Asiatic Society took only a sporadic interest. [15]

John Ferguson, the co-editor of the *Ceylon Observer*, also made a plea for an infusion of outside support in his book *Ceylon in 1893*. In Appendix VI, written 1891, an account of the monuments of Anuradhapura and irrigation works of the North-Central Province, he mentions some of the work carried out up to that time and continues:

> Further exploration and excavation cannot fail to meet with a rich reward throughout the area covered by both the 'sacred' and 'secular' cities, and the new departure taken last year at the instance of Sir Arthur Gordon by the appointment of so competent an officer as Mr. H.C.P.Bell, as Archaeological Commissioner, could not fail of important results, even though that officer has been most inadequately supplied with the means to carry on his operations. Very fortunate, however, Mr. Bell has been in securing the co-operation of the present Government agent, Mr. Ievers, who in the past was instrumental in bringing many very interesting ruins to light; and of Mr. A.Murray, provincial engineer...
>
> The ancient ruins in Ceylon have hitherto been supposed to be well defined - if not sufficiently cleared. But the fact is there is room and reward for a number of explorers and excavators. We cannot expect the Ceylon Government to do more than touch the fringe of the work. We want a 'Dr. Schliemann' to come to the rescue. Where is he to be found?... We turn for answer to out past Governors, Sir William Gregory and Sir Arthur Gordon, who yield to no Anglo-Ceylonese living in their interest in everything connected with Anuradhapura. Can they not excite enquiry on the part of 'English Society', the literary and antiquarian members of the 'Athenaeum Club'... and also get the metropolitan press to notice the subject, with the possible result of a thoughtful English millionaire or wealthy savant being roused to devote his attention to our great buried city, and to the advantage of bringing its far-extending ruins into the full light of day? We trust so. [16]

In a subsequent work *Ceylon in 1896* Ferguson said that some years ago an American Syndicate was anxious to take up work at Polonnaruwa, but was officially discouraged, and he hoped that the new Governor, Sir West Ridgeway, might be induced to take a more favourable view of American enterprise. [17]

No Jove descended with a shower of gold or outside expertise to expand the work of the Survey but, as Ferguson suggests, Bell was generally lucky in the support he obtained from colleagues stationed at Anuradhapura during the period of his work. Ievers was a personal friend who shared Bell's interest in sport. [18] He accompanied Bell on some of his early circuits and

The Anuadhapura establishment

his Administration Reports contain many complimentary references. He undertook supervision of the excavations going on when Bell was seriously ill in late 1892, and was removed to Colombo for treatment.

H.Nevill, the Acting G.A. in 1893, was a man of many interests, collecting birds and shells as well as Kandyan silverwork and Buddhist and Pali manuscripts. He edited and published the journal *The Taprobanian* which dealt with many aspects of Oriental learning, was a keen student of the *Mahavansa*, and was the first to deduce that the great dagabas Abhayagiriya and Jetawanarama had been given each other's names. On this he and Bell did not see eye to eye at this time, and it may be remarked that his Administration Report of 1893 does not refer to Bell's work but mentions only some discoveries of his own. According to Toussaint, Nevill had the reputation of being somewhat eccentric, and he says that this may account for his never rising higher in the Service than District Judge. [19]

Nevill was followed by H.H.Cameron, who recorded his appreciation of Bell's work in his Administration Report for 1894, and in 1895 supported Bell in his request for an increase in the Archaeological Vote. Cameron was one of the first to enjoy life in Anuradhapura, earlier Government Agents having reported unfavourably on its isolation and unhealthy reputation. In 1872 he had written that the air was bracing, better than anything which Colombo or Kandy could afford. There was, he said, 'an entire freedom from that damp and oppressive stillness of jungle in which the languid air appears to "swoon like one that hath a weary dream"'. He continued:

> In Anuradhapura I have found not only an entire immunity from all minor ailments but a positive recreation of the system, a more complete than which [recreation] could hardly be expected from the cool plains of Nuwara Eliya itself. [20]

According to Toussaint, Cameron was a scholar and a cultured man who took a deep interest in archaeology, finding full scope for this hobby when he was G.A. at Anuradhapura. Toussaint quotes a tribute to Cameron on the eve of his retirement:

> No-one can deny that Mr. Cameron, wherever he went, shed an aerial grace, a lightness, a Parisian *savoir faire* which was just as much needed as the iron despotism of a Dyke, the practical sagacity of a Dickson or the practical genius of a Fisher. [21]

E.M.Byrde, G.A. from 1896 to 1899, was active in promoting the creation of a museum at Anuradhapura. His Administration Report for 1896 deplores the want of a public reading room and a museum to house all the interesting pillars, statues and bronze articles which lay scattered about the Kachcheri premises. Bell also pressed for a museum in letters to Government and in his Annual Reports, and in 1900 a ward of the former hospital was partially converted to afford a slightly better store for the many objects found during excavation.

Byrde also writes of the frequent visits to Anuradhapura of scholars and distinguished persons, English and foreign. One such was the travel writer J. Leclercq, who left a charming picture of life in the 1890s in his book *Un séjour dans l'île de Ceylan*. We give a translation of some passages below:

Anuradhapura was made the provincial capital by Sir William Gregory, but it is only a group of huts close beside the ruins of the buried city, with a population of 2,500 Sinhalese, Tamils and Moors, in the midst of which live two Europeans, Mr. Cameron the G.A. and Mr. Bell, the archaeologist in charge of excavation... Mr. Cameron has a fine house, airy and peaceful, surrounded by jungle transformed into an English garden with tropical flowers. There I spent delightful hours, a visit made more enchanting by my hostess, a beautiful young woman dressed in frilly white, who spoke French like a Parisienne. She was not only a talented musician but a skilled water-colourist, and had employed her brush to depict every corner of the ruins.

As for Mr. Bell, at once scholar and artist, for years he has devoted himself with passion to the excavation and reconstruction of these ruins, and it is his pride and joy to show his discoveries to the rare visitors who reach these forgotten solitudes. He was determined himself to show me round the great circuit of the ruins, which we toured in a mode of transport truly indigenous. This was a 'bullock-cart', a cart covered with a rude thatch and drawn by two bullocks led by a Sinhalese who walks between the animals. This mode of conveyance is clearly so primitive that it must date back to the early days of the city of Anuradhapura. The cart halted at every ruin and every monument and Mr. Bell gave me full details of their archaeological interest...

What strikes one above all is the great number of conical mounds which arise on every side, those colossal constructions whose slopes have been covered with earth and on which has flourished luxuriant greenery which gives them the appearance of being natural features of the landscape.

It is only by climbing one of the mounds that one can obtain any idea of their enormous size. Mr. Bell conducted me to the summit of the great Abhayagiriya Dagaba, whose height, even though reduced from its original, is 73 metres. Under a hellish sun we clambered up the broken steps cut into the side of the building. The heat is unbearable and I never experienced so painful a climb. We arrived at the top dripping with sweat, as if we had scaled a peak of the Alps. But the wonderful view repaid our pains.

The plain of Anuradhapura spread itself at our feet and the eye wandered wide over the jungle, a sea of green under which slept, in everlasting sleep, the 'Babylon' city. From the depth of the jungle emerge the dagabas, their splendid silhouettes outlined against a sky as blue as that of Naples; at a distance one could see the holy mountain of Mihintale, and in the other direction swam into view the velvet outlines of the mountains of the south, easily visible in the clear air. A feature of this wonderful panorama is the number of lakes which shine out in every direction like pieces of broken mirror scattered haphazard across the jungle. The lakes are the remains of the immense reservoirs, constructed with great skill, which once supplied water for millions of people and irrigated their rice fields. [22]

Leclercq was conducted to all the principal ruins and describes the 'Bronze Palace' and the Thuparama with its elegant columns, moonstones, staircases and balustrades. He was particularly impressed by the Kuttam Pokuna, the twin baths, one of which had been 'restored by convicts working under the careful direction of Mr. Bell', and by the sedent Buddha on the Outer Circular Road.

There were other officers there besides the Archaeological Commissioner and the Government Agent. Their names are brought together in the introduction to the article on 'The Anuradhapura

The Anuadhapura establishment

Anthem' when the text was published in *The Times of Ceylon*, Christmas Number of 1917, probably with information supplied by Bell:

> With some difficulty we have secured a reliable version of this quaint Civil Service *jeu d'esprit* in verse, which we venture to think may fitly be rescued from oblivion. It is known to have emanated from the joint 'light effort' of the late Mr. Robert Wilson Ievers, and a certain retired Civilian (still with us), whose lot was cast for many years amid the 'Buried Cities'. The date of its production is fixed to about 1890 by the allusion to 'Royal Siam's silver', in connection with the rebuilding of the Mirisavetiya Dagaba; for that fiasco did not last much longer.
>
> Anuradhapura was fortunate in being, at the time, under the able sway of the genial 'Bob Ievers, of fond memory', Government Agent of the North-Central Province, aided by a sturdy 'crew' of brother officials who then manned 'the Captain's Gig', 'Provincial Administration' at that Ancient Capital of Ceylon - 'good fellows', pulling together most harmoniously in their semi-isolation (prior to the advent of the Northern Railway) and helped not a little by a judicious leaven of merriment in leisure hours.
>
> The 'crew' - so far as our memory serves - was composed of Mr. Alexander Murray (Provincial Engineer, afterwards promoted to the Straits Settlement); Mr. R.B.Hellings (Office Assistant to the Government Agent; now the Honourable, and Government Agent of the Southern Province); Mr. J.B.M.Ridout (Superintendent of Surveys); Mr. H.F.Tomalin, Mr. F.W.Johnson, or Mr. F.J.Pigott (District Engineers); Mr. E.R.Macdonell (Irrigation Officer); Mr. W.H.Clarke (Assistant Conservator of Forests), and Mr. H.C.P.Bell (Archaeological Commissioner). Of these officials Messrs. Ievers, Murray, Clarke, and Macdonell have all since 'crossed the Bar'; Messrs. Ridout, Johnson and Pigott have left Ceylon and Mr. Bell has retired on pension in the Island. Messrs. Hellings and Tomalin alone remain in harness.
>
> The 'Anthem', we are informed, was composed to supplement a merry 'Irish Ballad' sung by Mr. Ridout to the accompaniment of a swinging 'March' played on his ever-facile banjo. It is believed that Mrs. L.W.Booth (when Mr. Booth was G.A. at Anuradhapura) had both words and music printed; but we have been unable to procure a copy so far.

We print the text, with the notes as given there, in an Appendix. It seems unlikely that the music was ever printed, but the original text with an appropriate tune was preserved by Mrs. Booth and eventually sent to the authors of this book by Mrs. Booth's grand-daughter Hilda Thorpe, together with a letter from Bell dated January 27, 1934 in which he confirmed the above, saying:

> The 'short poem' - facetiously styled 'The Anuradhapura Anthem' - you refer to was a joint *jeu d'esprit* of the late Mr. R.W.Ievers, Government Agent, N.C.P., and myself when Archaeological Commissioner on the Ancient ruins of Anuradhapura. It was frankly a pure skit, wholly well-intentioned, but as fully sarcastic, and composed merely to be sung by a party of old friends stationed together to a rousing March of some British Regiment.

Satisfying work, congenial companions; those were happy days.

8

From Exploration to Excavation

The resources of the Archaeological Survey were limited; so at first were its aims. Gordon in his message to the Legislative Council in 1889 had proposed 'on a modest scale, before the rapidly disappearing monuments of the past have altogether perished, a species of Archaeological Survey resembling that carried out in India', and in the Preface to the Kegalla Report Bell quoted a Minute of January 22, 1862 from Lord Canning, Governor-General of India, defining such a survey as 'an accurate description - illustrated by plans, measurements, drawings or photographs, and by copies of inscriptions - of such remains as most deserve notice, with the history of these as far as it may be traceable, and a record of the traditions that are retained regarding them'. [1]

This was the pattern followed in the Kegalla Report and the idea of a general survey, with only very limited further exploration, was still in force in June 1890 when Bell wrote to Noel-Walker. He suggested a general survey of the Island to be followed by detailed work at the major sites, and thought that this might take two or three years, 'as it cannot be done piecemeal', and that he would like five years in order to match the thoroughness of the Indian Survey. [2]

Bell was certainly underestimating the period required, but it was always desirable to suggest to Government that work could be done relatively quickly and cheaply. Bell also wished to work systematically and thoroughly. His plan for Anuradhapura is laid out as follows at the beginning of the Annual Report for 1890:

> As a first step, it was decided to utilize the small labour force at Anuradhapura on a thorough and systematic exploration of the jungle between defined limits (e.g. the Inner and Outer Circular roads), with the preliminary object of ascertaining definitely what ruins still exist above ground. The excavation of likely sites can then follow with more economy of time, labour, and expense than under the irregular and spasmodic efforts hitherto employed.
>
> Such methodical exploration, if slow and barren of frequent startling discoveries, is the only sure means of satisfactorily carrying out that 'complete survey and excavation of Anuradhapura' contemplated by the Ceylon Government. [3]

Bell divided the whole site into sections labelled from A to G, and with X for the central area and Y for the northern area round the Jetawanarama. A map was published in his First Report. [4]

The exploration was gradually undertaken through the years, and by 1895 Bell reported that 'with the exception of tracing other roads and streets within, and leading from the ancient city, its environs may be now said to have been very thoroughly explored as far as surface indications disclose... Doubtless a good deal completely buried at the present day would come to light if time and means permitted of the whole area being exhumed. The greater part of it is still under forest and jungle'. [5]

From exploration to excavation

The work was necessarily slow, for even areas which had once been cleared were soon again overgrown, and impenetrable. In the First Report we read that a whole day was spent in trying to trace the ruins of a 'brick building' and the adjacent 'stone canoe' found by Burrows in 1886.[6]

There are many references throughout Bell's reports to the dense, prickly and exasperating nature of the undergrowth which had to be cleared. An entertaining account is given by John Still in *The Jungle Tide*, that classic of a real forest lover, of how he lost himself with the Governor in the uncleared jungle of Polonnaruwa, and the same conditions existed to a large extent in Anuradhapura in these early years, as may be seen in the charming pictures of overgrown ruins in early travel books. Still wrote:

> It all happened this way. The Governor wished to visit a certain ruined temple where some remarkable frescoes still retained their colours after six centuries of neglect, and he asked me to take him to see them. There were two ways to choose from: one led through the forest along a footpath, and the other crossed beautiful parklands where open glades alternated with woods, and where we were likely to see something of wild life. By cutting across these, the walk could be reduced to about three miles each way, and was more out of the ordinary run. In the event it proved to be very much out of the common routine of a Governor's life, for I mistook one cattle track for another, where all looked much alike, and went a shade too far to the north, thus failing to cut into the forest footpath which led to the ruin but no farther. On we went, and when we had been a couple of hours afoot I knew we had missed the frescoes, lost our way and were heading for very wild uninhabited country. There were plenty of game paths, and they bore the fresh imprints of buffaloes that might or might not be wild, and of elephant, leopard, bear, and several kinds of deer that certainly were; also there were damp hollows where wild pigs had dug, and in the trees above us endless tribes of monkeys moved. So the Governor had many interests added to what must normally prove a tedious career. But it was hot, he was more than sixty years old, and he became very tired and thirsty.
>
> Once, twice, and a dozen times I climbed trees to try and catch sight of some landmark; but those who have not tried to do this may not realise what an exceedingly difficult thing it is to do... Unless one can find a tree that rises above the rest - as a spire above a city - it is not of much use to climb it, for the actual tip-top cannot be reached, and any lower position is valueless...
>
> At last the Governor grew so thirsty that I had to climb one more tree to get him berries to eat. There were very few I could reach, and I gave them all to him. 'Weren't those delicious, Miles!' he exclaimed as he finished the last of them, and the most perfect A.D.C. in Asia replied, with a desiccated tongue,'Yes, Sir, quite delicious'.
>
> That Governor was a great gentleman. When at last I found the way out, and we stumbled wearily along to the door of the Circuit bungalow he occupied, I began to voice my apology; but he cut me short with, 'I have enjoyed my walk, and you must come to dinner'.

Still was a romantic and regretted the disappearance of the wilderness. He wrote:

The last time I visited that city was about twenty years after the adventures I have set down. Where I had gone slowly, we went in a car now; and we found the railway well advanced, and were told that two motor omnibuses called daily. I talked of the better days of old, and my friends envied me; for in the old days it had been an adventure to walk around those ruins that were now so spick and span, with their neat barbed wire fences to keep cattle from damaging the restorations... The place was spoiled. [7]

Although there are passages in Bell's reports which show his appreciation of the beauty of lonely places, his chief concern with the thickets of Anuradhapura was to clear them out of the way. For this he needed a larger force of coolies than the original twenty who started work in July 1890. It was his custom to employ Sinhalese workers on the clearing, 'it being found that the Sinhalese villager, in addition to a knowledge of these jungles, uses a *ketta* with far greater effect than the Tamil coolie'. [8]

On the other hand he found Tamil coolies better at excavating and in unearthing remains when he was on circuit. In his Seventh Progress Report he writes :

Experience of the apathy, superstition and passive obstruction of the Sinhalese villager, even when under definite orders from the Kachcheri through the local headman, to turn out for the slightest extra *rajakarija* ('king's service') involved in clearing the narrow paths to ruins, leaves me with no option but to fall back on my own resources, if the examination of the countless ancient sites scattered through the North-Central Province is to be thorough. The Tamil coolie has no fear of offending the *yakku* believed by nearly every Sinhalese *goiya* to haunt ancient Buddhist ruins... no qualms of conscience in exhuming or handling figures of Buddha in *deviyo*. [9]

Bell was allocated thirty workers in October 1890, but still felt this to be inadequate, as he explained in a letter to the Colonial Secretary on November 15, which is printed in the Third Progress Report as an Annexure. In it he described the difficulties of excavating in the site near the Abhayagiri, where the 'Buddhist Railing' was discovered:

Before commencing to dig it was necessary to fell and remove about fifty large and tough vera trees. This work alone occupied some ten days. Since then excavation has been carried round the exterior of the railing to an average width of 10 ft. and depth of 3 ft. to 4 ft., in order to lay bare the basement and recover the scattered members of the railing plinths, posts, rails, and coping. Owing to the hardness of the soil (much of it fallen brickwork), necessity of carrying to some distance the earth dug out, the ramifications of countless roots, and the care required in getting out the stones and slabs intact, progress has been tediously slow...

I am anxious to start excavation at a dozen other sites almost equally promising, but am met by the insuperable difficulty of want of labour.

I deem it my duty to point out that in my opinion it is useless proceeding with excavation under the present conditions. The tangible result can never be commensurate with the time and money spent; and I do not hesitate to say confidently that unless excavation on a much extended scale can be undertaken,

From exploration to excavation

it will be better to drop this portion of the archaeological survey altogether. That it should be held necessary to recommend the abandonment of this, the most important part of my work, will, I think, prove the gravity of the situation. [10]

He returned to the charge in March 1891, in a further letter to the Colonial Secretary:

I have recently had the advantage of explaining the nature and scope of my work and the difficulties attending excavation in Anuradhapura to several visitors fully competent to express an unbiased opinion, among others to Mr. J.J.Tylor, who has had experience of similar work in Egypt with Mr. Petrie. These gentlemen made no secret of their conviction that the magnitude and exceptional obstacles connected with the survey of Anuradhapura absolutely demand the employment of a far larger force than has been hitherto allotted for the undertaking as contemplated by my instructions. [11]

At first Bell was merely told that he could employ more men if he could pay for them out of the money allocated to the Survey, but in May the Government sanctioned the employment of a further 30 hands. On June 8, 1891 Bell wrote with satisfaction to Sir William Gregory that 'the Government has yielded to my exceeding bitter cry by giving me double the former force, viz. 60 men'. [12]

By 1893 the force numbered 100 men, women and boys. We have seen that exploration and the clearing of vegetation from the remains visible on the surface was only the first step of operations. From the first excavation proceeded side by side with exploration, whenever the ground was not too wet, nor alternatively too dry and hard-baked to make it practicable.

A complete list of the ruins excavated in Anuradhapura up to 1900 is given in the *Summary of Operations 1890-1900* as follows:

1. Vijayarama ruins 1890-1891
2. Abhayagiri ruins 1890-1893
3. Pankuliya ruins 1891-1892
4. 'Kiribat Vehera' 1892-1893
5. Tamil ruins.. 1892-1893
6. Jetawanarama ruins (portion) 1890-1893-1894
7. Toluvila ruins.................................... 1893-1895
8. 'Mayurapada Pirivena'...................... 1894
9. Ruins on Ayton Rd. 1894
10. Sela Chaitiya..................................... 1895
11. Shrine on Kurunegala Rd.................. 1895
12. Thuparama-Ruwanveli ruins............. 1895-1900
13. Mullegala ruins 1896
14. Puliyankulam ruins........................... 1896-1900
15. 'Elala Sohona'................................... 1896-1900
16. Shrine on the Y Rd........................... 1898
17. Citadel.. 1897-1898

A map showing the areas excavated and unexcavated by that time is appended by Bell. [13]

61

The fullest detail on these excavations is available for the period 1890 and 1891, for those years are covered in the first seven Reports, which were published with accompanying illustrations between 1890 and 1896. The first two were entitled Reports, then three to seven were Progress Reports. Thereafter, until 1904, the only records of Bell's work which he actually published were the brief annual accounts given to the RASCB and the three fuller Interim Reports on Sigiriya, which were apparently only ever published in the Journal of the Society. That he always intended to produce further detailed Progress Reports is indicated by the fact that the Annual Reports from 1890 to 1900, when eventually published in 1904, contain references to Progress Reports up to the numbers of 13, and the plans and plates to accompany the Annual Reports (which were not finally issued until 1914) also bear on their title pages references to the projected, but never published, Progress Reports.

In his report to the thirteenth Congress of Orientalists in 1902, Wickremasinghe picked out, as the most important of the excavations at Anuradhapura, those of Abhayagiriya, Vijayarama, Pankuliya and Toluvila. An account of these will also illustrate some of Bell's chief preoccupations and interests. [14]

Excavations were begun around the Abhayagiriya Dagaba in September 1890 and were gradually extended to unearth a large monastic complex and eventually to the clearing of debris round the dagaba and the excavation of the four entrance porches, altars and 'chapels'. Of the buildings first unearthed two were of exceptional interest. One was the Pilima-ge, an image house briefly described as follows in the Annual Report for 1891:

> It has proved to be a spacious and exceptionally handsome *pilima-ge*, or image house, of peculiar design - a large structure 75 ft. square with a bay portico in front. The whole site was raised some feet above the ground with a facing of limestone slabs in simple bold moulding. There were wide staircases on three sides, besides the chief entrance through the porch on the north. Upon this platform stood the image house proper, recessed on all four sides - in plan a broad cross. The distinctive features of this little shrine (which was roofed as an open canopy on twelve wooden clustered posts) are its chastely carved stone plinth, the lotus-leaf surface ornamentation, and specially the reversed position of the elaborate *makara* balustrades to its steps. Around the inner shrine were ranged three rows of limestone columns - sixty in all. [15]

Full details are to be found in the Fourth and Seventh Progress Reports. In the Fourth we read of the unusual form of the balustrades:

> The position of these rises at once struck me as quite unusual. Their peculiarity lay in their apparently reversed position. They seemed to face *inwards* towards some building buried in the low mound from which the heads protruded, much after the fashion of living crocodiles basking in a tank...

> Ordinarily, the fall of these artistic balustrades issues from the mouths of the *makaras*, and curves into a helix at the foot of the stairs. This form, varied in minor details, is universal among the richer Anuradhapura ruins. The present rises are unique and in more than one respect. It is the leafy tail of

the monster that trails down outwards ending in a fancy volute, from the centre of which depends a neat tassel, possibly symbolising the *dharmma-chakra* - a combination of the practical and symbolical [sic], as happy as graceful. The effect is somewhat marred by the shafts of the low relief pilasters (on which the *makaras* are made to stand) being formed of lotus stalks, awkwardly bent, and straightening up into plain capitals. As usual, the *makara* rises flanked by a flight of steps. [16]

Further excavation is described in the Seventh Progress Report, in which Bell writes of what the building might have looked like originally:

> In the days of its glory it must have presented a magnificent appearance exteriorly, with its milk-white basement and stairs of quartz glittering in the sunlight; whilst within, after dark, the chaste beauty of the carving of the shrine would have been immeasurably enhanced by lights coruscating from columns mica-cased. [17]

Of even greater interest to Bell was the discovery of the Buddhist Railing, a find of which he told Gregory on June 8, 1891, 'I am not a little proud', and which was the first building of which a restoration was attempted. [18]

The find is recorded thus in the Second Report in 1890:

> About fifty yards north-west of the *pokuna*, and abutting on the Outer Circular, were found an octagonal shaft and *puhul* capital (a type not hitherto noticed at Anuradhapura) and some narrow moulded slabs deeply morticed. These gave hope of further discovery. When the raised site, six or eight feet above ground level, and some 140 ft. in length by 110 ft. broad, had been cleared of scrub, search was rewarded by a valuable archaeological 'find' - a post with three rails attached, in two pieces - a genuine fragment of a structural 'Buddhist railing'. Fortunately the peculiar shape of the semi-convex rails had saved them from the fate of the shapely pillars of which but stumps remain in position. The tenons at both ends of the standard explained at once the purpose of the morticed slabs. Here were the rail, post, and plinth; only the coping seemed wanting. After continued search a portion of this was found, showing a few inches above ground, and close to it two slabs of a rounded basement, 10 in. in depth, as originally built at right angles to each other. This fixed the south-east corner and determined the plan of the railing which followed the lines of the oblong site. Trial excavation brought up more pieces of rails and coping, and two additional members - a stepped sub-plinth and a low socle below the quarter-round base. There is, therefore, every reason to hope that by running a trench along the foot of the mound more of this fine railing will be unearthed, and that it may yet be possible to restore it in part to nearly its pristine form. [19]

From the first Bell was determined that the scattered parts of the railing should be re-erected as far as possible in their original positions. At that time no part of the Archaeological Vote was assigned to restoration work, so Bell turned for help to the RASCB. On December 16, 1890 he wrote asking if the balance of the Excavation Fund originally raised for work on the Mirisavetiya Dagaba might be spent on several projects which he had in mind, including the re-erection of the Railing. After long consideration, on March 28, 1893, the Society voted that Bell could devote the money to whatever purpose he desired. [20]

The work was entrusted to the Public Works Department and carried out by A.R.Tocke and G.S.Goodman from 1894 to 1897. In 1898 Bell submitted an account of expenditure to the RASCB, meticulously refunding a balance of Rs. 1.33 out of the sum of Rs. 709.57 'placed at his disposal from the Anuradhapura Excavation Fund and spent on the rebuilding of the Buddhist Railing'. The Society published a picture of the restoration and Bell commented that 'the Railing as restored is among the most strikingly beautiful specimens of ancient architecture to be seen anywhere throughout the Island'. [21]

The Vijayarama monastery, a mile and a half north of the Jetawanarama Dagaba, had been partially cleared by Burrows. It was one of the first of the complete monastic complexes excavated by Bell and he reported on it in considerable detail in the Fourth, Fifth and Sixth Progress Reports. He summarised as follows in the Annual Report for 1891:

> By the more complete felling of the jungle which hid the greater portion of the 'Vijayarama' ruins, and by systematic excavation, the ruined buildings and their co-relation leave no room for doubt that here existed a typical *sangharama*, or Buddhist establishment, perfect in itself, with its shrines and meeting hall, its priestly residences, bath-house, storerooms, ponds, etc. [22]

Of great importance was the finding, in the debris around the basement of the dagaba, of thirteen copper plaques, votive tablets of the Mahayana cult. They were cleaned by soaking in oil and weak acid. Transcribed and translated by Wickremasinghe and Gunasekera, they appear in Appendix A to the Sixth Progress Report where their importance is indicated as follows:

> (i) The plaques afford indisputable proof that writing on copper plates was in vogue in Ceylon, at least as early as the ninth century, or several hundred years previous to the date of the oldest genuine *tamba sannasa* hitherto made known.

> (ii) For the epigraphist they supplement a knowledge of the Sinhalese character of the time, until now drawn only from stone inscriptions often too worn to be turned to palaeographical use.

> (iii) They prove distinctly the presence in Ceylon at the period of adherents of the 'Great Vehicle' (Mahayana) school of Buddhism as tainted by Tantric accretions.

> (iv) By enabling the age of the erection of the 'Vijayarama' Monastery to be fixed with fair approximation, a safe guide is obtained (independent of the intrinsic evidence deducible from the carvings themselves), for an examination of the style and forms of the ninth century architecture at Anuradhapura, as compared with other date-assured examples of Buddhist art, both in India and Ceylon. [23]

The Sixth Progress Report gives a detailed description of the great open hall connected with the temenos quadrangle, and contains drawings of the very fine bas-reliefs and carvings. It also illustrates various carved steps and guardstones found at Vijayarama, and contains the following comment of Bell on the dwarf figures which he always enjoyed finding:

From exploration to excavation

The sleek, well-fed dwarfs that figure on these slabs, and the merry little fellows found on the risers of staircases, or at the feet of the Naga janitors, have an unmistakable family likeness, despite the varying positions and styles of dress which they affect. Never burdened with a superfluity of clothing, what is wanting in ordinary covering is usually compensated by a plethora of heavy ornaments - necklaces, cords, chest-band, waist-chain, armlets, wristlets, earrings, and tiara, with or without some elaborate head-gear.

I am unaware whether these dwarf guardians have been satisfactorily identified. I take them to be *Yaksha kritiyas*, the slaves of Vaisravana or Kuvera, god of wealth. Part of the duties expected of these *ganas* appears to have been to act as sentinels at the outer portals to sacred precincts or buildings. Thus we meet with them at the eastern portico of the Thuparama enclosure, on the left and right of the broad flight of front steps to the south *mandapa* of Jetawanarama Dagaba, and, as here, posted at two of the main entrances to the 'Vijayarama' temenos. [24]

A further find made at the Vijayarama, by Bell's assistant Wickremasinghe, was the set of bronze figures found in brick cellas beneath the four porches at the cardinal points of one of the buildings. At each point of the compass there was a guardian deity and an animal: a lion at the north, an elephant at the east, a horse at the south, and a bull at the west. Bell argued that the animals represented the four great rivers said to emerge from the mythical lake of Anotatta, whose outlets were supposed to have been in the form of these animals. In Appendix B to the Sixth Progress Report he further suggests:

> In this theory may possibly be found an explanation of the band of animals - elephant (east), horse (south), lion (north), bull (west), which, with a further band of *hansas*, adorn the 'Moonstones' of the more important ancient shrines at Anuradhapura. May not the animals as representing 'the four directions' be held to signify that the doors of the temple, on whose steps they are carved, stand ever open to all Buddhist worshippers - the silent lithic symbolism of a later age, when structural viharas had superseded the rock cave with its brow-inscribed warranty to hermit 'monks from the four quarters, present and absent' (*agata anagata chatu disa sagasa*).

Bell, however, sharply criticised the execution of the bronze animals, saying:

> The elephant, in proportion to horse or bull, is much too small. The head is well moulded, with frontal depression marked, large true ears erect, but impossible goggle eyes. The trunk curls back into the mouth. The tusks are not fully developed; feet, fairly good; tail (carried down the right leg) of undue length.

> The horse is a sorry beast, recalling Hudibras' gallant steed:-
>
> > '...sturdy, large, and tall
> > With mouth of meal and eyes of wall.'

> A stallion, right ear gone, right foreleg (broken off at knee) larger than the left, short-cropped mane, and scraggy tail. The horse could hardly have been a familiar animal in ancient Anuradhapura.

Like the elephant, the lion, a male, is cast ridiculously small, and is further wanting in every attribute which stamps the 'king of beasts'. This bronze might pass for an ill-bred bull-dog:-

> 'If you think I come hither as a lion, it were pity
> of my life: no, I am no such thing.'

The head is raised, the mouth gapes displaying the gums; two teeth protrude from the upper jaw on either side; the ears stand out, and the eyes are very prominent. There is no mane; the feet are canine. The tail is curled back over the right haunch and down the flank. Conventionalism has in this instance degenerated into travesty.

Finally, the bull is hardly less faulty than the other animals. A rough dewlap, 'pommel', hump, and horns (both broken), alone prevent it from being written down an ass when viewed in flank. Fronting, the beast has the distinctly 'rakish' look of a bull at bay. [25]

The Pankuliya ruins had been visited by Ievers in 1887, and he had seen a sedent Buddha which had fallen forward and was too deeply buried to be examined in any detail. Bell's first, somewhat jocular, reference to this Buddha in his Fifth Progress Report, caused him to be taken to task in *The Buddhist*. Bell had written:

In the centre of the vihares, showing well above the ground, are the 'hind quarters' of a large sedent Buddha, fallen, like Dagon of old, headlong, in an attitude possibly befitting his worshippers but that ill becomes the *Tathagata*! [26]

The writer in *The Buddhist* had protested strongly against 'the insinuating and odious comparisons and language used by the Commissioner H.C.P.Bell, C.C.S., who is a paid public servant'.

Commenting on this in the *Monthly Literary Review, Notes and Queries for Ceylon*, January 1894, A.E.Buultjens wrote, 'I believe I have heard it said that in the course of Mr. H.C.P.Bell's work at Anuradhapura he has set up so many fallen "graven images" that I fear the common opinion is that he is a staunch Buddhist. It must be refreshing to him, therefore, to get this counterblast'. [27]

Bell's description of the Buddha when re-erected 'by fifty coolies and six Europeans' on July 19, 1892, may have been in the nature of an amende honorable. He wrote:

The image measures approximately 7 ft. from head to seat, and is as usual carved from quartz. The pose of the broken arms and hand shows that this sedent Buddha was sculptured in the *asirwada-mudra*, or attitude of blessing. As since raised and replaced with the hands fitted on, the figure is undoubtedly the finest of the large Buddhas yet discovered at Anuradhapura.

The classic features, simple expression, and life-like attitude of the Buddha, as represented in the act of blessing, render the Pankuliya figure a distinctly pleasing variation from the ubiquitous *dhyana-mudra* images with folded hands and vacant stare. [28]

From exploration to excavation

At the end of his career, Bell reported that 'the figure was in 1912 permanently set on its renewed *asanaya* within the shrine, and now offers one of the most taking and effective presentations of the seated Buddha to be met with anywhere in Ceylon'. [29]

In all, thirty buildings belonging to this complex were opened up in 1891 and 1892, and details of the excavations are given in the Sixth and Seventh Progress Reports. The latter contains a full description of the main steps of Vihare No. 2 and at their foot the moonstone, that semi-circular carved stone which is the glory of many Buddhist buildings:

> The execution of the 'moonstone' goes far to redeem the mediocrity of balustrade and terminal. At the middle is the customary conventionalised lotus flower, full-blown, with plain centre; then two narrow fillets, the first with foliage ornament, the other lined; beyond these a band of flowing arabesque pattern; outside this again, between plain thin fillets, a broadish band (except for arabesque strips at the end) of fauna carving - a procession of eight elephants and horses (four of each) passing listlessly from left to right, so arranged that horses occupy the corners and two elephants the centre. [30]

Bell noted that this moonstone lacked the lions and bulls almost invariably found on others in Anuradhapura.

The Report continues with an account of several 'finds' of exceptional interest. These included two bronze feet (apparently of a dancing figure), tiny offering figurines, a silver belt inlaid with spurious jewels and a crystal eye thus described:

> To light on one of the veritable eyes - the left - of the ancient stone image of the Buddha was a unique stroke of luck. The 'eyeball', so to speak, less pupil, was first found. Working on cautiously the following day we were fortunate enough to pick out from the debris the pupil itself. The eye is beautifully cut from transparent crystal, highly polished and slightly curved to fit the eye socket, with a central depression to take the pupil... The pupil, a thin circular chip of crystal, was stained dark blue. [31]

Another monastic site fully excavated was the ruins at Toluvila, near Nuwaravewa. It was here that in 1890 a huge sedent Buddha was found, which was sent to the Colombo Museum and still presides over the entrance hall. At that time Bell described it as 'the finest yet brought to light at Anuradhapura', and continued:

> In mere size it yields to the seated Buddha of the Outer Circular which measures 7 ft. 6 in. in height by 7 ft. across the knees. But in other respects it surpasses all three statues near the Jetawanarama. The wonderful sharpness and depth of the features, the softness of expression, the symmetry and repose of the body, give the image a *tout ensemble* which contrasts markedly with the stolid 'figure-head' appearance so characteristic of these Buddhas in stone. The eye-lids, under-lips, and ears are carved with a life-like reality not reached in the case of the other Buddhas already known. The nose is chipped, but so slightly as to be practically unnoticeable from the front; the fingers are somewhat worn, and there are a few cracks. With these slight blemishes the Sage sits as serenely contemplative as when votaries flocked to worship and make their offerings upon his altar. [32]

H. C. P. Bell

In his *Summary of Operations 1890-1900* Bell very briefly outlined the work he had done in the Kegalla district and at Anuradhapura, listing the chief ruins remaining to be excavated. He also mentioned the topographical surveys which had been initiated, the excavations at the remarkable site of Sigiriya, the projected work at Polonnaruwa and his extensive circuit work. All these had to be carried on simultaneously.

9

Jungle Trails

In the *Summary of Operations 1890-1900* Bell wrote:

> Every ancient site in the North-Central Province as far as ascertained by the Archaeological Commissioner at the time has been visited and examined. Hardly a nook or corner remains to be explored. [1]

This was achieved by circuits, sometimes two in a year, through jungle areas. The reviewer of Bell's Seventh Progress Report pertinently wrote:

> We commend a perusal of the latter part of the diary to those who look upon the work of the Archaeological Commissioner as a jolly picnic. [2]

An account of Appendix B of this Report, which chronicles a tour from September 5 to October 25, 1891, will support this comment on the hardships of Bell's circuits, and also indicate what they achieved. Though a baggage-cart was sent ahead, it could be nearly a month before it was rejoined, and everything necessary had to be carried on coolies' heads:

> The sun was now sinking well down, and the picture of the straggling line of coolies... heavily loaded, picking their way slowly through the tall *ramba* grass, and the stretch of level plain, with forest at back in the distance, instinctively recalled to my mind - *magnis componere parva* - pictures of African travel. [3]

Meanwhile Bell, accompanied at first by Ievers and the Acting Chief Surveyor, Ridout, and thereafter by his Assistant Wickremasinghe, often covered 16 miles and once as many as 20 miles in a day. A distance might be estimated by a far-reaching 'hoo-cry' from the Sinhalese, in 'clear long-drawn-out tones' echoing from the hills. For the earlier part of the circuit they might walk in dense shade but in deep sand, or else have a 'hot cheerless walk'. September 14 was intensely hot, and the labour of examining horizontal inscriptions on rock without any shade was 'exceedingly trying'. Bell more than once notices the difficulties of village women who had to get water from a murky pool, or trudge twelve miles in a day to fetch some.

The situation changed to the opposite with the breaking of the North-East Monsoon, which that year was exceptionally heavy:

> The rain fell in torrents, converting the road into a muddy stream and soaking through everything.... When we reached Maha-Kapu-Gollewa at dark it was in the condition of drowned rats. [4]

Nor was shelter for the night always adequate. After a blinding storm, Bell's *gaman-wadiya* or temporary leaf-and-straw shelter, 'leaked like a sieve'. The following night, 'the evening closed in misery and bed, with rivulets running riot among my baggage and the roof weeping piteously'. As a result, travel was impeded. Bell writes, 'The Ma-Oya too swollen this morning to admit of crossing, until I ordered a couple of trees (one on either side of the river) to be cut so as to fall inwards'. They had to cut and force their way through thick wet jungle, in which 'myriads of green caterpillars, which hung from every twig at the end of long silky threads, and fastened on to face, hands and body', were added to the dank vegetation and swarms of mosquitoes. All this had its effect on health. Bell had three bouts of fever in October, which obliged him during the two or three days' helplessness to rely on Wickremasinghe (also frequently drenched) to explore and measure ruins and copy inscriptions.

Among the discoveries which were hoped for on circuit were of course inscriptions, looked for in every cave and on every pillar found. In the Aliya-kada caves, one epigraph was twenty-five feet or so above the rock floor, but Bell notes:

> By 'swarming up' the only tree 'within range' and as straight as a mast, I was able to dictate the inscriptions to the Vel-Vidana, who, standing below, wrote it in Sinhalese characters in the sand with his finger. [5]

When Bell felt too weak for a long exploration walk, he spent a forenoon copying the fine inscriptions from 'Parakrama Bahu I's pillar' on the bund of the Padaviya tank. Bell was always interested in tanks and their workings; he spent a day at the almost unknown 'Great Tank' at Wahal-kada, measuring the rock-spill, the breach, and the high-level sluice. Former temples were always the objects of search, to be cleared enough to survey, make plans of and photograph. The 'Ella-vewa' temple, more correctly called *Vehera-gala*, 'the dagaba (crowned) rock', had a dagaba, flower altar, nicely carved *Sri patul* stone, stone steps, and the massive basement slabs of the old *pansala*, and to testify to its antiquity, an inscribed pillar of the mid-tenth century.

Ancient sites might be buried in forest, or have developed from the religious use of caves. The former applied to Kuda-amba-gas-vewa, found in such dense jungle that the guiding Vel-Vidana at first went astray. It had an image house with a Buddha black with age, which had frightened villagers who thought it a dread *yakka* (demon), also guardstones flanking steps, and a moonstone with eight elephants. Equally frequent were the ancient vihares constructed under caves. Local people could be unwilling to approach a cave, because there a villager had been killed by a bear. An Arachchi guide who felt responsible for Bell's safety carried a cudgel at Brahmanaya-gama, where they made their way to a cave, 'scrambling and bawling' to scare off possibly resident bears. Other animal life was less threatening. A small herd of half-wild buffaloes haunted an abandoned tank near the 'black Buddha' temple, but when they saw the party, backed slowly and stealthily away into the jungle; and in a small muddy tank during the drought 'buffaloes were wallowing with satisfaction'. Elephants could be intrusive. A pillar at Namba-kada had been raised with poles, which were snapped and trampled by the beast; and a priest complained that because some villagers had not mended his fence, 'elephants played pranks in his back-yard'.

Jungle trails

Bell gives details of sculptures found. He describes a variant on a carving often seen, this one near a tank at Talapat-kulama:

> At numberless tanks detached *naga-gal* ('cobra-stones') are found near the ancient sluices, representing the sacred guardianship of the water. In this case the figures are carved on the vertical face of the living rock on the tank side, and the addition of a pair of female 'supporters' - so-called *devas* - to the *naga* is distinctly uncommon. [6]

On another tank bund, that of Kon-vewa, was the image of 'a fine sedent Buddha overshadowed by the Snake-king Muchalinde' represented with nine hoods. The Buddha was sitting cross-legged on three coils of the snake. The figure had been moved from a neighbouring ruined monastery to the inappropriate location of the bund; this, some villagers believed, had deprived the tank of water. Bell was very ready to state their grievance to the Government Agent, and hoped that by the restoring of the image to its shrine, the tank and the fields lying fallow would revive. Of all the Buddha statues found in the jungle, however, Bell was most struck by the figure at Komarike-wala:

> When first seen, seated in impassive solitude amid forest trees and thick undergrowth, buried to the waist in the leafy deposit of centuries, the huge Buddha presented a strangely weird appearance, singularly impressive. Real awe has kept generation after generation of villagers from in any way meddling with the statue of 'the Sacred One'. [7]

Ruined shrines were not the only ones to be met with on circuit. At several places a 'working' vihare was encountered, and these afforded opportunities for Wickremasinghe to borrow ola manuscripts, and for Bell to describe their images and decorations. He also twice encountered complaints from priests of neglect by villagers. As we have seen, the latter could be moved by fear of the 'malificence of demons'. At Tammannewa they were reluctant to clear thorny shrub from some ruins, because after their doing so the previous year several deaths had occurred in the hamlet, which they attributed *post hoc propter hoc* to disturbed demons.

Bell's own sufferings from fever perhaps led him to sympathise with the villagers of Namada-vewa, who told him 'with grim resignation' that no old people were left - all had succumbed to fever! It was a village of *kandayo* of jaggery-caste, and Bell found humour at Rambewa in his guide's refusal to drink water given by villagers of another caste - until they were out of sight. Bell had to be dependent on local headmen for each *wadiya* shelter of jungle material lined with cloths, and for guiding his party. In spite of its highlights of discovery, the sheer toil of a circuit must again be stressed - getting in late 'as the moon rose to help us somewhat with faint light struggling through the boughs'. Yet there were moments to 'stand and stare' as at the Talapat-kulama tank:

> Looking over the tank from the bund the view of picturesque solitude is most striking. From the foot of the bund a beautiful stretch of open *ramba* grassland rolls back, with occasional wooded clumps to break the monotony, up to the fringe of dark green and brown forest in the distance. [8]

Travel in the Island was slow enough, even when not on foot. Jules Leclercq in his book *Un séjour dans l' île de Ceylan* gave details of a journey by Royal Mail Coach from Matale to Anuradhapura. The one hundred and thirteen kilometres were a twelve-hour trip in ten stages. A blacksmith was carried to re-shoe horses when necessary at staging posts, which took a quarter of an hour. A tent was stretched over two benches in the waggon, and there was a box seat above for the driver and officials - such as the Government Agent or District Engineer. On the principle that an omnibus can never be full, a dozen passengers were squeezed into a space which appeared capable of holding six. [9]

At that time there was already a railroad from Colombo to Kandy. The system was extended, but travel was still awkward enough in the later part of Bell's service. From A.T.G.A. Wickramasuriya comes an account in an article 'Are the toils of the archaeological pioneers forgotten?' of the experiences of his father P.Don Ambrose 'during the first quarter of this century, while working, living and travelling in those uninhabited jungle areas'. Wickramasuriya writes of his father's journeyings:

> The event that excited me most was the circuitous route and mode of transport he had to take, whenever he had to go from the Head Office at Anuradhapura to the work-site at Polonnaruwa during his very early years in the Department.
>
> The first lap of that journey was by train from Anuradhapura to Matale via Polgahawela, where he had to change train. The second lap was from Matale to Habarana in a horse-drawn coach (which took mail to Trincomalee). The third lap was from Habarana to Polonnaruwa in the double bullock-cart of the Department. The inside of the cart was benched and cushioned to serve as a sleeping cart. Under its foot-board was the locker for the trunk he carried. It contained the wages and pay roll of the popularly known 'Bell Party' working at Polonnaruwa.
>
> This last lap lasted from midnight to early morning, through thick jungle infested with elephant. The run was steady and continuous except for two halts at Minneriya and Giritale, where new pairs of bulls were kept in readiness to take over. The Department cart reserved for the 'Sudu Mahathaya' (Commissioner) had the same 'bull power' but was undoubtedly better furnished. [10]

In Bell's accounts of his circuits, among the difficulties of travel the theme of water - too little or too much - recurs. In the Gal-ge Wanni in 1896, Bell refers thankfully to 'a small rock hummock (Gala-wala) with a "pocket" of cool pure water - the only oasis in twelve miles of shadeless barren country'. On the other hand, when the monsoon broke, they were 'crossing the Malwatu-oya, now in flood, with great difficulty'.

Some circuits covered wilder and rougher, less inhabited country, which produced particular hazards. In August 1893 they had to cut their way through dense stunted jungle along the summit of the wild Ritigala-kanda range, and later use rope to negotiate precipices.

In the autumn circuit of 1896, after the dry Gal-ge Wanni, the Moragolle Wanni showed lakes and vegetation, but produced its own problems. Hunters had spoken of an inscribed pillar at Kukuru-mahan-damana, but after some days' search in the trackless jungle, it was found that,

Jungle trails

'elephants had thrown down the pillar and trampled it into the ground'. [11]

Besides the inhabited vihares and devales visited in late 1891, others were found on circuit both in forest areas and isolated in the hills. Bell investigated these, and gives impressions of the monks and priests heard of or encountered. The Fourth Progress Report speaks of 'an extraordinary accident' at Debal-gala a few years back when two priests at their devotions were struck by lightning, 'one being killed on the spot, the other stunned', and the mark of the electric current was still visible on the rock.

Kapiri-gama was a well-to-do temple with a comfortable pansala, the modern buildings on an ancient site. Bell was able there to borrow two olas; and indeed he was normally given scope for examining the temples in detail. At the Tambala-gallewa rock devale, one of the finest in the Province, since it was not a *kemara davasa* (worship day), the Kapurala was persuaded to show him an unusual figure of Vishnu, with snakes entwined round the neck and waist. After a simple ritual the concealing curtain was drawn back. [12]

Among Buddhist vihares, the one at Kammalapalliya 'a perfect forest retreat for ascetic monks', visited in an autumn tour in 1895, gave a rather attractive impression:

> The pleasant old incumbent.... his minor priest and three pupils tried to reconcile the 'Spartan simplicity' of the usually self-denying *Ramanna* fraternity with incongruous luxuries supplied by the liberality of pious villagers... modern furniture, vegetable garden, etc. [13]

Vihares not far apart could offer contrasts in characters. Whereas Mahagal Vihare, where ambitious building was proceeding, had an elderly incumbent 'a worthy Buddhist monk universally respected for his kindness, piety and medical skill', at Alut-gal Vihare the priest in charge, once fellow pupil with his brother monk and neighbour above, 'is zealous only in carpentry'. [14]

Bell's interest in tanks and streams flows through the accounts of his circuits. He admired the skill of the ancient engineers in constructing spills and sluices. The storage tank at Nachchaduwa, which had originally helped to fill Nuwara-vewa, one of the two great tanks of Anuradhapura, had a well-preserved spill with an ingenious bonding of its face. Where old sluices remained in order, as at Manankattiya, he found also 'a thriving village with a magnificent far-reaching tract of rice fields'. Unhappily tanks had often been breached by excessive floods. Repairs had been attempted, as seen at the great 'dam-built-by-demons' at Yakkabendi Amuna, where in 1895 Bell found carved stones had been used:

> These stones - dado of squatting lions, and cornice ornamented with a string of *hansas* (sacred ducks or geese) must have formed part of the basement of a handsome ruin. [15]

Where tanks had been breached and abandoned, as Bell noted in 1896 in the wild Vilachchiya Korale, the want of water in the dry months had destroyed the ancient prosperity of the area. Ancient indeed, for the picturesquely situated Giritale-vewa, seen in 1905, might well date from the days of Maha Sena (277-304 A.D.). [16]

Ancient images were often found in ruined vihares. In autumn 1897, at Nagala-kanda, a hill near Minneriya, in the remains of a once important monastery in thick jungle, 'a colossal standing figure of Buddha (nearly 12 ft. in height) was found prone and almost buried'. Bell liked to remedy such a situation where possible. In 1892 at Ayitigevewa, the parts of a standing Buddha and pedestal, found at the site of an ancient vihare, were set up with 'infinite labour'.[17]

These were forest sites, but caves could also yield finds. In the Spring tour of 1892 at Dunumadala-kanda, a large cave temple, 107 ft. by 36 ft. in depth, held a 'huge recumbent figure of Buddha, 29 ft. from head to foot, well-modelled, besides several other images'. Ritigala-kanda is a great region of caves. August 1893 was spent in this area, and the ancient cave temple at Na-maluwa deserves remark:

> The beetling rock, under which was built a vihare, rises some 40 feet to the *katare* alone. The shrine was shut in by a brick wall, plaster coated, which tapers in thickness - a marked peculiarity of the ancient walls. Inside, partly buried in bats' excreta, are several images, more or less worn, and all small. Six are of wood, not mere rough-hewn cores for after-fashioning with clay, but carved and originally painted. One standing figure with arms crossed above the breast recalls - *magnis componere parva* - the beautiful rock-cut statue of the mourning Ananda at Polonnaruwa.[18]

Two immense Buddha images not within rock temples, but carved from the living rock, seem to have been first seen by Bell in 1895. Seseruwa, an isolated modern temple, was viewed in September. Bell observed:

> Of chief interest is the erect figure of Buddha which stands at the head of the long staircase backed by the towering southern cliff of Maha-kanda. The colossal image stands on an unfinished elongated low pedestal (16 ft. x 2 ft. in height) and measures 39 ft. 3 in. from head to foot. It is cut from the scarp wall in high sunk-relief and united to the rock throughout, even the back of arms and hands. As at Awkhana, the Buddha is posed in the act of blessing (a*siva mudra*) - the right hand with open palm raised, the left bent and grasping the *sivura* or robe..... Grooves and mortices in the rock, and the remains of stone pillars utilized to form the oblong site in front of the figure, show that it was originally sheltered by a roof shelter.[19]

Bell compared this great figure unfavourably with the other colossal Buddha at Awkhana Vihare, which he saw later in the circuit. He wrote:

> This image is of much the same height as its mighty fellow at Seseruwa, but in every respect has the advantage, and impresses the gazer far more strongly. The Seseruwa Buddha is necessarily dwarfed by the cliff towering above, and being carved in semi-sunk relief is less striking from a distance; further it has weathered badly in places, and unconsciously wears a distrait look. In contrast the Awkhana statue, cut in almost full round from a boulder of about the same height, stands boldly forward, huge, assertive, awe-inspiring. The features, members and robe are better chiselled, and the expression is not wanting in placid dignity. Exclusive of the nimbus (*sirespota*, 3 ft. 8 in.) and pedestal (3 ft. 10 in. in height, 15 ft. 2 in. in diameter) the figure rises 38 ft. 10 in. The Buddha stands in the attitude of blessing (*asiva mudra*).[20]

Jungle trails

Bell's eye for detail on his circuits is frequently exemplified. He seizes on the odd item of interest, gives little set-pieces, speculates on a finding, but sometimes is compelled to confess puzzlement or yield himself to a sense of mystery. In his Fifth Progress Report, having tracked an ancient roadway from the Jetawanarama ruins at Anuradhapura to the Vijayarama Monastery, he noted at the site of a ruined building, 'a stone pier, 4 ft. in height, hollowed at top, intended doubtless for the *pin-taliya* or free-water chatty, still offered for travellers' use by the Sinhalese of the present day'.

When the Nalanda Gedige was eventually studied, Bell was caught by the carving in the tympanum of 'Vaisrawana, guardian deity of the north, as Kuvera, the podgy god of wealth'. He wore the *upavita*, or Brahminical cord, armlets and a rich necklace, and his pose is thus described:

> ...with his right foot resting on the cornice of the tower... and the left crossed in front on a cushion... He holds the right hand with open palm in front of his belly, as though engaged in complacent talk, and in his left hand, which rests on his leg, he grasps a closed fan (?). [21]

Less easy to identify was a carving on a slab at Velana-damana in the Moragolla Wanni, pointed out by a Wanni hunter. Bell writes:

> The sculpture, represented in sunk relief, is in two panels. In the upper is a king seated cross-legged with left hand in lap, the right resting against the knee: on either side are female *chamara*-bearers, one arm bent and raised. The large lower panel displays a spirited battle between a giant armed with sword and shield, aided by a kneeling spearman, against four foes (three of whom are dying or dead) whose weapons are bows and arrows. The giant has been hit by two arrows, but has just disembowelled one assailant. All the figures are almost naked. There is no tradition helping to explain this highly spirited and historically interesting bas-relief, so strangely placed in the trackless wilds of the North-Central Province. [22]

There was also a strangeness about something found, and restored, in Tamankaduwa in August 1897:

> At Morakanda, a hill about two miles south of Alut-oya resthouse, under heavy forest, is a deliciously cool spring called '*Nayipenna Ulpota*' from the hooded cobra guardian of the water, carved in limestone. The cobra is cut in the round - not as usually in relief on a slab - and fitted into a granite socket. Both were found half buried in the stream bed. Had them dug out and fitted securely on dry rock close to the spring. As set up the giant white cobra apparently issuing from its lurking place in the rock, amid dense shade, is startlingly 'uncanny' viewed from a short distance. [23]

They left it to its watch, and a month later reached another sight by water near Katupilana on the left bank of the Mahaveli-ganga: a *gal-aliya* or rock-carved elephant, thus described:

> This piece of animal sculpture is probably unique in Ceylon. Cut in full round from a rock, life-size, are the head and shoulders of an elephant whose feet the river washed when low. The elephant stands

in the water, looking slightly up stream, as though hesitating to cross. At present the river in semi-flood reaches its eyes. There are signs of 'sets' for some building's foundations on a boulder adjoining, but no ruins or inscriptions are known likely to afford a clue to the object of this solitary *tour de force* of a skilful sculptor. [24]

The sight so much impressed Bell that twenty years later he expanded the brief account from his diary into an article opening with a quotation:

'Insula Taprobane gignat tetros elephantos'.

The elephant, feared and wondered at in the West in ancient times, was always in the East, Bell wrote, familiar in war, in ceremony and in useful labour, and was reverenced rather than feared. So in the *Mahavansa* King Dutugemunu owed to his mount, the incomparable Kandula, the death of the usurper Elala. Bell gave many instances of the great animal in Sinhalese art: in relief on edifices, on moonstones, at the Ruwanveli Dagaba. Very rarely, though, did they appear in the full round, except surmounting pilasters on guardstone terminals at Anuradhapura.

It was rare to represent elephants realistically. Bell mentioned the bas-reliefs above the pokuna north of the Isurumuniya Temple at Anuradhapura. He then concentrated on the dark grey granite beast at Katupilana, virtually unknown because off the usual track. On September 23, 1897 he had crossed the river by canoe and the party cut their way upstream. Repeating his description of the elephant, he stressed that from a short distance it looked 'very much in the flesh as very much alive'. All but the head was buried, so he had the silted earth behind dug out, and found that six feet backward from the head had been carved, sloping down one foot in three. The elephant, facing SSE, was said by the guide to be in a kneeling attitude. Bell continued:

Photographed what showed of the beast with a merry Moor youth (who 'seemed to enjoy the ride') on its back.

The trunk was submerged but the ear is very clear in the plate and was 2 ft. 7 in. long; he measured every part meticulously. Bell wondered when it was made and why. Did it represent the petrified representation of some erstwhile 'Kandula' whose deeds his Royal Master desired thus to perpetuate amid environment so congenial to his living compeers? The author embodied the mystery in a quotation:

'Ille, velut pelagi rupes immota, resistit;
Quae sese, multis circumlatrantibus undis,
Mole tenet'.

'He standeth like some sea-girt rock,
Moveless, athwart the waters' shock;
And, anchored by his ponderous form,
Massive, resists the beating storm'. [25]

10

Jungle Dwellers

Most of Bell's own circuits through jungle to examine sites fell between 1890 and 1900, though he made others in 1905 and 1908, and included in his Reports tours made by his assistants. In later years he produced articles based on his diaries, which record his dealings with the wild creatures of the jungle and its primitive inhabitants. He met wandering gypsies and described these occasions in an article in 1916:

> Gangs of them have been 'struck' under all sorts of conditions - it may be whilst 'trekking' with donkeys, dogs, portable belongings, and the usual stock in trade (monkeys, cobras, etc.), to some other camping-ground - or more frequently as bivouacked on 'road reservations' and similar open spaces - or, perchance, when begging in outlying villages (where they are not unwisely restricted, during their temporary halt, to the *'tis-bamba'*, the thirty-fathom belt surrounding fenced-in dwellings forming the *'gan-goda'*, or hamlet) - and, even on one occasion, by great luck, a party emerging from a jungle belt, hunters and dogs in full career after game 'with hark and whoop and wild halloo'....
>
> 'Easy live and quiet die' is the motto adopted throughout their happy-go-lucky life of vagabondage by this restless tribe of Indian 'Ishmaelites', whose hand is against every man, and every man's hand against them, albeit peacefully. And who shall say that, on the whole, they be not 'good honest men and true, saving a little shifting for their living. God help them!' [1]

The article was accompanied by Plates, showing various gypsy types and their palm leaf dwellings, as well as two trackers squatting by a magnificent leopard which they 'do not fear to run down and kill without the aid of fire arms'. Bell also gave information on their snake charming methods, and in his circuit in 1891 he had been amused by some snake charmers who were willing to sell some of their 'infallible remedies... on condition that we never divulged the secret'.

On this same circuit Wickremasinghe, when going on his own to examine ruins at Alut-halmillewa, found a village, Bogaha-wewa, of which he noted, 'Its sole inhabitants are a few families, "*Wanni minissu*" - undoubtedly the descendants of Veddas, for some of them still used the bow and arrow in hunting'. [2]

In circuits later in 1897 through the wilder regions of the Egoda Pattuwa, Bell visited hamlets of the primitive Veddas. One was in the Vera-goda-gala, on the right bank of the Madara-oya, and he wrote of its headman:

> The *Patabenda* lives here; and there are altogether 42 inhabitants (names taken down) - 15 males, 14 females and 13 children. One or two families have gone into the jungle, and only return periodically. Dwellings (bark-walled) are naturally very poor: the only cultivation round the hovels is represented

by a few plantain trees... the *Patabenda*... is a comical, but rather foul-mouthed little fellow, who has not been improved in manners or talk by a 'free visit' to Colombo at Government expense a few years ago in connection with a Vedda murder case from Kohambalewa.[3]

Veddas often acted as guides in these wild regions and some appear in Plates to the Egoda Pattuwa article. A *Patabenda* was with Bell at caves near Kandegama-kanda in 1897, and 'walking ahead, was here bitten by a viper (*Ancistrodon Hypnale*, Sin. *kunu-katuwa*) which he called "*pingiti*". He treated the matter very lightly - only applying "chunam" to the wound as of little moment; but said that he would suffer to some extent for a day or two'.[4]

Bell's knowledge, from his circuit of 1897 and later visits, of the remote country of Tamankaduwa and its people, enabled him to help the Government to clear up unsettled boundary questions affecting the North-Central Province. In 1903 a 'bone of contention' arose from the proposal of the Superintendent of Topographical Surveys, backed by the Surveyor General and by Mr. S.Haughton, Government Agent of the Eastern Province, that the Egoda Pattuwa area of Tamankaduwa should be annexed to the Eastern Province. Haughton said that all the villagers wanted it, but Bell, strenuously countering the plan, said they were 'benighted' enough to assent to anything when asked, but had never *petitioned* to cut their connection with Anuradhapura. Granting that at present, to reach the headquarters of the Revenue Officer at Topavewa, they had to cross the Mahaveli-ganga, which sometimes flooded, Bell suggested they should be given three trees to make ferry boats. For all the villages except Vedda hamlets were an easy distance from Topavewa, whereas there were fifteen or ten miles of wild country to Onegama the nearest village across the Eastern Province boundary. The Government Agent of the North-Central Province, L.W.Booth, supported Bell, and the Government instructed the Surveyor General to adopt his boundary line.[5]

In 1905 Bell had toured the area and recorded the ancient boundary landmarks from the mouth of Talawarige Mattuwa, the old *Patabenda*, or chief of the Veddas of Tamankaduwa, 'whose simple statements could be relied on unhesitatingly'. Bell records that the chief 'plaintively stated' that true landmarks had been stolen by 'unscrupulous native headmen of the Eastern Province years ago, in order to "annexe" Kandegama-kanda with its rich annual yield of *bambaru* (rock-bees) honey and wax'. In his article on 'Archaeological research in the Egoda Pattuwa' Bell enlarges on the chief's complaint, saying, 'The rent for wax is said to be annually sold at Batticaloa (Eastern Province) and these North-Central Province Veddas are prosecuted if they take the hives'.[6]

John Still writes at length about the *bambaru*, the wild bees whose honey was of such value to jungle folk. The bees often nested under overhanging rocks where they 'hang in brown shimmering curtains that smell fiercely of the death that awaits their disturber, the scent of an infinite number of poisoned daggers'. He describes how the jungle villagers smoked them out 'before full moon, when, they say, the bees have a feast and drink their cellars dry'. He himself had had to flee from *bambaru* on perilous rock ledges at Sigiriya, and he relates an anecdote of a Royal Duchess on a visit there. She was compelled to escape into the jungle, while the Princess her daughter, and the Governor's daughter, were marooned on the top of the Rock. Looking down

Jungle dwellers

they saw the Governor 'the representative of the King, pursuing His Majesty's sister-in-law and beating her with her hat' - an obscure tactic, since the bees on her were invisible. [7]

Some dangerous wild life was larger, for example bears, though in photographs of slain ones they do not seem very big. They were readily encountered. Still wrote in *The Jungle Tide*:

> It interested me to find the requirements of monks and bears so nearly identical; and just as the earliest monks showed a preference for converting the dens of bears into hermits' cells, so do bears today prefer the sites of ruined monasteries, thus offering a very sincere tribute to men who had preferred to exchange the temptations of an over-luxurious world for a life of bodily simplicity and rigorous contemplation. [8]

The Veddas had a wholesome respect for bears. At the caves in the Egoda Pattuwa this appeared when they declared to Bell that some they had been sent to examine had no 'drip lines', the ledges carved by monks above cave entrances to channel off the rain. Bell thought that 'they probably did not care to "investigate" too carefully, for fear of bears who revel in these caves during rains'. Caves were a convenience in such weather, if they were empty. One such lodging Bell describes:

> Passed the night in the loftiest Cave (No. 1), making a jungle stick bed on which to spread my rug, etc. The coolies made shift in the adjoining Cave No. 2, keeping a fire alight to scare any bears who might seek to share our rock dormitory. Heavy rain from 5 p.m. till 9 (from which we were well sheltered by the overhang and drip ledge which kept the canvas as 'dry as a bone'); later the moon shone out brightly. [9]

Things were not always so comfortable, and Bell chronicles an adventure about the same time:

> Returning we had a surprise. We ran 'bang up against' a *tani aliya*, or 'rogue elephant', that *corruptio optimi pessima* known to the Veddas to be infesting the neighbourhood. He stood confronting us less than a dozen yards away in the only narrow path through the close-set jungle. Had nothing but my shot gun, and a couple of soft-lead ball cartridges (for bears) with me; but as the brute showed no inclination to move, risked a shot at his head. It did about as much damage as a pea from a pea-shooter striking the human face; but fortunately 'stung him up' enough to decide on retreating - let it be confessed frankly, to the general relief! - but sulkily, and without undignified hurry. Presumably our 'safety' must have lain 'in numbers'; for we were eight in all. On sight of the elephant the Tamil coolies stood not for a moment on the order of their going: each made, wisely, for the nearest tree! The plucky little *Patabenda* alone 'stuck to me'. The rogue, he said afterwards in his broken Sinhalese, had been awaiting us, and that we were well out of (*wantan beruna*) the encounter. [10]

The editor of the *Times of Ceylon* asked Bell for an article for his Christmas Number of 1917 on 'Bear shooting in Ceylon'. Bell, from his twenty years and upwards of intermittent experience over the wide area of his 'peregrinations', complied with accounts and criticisms of 'seven ways of circumventing Bruin'. Of two almost invariably followed by Europeans, the first was 'Water-hole shooting' from a *messa*, a jungle-stick platform in a tree overlooking the rock-hole or wooded pool in a river bed in the jungle. Bell disliked this, as it seemed to him 'virtually taking a mean advantage of the bear, with absolutely no risk to the man'. Many bears got away 'cruelly but not mortally wounded' because the light was too poor to hit a vital part, 'the head by choice', and with its wonderful stamina the bear could get miles away.

A second method involved shooting from a *sangar*, a low, slightly convex protection of stones, roughly put together near the *gal-wala* (rock hole) on a bare hill or rock. Europeans used this who got excitement from giving the bear a 'sporting chance', for he might rush the shelter. River-pool shooting was another, somewhat similar system, the stone *sangar* being replaced by a *korotuw*a, or low leaf-and-twig shelter; this also had its risks. In September 1896 Bell was sitting in one under dense shade and, firing, missed a leopard which sprang within a yard of him but being unwounded, dashed away - a lucky escape.

The fourth hunting method, tank-pit shooting, was a favourite of the natives, and involved digging a shallow pit in the dry bed of a tank at an approach track to the water. An hour's trial of this was enough for Bell, being 'eaten alive' by mosquitoes in a dirty, cramped and unsavoury pit. *Hadaram-messa* shooting was also on such a *handya* or beast-track, but from a stick-platform put up in some tree. Perhaps the platform or the human scent warns the thirsty prey, for Bell had never had a sight of predators by this method, though there was the 'indescribable charm of lying out under a tropical night of purest moonlight with the jungle "calling" all round one'. He did once shoot a wild buffalo this way, when his Moor baggage-coolies were in urgent need of food, but found more sport in stalking one in Tamankaduwa, when some villagers wanted it slain because it had attached itself to their tame herd.

'Rock-hunting' involved looking for bears in their caves in wet weather. Bell found this method sheer folly, for the bears 'quite probably will stalk the stalker'. Once when he wished to attempt it, the *Patabenda*, a 'brave enough little fellow', said that if the 'Suda Hura' (White Chief) ventured, he too would have to go *'to protect him'*; and tapped the tiny axe, his own sole protection.

The final method Bell considers, also mostly used when rain had ruined the chances of water-hole shooting, was 'Hunting-Buffalo Shooting'. The animal, the *dada-migona*, was employed as a decoy. The natives used the method for hunting deer, who were not disturbed by the buffalo so long as they did not get the human scent. This was Bell's favourite form of bear hunting, as the most 'sporting'. It takes place, he said, at night, and the buffalo, usually free from the 'nose-cord', moves on slowly, partially grazing, 'wandering aimlessly, as it were, and alone.... while the gun-armed hunter lurks behind it, half-hidden, urging the beast forward stealthily'.

Bell describes his own experience on September 11, 1897, on circuit in Tamankaduwa, while going to Veragoda rock, to examine ruins and inscriptions. Kawrala, a Sinhalese-Vedda hunter, led behind the decoy buffalo; then came Bell with a 'trusty double-barrel gun...besides a cheap Snyder carbine', and two Veddas following. They moved in full moonlight along the forest edge, then nervously through deepest shade - one bear appeared but fled - then in more open country:

Jungle dwellers

Just before we reached the rock, about midnight, whilst passing a copse, a she-bear came out to our right rear, and momentarily sat on her haunches. The Vedda behind me (I had not seen the bear) at once quietly touched my shoulder - the sign agreed on. Swinging round, I was just in time to 'get' my 'blow in first': as the bear charged, she 'got it in the neck' from the despised carbine, which I happened to be carrying. The shot stopped her, and, turning sharply, wounded unto death, she rushed back into the wood; whence, within a minute or two, the unmistakable strident 'death-wail' of a dying bear reached our expectant ears. *Habet*!

At Veragoda rock Bell slept on ancient altar slabs, and next day copied some unique inscriptions of kings: Buddhadasa (A.D. 341-370) and Mahanama (A.D. 412-434). The dead bear was retrieved, photographed with the buffalo and carried back to camp:

Thus ended an entirely novel, and most exhilarating episode outside the ordinary antiquarian official life of a Government Archaeologist. [11]

Now and again in his Reports Bell gives some impression of a jungle scene by day or night, but this was not their purpose, and we have to look elsewhere for pictures of the world of jungle folk. A description of the forest in Bell's area was given by A.Walters in *Palms and Peaks, or Scenes in Ceylon*, of the road from Dambulla to Mihintale:

For many miles we passed through dense *chenar* or thorny jungle, with tall *mana* grass growing amid almost impenetrable thickets, and a network of bush and brake and matted stems; thorny shrubs, spiny creepers, and innumerable prickly parasites caught our clothes and scratched our flesh at every step. Now and then the sultry silence was broken by the distant bark of a sambhur elk, the nearer tap of a woodpecker, the scream of a peacock or the grunting of a wanderoo ape; while now and then a flock of small chattering *rilawa* monkeys would dart along overhead and vanish with the speed of an express train. As we passed along our eyes were bewildered by a multitude of ferns, orchids, and climbing lilies with gaudy gold-red crowns, orange mosses and lichens, yellow purple-dashed hibiscus, whispering bamboos, brilliant convolvuli and huge trailing lianas as thick as a ship's best hawser. [12]

Constance Frederica Gordon Cumming, a much-travelled lady whose books contain her own delightful illustrations, published the account of her 'two happy years in Ceylon' in 1892. There was little which she did not notice, in many parts of the Island including Anuradhapura and Polonnaruwa when excavation there had hardly begun. We see in the following the artist's eye for colour in nature:

Glorious large butterflies skimmed lightly over the water, some with wings like black velvet, and others of the most lustrous metallic blue; and kingfishers, golden orioles, and other birds of radiant plumage, flitted over the waters....

Oh, the beauty of these water-lilies! - white, blue, yellow or pink - nestling among their glossy leaves on the still waters. The fragrant, large, pink *manel*... is certainly a beautiful object, as, with the first ray of the morning, it rises high above the surface of the water, and unfolds its rosy petals to drink in sunlight all the day, closing them again at sunset, when the blossoms hide beneath the great blue-grey leaves, and, I am told, sink beneath the surface of the water. [13]

The beautiful butterflies of Ceylon were described by many visitors, the incomparable riches of their colours and their mysterious migratory flights. Jules Leclercq, in his relation of the coach ride to Anuradhapura quoted in the previous chapter, speaks of soft clouds of their wings brushing the cheeks of travellers.

Open spaces in jungle country had to be man-made. Areas had been cleared for cultivation, and where ancient cities had been covered by the persistent tropical growth, vistas were being created between the ruins. In *The Lost Cities of Ceylon* G.E.Mitton writes:

> It is difficult to do justice to the beauty of Anuradhapura; it combines so much not usually found in an eastern town. The wide park-like spaces of short grass are shaded by the beautiful spreading 'rain-trees', so-called because their leaves fold together at night and, opening in the morning, drop dew on the heads of those who pass below. The grass is studded with ruins, showing many a specimen of exquisite carving in granite, fresh as the day it was done, possibly 2,000 years ago. [14]

The greatest open spaces are the 'tanks', which is too down-to-earth a name for the great artificial lakes. C.F.Gordon Cumming and John Still both delighted in Topavewa at Polonnaruwa, with the view across forest to the Matale range. Still says:

> The waters are very blue, and in the far distance, across a plain where men are rarer than bears, the peaks and ramparts of the mountain ranges tower into the sky to a height of six thousand feet or more. They too are vivid blue, but a different blue from the water. To walk round the tank may take two hours, or three if it be very full, and even now one is sure to see crocodiles there; but the most delightful part of it is in the forest of red lotuses, so full of birds that their voices mingle in a clatter like that of a children's playground. [15]

Bell, however, must have the last word. In 1896 he was at the practical task of measuring tanks in the Moragolla Wanni, and he had his reward:

> The calm beauty of these inland lakes is indescribable. The bright blue of the still water, the ring of white sand fringed with grass and forest, mingled greens and browns, the varied bird and animal life - and withal that wondrous hush which pervades and sanctifies nature uninvaded by man's encroachment -
>
>   'Oh! if there be an Elysium on earth,
>   It is this, it is this.' [16]

11

Sigirya : The Ascents

Sigiriya is an extraordinary place; it captures the imagination of all who see it; those who recorded its glory as the fortress of the parricide king Kasyapa I; those who left their poetic musings on the Gallery Wall when drawn to visit the incomparable 'ladies' painted on the rock high above; those who see it now as the water gardens at its feet are being gradually restored.

The exploration of Sigiriya was the most dramatic of the episodes in Bell's career, both in the actual danger and difficulty of the undertaking and in the peculiar interest of some of the discoveries made in the course of the excavations. There is an excitement and immediacy in his accounts of the first three years of the work as recorded in the Interim Reports read to the RASCB which is scarcely to be equalled in the rest of his writings.

It is noteworthy that he continually illustrates his remarks by quotation, always a sign that he is moved by his discoveries. Whether he is telling of his adventurous climbs, the harsh physical conditions under which the work was conducted, and the bravery and skill of his assistants, or wondering at the achievements of the ancient architects or the beauty of the frescoes, Bell conveys a feeling of enormous enjoyment. Here he does not complain of difficulties, he revels in overcoming them, and allows full scope to his imagination, whether in describing what the palace would have looked like, or in guessing at the characters and feelings of the 'ladies'.

Thus in the third Interim Report he writes of the palace on the summit:

Little wonder that the glory of a structure, towering to heaven on the dizzy heights of *Sigiri-gala*, 'white as snow' within and without, should call forth irresistibly the unalloyed admiration of the old chronicler, not given to spare its master-hand, King Kasyapa, 'that wicked ruler of men'. 'He built there,' so it is written, 'a lovely palace splendid to behold, like unto a second Alakamanda, and lived there like (its lord) Kuvera.' (*Mahawansa* xxxix, p.5.)

How little comparatively now remains to attest the ancient beauty and grandeur of *Sigiri-nuwara*, the parricide's stronghold:-

'Those golden pallaces, those gorgeous halles,
With fourniture superfluouslie faire;
Those statelie courts, those sky-encountring walls,
Evanish all like vapours in the aire'. [1]

When summing up the work that had been achieved by 1905 Bell gave the following general description of the rock, and particularly of the gallery which had originally provided access to the summit:

The huge isolated mass of gneiss rock oval in contour nowadays known locally as *Sigiri-gala* is situated in the Matale district of the Central Province, some 10 miles north-east of Dambulla, and nearly 20 almost due west of Polonnaruwa. It was at this 'rocky fortress in mid-air' that in the 5th century Kasyapa I , the parricide king, took refuge, making it his capital yet ever 'living in fear of the world to come and of Moggallana' (his brother and successor), at whose hands he ultimately met the just retribution of his crime...

Sigiri-gala rises to about 600 feet above the fields and tank lying beneath it to south-west and south. For about half its height the Rock towers sheerly, but the lower spurs and reaches are masked by a series of bare boulders, and of stone-banked terraces, much dilapidated. Immediately at the foot of the cliff masses of *debris*, washed down from the ruined outskirts of the Citadel which formerly crowned the summit of the Rock, still further conceal the base of the main Rock.

Forest trees, undergrowth, and patches of *mana* grass (*Andropogon zealanders*) extending up to the very face of the Rock, hid this talus and the terraces completely when the Archaeological Survey commenced operations at Sigiriya in 1895. This pall, so to speak, has since been pushed back steadily, season by season, with the object of leaving all open and visible in a wide belt several hundred yards in width...

The summit of *Sigiri-gala* is quite inaccessible without adventitious aid; and this necessary help the Gallery easily afforded in former days. Artificially built of brick, high walled, and paved with stone, the Gallery was made to run along the western and northern faces of the Rock. In its serpentine course up to the Rock's summit it clung to the cliff at the level where the Rock face has the greatest concavity; so that while resting upon the highest part of the downward slope, it was also, for much of its length, well overhung and protected by the beetling crag towering above.

In 1895 a hundred yards of the Gallery - wall, floor, and four staircases - still stretched almost perfect (with the ruins of two more landings and stairs, from which the flanking wall had fallen away bodily) along the western face of the Rock nearly as far north as the point where it formerly swerved eastward. Beyond the north-west corner of the Rock was a wide stretching breach. For a distance of many yards no remains of the Gallery had survived and further progress was impossible. At the far end of this gap the half buried ruins of a long, steeply rising, stairway, also wanting its outer wall, could be traced along the north face of the Rock. These stairs formed part of the original continuation of the Gallery where it formerly mounted east to the broad *maluwa*, or highest terrace, projecting from the Rock to the north.

Further on where the Gallery manifestly once zig-zagged up the sloping face of the Rock above the 'Lion Staircase-House' (which showed merely as a jungle-covered mound of brick *debris* until opened up in 1897) it has been completely washed away. Only ledges, grooves, and oblong 'keys', cut in the Rock, are left to suggest how its brick foundations were sustained; but these, with higher channelettes intended to pass off water, clearly mark its steeply inclined course onwards, in a north-easterly direction, from the head of the present iron ladders. [2]

Bell did not discover Sigiriya. It was not an unknown site, and although access to it was difficult it had been visited and described by Forbes in 1831 and 1833. Rhys Davids had contributed an article in the JRAS in 1875, commenting on the paintings, and in 1876 T.H.Blakesley of the

Sigirya : The ascents

Public Works Department conducted a survey of the rock and its environs.[3]

In 1893, although work at Anuradhapura had only begun, the Government ordered Bell to extend his operations, either to Sigiriya or to the ruins at Yapahuwa, and he decided to concentrate on Sigiriya. A swift reconnaissance in 1893 made it clear that operations could not be started until some kind of permanent ladders could be erected and fixed to the rock, but Bell made an ascent of the north face in April 1894, before he was taken away temporarily to act as District Judge at Kalutara from May to December. An improvised bamboo ladder was placed from the mound at the foot of the rock, but the final ascent was achieved by clinging to the grooves in the rock face. At the end of 1894 the P.W.D. erected a permanent ladder to replace the makeshift bamboo affair and a single handrail to cling to while climbing along the grooves.

Bell wrote in his Annual Report for 1894 that his was 'the last ascent by a European of Sigirigala prior to the erection of the iron ladders and railing'. The rock had previously been climbed by some half dozen Europeans in all. Messrs Adams and Bayley of the Ceylon Civil Service made the earliest known ascent.[4]

In the *Monthly Literary Register and Notes and Queries for Ceylon* of June 1894 we read:

> We learn that Mr. H.C.P.Bell has lately been climbing to the top of Sigiriya. He went there in connection with arrangements for starting work at the Rock early next year. He climbed the Rock as a matter of course (and we believe Mr. Bell can't understand where the real difficulty 'comes in' to anyone with a head for heights and ordinary pluck) and thoroughly explored the summit. Mr. Bell's Tamil coolies went up like cats, carrying his camera, tied to their backs, and he took photographs of the two pokunas at the top and a view of the Matale hills from the highest point. With the iron ladders and chain (or bar) that the Government are about to put up, the ascent of Sigiriya will become exceedingly prosaic.[5]

In September 1895 in the same journal there was considerable correspondence on the claims of various persons to have made the climb in early days. A brief account of the first recorded ascent, and description of the ruins on the top, was given by G. Wijeyekoon as follows:

> It was on the 23rd of September in the year 1853, that the late Mr. John Bailey, the Assistant Government Agent of Matale, Mr. A.Y.Adams, and myself with some natives of Sigiriya village, succeeded in ascending the Sigiri rock. Mr. J.Northmore, the then Assistant Government Agent of Anuradhapura, was also with us but he did not attempt to ascend. It was a very perilous undertaking; for we had to scramble on the surface of the steep rock, which was destitute of any plant or shrub that might have assisted us in the ascent. Near the top of the rock where it was less steep, we came across some remains of brick foundations. The surface of the rock was about two acres in extent and was covered with jungle, in the centre of which was a tank about 45 feet square. This tank, the sides of which were paved with stone, dried up subsequently during a severe and long-continued drought that prevailed in the district. At the southern end, there was a tank cut in the rock which measured about 18 feet by 15 feet, and which supplied good drinking water. To the west of it were to be found the remains of a dagobah. What struck us rather forcibly was, that on the top of the rock there were pieces of stones and bricks strewn almost everywhere. On enquiry from the oldest residents of the place we

learnt that excepting some natives we were the first outsiders who succeeded in ascending the top of the famous rock. [6]

The only other account of the climb to the summit is by A.V.Renton and appeared in the *Ceylon Literary Register* for 1889-90. He climbed by ladders as far as the frescoes on the west wall and then zig-zagged up the overhanging face and slantingly up, holding on by notches and finger-tension. He found his boots a great inconvenience and the strong wind made his position very dangerous, so he came down to wait for a calmer day. When he tried again, barefoot this time, a Sinhalese climber preceded him to the top and fixed a rope to a tree to hang down and act as a hand-hold. In the event, as the wind had died down, Renton managed to achieve the summit without the aid of the rope. He walked about on the summit and cut his initials on a banyan tree and descended safely once more to slake his thirst 'with I don't know how many cups of tea and jaggery'. He summed up his views on the unaided ascent as follows:

> Is the climb dangerous? Yes. Difficult? No, not to a climber, only one must go barefoot as I did. Is it worth it? Yes, a hundred times yes. [7]

When, in 1896, Bell wished to explore a possible cave in the east wall of the rock he also made use of a rope hanging from the top. In the Interim Report for that year he wrote:

> The Rock scarp below the caves, being nowhere less than 30 degrees in slope, and in places sheer, ascent without the aid of a rope is impossible. A 4-in. hawser was, therefore, let down to the ground over the brow of the caves. Up this stout rope 'swarmed' half a dozen of the strongest and most 'sure-headed' coolies - *it is 294 ft. measured distance, hand over hand pull up the whole way* - to the apparent mouth of the caves: *apparent* only, for the men found themselves still 50 ft. out from, and below, the actual floor, with no means of getting nearer owing to the projecting crag above, and the rope's own weight keeping it taut. Ultimately a brave Sinhalese lad with a light rope round his waist (the other end being held by men) crawled, crocodile-fashion, up the remaining steep smooth slope. Once in the caves he noosed the rope to a piece of fallen rock. Next day a strong iron ring was driven into the floor for greater security, and the hawser passed through it.

However, when Bell and Perera, 1st Draughtsman of the Archaeological Survey, climbed the rope up to the cave, they were disappointed to find no trace of previous human habitation, and Bell wrote that being virtually inaccessible it had 'to all appearance been left "from the dark backward and abysm of time" to bird and bat and mountain bee'. Bell found three eggs of the Peregrine Falcon which had never before been taken in Ceylon. He measured the cavern, photographed it and left a 'sealed record of its exploration by the Archaeological Survey in the year of grace 1896'. [8]

In the MLRC for September 1895 several men were reported to have climbed up to the frescoes, but the only detailed account is that given by A.Murray in *Black and White* No. 189, 1891 and in the *Ceylon Literary Register* of the same year. There he states that he made the attempt to reach and copy the frescoes 'at the request of Sir William Gregory and with the

Sigirya : The ascents

sanction of Sir Arthur Gordon'. He had holes bored in the rock and a rope ladder attached. It was very difficult to get the local inhabitants to help, as they feared the fortress as an abode of yakku, but he obtained the services of six Tamil stone cutters. The last part of the ascent was the most dangerous, as the rock face jutted out below the pockets in which the frescoes were located - but after a three-day fast the workers dared the final stage. [9]

In order to make copies of the frescoes Murray drove iron stanchions into the sloping floor and fixed timber staging. Even so he had to lie on his back while making the chalk copies. He only made copies of those in pocket 'B', and though Bell frequently praised his 'pioneer work' he felt that the copies failed to give anything like a true representation of the vividness and coarseness of the original colouring. [10]

In 1895 Bell climbed up to the frescoes on a makeshift ladder of jungle sticks, but had this removed before he left the site, to prevent unnecessary risk to life and chance of vandalism. It was not until 1896 that more permanent access to the frescoes was secured by fixing a vertical wire ladder, cane hooped. By this Bell mounted, with his youngest son on his back, and one of his daughters following calmly behind. Another photograph shows the children sitting contentedly on the bamboo raft slung out from pocket 'A', with Bell standing on its edge pointing dramatically to the frescoes in pocket 'B'. In another photograph the children rest on the slope of pocket 'B', and it is annotated on the back by Bell as follows:

> The 'troupe' resting in pocket 'B' after their 'turn'. *N.B.* Malcolm has not fainted: he is 'full up' with coconut water and fruit!!

The children also accompanied Bell to the top of the Rock and the family posed on the great *asanaya* (throne), hewn out of the gneiss rock core. Previously, in 1895, Bell's sister-in-law, Miss Fyers, had reached the top, the first woman known to have done so. It is not recorded which Miss Fyers did this, but it was probably the youngest child by Fyers' first wife - Kate Minnie Fyers, known to the family as 'Aunt Cuckoo'! [11]

For the excavation of Sigiriya Bell was eventually fortunate enough to secure a plentiful supply of labour, and to infuse into his workers something of his own enthusiasm. This was despite the fact that, as he wrote in his first Interim Report, the place had a bad name 'from its forest seclusion, the dread presence of countless *yakku* or *pisachikal* (demons), the unwholesome tank water, and the scarcity of food. The latter objection I partially overcame by arranging for advances of rice and cocoanut, in addition to a slightly enhanced rate of wages'. [12]

Moreover, the work itself was difficult, and not without considerable danger. As Bell wrote in his second Interim Report:

> Those only who know *Sigiri-gala*, have climbed (not without some misgiving) to the summit, and uttered involuntarily a sigh of relief on reaching the ground again safely, can fully realise the mental 'tenter-hooks' on which the officer is stretched, who for nearly four months has to be responsible for the safety of a hundred lives, daily risked - not in the ascent and descent of the Rock merely, but upon the summit itself. For despite every precaution to insure against ordinary accident, as well as foolhardy rashness, hair-breadth escapes must inevitably occur. [13]

Familiarity bred contempt, and Bell wrote in 1897 of the mad recklessness of the Tamil cooly disporting himself on Sigiri-gala, quoting Kipling to describe him as 'a veritable "indiarubber idiot on the spree" risking life airily a dozen times a day'. [14]

It must be said that Bell himself did not give a good example of caution; witness the picture of his posturing on the outer corner of the hanging 'raft' slung out from the frescoes, and another in which he lolls at ease at the very edge of the summit with the rock sloping away beneath him to a sheer drop. The latter is annotated:

> The 'A.C.' resting on the brink of the precipice.

The ascent to the top was arduous. Even the ladder, erected by the P.W.D. in 1894, at first lacked a handrail, and the climb above it along the grooves was protected only by a single bar, easy to slip under. There were frequent thunderstorms and in May of every year the high wind of the south-west monsoon swept around the fortress, creating a ceaseless cloud of blinding brick dust.

In 1895 the workers faced the additional hazard of attacks from the rock bees, the *bambaru*, which nested in the crevices and came forth to repel invaders. Bell says:

> The whole force - a strange and remarkably unpleasant experience - was for quite a fortnight harassed by the *bambaru*, or rock-bees, whose hives line the cliff. These aggressive little pests (with a sting considered almost as severe as that of the *debora*, or hornet) lay in wait for the approach of the coolies, and more than once, *suo more*, literally chased them down to their lines, inflicting stings that half blinded some of the men and laid them up for days together. Hardly one escaped, and work on the summit had to be temporarily suspended. After several ineffectual attempts to destroy the hives by riddling them with shot and ball, we at last succeeded by slow-burning fire balls (Sinhalese, *vedi dodan*) in burning them out from their main hive a hundred feet or more up the west cliff. The rest of the bees then gave comparatively little annoyance. [15]

The work on the top was every bit as tough as in the jungle round Anuradhapura, for there were tall trees and a dense undergrowth, neck high, growing on the mounds of debris, and all had to be cleared and thrown over the edge before excavation could begin. Bell wrote in his second Interim Report:

> The one great trial - how great nobody who has not experienced it can *grasp* - was, and will always be the terrible exposure to the tropical sun on the summit of *Sigiri-gala*. Save for three or four trees still standing, there is no 'shadow' from the heat on that 'great rock in a weary land'. To allow the coolies to descend the Rock for a mid-day meal was out of the question: it would have entailed undue waste of time and energy. The working hours were therefore fixed from 6.30 a.m. to 3 p.m. at a stretch - as honest and hard a 'eight-and-a-half-hours day' as could justly be demanded by any taskmaster. [16]

The first year there was little or no water to drink, and the supply was impure, but by 1896 the cistern on the south-west edge had been cleared of some 7 feet of brick and mud and provided a sufficiency for the whole four months of work. In that year a second cistern was found in the

Sigirya : The ascents

south-east corner and cleared for future use, and finally the great central pokuna was excavated.

The health of the coolies was a matter of continual concern to Bell. For the first three years he reported with great satisfaction that there had been no accidents nor any deaths from disease, although there were cases of dysentery and fever and ulcerated sores caused by bad water. In 1897 he wrote:

> The climate of Sigiriya has usually proved bracing to the coolies, the majority of whom live for two-thirds of the year in the jungle-bound chenas and low-lying lands about Anuradhapura. Month by month they 'put on flesh' despite the unspeakable heat which an eight-hours' spell of work upon the bare Rock involves; and return after the four months' absence, robust and sleek, with a stock of health that enables them to battle the better against the insidious malaria of the North-Central Province. [17]

That year saw two mild cases of measles, but the patients were isolated and no further infection followed. Sadly, there were deaths in 1898 and 1899 caused by fever and pneumonia, resulting from exposure on the wind-blown slopes and from damp quarters. In 1897 there was a mild case of incipient small-pox, but the sufferer was sent to the Dambulla hospital and his hut and adjoining 'lines' were burnt, so that no further cases ensued.

The chief sufferer from the harsh conditions was certainly Perera, whose eyesight was severely affected by the long hours he spent in the intense glare beating upon the rock-face, while he carried out his meticulous copying of the frescoes. In 1896, when he started the work, his sight was so affected that he was ordered complete rest for six weeks, and Bell notes in the third Interim Report for 1897:

> Altogether, from first to last, in 1896 and this year, Mr. Perera spent nineteen weary weeks - practically five months - in the cheerless 'pocket' caves of *Sigiri-gala* working on day after day from morning to evening - exposed latterly to the driving force of the south-west wind, and sorely tried at times by inflammation of the eyes and attacks of fever - before the final touch could be put to the last of the twenty-two paintings. [18]

It is true that extra pay was given to those working at Sigiriya, but this cannot have been the sole reason that in 1896 Bell was able to write with satisfaction that those who had come from Anuradhapura the previous year brought back with them their family and friends to swell the force the next year. It was necessary to bring Tamil workers from Anuradhapura for the actual excavation work, although local Sinhalese labour was employed in the extensive clearing of the whole area of the ancient city, *Sigiri-nuwara*, and in 1896 it proved possible to induce 'a sprinkling of Sinhalese to work as earth-carriers upon the top of the rock, in consideration of a higher rate of wage than that paid for jungle-clearing below. For the timid and superstitious Sinhalese villager to scale the dread Rock daily was an entirely "new departure" due to final conviction that the Archaeological Survey had effectively routed for ever the *yakku*, or demons, of *Sigiri-gala*'. [19]

Bell was very proud of his team of workers and of their loyalty to him. He used to tell his children that they reverenced him as the re-incarnation of King Parakrama Bahu the Great. There is a photograph of 'Labour Force, Sigiriya, 1896', a group seated below the Rock, men, women and boys, with Bell and Perera at the back. Bell stands with arms akimbo, at the peak of the pyramid. The photo is annotated in his handwriting with yet another of his quotations, this time from Scott's *Lady of the Lake*:

Note the graceful pose of the 'Chief' at the back.

> 'These be Clan Alpine's warriors true,
> And, Saxon, I am Roderick Dhu!'

It is perhaps his happiest memorial that 'diggers' in Sri Lanka are still known as a 'Bell party'.

Sigiri-gala, view from the North

Perera photographing
the frescoes

'Viewing the frescoes'

Bell and his children in
Pocket 'B', Perera copying
the frescoes

Sigiri Lady

Bell climbing Sigiri-gala with his children

'The A.C. resting on the brink of the precipice'

Labour force, Sigirya, 1896

Bells on Kasyapa's Throne

Lion's right claws

12

Sigirya : Glories Revealed

In 1898 Bell summarised the work carried out at Sigiriya as follows:

> In brief, the three previous seasons had witnessed the first clearing of most of the forest undergrowth overlaying the site of the extensive ancient city, the completion of a topographical survey of the whole area with the *vil-bemma*; the thorough excavation from end to end of the citadel which stood on the summit of Sigiri-gala and of the two staircase approaches to the gallery along its western face; the securing facsimile copies in oils of virtually all of the paintings which have survived to this day in the Rock 'pockets', and the carrying out of other minor but essential work with a view to the conservation of the ruins of Sigiriya. [1]

Some excavations took place around the base of the rock and among the great boulders which had supported further buildings, but excavations on the summit took precedence. In the first season of 1895 about an acre was cleared in the north-east corner; ruins of two periods were found, 'spacious rooms separated by passages paved with quartz flags and joined by quartz stairs - quartz everywhere - a striking feature of the Sigiriya ruins'. [2]

In the second season the eastern section was dug, exposing a series of terraces north and south of the great pokuna, with small rooms and staircases all taking advantage of the limited space available and the varied levels of the summit. The whole area dug was completely cleared of earth, all debris being thrown over the side. Bell writes:

> The ultimate benefit of this wholesale 'sweep' of the *debris*, laborious and slow though it be, cannot be exaggerated. Nothing is missed; walls and foundations can be perfectly differentiated; forms of moulding examined properly; above all, thus only can there be got a comprehensive and intelligible view of the trend of walls and cross-walls, and the intercommunication of a perfect labyrinth of stairs and passages. [3]

The pokuna itself was cleared out at the end of the season, a most laborious business, which Bell describes as follows:

> Undug, the pond had the appearance of a shapeless pool, with ragged sloping sides, due to the collapse of the surrounding brick walls. It contained some 5 ft. of half-stagnant water, so sour from rotting vegetation that even the hardened Tamil cooly shrank from drinking it. As clearing proceeded it became evident that the *pokuna*, like the smaller cisterns, was rectangular, and of dimensions considerably in excess of anticipation...
>
> An effort to pump the water out of the pond over the high bund, and to pass it down the east cliff, proved a Sisyphean task - utterly futile. The black, viscous mud of ages choked the draw-pipe, and the

borrowed hose split everywhere. With infinite labour of days we reduced the water by a foot and a half: in two nights the rain put as much back! Then, as a last resource, the brick wall was cut through on the south-east down to the rock, and wooden *yoto* (Sinhalese hand-worked scoops) tried - with complete success. These simple and effective implements emptied the pond in a few days. The subsequent removal of mud and *debris*, with which the *pokuna* had silted up, occupied some time, owing to the numerous steps and pavement slabs that the washaway of centuries had deposited at the bottom. In the silt nothing of interest was found embedded.

The *pokuna*, now scoured and clean, should furnish abundance of pure drinking water for our next season. [4]

Filled yearly by the rains of the north-east monsoon, the pokuna must have supplied the needs of the great palace, with supplementary drinking water from the smaller cisterns located near the edge of the rock.

The third season saw the clearing of the higher ground to the west, which contained the larger rooms. It was also revealed that rooms had been built even below the actual edge of the rock summit:

On clearing the tangled *mana* grass and low jungle off the west edge of the Rock a surprise awaited us. It became for the first time evident that the whole side of the slope - here more prolonged than on the other faces - had been grooved deeply to hold the foundations of a lower reach of rooms and passages, and drain the summit speedily of the heaviest rainfall.

The boldness of conception and pre-eminent skill which enabled these old architects to make even the steepest slopes of *Sigiri-gala* subservient to their will, led them to annexe profitably every inch of possible foothold. The exterior wall of the citadel, which wholly engirdled the Rock (except on the south-west), was built everywhere several feet - indeed for a great part of the circuit some yards - below the flat summit, and must have risen majestically all round from the very brink of the precipice. [5]

The whole plan of the citadel had now been laid bare, with its paved way, leading from one flight of steps to another down the centre, and smaller passages leading through the maze of rooms. All were paved with quartzose, but above floor level the builders used brick or wood, with no pillars nor stone-carved doorways. Bell assumed that the buildings were roofed with wood and flat-tiles, as at Anuradhapura.

The great work of 1898 was the clearing of the oblong *maluwa*, a tableland terrace which stretched out on the north at the point where the gallery once swerved up, and from which access was gained to the summit. It was the excavation of the mound on the terrace from which the ladders led upwards which produced the greatest surprise. It turned out to be the ruins of a huge brick building, itself containing a staircase which led towards the summit, and the building had been shaped in the form of the head and shoulders of a great lion. Of this enormous animal only the claws remain and Bell thus describes the discovery and the conclusions drawn from it:

Sigirya : Glories revealed

When following the curved ground line of the north façade to the massive brick structure some stucco-covered work was uncovered. This at first seemed to represent very roughly moulded elephants' heads - three on either side of the central staircase - projecting from the brickwork in high relief, life size. Closer examination and the presence of a small boss further back than the 'heads' gave the clue to a startling discovery - the most interesting of many surprises furnished during the four seasons' work at Sigiriya.

These *alto relievos* were not a variant form of the 'elephant-head dado' of the chapel 'screens' at the large dagabas of Anuradhapura. They were none other than the huge claws - even to the dew claw - of a once gigantic lion, conventionalized in brick and plaster, through whose body passed the winding stairway, connecting upper and lower galleries. The monstrous *Sinha* - suggestive of the legendary founder of the Sinhalese race - towering majestically against the dark granite cliff, bright coloured, and gazing northwards over a vista that stretches almost hilless to the horizon, must have presented an awe-inspiring sight for miles around. Thus was clinched for ever to the hill the appellation *Sihigiri*, 'Lion Rock'.

Here then is the simple solution of a crux which has exercised the surmises of writers - the difficulty of reconciling the categorical statement of the *Mahawansa*, and the perpetuation to the present day of the name 'Sinha-giri' (Sigiri) with the undeniable fact that no sculpture or paintings of lions exist on Sigiri-gala. That strange conceit the 'lion-staircase-house' - the quaint, grandly conceived break in the weary continuity of the tortuous gallery ever ascending - backed by the frowning rock, and crowning the highest terrace above the tallest forest trees, worthily emanated from the master mind that designed the marvellous gallery and the complex citadel on Sigiri-gala. [6]

In the years that followed there were further explorations and excavations in the area surrounding the rock, up to and beyond the enclosing fortification wall, or *bemma*, but the main thrust of the work was concerned with keeping the excavations clean, repairing the staircases and gallery and protecting the frescoes. It was found best to leave the renewed growth of *mana* grass undisturbed. In the Annual Report of 1905 we read that:

> On the Rock's summit and its steep slopes the carpet of strong grass, which has gradually sprouted since excavations were completed in 1897, helps to hold together the banks of crumbling brickwork, and check further washaway. This grass is, therefore, every year merely freed of plant growth and burnt. A wholesale sweep of all vegetation would but result in a continuance of the heavy scour which occurred each monsoon until this grass grew and began to protect the ruined walls fringing the summit from rapid denudation. [7]

Bell did nothing to preserve or restore the buildings excavated on the top of the Rock, except by allowing the grass to grow to hold the brickwork together. When conservation proper commenced in 1948, Paranavitana, then Archaeological Commissioner, commented in his Annual Report for that year:

> Bell did not make any attempt to conserve for posterity the interesting structural remains that he, with such heroic an effort, had brought to light after they had lain hidden from human sight for a thousand

years. The conceptions of archaeology then prevailing did not take this to be an imperative need. Bell's successors, too, did not make a concentrated effort to preserve these remains. It was not that they did not realize the importance of the work. The meagre resources that they had at their disposal and the pressing demands of other monuments made the claims of Sigiri to go unheeded. The most that they could do was to prop up a wall threatening to collapse, to re-build a flight of steps that had fallen down and such other works of a limited scope. For fifty years, these remains thus lay exposed to the destructive forces of the annual monsoon rains and some damage was sustained by them every year. [8]

Even in 1948, however, expense precluded the use of machinery to transport materials to the top, and human labour had to be employed as in the old days. Paranavitana describes the methods employed as follows:

> The conservation work was started with the remains in the southern sector. It is here that the walls are preserved to a greater height than elsewhere and, consequently, stand in greater danger of collapsing during an abnormally heavy downpour of rain. It is also the structural remains in this area that contain interesting architectural details. The conservation methods adopted are: to grout the joints of brick masonry with lime mortar, so as not to show from outside, to replace the decayed bricks and to rebuild such portions of the walls which are out of plumb or of which the masonry cannot be strengthened otherwise. The tops of the walls are to be made waterproof. By the close of the year, the conservation was completed of a large hall. It is hoped that the department would continue in its present affluent position so as to complete this work, which it is estimated will take about five years with the number of masons and labourers now employed in it. To employ more men would be to exhaust the water supply on the rock within a few months and to limit the work to a fraction of the year. [9]

One cannot but feel that had Bell been able to command sufficient resources he would have been overjoyed to have undertaken such a work himself. What he did undertake was the restoration of staircases and gallery on the east of the rock. He said:

> Until the present iron bridge was thrown across the gap in the Gallery round the north-west corner of the Rock between the 5th and 6th stairs, and the broken Gallery connected with it on both sides, the ladders at the foot of the final ascent to the Rock's summit could only be reached by a long and devious ascent winding up a series of terraces on the lower reaches of the hill side to west and north-west of the Rock. This rough narrow path, lined by sharp *mana* grass and strewn with loose stones and broken brick, proved ever 'bitterness to the flesh' for those essaying the climb. [10]

The work necessitated the clearing away of the foot-thick layers of granite chips and fine dust from the floor of the remaining portions of the gallery, the re-pointing of the irregular limestone flooring revealed, the filling in of gaps with concrete, and the rebuilding of sections which had broken away. As this was along stretches of bare rock face many feet above the ground it involved 'great labour and no small risk to life'. Where necessary iron railings were fixed and the wider gaps were joined by iron bridges. Of one of these, joining the western portion of the gallery with that hugging the northern scarp, Bell says in a note:

Sigirya : Glories revealed

The construction of this bridge in such a situation reflects very great credit on its builder, the 'village blacksmith', Gamagedara Salmanhami of Lenadora (Matale District). Strong, neat, ornamental, it is justly commended by all visitors to Sigiriya. Given the design by the Archaeological Survey Department, this humble, self-taught, villager has worked out, under supervision, all details excellently. The bridge is affixed to the Rock in cantilever fashion. Five lengths of iron planks rest upon cross horizontals - round iron rods (bent half way to form the uprights for the railing) jumped into the Rock strongly, and doubly secured by raking struts. [11]

By 1904 the work was so far completed that Bell could say:

In the ascent to the summit of *Sigiri-gala* progress has thus been rendered once more possible and easy along the whole length of the existing Gallery as far as the northern terrace, the half-way point of its original stretch whence, in zig-zag course, it of old struck upwards through the lion-shaped *Mura-ge*, or Guard-house. [12]

Thus the summit was made reasonably accessible not only for the workers but also for the ever-increasing number of visitors to the site. The greatest attraction was naturally the series of paintings of the 'ladies'. Bell was much concerned to ensure that they could be viewed without difficulty and that they should be secured against further damage. But first of all he arranged that they should be copied.

The beautiful facsimiles in oils were completed by D.A.L.Perera in 1896 and 1897. The wire ladder and the handrail in front of the frescoes was not fixed until the end of March 1896, so that in the first year only six of the ladies were copied. An attempt was made to obtain a photograph of the whole series from a chair suspended in mid-air in front of them. Bell writes:

The height of the 'pockets' from the ground and the 'gallery' prevents a complete view of all the frescoes together being got from any one point, except at such a distance that even a tele-photographic lens failed to bring them reasonably close. It was therefore decided to photograph and paint the two fresco caves from mid-air.

The 4 in. hawser was transferred from the east to the west edge of the summit, the rope lowered to the ground over the cliff (which on this face projects considerably), and a strong iron block bound to the end. Through the block a new 2 in. rope was then passed, and an improvised chair firmly tied on to it: the hawser was then pulled half way up the west scarp; and all was ready.

Hauled up, one swung in the air 150 ft. and upwards above the ground, and 50 ft. clear of the cliff. Swaying in mid-air from the force of the wind, the instantaneous shutter used for photography worked too slowly, and the pictures were more or less blurred.

On the other hand, after a week's 'rocking' in space, Mr. Perera completed an excellent little oil painting, to scale, of the two fresco 'pockets'. This shows at a glance the relative position of the several figures. [13]

A composite photograph exists showing Perera suspended in this perilous position. To the 'singular talent, unflagging patience and real courage' exhibited by Perera, not only in obtaining the photographs but in completing the full set of oil paintings, Bell continually recurs. When the paintings were first displayed at a meeting of the RASCB, Bell commented:

> Mr. Perera's copy in oils of the double-figure frescoes, Nos. 3 and 4 in 'pocket' 'B', is forwarded as a sample of his work. *Ex uno disce omnes.* It is hardly going too far to assert that this specimen, as well as the other four copies already made, represent the original frescoes, as they may still be seen at Sigiriya, with a faithfulness almost perfect. Not a line, not a flaw or abrasion, not a shade of colour, but has been patiently reproduced with the minutest accuracy. [14]

From 1899 to 1904 minor restoration work was undertaken and the whole area was screened off, to exclude birds, bats and bees, while not hiding the paintings from view. Holes made in the clay ground by mason bees, seeking material for their nests, were filled in and retouched, and the white marks left by the tracing paper attached by Murray, when making his copies in 1891, were blocked out. The floor in front of the paintings was levelled out with concrete and iron standards bedded in to hold the wire cage. A gangway was made between the two caves and a handrail fixed. The only entry to the caves remained a wire rope ladder. Bell added a note to this effect:

> This wire rope ladder is slung only for two or three months during the short season early in the year when the Archaeological Survey is at work at Sigiriya, to enable the pockets and netting to be annually cleaned, and to permit of any visitors desirous of inspecting the paintings closely climbing into the pockets.
>
> To leave the ladder permanently in position, and the door unlocked, would be to court certain mutilation of the paintings by 'furtive scribblers', such as the hundreds whose names crowd the plastered wall of the Gallery to its lasting disfigurement. [15]

It is sad to have to record that in 1967, when a permanent spiral staircase led to the pockets, one of the paintings was damaged by vandals. [16]

The 'ladies' of Sigiriya are one of the glories of the art of Sri Lanka, and much has been written about them since Bell's time. The technique of the paintings has been studied and different theories have been put forward as to what the ladies represent. The Sigiriya paintings have been set in the framework of the development of wall-painting in mediaeval Ceylon. Some of Bell's conclusions have been confirmed and others questioned. [17]

In the third Interim Report Bell writes:

> Like the so-called 'frescoes' at Ajanta, those of Sigiriya are strictly *paintings in tempera*, that is, the pigments used were mixed with some liquid vehicle and laid on a dry surface. The groundwork at Ajanta 'appears to be composed of cow dung, with an immixture of pulverized trap, laid on the roughish surface of the rock to a thickness varying from quarter to half inch. Over this ground was laid (the *intonaco* of) thin, smooth plaster, about the thickness of an egg-shell, upon which the painting was done.' [18]

Sigirya : Glories revealed

At Sigiriya - and to support my examination I called in the aid of the most skilled Sinhalese *'sitiyaru'* (painters) from Nilagama, in the Matale District, the village upon which has devolved for centuries the hereditary 'service' of renewing the paintings of the ancient cave vihares of Dambulla - an analysis of the plaster showed a groundwork of tempered earth and kaolin of a reddish brown hue and 1/2 inch in thickness, coated with at least two layers of white chunam, 1/4 to 1/2 in. thick. The clay base, strengthened by the admixture of *'dahiyava'*, or paddy husk, and perhaps shreds of cocoanut fibre, was first put on by hand, the chunam coating being (as at the present day) smoothed over it with a trowel.

Only three pigments were used, *yellow*, *red*, and *green*, though *black* seems to have been given a trial as background to one figure, No. 14 'B'. The particular shades of these colours predominating in the paintings may best be realized from the modern corresponding media employed by Mr. Perera in copying them, viz., chrome yellow, yellow ochre, raw sienna, burnt sienna, raw umber, light red, Indian red, sap green, terra vert, lamp black, and flake white. The entire omission of *blue* is very remarkable, and difficult to account for, as this colour enters freely into the sister paintings at Ajanta.

No one who chooses to carefully compare the Sigiriya paintings with those found in the Ajanta caves will fail to be convinced that *artists trained in the same school, if not the very same hands, must have executed both Indian and Ceylon frescoes*. The evidence to be drawn from dress and ornament, no less than from the quaint 'tricks' of pose and colouring common to both alike, for differentiating race and complexion and representing expression, is irresistible. [19]

The Indian origin of the artists responsible for the paintings was questioned at the time by C.M.Fernando. He raised the matter in discussion after Bell had reported to the RASCB in 1897 and the controversy continued in letters to local journals. [20]

Bell did not repeat his assertion as to the Indian origin of the paintings in the 1905 Annual Report and modern writers take for granted that the Sigiriya paintings are part of a Sinhalese tradition. W.G.Archer in his Preface to the Unesco monograph on *Ceylon Paintings from Temple, Shrine and Rock* finds the paintings of Sigiriya essentially different from those of Ajanta in their depiction of the female form:

> At Ajanta, women are depicted with brief waists and vast rotund hips, while even at the Buddhist *stupa* of Amaravati in South India, a relic-mound which was made in the first to third centuries A.D., sculptures of women conform to the same physical pattern, expressing, through rounded smiling faces, an air of gay exuberance. In the early painting and sculpture of India, in fact, woman is constantly shown as blandly acquiescing in sensual pleasure and wilting when denied the admiration of her lovers. At Sigiri, on the other hand, not only is the physical type somewhat different - the waists are long, the hips narrow, the faces thin - the expression itself suggests a seriousness of purpose, a calm and solemn realisation of sinuous majesty, even at times an enigmatic mystery. The female body is the acme of glowing splendour but the bland and jolly faces of Karla, Mathura, Sanchi and Amaravati are totally absent. An element of conscious gravity is present and this we can only define as Sinhalese. [21]

The frescoes that remain are only a small proportion of those that once adorned the rock. Rhys Davids had deduced that those that survived were those fortuitously protected by the overhang of rock, and Bell found a few faint remains in other places during his excavations. When

Paranavitana deciphered the many inscriptions concerning the ladies he found reference to five hundred 'golden-coloured ones' depicted on the Rock. Paranavitana differs from Bell, in thinking that those portrayed are 'cloud damsels' and 'lightning princesses' rather than human, and considers that this view is supported by the fact that each figure appears to rise out of swirls of cloud. Bell, however, was determined in his view that they are portraits of real queens and princesses, saying that 'conventionalism rules the stiff disposition of arms and hands; yet each figure is imbued with divergent traits in face, form, pose and dress, which seem to stamp it as an individual likeness'. He continues:

> So skilfully in truth has the portrait painter worked that it appears possible not merely to gauge approximately each lady's age, but even, in great degree, 'to find the mind's construction in the face'... Here they live, they move, they have a being; all is instinct with life and spirit.
>
> Mark the fair princess (No. 1 'B') who has purposely taken the lead in the procession with her lady-in-waiting (No. 2). That dainty head saucily tossed back surely betrays, plainer than words, full consciousness of her undoubted charms...
>
> Following her demurely at some distance is a second princess (No. 3), perhaps the staid elder sister, accompanied by a dusky maid of unattractive mien, carrying a rolled ola book.
>
> Next, come two more court attendants (Nos. 5,6), manifestly importuning a matronly queen (No. 7) to hasten her steps. The impassiveness of the royal lady is admirably brought out by a slight, but expressive touch - the deliberate unfolding, petal by petal, of a lotus bud she holds in her hand.
>
> Or observe the impulsive eagerness of No. 9, another lady-in-waiting, chafing at the delay and appealing to the queen immediately following (No. 10), who with right hand uplifted gently checks her impetuosity.
>
> Succeeding No. 10, attended like Nos. 3 and 7 by a servant maid bearing a tray of flowers, is a princess of seventeen or eighteen years (No. 12), who may well be Kasyapa's daughter. Excellently has the artist caught the young girl's
>
> > 'Embarrassed look of shy distress,
> > And maidenly shamefacedness'
>
> on the occasion of this - not improbably her initiation into a - public Court procession.
>
> The figure behind is perhaps her mother, the queen consort, from whose well-chiselled face 'Decay's effacing fingers' have still not 'swept the lines where beauty lingers'.
>
> Last of all, calm and sedate, walks the queen mother (No. 14) absorbed in silent meditation. Can we doubt that that fixed gaze and dreamy look sadly speak to 'thoughts too deep for tears' - a royal husband slain at Kala-Vewa; a son, his slayer, ruling, but not reigning, at Sigiriya; to a 'past' no longer 'sighed for, and a future sure'. [22]

Sigirya : Glories revealed

In a note to his account of the paintings in 1905 he reaffirms his view that the fact that the ladies were not portrayed at full length indicated nothing but the necessity imposed by the space available, saying that:

> The conformation of the rock left the artists no option but to 'dock' the ladies of their lower limbs to avoid the comical effect extremities distorted by the concavity must necessarily induce. Equally undesirable would have been the compression of full-length figures into the limited space available, in as much as details could not be distinguished from the terrace below the Rock. No small ingenuity was exercised in putting to full use the peculiar badly adapted surface (wall and roof) of the chambers, so as to exhibit to the best advantage a series of half figure portraits ranged in possibly three to four rows originally. [23]

Bell also was convinced that the figures were not, as they may appear to be, naked above the waist, saying that 'every court lady depicted in the frescoes is in reality fully clothed: in coloured *kambaya* from the waist downwards, and above in a short-sleeved jacket of finest material - so thin, indeed, that the painter has occasionally contented himself by indicating it by a mere line of deeper colour'. [24]

Finally we come to the Sigiriya graffiti - those comments and poems inscribed on the Mirror-Wall of the gallery, which have been so painstakingly transcribed and translated by Paranavitana. Bell and Still had deciphered a few of the writings and Bell gives a small selection in Appendix C of the Annual Report of 1905. His introduction opens as follows:

> 'The insatiate itch of scribbling, hateful pest!
> Creeps, like a tetter, through the human breast.'

The tombs of ancient Egypt, of Rome, of Pompeii, have known the curse: today it is epidemic wherever antiquities are accessible. 'The trail of the serpent is over them all!' To this universal craving for cheap notoriety the innumerable writings scratched on the highly polished plaster of the Gallery at Sigiri-gala too amply testify.

The 'inscriptions' in Sinhalese date palaeographically from the 6th to 15th century. Despite their brevity and ephemeral import, they merit careful study, no less on epigraphical than linguistic grounds, providing as they do a valuable field of research into the gradual mutation and development of the Sinhalese script and language from archaic and obsolete characters and word-forms.

But the task of deciphering the vast majority of these *graffiti* is rendered extremely difficult, in as much as (unlike the modern vandal striving commonly to spoil as much wall space as possible with ignoble name and date) the native 'scribe', albeit with more sense of propriety, usually left his record, neatly incised by *ulkatuwak* (metal style), in ordinary manuscript size, now weathered and blurred by age.

Add to this that the writings bristle with clerical errors only to be expected of 'the general', ever more or less illiterate. [25]

H. C. P. Bell

Bell's hostility to those who deface ancient monuments appears in this extract. It was with shame that his friend Ievers, when proposing the vote of thanks on the occasion of the reading of the first Interim Report, admitted to the crime of having scratched his own name on the gallery wall.

Bell having read only a few of the Sigiriya graffiti, it was left to Paranavitana to publish as haunting poetry those comments on the 'ladies with the golden skins' which Bell tersely describes as 'homely stanzas, to the pedant "so sweetly mawkish and so smoothly dull"'. [26]

But despite their differences of interpretation Paranavitana pays the following tribute to his predecessor:

> By his sustained work at Sigiriya Bell has earned the undying gratitude of all students of Sinhalese history and culture. This work he carried out at great risk to his own health, with no desire nor expectation of gaining any personal advantage, but impelled by a pure love for the advancement of knowledge, making himself liable to be misunderstood and found fault with by the very people who stood to be benefited by his labour. The joys and thrills of discovery he no doubt considered to be enough recompense. [27]

It was by reporting on his work at Sigiriya to the RASCB that Bell's name first became known to a wide public. The first two Interim Reports, which were read at the Annual General Meetings on September 10, 1895 and January 9, 1897 respectively, although received with considerable interest by those present, did not attract a wide audience. For the first there was an attendance, besides members of the Society, of twelve ladies and eighteen gentlemen, and for the second only ten gentlemen. But the news got round, the site had been visited by a number of people, including Mr. and Mrs. Cameron from Anuradhapura, and it was decided to hold the next Annual General Meeting, at which the third report was to be given, in the Colombo Public Hall. At this meeting, on December 22, 1897, were exhibited plans, drawings, photographs, as well as the whole set of facsimile copies in oils of the frescoes; and Bell himself read his paper. On this occasion, as well as members of the Society, there were seventy-five ladies and a hundred and twenty-five gentlemen present, certainly a record for a meeting of the RASCB up to that time. In his account Bell had included the somewhat fanciful description of the frescoes which has been quoted, and this accounts for the arch remarks in the following warm tribute which he received from the new Governor, Sir J.West Ridgeway, who put the vote of thanks when it had been proposed:

> My Lord, ladies and gentlemen: I now invite you by hearty acclamation to pass the vote of thanks to Mr. Bell which has been proposed and seconded. Mr. Ferguson and Mr. Fernando have evidently interpreted the feelings of this audience with the same accuracy and sympathy as Mr. Bell has the 'maiden meditation' of the beautiful young ladies on the frescoes (*laughter*). [To Mr. Bell:- as your official chief I was rather shocked for a moment at your intimate acquaintance with the feelings of these ladies, and I began to fear a Breach of Promise case until I remembered how very much older they were than yourself (*renewed laughter*). In conveying to you the thanks of this Society, the thought occurs to me - how often have you received the thanks of this Chair; how often have you read Papers and done other useful work, and earned and received their thanks?] However, I have no doubt Mr. Bell has been well rewarded. I can imagine, enthusiastic as he is, how pleased he has been to break away from the

> trammels of 'red-tape' which usually surround him, and escape from cold official control; when he finds himself in this hall of culture, in the presence of a sympathetic audience, how he must revel in delight. The icy *douche*, with which Government may occasionally quench his archaeological ardour, is forgotten: he can dream, he can build magnificent castles - or shall we say dagabas - regardless of expense, knowing that he has the entire sympathy of his audience (*laughter and applause*). [28]

The members of the Society also showed their appreciation of Bell's work and the Bishop of Colombo said the following, when thanking the Governor for his attendance as Patron:

> I am very glad to think Your Excellency's presence today is in great measure, not merely to show your sympathy and to discharge your duty of patronage to this Branch of the Royal Asiatic Society, but also to show your approbation of him whom I shall not hesitate to call '*our* Mr. Bell' (*hear, hear*). He belongs to you, Sir, as a servant of the Government but he belongs by extraction to the Royal Asiatic Society (*hear, hear, and laughter*). And we hope we may be able to make further requisitions on him for services like those which he has performed this evening (*hear, hear*) - services which demand such extraordinary combinations in himself and Mr. Perera. It has been shown that they require, not only minute scientific knowledge and accuracy, but heroic efforts, which belong rather to the sphere of the athlete, or even of the aeronaut. [29]

It will be remembered that it was in 1898 that Bell was elected as an Honorary Member of the Society; in more ways than one Sigiriya was the peak of his career.

13

Protection of the Heritage

Excavation is only the beginning of the work for the archaeologist; what is excavated must be conserved. Repairs to fallen monuments and, in some cases, their restoration, may follow. First it must be noticed that at this time the term 'Conservation' was used in a somewhat different sense from that in which it is used today. It meant neither the preservation of objects and/or monuments nor their restoration. Scientific conservation was as yet undeveloped, and although we read of the cleaning of finds with acid there were no laboratories, no trained scientific workers. The annual clearing of growth on sites once excavated was intended to preserve the monuments from disappearing under rank vegetation, but it became a moot point as to whether this did not cause further erosion, and at Sigiriya, at least, the grass was left to hold the brickwork together.

'Conservation' in the early Annual Reports and in files in the Colombo Archives referred to the purchase of land round major monuments so that they could be protected either from treasure seekers or from those more simply wanting to use stones for building purposes. In a letter to the Colonial Secretary on June 1, 1895 Bell added a further argument in favour of the acquisition of an area around the Abhayagiriya Dagaba, saying that land purchased would add to the 'lungs' of a jungle-bound town which was being invaded by a growing stream of visitors. He wrote that but for the action of Sir John Dickson in earlier years there would have been 'an incalculable loss which must have resulted from cutting up for private gardens and building lots of the beautiful stretch of park dotted with ruins lying between the Government Agent's residence and the Thuparama'. [1]

In the *Summary of Operations 1890-1900* we read that 'since 1891 the following areas and ruins at Anuradhapura have been set apart for conservation by the Crown: i) Abhayagiriya, ii) "Elala Sohona", iii) Jetawanarama and Lankarama, iv) "Kiribat Vehara", v) Mirisavetiya, vi) Moated site below Nuwara-vewa, vii) Pankuliya, viii) Puliyankulam, ix) Shrine on the "Y road", x) Toluvila, xi) Vijayarama'. [2]

Other areas were designated from time to time, for example eleven acres around Vessagiriya were finally bought in by 1903, and in 1912, just before Bell's retirement, the Survey Department redefined the boundaries of most of the Crown reservations at Anuradhapura and marked the areas with concrete posts, counter-sunk in the top with the royal crown below A.R. and dyed red. Bell noted in the Annual Report 1911-12 that other areas were still to be defined, notably the Jetawanarama-Lankarama area, which covered 300 acres and upwards. [3]

In the same year Bell reported that the survey of the areas to be reserved at Polonnaruwa had been completed, and in a note added that by Final Order no. 728, *Ceylon Government Gazette*, October 23, 1914, 2,413 acres, 0 roods, 13.36 perches at Polonnaruwa were declared the property of the Crown as an Archaeological Reserve. [4]

Persuading Government to pay out money to acquire land, and negotiating its purchase, often, as Bell put it, 'dragged its slow length along'. At Nalanda, which Bell first visited in 1894, the Surveyor General was asked to make a plan of the land around the 'Gedige' in that year, but it was not until November 15, 1901 that the certificate in question was finally issued. [5]

The whole area within the fortifications at Sigiriya was declared a conservation area in 1898. In a letter to Government on March 2, 1901 Bell estimated that Sigiri itself covered about 10 acres and the total area designated as an archaeological conservation area, 250 acres. At this time Bell made a determined effort to get the responsibility of the care of the wider area shifted to the Forest Department, saying that they might usefully reafforest some portions of it. He said that the area was 'easy of access to any Forest Officer who will take the trouble to inspect it' - for example by bicycle! But the Assistant Conservator of Forests, A.Clark, replied that it was too far off main roads to be usefully exploited. [6]

One of the purposes of declaring conservation areas was to protect the monuments from treasure hunting. This was also the aim of two Ordinances passed during Bell's tenure of office; the 1891 Ordinance to amend the Law relating to Treasure Trove and the 1900 Ordinance for the Better Preservation of the Antiquities of the Island. With both Bell was closely concerned.

In 1887, Ordinance 17 had been passed with the stated purpose of providing against 'the concealment of treasure trove found in the island' but the definition of treasure was limited to 'money, coin, gold, silver, plate, bullion or precious stones found hidden in the earth or in any private place'. [7]

On August 20, 1890 F.H.M.Corbet, joint Secretary of the RASCB with Bell, wrote to the Colonial Secretary suggesting that Ceylon might with advantage adopt the rules for the protection of objects of archaeological interest in force in India, and enclosing a copy of the relevant State Paper published by the Government of Madras on April 27, 1809. The suggestion was passed to Bell for his comments and he wrote to the Colonial Secretary on November 20, 1890 from Anuradhapura, supporting the proposal. In particular he recommended that the scope of the definition of treasure trove might be extended to cover 'antiquities or anything of value found hidden in the earth, or in anything affixed thereto'. He also suggested that an increase in the reward offered would give a greater inducement for the reporting of finds, and proposed that payment should be made equal to the 'full value of the *materials* of any treasure trove (as distinct from their adventitious value as objects of archaeological interest) *plus one-fifth of such value*, whenever it is decided by Government to acquire such treasure, or any portion of it'. [8]

Sir Arthur Havelock, in his Address to the Legislative Council on August 20, 1891, said that he was adopting Bell's suggestions, and an amended Ordinance (No. 3 of 1891) was duly passed. [9]

Bell then drafted a circular which Government sent out on June 26, 1891 as General Circular No. 57. Printed in Appendix C to his Sixth Progress Report, it placed the responsibility for reporting discoveries of archaeological interest on the Government Agents. It laid down that objects still *in situ* should not be removed, but that isolated finds, or those liable to be mutilated, might be sent to the Colombo Museum. [10]

Bell continued to record instances of damage by treasure hunters, and finally persuaded Government to enact in 1900 *An Ordinance for the Better Preservation of the Antiquities of the*

Island. This, as its title implies, was concerned with establishing a policy for the safeguarding of the total cultural heritage of the Island rather than merely regulating the reporting of finds. This Ordinance defined antiquities as follows:

> 3. The expression 'antiquities' shall mean and include any of the following objects, lying or being found in the island, which date or may reasonably be believed to date from a period prior to the annexation of the Kandyan kingdom by the British; that is to say:
>
> (a) Statues and statuary, sculptured or dressed stone and marble of all descriptions, engravings, carvings, inscriptions, paintings, writings, and the material whereon the same appear, all specimens of ceramic, glyptic, metallurgic, and textile art, coins, gems, seals, jewels, jewellery, arms, tools, ornaments, and generally all objects of art and movable property of antiquarian interest.
>
> (b) Temples, churches, monuments, tombs, buildings, erections, or structures and immovable property of a like nature or any part of the same.

All movable antiquities, as defined in 3(a) above, were declared to be Crown property; permission from the Government was required before any excavation was allowed to take place, and a penalty was prescribed for the purchase of illegally excavated antiquities. The export of antiquities was prohibited without express leave, and this was not to be granted if any Museum in Ceylon wished to acquire the object or objects. A penalty was laid down for the wilful damaging of antiquities. [11]

Needless to say, even the more stringent law failed to prevent treasure hunting or to discourage applications for permission to excavate. Bell refers to both forms of activity in his Annual Reports for 1909 and 1911-12 under the heading of 'Destruction of Ruins'. Of illicit treasure hunting he complained, in 1909, that 'in no case were the culprits detected - or rather, "given away" - by the minor headmen, themselves usually aware of such actions, if not joint perpetrators therein'.

On one treasure-trove application he had minuted in October 1908:

> This is one more of the increasing number of applications to Government Agents and the Archaeological Commissioner to search for treasure. The present applicant desires to be granted what amounts to 'a roving commission' to hunt for treasure throughout a good part of the extensive Hurulu Palata, North-Central Province. He ingenuously admits that he is not the first in the field in 'excavating these places' - a euphemism for breaching ruined dagabas, blasting rock inscriptions (of great palaeographic and literary, if not historical, value), and breaking up inscribed pillars and slabs, fatuously believed to conceal hidden treasure.

He believed that all such applications should be refused unless one should come from 'a recognised Syndicate or Company prepared to offer adequate security to ensure the Government against all damage to ancient monuments'. [12]

Bell was firm in upholding the aim of the Ordinance to keep Ceylon antiquities in Ceylon.

Protection of the heritage

We read as follows in the Annual Report for 1910-11:

> The Director of the Museum at Munich, during a recent visit to Anuradhapura, interviewed the Archaeological Commissioner with the object of securing 'specimens of archaeological interest' for that German Museum.
>
> Courteously, but with no hesitation, the Professor was informed that his application, like others of a similar nature in previous years, could not be acceded to, but that he was at liberty to make drawings, or plaster-casts, if desired.
>
> More than one attempt has been made in past years (e.g. by an American syndicate, and a distinguished Professor of the Berlin Museum, since dead) to induce the Ceylon Government through its Archaeological Department, to part with antiquities of the Island: every application has failed.
>
> Unlike India and Java, Buddhism is still a living religion in Ceylon, and, for that reason alone, the Government would never consent to hurt the susceptibilities of the Buddhists by permitting reverenced relics of their cult to be removed from the Island. [13]

In Bell's last Report he reaffirmed the Government policy of leaving antiquities where they were found whenever possible. Admittedly Sir William Gregory had formerly authorised the moving of the great lion from Polonnaruwa to the Colombo Museum, and even Bell had permitted the transfer of the Toluvila Buddha, but as years went by it became more usual to attempt to replace statues in their original position. In 1906 most of the small antiquities stored in the Anuradhapura Museum were taken to Colombo, and listed by John Still, and a further selection was made by the Director of the Museum, Dr. J.Pearson, in 1911 and transferred in 1912. These included some sculptures and sculpted slabs, but Bell defended their selection by asserting that 'hardly a single specimen of these sculptures has been removed from any ancient building, however ruined, which is both worth preserving and capable of due restoration'.

He then went on to list certain sculptures that *had* been transferred to Colombo, which he thought should be restored to position. He had discussed the question with his successor, Mr. E.R.Ayrton, who agreed with him. Bell was particularly insistent that the ornamental granite window from the Porch at the head of the staircase at Yapahuwa should be returned:

> This is one of a pair of beautiful pierced stone windows (Sinhalese *siv-meduru-kavulu*) - of the other only fragments are left - which lighted the handsome Porch at the head of the magnificent staircase at Yapahuwa. The highest staircase and Porch were restored by the Public Works Department in 1885; this year (1912) the middle stairs have been partially reset, and made serviceable for mounting to the uppermost stairway. Additional repairs were at the same time effected at the Porch to the 'Raja Maligawa'.
>
> The ruins of Yapahuwa (only three miles from Maho Railway Station) are being yearly rendered more accessible, and attractive, to visitors, by the Archaeological Survey Department. It is most undesirable that any prominent functional member of the fine Porch at the head of the grand staircase should be separated, as it is at present, from the rest of the structure. [14]

Bell's desire to see antiquities retained in their own country, and restored when possible to their original position, might well have made him support the return of the Elgin Marbles to the Acropolis at Athens. However, in Ceylon, there was a particular problem facing the archaeologist, the undoubted fact that most of the monuments were religious in origin, and some of them still in use for religious ceremonies. In 1869 the Temple Lands Commission had handed over responsibility for the 'Eight Sacred Sites' at Anuradhapura to the Buddhist Committee of the Atamasthana. These sites comprised:

1) Jetawanaramaya, 2) Lankaramaya, 3) Thuparamaya, 4) Abhayagiriya,
5) Lowa-maha-paya ('Brazen Palace'), 6) Bodinwahanse (Sacred Bo Tree enclosure),
7) Mirisavetiya, 8) Ruwanveli. [15]

However, this was not enough for some Buddhists, who opposed any excavation, particularly in or around the dagabas. The Maha Bodhi Society, with its active Secretary, Walisinha Harischandra, aimed to control all religious sites in Anuradhapura and even complained when Bell filled in two small pokunas which he had found of no archaeological interest. Friction with the Christian community led to the outbreaks in 1903 known as 'The Anuradhapura Riots', and Bell was one of those called as a witness during the trial which followed. His own operations were not, however, called in question. [16]

On other occasions Bell encountered criticism - and replied to it. In 1895, when excavating the already rifled relic chamber of the Sela Chaitiya Dagaba, he faced a hostile crowd and was later attacked in *The Buddhist* for 'committing a piece of vandalism in the eyes of the scientific and an instance of sacrilege in the eyes of the Buddhists'. But Bell insisted that he had permission from the High Priest of the Atamasthana, 'who might be compared to the Archbishop of Rome'. [17]

In 1901 Bell came under fire in the Legislative Council, when S.N.W.Hulugalle suggested that not only were his excavations acts of sacrilege, but that they 'tended in the direction of endangering the stability of those structures which are sacred in the eyes of the Buddhists'. In a written reply Bell defended himself briskly:

> The charge is vague, general, and made only on hearsay, but being put forward above the name of the member for the Kandyans it becomes serious. On behalf of the Government, therefore, under whose authority I have the honour to conduct the Archaeological Survey, I am bound to meet it at once. I am able to give the charge an unqualified denial and to challenge the Buddhists of the Island to quote a single concrete instance in which the Archaeological Survey Department has by its excavation at any site during the past ten years of its existence impaired the stability of edifices. The utmost care has always been exercised by myself and my several assistants to carry out excavations so as to avoid causing damage to ruined structures, and this as much in the interests of the public and the Buddhists themselves as for the credit of the Archaeological Survey. Nay more; wherever practicable, ruins have been restored and their stability thereby greatly strengthened. Since 1890 as Archaeological Commissioner, I have carried on excavations according to my lights; and with the accumulated experience of a decade and upwards I have seen no reason to alter or modify a single line on which the Archaeological Commissioner proceeds. [18]

If Bell came under attack from the Buddhists for interference with sacred sites he was not slow to counter-attack when wandering priests set up residence in archaeological conservation areas, or requested permission to erect modern additions. Some petitions made on this subject have been studied by L.A.Wickremeratne in a article on the functions of petitions in colonial government, and he quotes various tart comments by Bell. On a petition from a priest in Kotahena to occupy the Gal Vihare in Polonnaruwa he wrote, 'It is not desirable to allow any priest to occupy and inevitably "modernise" the Gal Vihare... the sad experience gained at Isurumuniya rock temple in giving an ignorant priest a free hand to disfigure the grand old rock by... minarets and a hideous belfry should be sufficient warning'. [19]

In response to another petition Bell showed that he was very aware of latent criticism of excavation as intrusion. He remarked that 'from paragraphs 2 and 3 of the petition it would appear as though the Archaeological Commissioner was the officially recognised "Bill Sykes" of the Ceylon Government - a brutal burglar of Buddhist buildings'. [20]

In many ways the archaeologist and the worshipper had different priorities. Bell deplored the results of the increasing popularity of pilgrimages to Anuradhapura, writing:

> To those lovers of antiquity undisturbed who can remember the days, not so long ago, when it was possible to approach all the ruins at Anuradhapura without having one's eyes and nose offended by incongruous sights and smells - makeshift tables (mostly packing-cases), curry-and-rice, *kevun* (cakes), plantains, bread, tea, coloured drinks - any cheap comestibles, in fact, except spirituous liquor - at one point openly provided under the very shadow of the saintly Buddha, sitting *saxeus* in silent sorrowful reproof, as it were, at such desecration, these ancient sites may well seem to echo the cry, '*Ichabod, Ichabod.*' [21]

An incident at Mihintale which came to a tragic end is reported thus by Bell, in a note on his description of the caves in the area known as Raja-giri-lena-kanda:

> The most recent occupant came from Northern India. Unable at first to speak a word of Sinhalese, he was allowed by the Government Agent of the time to settle in these caves as a hermit, at a nominal rent. For some years (until he learnt the language and became sufficiently familiar with the neighbouring villagers to earn their confidence) the man lived the most orderly of lives in virtual solitude. Subsequently he assumed the robes of a Buddhist monk to secure greater assistance in his real object - the gradual conversion of the caves into a *Gal Vihare*, or Cave Temple. Of late, by assaying so-called 'restoration', he has exhibited objectionable effort to run counter to the Crown intention to leave the caves and surrounding jungle in their existing ruined picturesqueness. The Government Agent was warned that such Jeshurun proclivities would lead to trouble, unless this 'irresponsible adventurer' (A.C., No. 528, August 28, 1911) was promptly ousted. (Whilst this Report is passing through the press the man has been convicted of a murderous assault on the Government Agent, and sentenced to 16 years' imprisonment). [22]

In a letter to Government on the subject it is clear that Bell was present when the priest was ejected, for he says that 'the Government Agent was attacked with axe and knife, but there was little damage to myself'. [23]

A lighter note is struck by Paranavitana, when he reports the following tradition that Bell was frustrated in an attempt to excavate the dagaba then known as 'Elala Sohona' by divine intervention in the form of a swarm of hornets:

> Mr. Bell, towards the close of the last century, carried out investigation at this site by opening trenches on the eastern and northern slopes of the mound, and by levelling its top. The ordinary man of the day, no doubt, considered this work of Mr. Bell as sacrilege of a very heinous character, and would have restrained him if he had been able to do so. But what he was incapable of doing, he credited the gods with having done. Moved by his resentment, and possibly acting on their own initiative, the gods, he fancied, decided to teach the impudent archaeologist a lesson that would never be forgotten, and sent from nowhere a huge swarm of black hornets, at the approach of which Mr. Bell and his men were said to have run away for their very lives, and given the place a wide berth ever after. This 'discomfiture of an archaeologist' is, to the villager in and around Anuradhapura, as true a narrative of history as the fight between Dutugamunu and Elara, and is at times given credence even by people who ought to know better. [24]

It was not only against native treasure hunters and 'trespassers' on sacred sites that Bell waged war; he conducted fierce battles with the Public Works Department. He criticised their attempts at restoration and he accused them of damaging archaeological sites by blasting slab rock when building roads near the Vessagiriya in Anuradhapura. Central Government officials were inclined to discount some of his complaints, remarking that 'Mr. Bell is apt to be a little hysterical', and 'This is a storm in a tea-cup. Mr. Bell is morbidly sensitive when his ruins are in any way affected'. [25]

Morbidly sensitive perhaps, certainly extremely proprietorial. The ruins were his ruins and only he knew what should be done.

14

Restoration : The Great Dagabas

The actual restoration of monuments, the re-setting of fallen stones or bricks, or even the complete dismantlement of a ruin and its rebuilding, was not included as one of the original objects of the Archaeological Survey, nor was money provided for the purpose. We have seen how Bell drew on the Fund collected by the RASCB for the restoration of the Buddhist Railing at Anuradhapura, and at Sigiriya found sufficient money and labour to rebuild the Gallery. From 1900 onwards he was urging Government to provide a special Vote for restoration.

The only major restoration work authorised by Government up to that time had been the work on the Abhayagiriya begun by Sir Arthur Gordon, and that on the Mirisavetiya, largely funded by a Siamese prince. An independent operation on the Ruwanveli dagaba had been started by the monk Naranwita Unnanse, with the support of Sir William Gregory. The question of further repairs to these enormous structures continued to be an issue throughout Bell's career, but his attitude towards this was curious, and indeed often decidedly unhelpful. Although he kept a careful watch and always reported dangerous cracks or slips, he was extremely critical of anything done either by individuals or by the Public Works Department. He continually maintained that as the three dagabas had been handed over to the Buddhist Committee of the Atamasthana, responsibility for their upkeep rested there and not with the Archaeological Survey nor indeed with Government.

The work on the Ruwanveli continued spasmodically during the whole of Bell's period of office, until in 1910 there was an extensive slip and a large section of the restored facing fell away. In a Memorandum to Government on November 9 Bell reported the matter and gave his opinion on the reason for the disaster, but advised against Government interference.

> That the 'restoration', so-called, should have proved abortive (as shown by the partial collapse on the 7th instant) - however much it may be regretted - was not unforeseen by impartial critics of the work already done on the Dagaba. The thinness of the brickwork shell, the want of due bond, the undulating slope noticeable on the wall line (due to pressure from behind of packing, rain-sodden yearly for months at a time) - these and other causes patent to ordinary observation have doomed the new work to certain fall, sooner or later. It would be as officious to call upon Government Officers to report on the 'slip' as it would be unwise... It is essentially a case for the Atamasthana Committee to deal with, and that without delay, if that body cares to interfere with Naranwita Unnanse.[1]

The Government was already, however, involved in the repairs to the Abhayagiriya and the Mirisavetiya. Gordon, who had become Lord Stanmore in 1893, maintained his interest even when retired, and in 1895 contributed Rs. 1,000 towards continuing work on the Mirisavetiya Dagaba. By 1896 the money had run out and a proposal was made that Government funds should be allocated to the work. This Bell strenuously opposed in a Memorandum dated October 9,

1896. He put forward arguments under two headings 'ad religionum' and 'ad architecturum'. Under the former he gave the history of the work to date and repeated some of the arguments put forward by H.Bois long ago in the Legislative Council in 1886, to the effect that it would violate the principle of strict impartiality of the Government towards all religions, should Government money go to the restoration of a Buddhist shrine. On this, one of the officials in the Colonial Secretariat office minuted that 'I have seldom read greater trash than Bell's argument "ad religionum"'. Bell's criticism of the architectural merits of the restoration was given more weight by Government. He had written:

> But admit - for the nonce - that Government is justified in throwing to the winds the policy of abstention from direct support to religious denominations; that it can consistently grant public money to one religious sect and refuse it to others; that it deems the Mirisavetiya Dagaba a monument worthy of restoration on exceptional grounds, historical, antiquarian or artistic. What then? Is it possible to *restore* the Mirisavetiya Dagaba, i.e. to rebuild it on the original lines and in conformity with the architectural and ornamental style of the period when it was constructed, by Dutugamunu Raja circa 80 B.C.? Unquestionably it is *not possible*: requisite data are wanting and may never be forthcoming. To renew an ancient structure of a special type, i.e. to rebuild it after a more modern design, is admittedly unjustifiable on every ground. And yet such *renovation* of the Mirisavetiya Dagaba has been going on for some years past under the pseudonym of 'restoration'.
>
> The architectural history of 'stupas' shows them to have known, like other structures, periodical modifications of 'style'. As in India, so in Ceylon. The early dagabas of Anuradhapura must have followed the general type and sculptural designs ruling at the period of their respective constructions, whilst those built at Polonnaruwa belonging to thirteen hundred years subsequently would inevitably conform to mediaeval forms and ornamentation in vogue at that time...
>
> The restoration of the Mirisavetiya Dagaba having been decided on, the Public Works officers entrusted with the preparation of necessary plans were thrown on the horns of a dilemma. On the one hand the orders of Government had to be obeyed; on the other no reliable data existed as a guide to the true original style of the Dagaba. Responsibility could not be shifted to the Archaeological Survey Department, for it did not then exist. Incontinently the difficulty was solved by a bold stroke - *a gap of twelve hundred years was lightly leapt over 'ad saltem'*, the Mirisavetiya Dagaba at Anuradhapura dating from the first century B.C. should be renewed after the design of the Kiri Vehara or Rankot Dagaba at Polonnaruwa, albeit structures of the twelfth century. Whatever the original design of the Mirisavetiya Dagaba may have been it may be positively asserted that it must have differed and probably differed considerably from that of the middle-age Dagabas of Polonnaruwa.
>
> The Mirisavetiya Dagaba has been steadily rising, course by course, during the past few years, *to perpetuate in brick and mortar an anachronism of one thousand two hundred years and upwards, a standing architectural fraud*, the gradual growth of which the Government has been placidly countenancing, and would now (but for timely warning) further support from Government funds.
>
> The 'evil' cannot be undone, but it can be promptly ended. No further work on the Dagaba's bell or dome should be permitted.[2]

Restoration : The great dagabas

Work was not resumed on the Mirisavetiya, but this was partly because on December 27, 1896 the whole of the west front of the tee of the Abhayagiriya Dagaba had collapsed and this had raised fundamental questions as to the methods of reconstruction being employed. There followed a series of investigations into the state of the two dagabas, and feasibility reports by experts on the possibility of repair and restoration. The first of these was conducted by F.A.Cooper, the Director of Public Works for Ceylon, and his report of June 3, 1898 concluded that the total collapse of the tee of the Abhayagiriya was inevitable and that nothing could be done to avert it, but that, with certain modifications, work could continue on the Mirisavetiya.

At this point the matter was taken up by the Royal Asiatic Society in London. A copy of their letter, urging the Ceylon Government to action, was passed on by the Colonial Office. Its tone was decidedly patronising, opening as follows on the subject of the Abhayagiriya Dagaba:

> This monument, as you are no doubt aware, is one of the most remarkable in the East. Almost vying in size with the Pyramids, and containing bricks sufficient, as has been estimated, to build a large English provincial town twice over, it may be reckoned among the chief buildings of the world. The Royal Asiatic Society is deeply impressed with the opinion that such a structure cannot be allowed to perish or become a mere pile of ruins through neglect without discredit to the Government both of this country and the colony.

The letter went on to refer to 'personal and professional jealousies and squabbles on which it is unnecessary to enter, but which had the effect of making it doubtful in whose charge the dagaba was', and also suggested that as 'the revenues of Ceylon were never in a more flourishing condition' there was every reason why 'a small portion of this should be devoted to the preservation and repair of a historical and architectural monument of the highest interest and value'. [3]

It is hardly surprising that Sir West Ridgeway replied on July 7 in a tone of some dudgeon:

> The Royal Asiatic Society may rest assured that this Government is not indifferent or lukewarm in the cause of the preservation of National Monuments at Anuradhapura or elsewhere in this Island and that it has expended, and continues to expend a considerable amount of money to that end.

> It is, however, necessary that the Government in selecting the monuments to be preserved should be guided by the advice of its professional advisers as to the possibility, and the possibility within reasonable limits of expenditure, of restoration and preservation. [4]

He went on to say that he had already authorised a report on the subject and gave details of Cooper's opinion. Lord Stanmore, who had been behind the action of the Royal Asiatic Society, was deeply disturbed and on August 24 wrote to Sir Arthur Havelock, his successor in Ceylon, who was now Governor of Madras: 'Sir West writes to me that he means to allow the dagabas to go to utter ruin. Why, *why* didn't you go on with my restorations?' On December 21, 1898 he wrote even more despairingly:

> Oh Havelock, there is one thing I find it difficult to forgive you and the results of which give me really

111

serious distress and pain. I mean your abandonment of my arrangements for the restoration of the Mirisavetiya and the preservation of the Abhayagiriya. If the work had gone on on the lines on which I left it all would have been finished during your government. You *did* go on with the work, but on an altered system which got little done in your six years, and now West Ridgeway has doomed them to ruin. What has been done has of course only made that ruin more easy and more certain. When they were covered with piles of debris and earth they were comparatively safe, but when the platform of the Abhayagiriya was cleared, of course it required keeping in order and the cracks stopping. This has never been done, the water has got in everywhere - one side of the tee has already completely fallen (old work as well as new) and three others will certainly follow. *Nothing* is to be done to check the progress of decay. At the Mirisavetiya the suspension of working, now that the earth is cleared away, makes the interior a huge *cup* to receive the rains, which of course will in a few years destroy the whole structure. So my efforts at restoration and preservation will have been the direct means of effecting destruction and the reflection is a bitter one to me. I really cannot bear to dwell upon it. I fancy the new Director of Public Works looks on these structures as 'magnificent quarries'.

However, West Ridgeway decided to get another opinion, and on August 26, 1899 Lord Stanmore wrote again to Havelock:

It is only *now* that I have received your letter telling me that you had sent your best expert archaeologist to look at the Abhayagiriya Dagaba at Ridgeway's request. I wonder if you saw him before he left India. You will have found out for yourself before now that in any case where the pros and cons are pretty equal the most honest report is apt to be influenced more or less unconsciously by the known wants of those to whom it is to be made. *You* would wish for a report in the sense that the Dagaba can be preserved. The Ceylon Government wish for one in the sense that it cannot. [5]

The man sent by Havelock was G.Harris, of the P.W.D. in Madras, and he had made his report on August 25, 1899. He concluded, as Cooper had before him, that the tee of the Abhayagiriya erected in 1890 was far too heavy and could not and should not be repaired. The only method of restoring the whole bell that he could envisage would be to encase it in solid masonry from the bottom to the top and he thought that the expense would be prohibitive. Harris accepted Cooper's view on the Mirisavetiya; he had said that it would be possible to continue the work, if the overall construction were much lighter and deeper foundations were laid for the tee and pinnacle. [6]

Lord Stanmore was still unsatisfied and in 1900 arranged that another expert, a fellow of the Royal Institute of British Architects, F.O.Oertel of the Indian Public Works Department, should visit Ceylon on his way back from leave in England. The expenses of the survey were to be borne jointly by the Royal Asiatic Society and the Ceylon Government.

Oertel's report, which was written in July 1902, but not published till 1903, is long and interesting from several points of view. His description of the causes of the gradual erosion of the bell of the Abhayagiriya and the consequent instability of the tee is given below:

The early explorers unfortunately thought less of the preservation of the monuments than of tracing their shape and meaning. The spade was freely used to clear away the fallen debris around the dagabas, but as this debris formed the toe of the natural slopes assumed by the ruined dagaba mounds, its removal resulted in slips, threatening the structures with further ruin. We see this exemplified in the Abhayagiriya. After its abandonment on the desertion of the capital, the protecting facing of the ruined dome gradually crumbled away under atmospheric influences and the action of roots piercing it. Loosened bricks slid down with each heavy fall of the monsoon rains, and by degrees covered up the steep base until a sufficiently gradual slope had been formed to ensure future stability. The pile had now reached, as shown in the sketch below, a state of almost complete rest, in which, if left alone, it might have remained for centuries without any appreciable change. Trees and undergrowth were sufficient to protect the slope from further damage by the rain. As soon, however, as the toe of the slope was cut away, further destruction was bound to occur. The rain penetrating into the brickwork loosened the joints and swelled the clay, causing slips at the top of the base, now deprived of the support before given to it by the debris. Small slips of this kind must have taken place in each rainy season, and have gradually extended upwards until the stability of the 'tee' was affected. This process of destruction being gradual, many years might elapse before the full extent of the mischief would be realised and traced to its source. [7]

Oertel thought that the only way to restore the dome thoroughly would be to renew the outer casing with brickwork and plaster it over, a feasible but impossibly expensive operation. He therefore suggested that further collapse might be avoided by filling in the trenches round the base of the dome and allowing vegetation to grow up once more to hold the surface together. He also proposed to give new foundations to the tee, which he found had rested partly on loose debris, and estimated a total cost of Rs. 10,983 for the work.

On the viability of the restoration of the Mirisavetiya he agreed with both Cooper and Harris, though proposing some modification of plan. It seems likely that he discussed the matter at some length with Bell, for he mentions that Bell provided him with a copy of the original plan of restoration drawn up by A.Murray in 1891, and he strongly supported Bell's proposals that money should be voted regularly for the preservation of monuments. However, he disagreed with Bell over the advisability of continuing repair work. His modified plan proposed an overall reduction of height from 205 to 167 ft., leaving the *pasadas* and dome unchanged but with a reduction to the tee. This, he said, 'will not only make it lighter and more stable, but will also result in better proportions and make it easier to construct'. He continued:

> For the outline of the 'tee' I have adopted the proportions of the miniature stone dagaba near the Ruwanveli, the only authentic guide to the shape of the ancient dagabas at Anuradhapura, and to which Mr. Bell was kind enough to draw my attention. But being only small in size and of stone, some slight modifications were required, as to which I have consulted the Rankot dagaba at Polonnaruwa. The Mirisavetiya, when restored, will therefore be as correct a reproduction of an ancient Sinhalese dagaba as it is now possible to obtain. [8]

The cost for the work on the dagaba would be Rs. 86,496.

On November 25, 1903, there was a debate in the Legislative Council, when S.N.W.Hulugalle urged the Government to follow up Oertel's report by carrying on the restoration of the Abhayagiriya. The Acting Colonial Secretary, F.R.Ellis, however, jibbed at the possible cost which he estimated at twice that proposed by Oertel. Moreover he questioned the advisability of the proposals:

> The next question is whether, if we are successful, it will really leave this building an object of interest to antiquaries. If we are going to plaster up these old monuments with Portland cement and Aspinall's enamel and put a top on it made at Messrs. Walker's foundry, the question is whether that monument will still possess that antiquarian interest which we are justified in presuming. To me, I am afraid, it seems it will be something like the axe which was exhibited by the showman who explained that with the exception of the blade and the handle, which were new, it was identically the same axe with which Charles the First was beheaded. [9]

The cost of implementing Oertel's report was clearly prohibitive. The Royal Asiatic Society in London, although they had initiated the report, were unwilling to make any contribution, as was the Buddhist community generally. That the Ceylon Government was not prepared to adopt Oertel's report as a blue-print for action is made quite clear by the following comments on the situation in Sir J.West Ridgeway's account of his work in Ceylon from 1896 to 1903:

> The results of Mr. Oertel's mission... confirmed the conclusions previously arrived at that the complete restoration of the dagabas would involve a very large expenditure; the cost, for instance, of restoring Mirisavetiya being between eighty and ninety thousand rupees. The Secretary of State has agreed with the Executive Council that the appropriation of so large a sum of money from public funds would be unjustifiable, and we can only continue to afford such temporary relief as is possible. There is some reason to believe that a partial restoration, at least, of Abhayagiriya is more feasible, and the Public Works Department are at present engaged in further investigations to this end. [10]

On December 6, 1904 the Government arranged for the sum of Rs. 2,800 to be allocated to the repair of the Abhayagiriya Dagaba. It is evident, however, that no major work was put in hand. From 1904 to 1907 there are brief references to the 'maintenance of the Mirisavetiya and Abhayagiriya Dagabas' in the Administration Reports of the Public Works Department, but only to the repair of ladders and handrails or to the clearing of vegetation. [11]

In the Annual Report of 1910-11 Bell recorded that the Public Works Department had been given an annual vote of Rs. 500 for the 'general upkeep' of the two great dagabas, but that in 1910 the Government Agent of the North-Central Province had written to Government saying that he saw no reason for this grant to continue as they were in the charge of the Atamasthana Committee. Bell had added the following comment:

> From an archaeological point of view the sum expended on the Mirisaveti Dagaba by the Siamese Prince, and upon the Abhayagiri Dagaba by the Ceylon Government, has been money to [a] great extent misapplied. The so-called 'restoration' prior to the initiation of the Archaeological Survey was, in the case of Mirisaveti Dagaba, carried out on wrong lines, is left incomplete, and is scientifically unprofitable in result; whilst in that of Abhayagiri Dagaba it was only partially successful, proving insecure and *pro tanto* futile, as borne out by the total collapse of the west face of the *hatares kotuwa*, or square tee, in December 1896.

Restoration : The great dagabas

He went on to report, not without a certain satisfaction, that the Government had decided to reduce the grant to Rs. 300 per annum. [12]

It appears, therefore, that any complete repair of the great dagabas was postponed *sine die*. On the other hand the general question of the need for restoration had been raised and of this Bell took advantage. Oertel put the case strongly for him in his report, saying that 'Mr. Bell has from time to time drawn the attention of the authorities to the matter, and my remarks on the subject arose from a wish to strengthen his hands'. Oertel pointed out that not only was it necessary to replace fallen or dislodged stonework, but that buildings once uncovered had to be kept clean of encroaching vegetation, and that the cost of this inhibited further excavation. He proposed that:

> If the Ceylon Government wish [sic]- and I know it does wish - to see its historical monuments duly preserved for future ages, the question of the systematic conservation of the most important and striking remains (other than those which the Buddhists should themselves undertake, if so disposed) must be faced, independent of the annual vote for archaeological research, and a special sum, however small, set apart for this particular object, to be expended under the direction of qualified officers, ere the fatal ravages of time render restoration either hopeless or prohibitive financially.
>
> What I would propose is that lists be prepared, as has been done in India, of all the monuments in each Province worthy of preservation on account of their historical or other interest, and that these monuments be made over to the Public Works Department, who should do what may be needed for their conservation, in consultation with the Archaeological Commissioner. The monuments on the list should be inspected at least once a year to ascertain whether any repairs are required. In addition to this, for purposes of 'first aid', I would set apart a fixed sum annually (separate from the present archaeological vote for research) to be expended by the Archaeological Commissioner in such restoration as should be done immediately after excavation, while he and his staff are still on the spot to supervise the operations. These measures would at a minimum outlay enable much good and lasting work to be accomplished towards the worthy preservation of Ceylon's ancient monuments. [13]

This part of Oertel's recommendations was agreed to by Government, and thereafter a special grant was provided for restoration work which was gradually raised by 1910-11 to Rs. 21,875. [14]

With this money Bell was able to carry through some extensive restoration work in his last years of service, particularly at Polonnaruwa and Yapahuwa, and to tidy up his excavations at Anuradhapura. There he also undertook some major work on the great Northern Dagaba, which was still known as the Jetawanarama. This he did despite the fact that it was one of the Eight Sacred Sites.

At Bell's request Oertel had inspected the Jetawanarama while at Anuradhapura, and included his comments in his recommendations to Government in 1902. According to Oertel, Bell had been concerned about the state of the tee of the dagaba since 1897, and had pointed out its dangerous state to both the Government Agent and the Provincial Engineer. But, Bell told him, 'Nothing has been done since, as the Public Works Department Officers have found themselves unable to undertake the extra work whilst my own limited vote and want of suitable plant have not allowed of my attempting to carry out the necessary work single-handed'. [15]

Oertel made suggestions for immediate repairs, but in these included the building of sloping buttresses of new brickwork to support the faces of the tee. Bell did not approve of this plan and so did not immediately press the case for repairs. He said later that, 'Such necessarily hideous, and wholly incongruous, subterfuge did not appeal to the Archaeological Commissioner, who allowed the matter to drop temporarily rather than be connected with a consummation devoutly to be opposed'.

In 1909, however, Bell was engaged in work around the dagaba, undertaken with the permission of the Atamasthana Committee, which resulted in the discovery of the inscription which finally fixed the fact that the so-called Jetawanarama was really the Abhayagiriya. [16]

He then decided to raise the question of the restoration of the tee and sent a copy of Oertel's report to Government. The Government acted promptly, determining on July 14, 1909 that the Public Works Department should estimate for repairs, and after H.T.Creasy, the Provincial Engineer, had made a report, sanctioned his estimate of Rs. 1,500 on October 26. Creasy, like all engineers, believed that the only way that the foundations of the tee could be permanently secured was by restoring the dagaba from its base, but proposed as a temporary measure 'filling in the weathered and undercut portions of the pinnacle with brickwork'.

Bell, as usual, did not wholly agree with the Public Works Department's plans, sending in a plea on November 27, 1909 that no complete restoration should be attempted, and on January 19, 1910 begging that the work should not be made too 'smooth', and no 'trim smugness', which the Public Works Department were apt to achieve, should be countenanced. Again he stressed that the Dagaba was the property of the Buddhists. In a letter dated January 5, 1910 and printed in the Annual Report for 1910-11, he set out his views as follows:

> The repairs should be done in the simplest possible manner consistent with the old work and regard for due strength. The pinnacle is, more or less, in a ruined condition exteriorly. *Qua* a ruin, abraded, irregular, and rough on the surface, it would be, archaeologically, most objectionable to renew its ragged outlines smoothly in any way, except to some extent at the base.

> The most that can be expected of the Government in aiding towards the preservation of this 'historical monument' - the admitted property of the Buddhists - is to *undertake certain immediate repairs to the face of the pinnacle (kota) and square tee (hatares kotuwa)*, in order to partially make good the damage caused by the weathering of centuries; and thus materially delay for a considerable period the fall of the pinnacle, which has survived the ravages of time for nearly two thousand years, but is now in a critical condition.

> The only improvement in the existing rough, irregular face of the pinnacle justifiable is to fill in small holes and crannies, and to ensure as far as possible that no course of bricks overhangs those below - at least up to the point to which work is carried.

> At the south side of the pinnacle its base has survived in almost perfect condition for a stretch of some ten feet, save that the plaster facing and a brick-and-stucco figure which once stood out in relief from

the wall line have disappeared. This strip being so well preserved it would be easy and inexpensive to restore its pristine outline from plinth to coping. To deal effectively with this section will be a piece of legitimate 'restoration', and should be executed *pari passu* with the more rough and ready repairs to the rest of the pinnacle's periphery at its base. [17]

He then offered that the Archaeological Survey should itself carry out the modified plan of repair and this offer was accepted by Government on February 6, 1910. The Annual Reports of 1910-11 and 1911-12 give full details of the work achieved in these years, and the latter has a number of plates showing the unrestored tee, drum and pinnacle, and others of the repairs in process. A telephoto view shows the ladder reaching right to the top of the pinnacle.

The work was hazardous. Bell writes:

It was of the highest importance to ascertain the condition of the *kota* at the top where broken off; but to carry a ladder up the steep and crumbling face (especially in the strong wind prevailing at the time) was an undertaking involving very considerable danger. No local workmen could be induced to venture their necks; and it was decided to bring to Anuradhapura some of the fearless village blacksmiths from Lenadora, nearly 50 miles away in the Central Province - men already accustomed at Sigiriya to such dizzy nerve-trying work. By gradually drilling deeply into the brickwork 1-in. round iron staples at every 10 ft., a ladder of stout jungle-timber was at length erected and tied fast.

It was P.D.Ambrose, son-in-law of W.M.Fernando, who had joined the Department on February 20, 1908, who climbed to the top, to the height of 250 feet, to take the necessary notes and measurements for preparing the conservation drawings. [18]

Bell felt that enough had been done to ensure reasonable stability to both the tee and the pinnacle. In accordance with his oft stated principles, he said that fuller restoration should be left to the Atamasthana Committee and the Buddhist Community generally.

15

Delay : Reasons and Remedies

When we study the bibliography of Bell's writings, looking primarily for his reports on his work as Archaeological Commissioner, a pattern emerges now to be considered and explained. After the first six years of his appointment, during which publication of his results was kept up with fair regularity in seven Progress Reports, there intervened a period when no reports were made to Government, and the only records of his work which appeared were the annual reports to the RASCB and the three special Interim Reports on Sigiriya, which were only published in the JRASCB. Then in 1904 appeared the *Summary of Operations 1890-1900* and the whole series of Annual Reports, not so detailed as the Progress Reports, covering the same decade. How do we account for the delay in official reports and how far can Bell be excused for his inaction ?

Initially we find Bell interested in the wider dissemination of his publications. He sent copies of his and Gray's translation of Pyrard to journals and influential people. Early in June 1891 he wrote to Rost of the India Office Library, sending him the first and second of his detailed Reports and asking support for obtaining publication in England. He sent the same Reports, expressing the same hope, to Sir William Gregory and wrote, 'My heart is so deep in the work that I yearn to have it taken up by people at home interested in archaeology'. [1]

However, not even the JRAS noticed the first two Reports. Still, reviews of the First and Second Reports did appear in the JRIBA in 1891. The reviewer, William Simpson, while praising Bell's efforts and the fine plans included of the remains, noted the fact (which had arisen because Bell was working outwards from a cleared centre) that the discoveries contained 'little that can be called an addition to our architectural knowledge'. [2]

In 1892 the Third and Fourth Progress Reports were also reviewed in the JRIBA, with architectural details reported of three monasteries near the Lankarama Dagoba, and praise of the Vijayarama Monastery for its solidity of structure and simplicity of ornamentation, which 'differentiate it from the ruins hitherto discovered in the city itself'. [3]

The Kegalla Report was reviewed in 1893 by Simpson, who later wrote to a Ceylon journal, the *Monthly Literary Register*, that he felt that 'my notice of it is scarcely worthy of its great merits'. [4]

The Fifth Progress Report was also reviewed in the JRIBA, but the Sixth Progress Report only in the MLRC, which had previously been reprinting Simpson's reviews. In this, in 1896, a hint of trouble appeared, for the Report had only reached the work of July to September 1891:

> Delay is doubtless partly due to the Surveyor-General's office where the plates which accompany the report were lithographed, but as they were executed in 1893 and 1894 we cannot see why two more years should have elapsed before the report was issued. [5]

Delay : Reasons and remedies

What other factors were operating, first to slow and then to stop Bell's Progress Reports? He wrote occasional articles for the MLRC, and it must be remembered that through this period he was carrying the editorship of the JRASCB, with all the reading and selection of contributions which this entailed.

The account by Jules Leclercq has shown that Bell enjoyed guiding visitors to Anuradhapura, but did so with a thoroughness that was time-consuming. Official visitors frequently required attention; the Governor Havelock, and those he introduced. In 1896 we hear of many 'scholars and distinguished persons, English and foreign'; royal personages included the Empress Eugenie in 1908. Entertaining unofficial and stranded visitors also involved expense, which led Bell in 1898 to complain to Sir Edward Noel-Walker. [6]

The illnesses which dogged Bell's work force and assistants did not leave him unscathed. He suffered from fever at Padaviya in September and October 1891, and on December 9, 1892 Albert Gray wrote to sympathise over a liver attack, 'Try to get to the hills if you can't get leave home. It does not do to try nature too far'. Though he never went 'home', Bell took some leave. He wrote to the Governor on December 12, 1894, 'Leave at the seaside sent me back to my hobby-horse like the proverbial giant refreshed'. [7]

An extensive absence from archaeology was the period from May to December 1894 when Bell was acting as District Judge at Kalutara. A letter of tribute to him as Police Magistrate, from his staff on his departure, is notable for its inflated enthusiasm:

> Sir, we beg leave most respectfully to offer you our sincere and heartfelt thanks for the kindness and courtesy shown to us during the time we have been fortunate to work under you. The highest esteem, regard and appreciation of your work: official, public, social, private, recognised by the Public, the Bar, and your subordinates, will ere long be proclaimed at the contemplated Demonstration got up in acknowledgement of you. The brush of the greatest painter Raphael could not adequately paint or describe a lily. In like manner we have no words to adequately sing psalms of praise and blow *tirra-lirra* to the highest encomium you richly deserve from us. Severance of your connection with this department is a cause of regret to us, but as the archaeological work demands your excellent services as none equal to you is procurable, and that special and laudable work will pave your way to build a tower of Fame not unequal to the one gloriously won by Col. Layard at Nineveh, we have the satisfaction of knowing that to us and our posterity the history of the buried cities of the colony and her hidden treasures will be told by your able, scholarly and masterly pen. Wishing you and your family abundance of blessings from Heaven. [8]

In 1891 Bell, between achieving the Third and Fourth Progress Reports, had told Gregory that he would like six months to organise each of such reports, as had his counterparts in India; but he had no reliable overseer to relieve him of duties while he wrote. European Assistants stayed for only short periods, and in 1898 Bell was to write, 'Since June 1895, or for three and a half years, the Archaeological Commissioner has had to conduct the Archaeological Survey without the aid of any Assistant'. [9] In such circumstances the need to report had to compete with the need to press on with the Survey, the completion of which was a horizon continually receding. By 1897 little more than Kegalla and the North-Central Province had been covered, and perhaps half of Anuradhapura and three quarters of Sigiriya had been excavated. Polonnaruwa was still a buried city, also Tissamaharama, which he called '*nominis umbra* - the shadow of a glorious past'. Circuit work occupied the dry months of the year, between August and October, as the plan was to survey a province generally, then areas in detail, before excavation could commence. [10]

In 1898 the Government realised with dismay that they had received no report on work performed at Anuradhapura later than 1891. Consequently Bell was called upon to furnish annually a general Administration Report. [11] He responded that he could not be set free to write without an European Chief Assistant who could manage coolies and who was not an 'unwilling tiro'. Otherwise there could be danger of the Archaeological Survey dying with him. His need for staff was increased because his estimate for 1899 envisaged work at the three sites of Anuradhapura, Sigiriya and Polonnaruwa as well as the Circuit. [12]

The time was ripe for an official response, which came in 1899 with the report of a Committee appointed to consider and report upon the question of the Archaeological Survey of Ceylon, in particular 'the system which should be adopted and the extent to which it should be pursued'. They commended the results so far achieved, believing 'that the success hitherto attained has been mainly due to the rare union in Mr. Bell of the necessary qualifications - scholarship, power of organisation and physical strength', and also due to his unflagging devotion to the work.

The Committee showed itself aware of the loss of efficiency caused by Bell's recurring lack of an European Assistant. For example he had had to undertake the necessary photography, besides all the direction of the working parties. It seemed that Mr. Wickremasinghe would be best employed in London on the literary treatment of inscriptions, and Gunasekera, Mudaliyar, as his correspondent in Ceylon; and an European Labour Assistant should be appointed. [13]

Although in 1899 Mr. C.E.Dashwood was appointed, in 1901 he was absent on sick leave. This impelled Bell to suggest remaining himself at Anuradhapura and working at Polonnaruwa only in the dry months. In August Bell attributed his continued delay in producing a report to illnesses of his clerks. He also stressed the absence of Dashwood, but this did not satisfy the Colonial Secretary's Office, which was therefore reluctant to promote him to Class I. On his part, when Dashwood resigned in October, Bell commented that the Assistant's post carried insufficient pay to attract good men. [14] In November 1901 Bell submitted in a Memorandum that instead of immediate detailed reports he should submit annual summaries to cover 1890 to 1900, and in addition continue his Progress Reports from number Eight, for, he said, several were ready. The situation was serious enough for Bell's friend Ievers, now in the Colonial Secretary's Office, to intervene. He approved of the plan and urged Bell to divide his work more evenly between office and 'field'. He told the Governor that he had pointed out to Bell that except for the clearing of the sites and excavations there was nothing to show for the Government expenditure on archaeology for the past ten years, and that, if he died, or was invalided, his field-work, without information on record, would be more or less useless. [15]

Late in April of 1902 Ievers wrote a long and frank private Memorandum to Government. He was obliged to make some severe remarks, for though Bell was a very old friend he was absolutely unbusinesslike, and was 'much astonished when his manifest delay is pointed out'. He had been warned that 'there was no record to show antiquarians your results'; and, by

Delay : Reasons and remedies

Government, that he would forfeit promotion unless he sent in brief annual reports. Yet, though he had promised summaries in three months, he had not sent them. Ievers found his excuses 'very disingenuous', and his claim that he had been promised a trained assistant was 'what in any other man would be impudence'. Ievers continued:

> I don't want to be hard on him, but I cannot swallow all this, and I think when the Lieutenant-Governor sees him he might point out that Mr. Bell has been treated in a most exceptional and considerate manner, and that he has failed to realise this.
>
> The fact is that Mr. Bell is a compound of Harold Skimpole and Mr. Micawber (if we go to Dickens for a sample of him). He is very keen on his work, but 'dilettante', and having had so long 'a free hand' he has got into that sort of *laziness* that he will only interest *himself personally* in his excavations and inscriptions and cannot endure the trouble of conveying his acquisitions and discovery to others. His plausibility is great, and he is quite childlike in inventing any reasons to show he is right and everyone else is wrong.
>
> At the same time I know he has done good work in his special branch, and what we want is to have some record of it. [16]

Ievers concluded by advising that Bell be prohibited from any more field work, that his labour force be dispersed, and his promotion be held in abeyance till he had given the Government all the reports due.

In the event, in May, Bell was summoned and told that field work would be stopped unless provisional reports were produced in the next few weeks. Bell promised something for June, and indeed by August something was forthcoming (though not published) on the period 1890 to 1894. [17] For Bell had not been unassisted in 1902. When the post of Labour Assistant had been advertised at the end of the previous year, despite Bell's pessimism, there were more than fifty applicants. Out of the short-listed twelve Bell preferred John Still and H.S.Cameron (the latter a Cambridge graduate).

John Still had been a tea-planter since 1897 under Mr. Arthur Anson. In November 1901 Anson recommended him in these terms:

> He has good health and leads a life which should ensure his retaining it. He has unusually good natural ability; great powers of observation, a good ear for languages, and great tact in dealing with natives. He is an excellent photographer and has great interest in anything to do with native life and customs. He has not had very great education from the school point of view, but is a great reader, and would make a point of acquiring all historical and archaeological knowledge bearing on the work.

Alfred Clark, Assistant Conservator of Forests, who also sent a testimonial, dwelt on Still's enthusiasm, his fluency in Tamil and his steady character. In fact, he thought him really too good for the lonely ill-paid post. [18] Still himself in his application asked whether the post would lead to similar work, as he was now in regular planting, but thought the interest of the work would compensate for less pay. Bell advised the employment of Still, and he was appointed from

January 1, 1902. After ten months service Bell recommended the grant of an increment to his Assistant, saying:

> He has from the first shown a keen and intelligent interest in his work and has worked loyally and with unflagging zeal... with more experience and perhaps a closer attention to the petty monotony incidental to his work he should make an invaluable assistant. [19]

The danger voiced by Ievers that Bell would forfeit promotion receded when in 1903 the Governor, West Ridgeway, asked for permission to promote him in the Service from Class II to Class I, writing:

> It is necessary that he should again be seconded for archaeological work, as it would be difficult at present to find a substitute to carry on the work of the Archaeological Department, and meanwhile Mr. Bell's special qualifications would be practically wasted in Revenue and Judicial appointments. On the other hand, it would be unjust to deprive him of all prospect of promotion because it is to the interest of the Government to have him employed upon special work. [20]

The request was approved in August and thereafter Bell moved up in the service according to his seniority.

Though Still had thought the interest of his work would compensate for less pay, he was not entirely settled in it, and in September 1903 went home on leave to check a possible position in a solicitor's firm headed by his uncle. While in England he approached the Colonial Office about a post in Egypt or the Sudan. The Governor, Sir Henry Blake, in a testimonial stressed his excellent mental and physical qualities, and said that it was 'impossible to get a better man for the very special duties he has been discharging as assistant to Mr. Bell'. However, Still found no other post and returned to Ceylon. [21]

Bell also valued Still, his colloquial Tamil, his experience with coolies, tact and strong constitution, enough to propose, in July 1904, increments to his pay and a change of title to 'Assistant to the Archaeological Commissioner'. Bell thought Still might even succeed himself, though a little doubtful whether he would face the burden of office work. He would need to study more archaeology and epigraphy and pass examinations in Tamil and Sinhalese. Still accepted the conditions leading to promotion, passed an examination in Tamil and aimed at one in Sinhalese. He was prepared to undertake scholarly work and indexed the English version of the *Mahawansa*, carrying this through in a most thorough manner, as Bell remarked in the Annual Report of 1905:

> The Index comprised every name, whether of persons, places, buildings, tanks, channels etc., arranged alphabetically, besides a chronological list of wars, campaigns and battles as well as genealogical trees of the several royal families. [22]

Unhappily, despite help from Still in his work, Bell's promises in 1902 of progress with his reports had been insufficiently realised. By May 31, 1903 Annual Reports for 1895 to 1900 had

Delay : Reasons and remedies

reached the Lieutenant-Governor, Sir E.F. im Thurn, and rough drafts of the full Progress Reports 8 to 12. However, on April 12, 1904, Sir Henry Blake heard that the latter had not been printed.

Even Ievers had reluctantly suggested in 1902, when he was Acting Colonial Secretary, that Bell should be told to stop field work. Since then Ievers had gone home on sick leave and resigned from the Service - his death was to come in 1905. So in the crisis of Bell's affairs he had lost a friend, and he was told that operations must be discontinued, apart from jungle clearing by a small group of expert coolies supervised by Still. Meanwhile, under threat of his increments being stopped, Bell was commanded to complete all promised Reports. [23]

Bell's reaction was strong. On May 19, 1904 he submitted a Memorandum, apologetic but defensive, and pleaded earnestly for continuance of the work, with himself overseeing only.

Sir E.F. im Thurn was unconvinced, though he regretted the clamp-down, writing:

> I have great sympathy with the enquiring turn of mind which makes Mr. Bell thirst for further field work and fresh discoveries, but in the interests of the Colony and of the Archaeological Survey in general, I feel that I must harden my heart and recommend that no further destruction of antiquities, for the sole information of Mr. Bell, be permitted until his record of all the work for all the past years is brought up to date. He is now 53 and not in good health and not a rapid literary worker. Before retirement he may not do much more than record properly what he has already done. On the other hand Mr. Bell is wrapped up in his field work and is used to an active and out-of-doors life, and it is probably true that it would be unwise in our own interests suddenly to cut him off from this. [24]

He advised that Bell should keep an eye on limited work at Polonnaruwa, devoting himself to reports while Still, with a small staff at Anuradhapura, could keep the ruins clear there and at Sigiriya. The Governor, Blake, agreed to all this for otherwise 'most valuable investigation' would be rendered useless.

Bell made the best of the suspension of field work in 1904 and 1905, in his report on 'Archaeology' for 1905 to the RASCB, saying:

> By staying his hand for the time from further excavations, the Archaeological Commissioner was able to advance substantially the record of the Department's work. The belated Annual Reports of the Archaeological Survey for the eleven years 1890 to 1900 inclusive, with the *Summary of Operations 1890-1900*, have been issued together. [25]

However, the plans and plates to go with the new issues were long postponed, and only rough drafts were seen of detailed Progress Reports - the eighth to the twelfth - which never appeared.

Besides the duties at the sites that fell to Still, he was able in 1905 to make an archaeological tour of East Wanni, a form of activity congenial to him. His descriptions in the Annual Report for 1905 show the variety of his interests:

> It is impossible to explore such hills as those at Periya Puliyan-kulam and Erupotana without attempting to form some idea of the manner of men who lived in the rock cells. Their wants were simple and few, and their lives must to some extent have been influenced by the stern wildness, and in places

123

grandeur, of their surroundings. The mistakes that occur in the inscriptions seem to argue that they were illiterate, for even a hermit would probably prefer to have his label written correctly.

Buddhism must have been real indeed when the priesthood, holding as they did most of the power in the country, were content with these simple abodes, in which there can have been nothing of magnificence and little of comfort, however they were embellished.

At several places, for example at Yaku-madu-yawa, he observed possibly 'primitive' stone circles. Of Bogaha-vewa, 'the tank of the Bo-tree', he wrote:

My guide, an old man, told me that in his father's time this tank was the haunt of a clan of Veddas; and in one place he showed me where they had used bricks from the neighbouring ruins to build their little fireplaces with. The Sinhalese conqueror built and decayed and the Vedda, who was before him, uses his ruins after him. [26]

On a small rocky hill, Kandasami-malai, Still found a little temple only thirteen foot square, saying 'it must have been a little gem of stonework'. He continued:

Of all the ruins I have visited in Ceylon the little temple on this hill occupies the most charming position. It is situated on the end of a low wooded promontory that runs out into the lagoon, nearly opposite to, and three miles distant from, the opening into the sea. It is thus almost surrounded by water, and the view from the summit is exceedingly beautiful.

The immediate foreground is pale blue water and low-lying wooded spits that cut up the lagoon into bays, which are dotted with tiny wooded islets and with little archipelagoes of pink white-topped rocks. Beyond these the far shores of the lagoon shimmer in the mirage; and beyond them the sea on one side and the forest on three fade into blue, and imperceptibly become one with the sky. [27]

Although in 1906 a severe attack of malarial fever had sent Still on six weeks sick leave in the hills in May and June, excavation had been resumed and the annual grant, which had been reduced, was restored. Still worked in Anuradhapura at Vessagiriya in July when Bell was at Polonnaruwa. However, from 1905 to 1907 Bell had been much involved in a correspondence with Wickremasinghe in England over the production of *Epigraphia Zeylanica*. No Annual Reports were published in 1905 or 1906, but in 1907 those for 1901 and 1902 appeared. [28]

This progress was not quite good enough, though, for the new Governor, Sir H.E.McCallum, for he told the RASCB in the following year:

In view of the fact that Mr.Bell is getting on in life, as several of us here are doing, I thought it was very much more desirable that the Annual Reports should be put on record, rather than that he should, by continuing excavation, accumulate an additional mass of undigested matter. [29]

Fieldwork was, therefore, again checked for Bell to make up leeway. It was in any case handicapped, as he himself was to write in the Annual Report of 1907:

Delay : Reasons and remedies

The Archaeological Commissioner was again left single-handed for the last six months of the year, owing to his Assistant's absence in England on leave. From July, therefore, no fresh excavations were undertaken at Anuradhapura. [30]

Still was in fact initially on sick leave, but in November 1907 he wrote to the Under Secretary of State of his intention to resign his position. This was because Anuradhapura was a notoriously malarial place, and his post had no pension attached. He decided reluctantly, for he had loved the outdoor life and the keeping of pets (seven leopards, three bears, deer, etc.). Still was applying for a job in British East Africa. His original planter employer, Arthur Anson, in a testimonial stressed his excellent relationship with natives, as also did Lord Elgin, the Secretary of State for the Colonies. However, Still did not get this post but instead was re-employed in Ceylon as Additional Assistant Land Settlement Officer. [31]

Bell was appreciative of Still's useful services and wrote in the Annual Report of 1908, 'Mr. Still's resignation was a great loss to the Department, as he had proved himself a most zealous and capable officer'. [32]

The problem of an Assistant to the Archaeological Commissioner had now re-surfaced, and with it Bell's proposal in his Memorandum of February 15 that the two Draughtsmen, D.A.L.Perera and W.M.Fernando, should replace a single more highly paid European Assistant. They had already often done the work and knew it well; they could continue as draughtsmen provided two others assisted. [33]

The plan was in fact approved, and the Governor, McCallum, told the RASCB in 1908 that he had consulted Bell with this result, adding, 'I am glad to say that he has reported to me that two native gentlemen, who have been assisting him for years past in the work, are qualified to carry on the work which Mr. Still has been doing. I have, therefore, assented'. [34]

In his Memorandum Bell had noted the advantage in his proposals of his being freed of Assistant's duties, the 'petty mechanical details', at two of the three sites being worked. This should, of course, expedite the production of Annual Reports, and in 1908 Bell achieved those of 1903 and 1904, but they remained in arrears, only that for 1905 appearing in 1909.

Alongside the continual work at the three main sites, between 1909 and 1912 the operations of the Archaeological Survey were more widespread, embracing also work at outlying sites such as Nalanda and Yapahuwa. In the circumstances it is not surprising that Bell's Annual Reports remained annual but still in arrears; 1906 and 1907 appeared in 1910 and 1911 respectively, and none in 1912. A clue to a contributory cause is that Bell was in the Victoria Eye Hospital, Colombo, from October 1911 to January 1912. After his retirement Bell remained at Anuradhapura to finish the work on his Annual Reports 1908 to 1912. [35]

16

Anuradhapura and Mihintale

At Anuradhapura, in the years after 1900, the circle of operations extended steadily, the chief objects of which were to uncover the monastic remains around and between the great dagabas, and to explore the very ancient buildings and cave dwellings of the southern site of Vessagiriya. Thus the area between the Thuparama and Ruwanveli was explored from 1900 to 1903 and that round the Mirisavetiya from 1902 to 1903. After the halt in operations decreed in 1904 and 1905, the work was completed in 1906.

In 1901 Bell had decided that one of the vihares south of the Thuparama Dagaba, first excavated in 1897, merited restoration. In his report to the RASCB on the work of 1903 he wrote:

> One of the finest of the ancient vihares of Anuradhapura lies a little south of the Thuparama Dagaba. It stands out pre-eminent from the generality of the ruins of this area, in the massiveness of its moulded basement slab, and, specially, for the fine moonstone and quaintly ornamented balustrades of the entrance stairs. The chaos of its slabs testified to the mighty convulsive power of the forest trees which formerly covered the site.
>
> In 1901 this vihare was taken in hand for restoration, gutted to its foundations, and all slabs and broken pillars laid outside ready to be replaced. Last year the ruin was partially rebuilt on the old lines, and the restoration will be completed gradually. [1]

In his Annual Report for that year he said that the work could not be completed until the Department was supplied with the requisite lifting gear. It was the lack of this sort of equipment which Oertel had pointed out when recommending a proper vote for restoration work.

Bell found that the fourteen monasteries surrounding the Mirisavetiya Dagaba were markedly uniform in plan and built in a simple style. In his report to the RASCB on the final season in 1906 he summarised as follows:

> Each has its own entrance porch, directly behind which stands the vihare with satellite *piriven* (here only two instead of the usual four) lying off the front angles, and an occasional extra building or two. The stonework is in the simplest style. There is a marked general absence of that elaboration in the carved accessories to stairs (moonstones, terminals, balustrades), so noticeable elsewhere. [2]

In the southern part of Anuradhapura, before moving on to the Vessagiriya, Bell had excavated some ruins below the bund of the Tissavewa. He says:

> Immediately below the embankment of Tissavewa, and two to three hundred yards north of the Issurumuniya Rocks and temple, is a smaller line of boulders. The overhanging sides of these rocks

were utilized as cave shelters, and their summits for superstructures; whilst at their foot, on the east, other buildings were erected.

The chief interest of this small group of ruins (now isolated, but formerly without doubt connected with Issurumuniya and the Vessagiri caves, situated still further south) lies in the two beautifully designed baths, with attached dressing-rooms (still in excellent preservation), built of dressed stone. The semi-arched recess, rock-cut, at the smaller bath is flanked on either side by realistic carvings in low relief of elephants emerging from a lotus pond.[3]

The Annual Report for 1901 has the following appreciation of the lively carvings on either side of the 'dressing-room' of Pokuna A:

> The sloping face of the rock (a breadth of 32 ft. in all) on either side of this strangely cramped, round-back, chamber has been carved into wondrously realistic bas-reliefs in perfect keeping with the *pokuna*. These represent elephants in a lotus-covered tank. On the rock slope to the right three elephants are shown lazily disporting themselves in the water, undisturbed, amid lotuses and fish. On the left the scene is vividly changed. Some sudden alarm has roused the elephants; one seems to be scenting danger, the other two are already in full flight. This absolutely unique piece of carving is without exception the most spirited and life-like to be seen anywhere among the ruins of Anuradhapura.[4]

On the wall of an adjacent cave was traced a representation of the *Sakvala Chakraya*, or ancient 'world map'. Bell gives a very detailed description of this, beginning as follows:

> Cut shallowly on a steeply projecting rock face, a great *chakra*, or circle, 6 ft. in diameter, scored by rectangular divisions containing figures (mostly small circles), the whole girt, as a tyred wheel, by a band on which is displayed variant piscine and crustacean life swimming round from right to left.

In the centre of the circle there are seven concentric rings. The space between these central rings and the outer circular band is, as Bell says, divided up by vertical and horizontal lines into different shaped boxes, or oblongs, and in these other signs are placed, irregularly. These signs and symbols are mostly tiny circles with a cross superimposed, which Bell identifies as the astrological symbol of the earth. But there are other unexplained empty circles, concentric circles, umbrella-like emblems and phallic symbols. Bell does not attempt to elucidate all of these figures, but comes to the following general conclusion:

> This weird circular diagram, incised on the bare rock - even more unique in a way than the elephant bas-reliefs of Pokuna A - may with every show of reason claim to be an old-time cosmographical chart illustrating in naivest simplicity the Buddhistic notions of the universe.

> The concentric circles with their interspaces at the centre of the *chakra* can assuredly mean only the *Sakvala*, in the centre of which rises *Maha Meru*, surrounded by the seven seas (*Sidanta*) and walls of rock (*Yugandhara etc.*) which shut in that fabulous mountain, 1,680,000 miles in height, half below, half above, the ocean's surface. Sun and moon (in the second strips) lie on either side of the *Sakvala*:

round about in space are scattered innumerable other worlds represented by quadrisected circles. Below and around is the 'world of waters' (i.e. the circular band) in which swarm gigantic uncouth denizens - fish, turtle, crab, chank, and other marine fauna.

This ancient 'map of the world' - perhaps the oldest in existence - is of quite extraordinary interest. Its presence here, within an eremite's cave at an out-of-the-way nook of ancient Anuradhapura, testifies to the antiquity of that astronomical lore still pursued in some of the Buddhist monasteries of Ceylon. [5]

The excavations at Vessagiriya, begun by John Still in 1906, continued until 1911 with a break in 1908, gradually moving south, on and between the three upstanding groups of boulders named Rocks A, B and C. Of the site as a whole Bell said in 1911 that, 'before mattock and axe combined to rob it of its beauty, no more picturesque spot existed at Anuradhapura than this thickly wooded medley of rock and tumbled boulders, rising clear of the grass and mudland which surrounds it. [6]

In his brief report on the first year's work here Bell dated the ruins to an early period:

There can be no question as to the period when the buildings which once occupied this site were erected. Everything recalls the citadel on Sigiri-gala constructed by the parricide Kasyapa I in the fifth century A.D. Steps, walls, mouldings, all bear out the comparison. The two inscriptions of Mahindu IV (975-991 A.D.), found at Vessagiriya some years ago, allude to 'Bo Upulvan Kasubgiri Vehera', which the *Mahawansa* records was built by Kasyapa I (A.D. 479-497). So that architecture, lithic record, and ancient chronicle unite perfectly in confirming the identification of this site nearly fifteen centuries old. [7]

In 1907, when caves 9 and 10 in Rock B were explored, additional evidence appeared:

An inscription in Brahmi writing occurs below the drip (*katarama*) of both these caves. Both too still bear traces of frescoes which once covered their faces, affording additional testimony to the period (5th century) when the Vessagiriya Monastery, highly favoured by the parricide king Kasyapa (479-497 A.D.), was perhaps at the zenith of its importance.

On the rock wall of cave No. 9 may yet be seen, though very greatly weathered, the outline of a female figure, measuring 3 ft. by 2 ft., painted in yellow with dashes of red here and there and a touch of green. Seated, resting on her right palm with the right leg crossed horizontally, the lady has her left leg raised and knee bent, and is emphasising an animated discourse by left arm half outstretched and hand with open palm - a favourite attitude in Indian sculpture and painting.

A smaller figure - a prince with jewelled headdress, armlets, etc. - is just distinguishable on the worn plaster of cave No. 10. This figure measures 2 ft. by 1 ft. 6 in., and is coloured in red and yellow. The delineation in these paintings exhibits equal spirit and level of art as the corresponding and better-known frescoes at Sigiriya, very probably executed by the same artists. [8]

Bell's work at Anuradhapura in his final years was largely concerned with excavations around the Jetanawarama Dagaba and the restoration of its summit. But he also devoted much of the 1911-12 Report to a description of the remains to be found to the west of the Jetanawarama-Lankarama area. Drawing on earlier descriptions by Smither and Burrows, and supplementing them by extracts from his own Progress Reports, together with the results of subsequent personal exploration and some small excavations, he came to very definite conclusions as to their purpose.

Originally they had been supposed to be secular buildings, but Bell identified them as a type of monastery, saying that, 'the grounds upon which these isolated ruins (despite their divergence from the type of stereotyped sacred buildings scattered broadcast in Anuradhapura) are considered by the writer to be veritable *ecclesiastical structures*, and integral components of Buddhist monasteries of their own special class, are set out at the end of his Notes'. [9]

He sets out twelve 'characteristics of the Western Ruins'. Most distinctive was the fact that the buildings were situated on rocky sites, and that the central building consisted of a double-platformed structure, connected by a stone bridge, and the fact that the back platform was encircled by a narrow ditch or 'moat'. Bell says:

> The object of these 'moats' - for such they would become practically during the wet season - is left to conjecture, as much as is the unexplainable location (perhaps from pure ascetic motive, unless for some occult reason) of these monastic buildings, generally on *bare rock*, exposed daily to the fiercest heat of the tropical sun.

The buildings were all very plain and unornamented, with the exception of the highly decorated lavatory stones or 'mutra-gal' which were covered with representations of buildings and sometimes animals. Of the elaborate lavatory arrangements he writes:

> One outhouse (often approached by curling path) specially dedicated to Cloacina was relegated, almost invariably, to a fixed position at a suitable distance from habitations. This was the *vesakiliya*, or jakes (with its double row of eight short stumps for wooden flooring) which was located to north-west. As this quarter would escape both south-west and north-east monsoon winds, sanitary, not religious reasons probably ruled its relative position. These latrines were supplemented by separate urinals (*kesakuti*), behind the *prakaraya* but close.

Bell had found monasteries of a similar type elsewhere in the North-Central Province, and in particular in the remote hills of Ritigala. He identified the sect which inhabited them as follows:

> What ascetical monks, then, once bore with the isolation and physical discomfort of habitations built on exposed sun-smitten rock, rather than accept shelter at better-found, cool, and shady Monasteries of gregarious, if less austere, brethren of the robe ?

> The *Mahawansa* furnishes the answer. It was for the 'Pansukulika brethren' - the rag-robed fraternity - that Sena I (846-866 A.D.) 'built, as it were by a miracle, a great Vihara at Arittha Pabbata (Ritigala), and endowed it with great possessions', giving to it 'royal privileges and honours'...

The Pansukulika monks, like the 'Theravansaja brethren', were of the Maha Vihare fraternity; and the old chronicle records that Kasyapa V (son of Sena II, 929-939 A.D.) 'rebuilt the Marichavatti (Mirisaveti) Vihare' and gave it to the latter fraternity.

From this he goes on to trace the gradual change of the types of monastery in Anuradhapura from the highly decorated to the bare and simple:

> Now, it is in the Mirisavetiya ruins to the west of the *Uda Maluwa*, or Sacred Bo Tree enclosure, that is found the penultimate link of the architectural chain which connects the *quincunx* type of monastic buildings (*vihare* and four *piriven*), so universal at the northern, central, eastern, and southern ruins of Anuradhapura, with the isolated groups situated still further west on the Arippu and Outer Circular Roads.
>
> At Mirisavetiya the five grouping has dwindled to *three* (vihare and two annexes), and of these some few had not finally discarded, for plain unadorned accessories on simple lines, the *Naga doratupala* guardian terminals and the curling *makara* balustrades so greatly favoured at the older Monasteries of Anuradhapura.
>
> The final link in the chain is found at the northern Block G, where the triple arrangement of the buildings - *vihare* and pair of *piriven* - yet survived; but had so far yielded to the influence of the 'Western Monasteries' as to surround the ordinary type of single buildings with a *prakaraya* - here not yet of stone, but brick-walled - entered by a stone-built portico of the pillared and slab-ceiled design adopted at - and only at - those Monasteries.
>
> The Buddhist monks who occupied the inclement rock stretches, apart from other fraternities, may well have been a Pansukulika schism which had cut itself adrift from their Buddhist brethren, and shunned haunts of men. That such semi-isolation in no way lessened, but only increased, the power they exercised and the respect they received is amply borne out by the *Mahawansa*, which emphasizes the deference shown to, and the favours conferred upon these jungle-haunting monks by the Ceylon Rulers of the 10th century. [10]

In 1909 a grant of Rs. 5,000 was allocated for clearing work at Anuradhapura, and some surplus was set aside for operations at the near-by site of Mihintale. Bell said:

> In the recollection of Mihintale hill and ruins carried away by the ordinary visitor, the sights begin and end with the long stairways, the stone boats and inscription-flanked vihare ruin, the picturesquely placed Ambastale Dagaba ringed in by graceful columns mid coconut palms (bringing to mind the similar Thuparama and 'Lankarama' Dagabas of Anuradhapura), the bold roundness of Maha-seya Dagaba which crowns Mihintale-kanda, the rock-cut *Naga pokuna*, with may-be - *si Dis placeat*, if the guiding 'gods' are complacent! - descent to that cool rock-retreat, 'Mahinda's bed' so-called, and a cursory look at the ornamental, but far less ancient, 'stone bath', fatuously connected with the same Apostle of Buddhism, near the half-way terrace.

Anuradhapura and Mihintale

Bell was determined to open up the whole area of outlying caves and ruins which, he said, 'have remained to this day "a sealed book", except to a few adventurous spirits, determined to grope here, there, anywhere for the rock shelters of eremites and the structural monasteries of the monks who have lived and died there'. But he gave the following warning of what would be his methods in describing his finds:

> It is not the province of a cut-and-dried Archaeological Report to 'spread itself' in delightful flowery 'word-pictures' of ruins. Are not such lightsome descriptions (often engrossing enough, albeit liable to rise at times to high falutin nonsense) written in the pages of many a modern 'guide-book' and popular magazine, where he who runs may read all - and more than - he expected.

> Official Archaeological Survey Reports, *qua* permanent technical documents, are strictly concerned with the *accurate record in detail* - frequently *ad nauseam* - of characteristic forms of ancient architecture, art, and palaeography, the practical, dry-as-dust side of archaeology rather than the aesthetic.

In a note he adds:

> This hard and fast rule of self-restraint to *severely condensed account* of ancient ruins in the Archaeological Survey Reports, issued by the Ceylon Government since 1890, the Archaeological Commissioner has studiously set himself to follow during his long tenure of the office. Much easier, and far more pleasant, would it have been to give full rein to the Pegasus of description, had official limitations justified excursion into popular narrative.[11]

Nevertheless, when he comes in his account to describe the stone bath to the right of the steps half-way up, he does not stint hyperbole, saying that, 'there is probably no more handsome specimen of bold artistic work of its kind in granite to be found in Ceylon than this finely conceived piece of sculpture'. After explaining the construction of the bath, one side carved out of the rock itself, and with the remaining three sides built up and ornamented with various human and animal carvings, he says:

> The striking *tout ensemble* combination of the delightful moulded lines of the whole structure, the quaintly carved reliefs of its dado, and the life-like rampant lion guarding the bath, cannot fail to win unalloyed admiration for this masterpiece of sculpture, as boldly designed as it is perfectly executed...

> The escape-water from the bath was made to pass out of the jaws of a fearsome *sinhaya* rising on its hind legs as though about to spring. The lion, a beast 7 ft. 4 in. in height and a pronounced male, is cut in very high relief, standing out from the ramp 1 ft. 9 in. This is perhaps the best executed piece of spirited animal sculpture *in the round* to be seen anywhere in the Island.

Under the heading of 'Restoration' he adds, 'The rampant lion at the Stone Bath, which had been badly broken, was strongly renewed as it stood of old. It now presents a wonderfully lifelike presentment of petrified leonine rage'.[12]

Operations at Mihintale were held up by a dispute over claims by the Mihintale-kanda monks to certain Crown lands, and in the 1911-12 Report Bell had to list those areas which he had not 'yet exploited by axe, pick and spade'. These included the more distant Kaludiya Pokuna ruins, which lie to the south. Here again Bell was tempted to allow himself the luxury of giving 'full rein to the Pegasus of description'. He writes with enthusiasm as follows:

> The first peep of this delightful glen, as it suddenly bursts on the charmed gaze, is entrancing in its quiet picturesqueness. A more perfect sanctuary for 'the sons of Buddha' could not be found anywhere throughout the length and breadth of Ceylon.
>
> Lying in the valley between Et Vehera-kanda towering to north-east, and the detached Anaikutti-kanda - the 'elephant-calf hill' to the high elongated Mihintale 'tusker' (*eta*) range - this dell nestles happily in unmarred loveliness all its own. Fringed by umbrageous trees, which dip their boughs in its placid depths, and with the hills offer inviting shade, the sheltered tarn has acquired for all time the pertinent designation *Kalu-diya Pokuna*, the 'Black-water Pool'.
>
> Around the marge of this winsome little lake was laid out, with skilful adaptation to the varied layers and interspaces between the foot-boulders of the guardian hills, a complete Monastery - isolated, 'so near and yet so far' - from the gregarious Buddhistic Establishments of Mihintale. [13]

Bell could not indeed complete his plans for the excavation of Mihintale, and there were large areas of Anuradhapura undug, and to some extent unrecorded. Time was running out. From October 1911 to January Bell was under treatment at the Victoria Eye Hospital, and from September 1912 he went on leave preparatory to retirement. In his account of the years 1911-12 his frustration at being unable to finish his work, and his desire to direct his successor to those areas which he felt to be most important, may clearly be read, particularly in the pressing footnotes.

Ayrton, the next Archaeological Commissioner, did carry on with the excavation of some of the Western Monasteries. He came to a conclusion about them similar to that outlined by Bell. In his Annual Report for 1912-13, the only one he lived to complete, he wrote:

> The complete excavation of so many buildings of one type should, one would think, have yielded some clue to their origin and the purpose for which they were built, but this was not so, and even the dating of them is uncertain. The only inscription found was a line of five letters on a coping stone of the moat round the second platform of one of the larger buildings, the letters of which date to about the tenth century A.D. In the Memoir on these buildings reasons were given for considering that these buildings were not secular palaces, but the monasteries of the Pansukulika monks who dwelt on the Tapovana, or 'Ascetics' Forest', and who were at the height of their power at Anuradhapura from 700-950 A.D. This theory is supported by a poor array of facts, but as it is the only satisfactory one yet put forward is worth serious consideration. Further excavations at Ritigala, Manekanda, and the numerous other sites where such buildings as these exist may throw more light on this interesting subject. [14]

Anuradhapura and Mihintale

Ayrton never published the Memoir to which he refers, but when Hocart took over the Survey in 1920 Ayrton's papers were collected together. The material on 'The Western Monasteries of Anuradhapura' was published in the first of the new series of Memoirs which Hocart edited. [15]

Since that time many other parts of Anuradhapura have been excavated and re-excavated, and some of Bell's work criticised and his conclusions questioned. But his connection with the great buried city will never be forgotten - and the house that was built for him there has itself been listed as an historic monument.

17

Outlying Sites

Bell was not exclusively concerned with the larger sites. In his Circuit reports he had recorded many isolated remains and made deductions and recommendations for action. He prided himself on always referring to discoveries made and excavations undertaken before his time, though often only to point out what he believed to be mistaken interpretations. This habit makes his reports a mine of information on early records. It was, however, perhaps a little excessive to insist on interleaving Still's account of his circuit in East Wanni in 1905 with extracts, in square brackets, from J.P.Lewis's *Manual of Vanni*, published in 1895.

One site in which he was particularly interested was that of Tantri Malai. He visited it in 1896 and in the Annual Report for that year he briefly described the square building known as the 'Potgula', which he calls a 'campanile', the small dagaba and the sedent and recumbent Buddhas, remarking that 'the execution of the whole falls short of the finish and magnitude of the not dissimilar *ot pilimaya* at the "Gal Vihare", Polonnaruwa'. [1]

In the Annual Report for 1907, possibly because it treated at length the Polonnaruwa Gal Vihare, Bell issued in Appendix B a full description of the two Buddha figures at Tantri Malai and suggested that they were copies of those at Polonnaruwa which 'were undoubtedly executed by Parakrama Bahu the Great (1164-1197 A.D.)'. He continued:

> The rock-sculptured figures at Tantri Malai were almost certainly carved, if not by the same ruler, at least by Nissanka Malla (1198-1207 A.D.), his only worthy successor prior to the subjugation of the Island by the Southern Indian invaders under Kalinga Magha, which followed within a few years. That sudden inroad, and the chaos that ensued, probably prevented the completion of the images etc., and brought about the final abandonment of Tantri Malai as a Buddhist monastery. [2]

It was John Still who next visited the site, after he had left the Archaeological Survey. He spent a week there in December 1909, living in a cave, and gave an account of this in an article in the JRASCB. He had found an inscription of single letters, lightly traced on the stones of the 'campanile' and, ascribing the form of the letters confidently to the latter half of the eleventh or to the twelfth century A.D., he confirmed Bell's estimate of the period of this 'Gal Vihare'. In this dating Bell had differed from Parker, who in his *Ancient Ceylon* had placed the ruins in the second or first century B.C. Still also found reason to disagree with Parker's use of the external size of bricks to date ruins. Bell, as editor of the Journal, added the following note:

> Mr. Still's view is supported by the Archaeological Commissioner. After many years' examination of brick ruins of all ages, mostly in the North-Central Province, Mr. Bell has had reluctantly to abandon 'the brick theory', except to the very limited degree of the broad generalization, arrived at by Mr. Still

independently, that 'old bricks are larger and newer bricks are smaller'. All bricks of 18 in. in length and upwards indubitably belong, with extremely rare exceptions, to an early period.

Bell then added an Appendix giving extracts from the diaries of the various Government Agents who had visited Tantri Malai, and another, entitled 'Additional archaeological notes', in which he gave his own descriptions of the 'Potgula' cave shrine and the two Buddha figures. He included pictures of these, which were also published in the Plans and Plates for 1896. [3]

Another site in which Bell took great interest, and which has since been reconstructed, is the isolated *Wata-da-ge* at Medirigiriya. Bell first visited the site when on circuit in 1897 and remarked that it had been previously inspected only by J.W.Birch and R.W.Ievers. He reported on it thus on August 19 in his diary:

> This beautiful shrine stands on the highest point of the rock, surrounded, like its known prototype at Polonnaruwa, by a slab wall carved with surface ornament and three concentric rows of graceful columns (sixty-eight in all) of the type seen at Thuparama and Lankarama, Anuradhapura. The inner and second row of pillars bear single lions and pilasters on their capitals, the outermost posturing *ganas* (dwarfs). In height this row of columns is but 9 ft. 9 in., while the two inner rows reach 16 ft. All are octagonal, and all are unbroken, save four; but several have lost their spreading capitals. Within the circle of pillars, seated on an *asanya*, is a Buddha in stone; probably one of four, cardinally placed, with their backs to a small central dagaba; the design on the stone slab wall encircling the dagaba and columns is the 'Buddhist-railing' pattern, in this differing from the flowered ornamentation of the Polonnaruwa *'Wata-da-ge'*.
>
> Undoubtedly Medirigiriya merits thorough clearing, excavation, and the restoration of its choice *'Wata-da-ge'*. [4]

In 1907, when the restoration of the other beautiful Wata-da-ge at Polonnaruwa had been largely achieved, Bell sent Perera to clear the site at Medirigiriya, to take photographs and make drawings. Perera spent three days there and his report is printed in the Annual Report for that year, preceded by a repeat of Bell's original account. [5]

But it was not until the 1940s that, despite the difficulties of the war years, the Archaeological Survey undertook the restoration of Medirigiriya, or as it is now known, Mandalagiri. The work was entrusted to W.E.Fernando, son of W.M.Fernando and thus one of the Fernando 'dynasty' of officers in the Survey. Paranavitana in the Report for the years 1941-6 pays tribute to his energy, resourcefulness and devotion to duty. Paranavitana also wrote an article on the work at the site for the *Illustrated London News*, which has excellent pictures of the shrine, before and after restoration. [6]

The Nalanda Gedige has also been recently restored. Bell had recommended it for conservation in a letter to Government on September 26, 1894 when he said:

> The ruin is of very great interest as, if it be not premature to hazard a conjecture, it appears to exhibit clear signs of the Mahayana or Northern Buddhist sect - the existence of which in Ceylon has hitherto been generally denied. [7]

H. C. P. Bell

Eventually in 1911 Bell felt able to start work. The following brief account appears in the report to the RASCB:

> As far back as 1893 land was acquired round this little known and solitary shrine of granite construction, popularly styled *'Gedige'*. It is situated on raised ground in paddy fields, picturesquely surrounded by low hills and wooded hamlets, about a mile north-east of the Nalanda Resthouse in the Central Province, half way between Matale and Dambulla.
>
> So long as Sigiriya demanded sole attention, the Archaeological Survey could not do any work here. In 1911 a small gang was detached from the labour force at Sigiriya to thoroughly root out all the jungle growth upon and around the ruin, besides cutting still further back the earth silt hiding the bold stylobate upon which the fane stands. The many slabs etc. fallen from the structure were stacked in heaps ready for future use.
>
> The ruin is manifestly Hindu in cult from its architecture and other evidence. The south facade stands nearly perfect: its upper part is filled by a semicircular niche containing in high relief a squat figure of Kubera, seated and bedecked like a prince.
>
> If the stones, when sorted, yield enough of the old material, the restoration of much of this unique and curiously placed shrine can be effected.[8]

The Annual Report of 1910-11 gives a very detailed description of the shrine as it then appeared, and of the surface ornaments and sculptures dug up around the temple. Bell says that, 'half are Hindu, half Buddhist - a combination which examination of the *"Gedi-ge"* temple led one to expect', and adds that 'very special importance attaches to this unique temple, as it is the *sole example* yet discovered in Ceylon of *composite styles of architecture judiciously blended* to form a delightfully homogeneous edifice'.[9]

In 1912 D.A.L.Perera made drawings to scale of the temple as it then stood, and of the pillars and sculptured slabs so far unearthed, and supervised further digging round about. Bell wrote:

> It will be necessary to gradually extend the open space to north and east of the 'Gedige' ruin, so far as practicable, in reasonable expectation of discovering other buried members of the structure, before it is partially dismantled with a view to correct reconstruction. For this fine edifice cannot be allowed to remain in its present semi-deceptive elevation, when all stones still on the ground have been recovered from the earth.[10]

In a note he adds that the work was commended to his successor, but that nothing other than routine weeding was done at Nalanda in 1913 and 1914.

The story is brought up to date in a small pamphlet by P.L.Prematilleke, who undertook the complete rebuilding of the shrine in the 1980s. It had become a matter of urgency, as the area was threatened with inundation by the waters diverted in the Mahaveli Project. The opportunity was taken to dismantle the ruin entirely and to rebuild it on a mound high above the waters. It stands now, reconstructed, approached by a flower-edged causeway and backed by the surrounding tree-clad hills.[11]

The only outlying site where Bell undertook any extensive restoration was Yapahuwa, an isolated fortress, built round and upon an outcrop of rock, utilising a position similar to that so majestically exploited at Sigiriya. But it is of a later period, dating from the thirteenth century and was probably only occupied for a short time. Within the outer walls of the city there was a small temple, the Dalada Maligawa, which had temporarily housed the Tooth Relic, and this Bell felt it was worth while to restore. But the site is chiefly remarkable for the three flights of stairs mounting to the Palace, the Raja Maligawa, and the richly decorated Porch at the head of the final staircase.

The Annual Report of 1910-11 devotes considerable space to this site. Bell as usual quotes extensively from previous descriptions, in particular from an article which he says is by J.Bailey of the Ceylon Civil Service, which appeared in a journal with very mixed subject matter entitled *Once a Week : an Illustrated Miscellany of Literature, Art, Science and Popular Information.*[12]

The original gives no author for the article, the anonymous writer merely saying that he was accompanied on his visit in 1850 by J.Woodford Birch of the Civil Service, but it is possible that Bell had private information on the subject. It is, however, an excellent short account, well illustrated, and Bell frequently draws on it in his detailed description of the carvings of the highest stairway and Porch.

In the Annual Report of 1910-11 Bell writes:

Along the top of the wing-walls lining the staircase, in gradual ascending order above the piers at bottom, are ranged, in couples, sculptures of demons' heads, 'Oriental' lions and mythical beasts, beasts in *messo relievo*, in high relief, and even in the full round.

Lowest, to each side of the higher steps of the first flight, is placed a scroll balustrade issuing from - not a *makara's* mouth as elsewhere universal, but - a *kirti-mukha* or face of the demon Rahu.

Above these, a pair of formidable lions with snarling jaws (quite possibly executed by a Further East sculptor) squat on their haunches guarding the short landing. These male *sinhayo* are cut wholly in the round except where their front feet and hind legs rest on pedestals. They stand 3 ft. 10 in. above the wall. Despite their weird conventionality the attitude of the enraged animal, half rising for attack, is admirably expressed.

Finally, where the last few steps reach the vestibule, the wings are formed by a sinuous balustrade on either hand terminating in a volute formed by the curling trunk of a tusked *gaja-sinha*, or fabulous elephant-headed lion. The mythical beast - carved deeply on both faces of the slab - is, as always, shown looking well back, the trunk here falling away over the rump to rest on a moulded pedestal.[13]

Of the sculptures which decorate the Porch at the head of the stairway Bell says:

The sculptures which delight the eye and instinctively command special meed of admiration for their marvellous symmetry and grace, are not the boldly executed animal warders of the staircase (lions etc.), which add much to the general grandeur of the whole scheme, but the more delicate efforts of the stonemasons as displayed in the chaste conception and artistic finish of the carved members of the Porch - the spirited frieze or dado of the vestibule's stereobate, the windows in its facade, with their elaborately embellished pediments, and, finally, the rich complex columns which sustained the roof.

Bell quotes Bailey for an impression of the ornamental dado:

> Both the terrace which projects in advance of the main building and the main building itself, are ornamented with carved stone mouldings, below which are groups of figures in bold relief, resting on a lower moulding designed to represent the upturned leaves of the lotus. The figures are excellent, and in great variety of attitude. They represent nautch girls, not oppressed with clothing, who are dancing with great spirit to the energetic music of tom-tom beaters and flageolet players, whose whole souls are in their work. The intense gravity of their faces is admirable; while the whole scene is so well 'told', that you can almost fancy you can see their heads nodding in time to their music, and hear the castanets in the girls' hands. The overhanging moulding has protected these figures from the weather, and the details are perfect. The ornaments of the female figures and the expression of their faces are as though the sculptor had but just completed his work.

Bell describes the musicians and dancers in rich detail, calling it 'a veritable cinematograph in granite of the most vivid and entrancing character'. A striking example is the third panel of the west dado:

> At the left end, a castanets player; then two women executing a 'can-can' dance in all its abandon, their left legs raised so as to touch the head; next a tom-tom beater with moustache and well-pointed beard of the mediaeval European type; then two female 'stick-players' clashing their short staves together, what time a woman plays the castanets on their left and another to right beats a *bera*. [14]

Bell then moves on to the stone windows which originally flanked the doorways of the Porch. A fragment of the east window was then in the hands of the priests of the neighbouring *Pansala*. The complete west window had been removed to the Colombo Museum, but in Bailey's time it had been still in place. Bell wrote that Bailey had devoted special care to the elaborate minutiae of this beautiful granite window and quotes him as follows:

> It consists of one slab of stone, measuring 4 ft. 7 in. by 3 ft. 3 in. and 7 in. thick. This thickness, however, is only preserved along the mouldings at its outer edges. Within the mouldings it has been reduced to a uniform thickness of 3 in. The name given to it by the natives exactly describes it, *siwoomaedurukawooloowa*, 'the perforated palace window'. The surface of the slab of stone has been perforated into forty-five rings, or circles, which admitted the light into the Entrance Hall, somewhat in the fashion of the tracery work at the Taj at Agra. In each circle is a sculptured figure, and scarcely two figures are alike.

There were rows of grotesque Bacchanalian figures, of nautch girls in different attitudes and of animals: the *gaja-sinha*, an elephant-headed lion, the lion itself, and in the top row, geese.

Outlying sites

Flowers, or stars, marked the angles. Bailey continues:

> The peculiar beauty of the window consists rather in the general effect produced by the arrangement of the figures, with which it is so profusely decorated, than in the ornamentation itself. Seen from a little distance the details are lost; and the window appears to be of beautiful tracery work, and a regular pattern. It is only when closely examined that the quaint designs are observed...
>
> It is much to be regretted that the rough texture of the stone should be so unworthy of the skill of the sculptor. Had it been executed in white marble, or even in the magnesian limestone which abounds in Ceylon, the effect would have been infinitely more lovely.[15]

It was in 1910 that Bell had conducted one of his usual running battles with the Public Works Department over the restoration of the three stairways. His diary entries on the subject are printed in Appendix A to the 1911-12 Annual Report. He agreed with Mr. Crabb, Provincial Engineer of the North-West Province, that there was no immediate need to undertake major work on the third stairway, although he could not wholly approve the earlier repairs by Williams. But he disagreed with the view of Mr. Moraes, District Engineer of Yapahuwa, who felt that the second stairway was too ruined to be reconstructed. Moraes was supported by Crabb, and by his successor Mr. Rothwell. Bell finally persuaded Rothwell that restoration of the second stairway was feasible. The P.W.D.'s estimate for the work was, however, too high for the Government to accept; so Bell got round it by offering to perform the work departmentally alongside other excavations at the site.[16]

In 1911-12 the second flight of stairs was partially restored, thirty steps and six platforms on either side being rebuilt. Even for Bell, expense prevented the restoration of the whole seventy steps, so the gap to the beginning of the third flight was bridged by an iron ladder, and cracks in the upper flight were filled in.

Excavation on the top of the rock proved disappointing, though some Chinese coins dating from the middle of the tenth century to the beginning of the thirteenth century were found. Bell compares the superficial construction of the 'Palace' on the rock with the elaborate buildings on the summit of Sigiriya, and concludes:

> In the 5th century the sovereigns of Ceylon had naught to fear from foreign foes, and could devote attention to civil and religious architectural monuments of their rule. When Yapahuwa was fortified, the most recent of many a flood of Southern Indian invasion had but recently been driven back, and men lived in restless fear of that recrudescence, which ere long put an end to the short-lived existence of this fortress Capital at *Subha-pabbata*. Little wonder then if the erection of the magnificent staircases and Porch, intended for a Palace yet to be constructed worthy of such adjuncts, alone occupied the later days of an always more-or-less uncertain rule at Yapahuwa, before - with the removal by death of the strong hand that had for twelve years held the foe in check - another and final inroad of Pandyan forces ensued, which, added to the horrors of a famine, proved resistless. Then fell Yapahuwa for ever.[17]

It was not until the 1950s that further work was carried out at Yapahuwa. A poetic description of how it then appeared was published in the *Illustrated London News* on December 20, 1952, and a small pamphlet on the restored site by W.B.Marcus Fernando was published in 1969. By that time the famous window had been brought back from Colombo, and placed in the Yapahuwa Archaeological Museum. [18]

18

The Lithic Quest

Especially in Sri Lanka, epigraphy has been an important aspect of the work of archaeologists. The study and its value are thus defined by H.A.I.Goonetileke:

> Epigraphy, by which we mean the discovery, collection, decipherment and study of inscriptions, generally engraved on stone and metal plates, seems a singular and unparalleled source for the reconstruction of the past history of Ceylon. In few other countries is there such a valuable source of information, very often buttressing, sometimes supplementing and in a few cases correcting and modifying the evidence of the chroniclers. Archaeological studies in Ceylon, especially the dating and identification of antiquities, have depended to a large degree on the evidence of epigraphy. Where identification and dating of monuments, on grounds of architecture and styles of development alone, are at best hesitant and hazardous, the authority of the inscriptions overrides other considerations in helping to reach a decision with much greater exactitude. They also provide an almost complete epigraphical record of the development and gradual evolution of Sinhalese characters from the Brahmi script to the present form.[1]

The official quest for inscriptions to copy or photograph, initiated by the Archaeological Commission set up in 1868, culminated before 1890 in the work of Goldschmidt and Muller. Paranavitana, in the preface to his *Inscriptions of Ceylon* Vol.I., writes of J.W.Robertson, a Superintendent of Surveys in Bell's early years as Archaeological Commissioner, as 'the first to make eye-copies, which were passed on to the Archaeological Department, of nearly two hundred cave inscriptions at Situlpavu and other sites in what is now the National Park'. Paranavitana mentions other residents of remote regions, 'incumbents of ancient temples and schoolmasters serving in areas where antiquities abound, who have supplied information about the existence of Brahmi inscriptions in caves'.[2]

D.T.Devendra in his article 'Seventy years of Ceylon archaeology' mentions also Headmen of the minor rural administration, passing on information to Government Agents. He describes valuable documents brought to light by the general public, such as the unique Panakaduva Copper-plate Grant of Vijaya Bahu I (a few years older than the Domesday Book) which not only confirms some of the *Mahawansa* facts recorded of him, but is also a document of rare human interest. He says that 'it gives the details of his sufferings when as a boy he fled before the invader and was hiding in inaccessible country under the care of a devoted chief solicitous for the safety of the country's future king'.[3]

Goonetileke's article and its bibliography chronicle the work from 1827 onwards of scholarly writers, for example A.O.Brodie, who in 1853 and 1855 treated some records in Puttalam and the North-Western Province. Paranavitana refers to Brodie, as do Wickremasinghe in the Preface to the first volume of his *Epigraphia Zeylanica*, and C.E.Godakumbura in his article 'History of archaeology in Ceylon'. These three also write of the prolific T.W.Rhys Davids, who between 1870 and 1875 wrote of inscriptions, including those in the Cave of the Golden Rock at Dambulla. The JRASCB published the work of Brodie and others. The many articles by Hugh Nevill between 1885 and 1894 were often published in *The Taprobanian*, which he edited himself. These included, in 1886, 'Inscriptions in Asoka's alphabet, reading from right to left'. He also wrote on Tamil inscriptions. [4]

With the beginning of the Archaeological Survey in 1890 the search for epigraphs became more systematic. The road was a long one before eventual publication could reveal their interest, linguistic, historical and social. First must come discovery, and not only from fairly accessible ruins. Goonetileke writes that, according to C.W.Nicholas in *A Concise History of Ceylon*, the earliest inscriptions were in caves. From the first century B.C. onwards they also appeared on separate rocks, but all were rare from the fifth to the seventh centuries A.D. In the eighth century they began to appear on pillars and slabs, and thereafter there were many of these, but comparatively few in the eleventh century of strife. From the thirteenth century onwards there was a general decline in numbers. [5]

We have seen, while tracking Bell along his circuits, how inscriptions figured among his targets, both on ruins and in caves of the wilder regions. Paranavitana writes feelingly of the manner in which the most diligent collector might fail to discover all possible material:

> Among the scores of boulders of different sizes and shapes which litter the hill-sides of many ancient sites like Situlparvu in unimaginable but picturesque confusion, with trees and shrubs, very often thorny, growing luxuriantly on every patch of soil that lie between them, it is very difficult, even for one who had been to these sites on numerous occasions, to find his way to a cave he had previously seen... Even in those caves visited by him certain inscriptions might have escaped his notice, due to the diminutive size and lack of depth of the letters, or for the reason that the light falls to a cave from the wrong direction, or that the letters are made invisible from the ground due to vegetation or moss. [6]

The difficulties of the search were enhanced by its discomforts. All necessities had to be moved twenty or thirty miles by bullock-cart. The campers were subject to the bites of ticks and the malarial mosquito, not to mention the threat of wild elephants, buffaloes, bears and leopards. Paranavitana writes:

> Arrived at a cave which two thousand years ago gave shelter to a *bhikku* who suffused the whole Universe with thoughts of good will, one might today be rudely confronted by a she-bear anxious about her youthful progeny, and prepared to defend them with all the ferociousness at her command. [7]

The three methods of recording inscriptions were photography, making eye-copies and the production of estampages. In caves it was at least easier to make eye-copies. Paranavitana writes:

> The early cave inscriptions lend themselves, more than any other class of epigraphs in Ceylon, to satisfactory eye-copies being made of them. These records are engraved in characters of large size to

The lithic quest

a considerable depth, on hard granite rocks protected from the rain by drip-ledges, and in positions beyond the reach of those who would have caused damage to them...Though few of these cave inscriptions are within the reach of one standing on the ground, very few of them are carved at such a great height as to make them indistinct from ground level. [8]

Not all inscriptions were physically easy of access. The Annual Report of 1905 chronicles John Still as obliged to climb barefoot down to a ledge of rock, and there, hanging on to a root, lean out and copy a letter at a time. [9]

To bring out letters there were expedients. In March 1891 at Welwelketiya, by rubbing a slab with burnt straw and oil, Bell was able to bring up more letters than Muller had done, and confirm his impression that the king making a grant was Siri Sanga Ba Abaya (Mahindu III). Bell and Ievers also found two ancient inscriptions on a rock south-east of Bandare Ratmale, and traced out the letters most carefully with lime, securing a good photograph of a short Sinhalese record. Ievers wrote in his Diary about tracing the larger epigraph:

> Lying on the bare rock in the mid-day sun was by no means agreeable, and when our task was half done, to our vexation a heavy shower... not only wet one to the skin, but washed out all the lime tracing. [10]

This prevented photography, but the deep-cut letters became fairly readable.

The method of recording epigraphs by 'squeezes' or estampages appeared in the JRASCB in 1884. Dr. Burgess of the *Indian Antiquary*, dissatisfied with some eye-copies forwarded to him, wrote a letter explaining an estampage-taking technique:

> First, the stone is well brushed to clean it, and then a little common soap is rubbed on the brush, and by it over the stone. Next, common country unsized paper (whitey-brown) is dipped in water and laid carefully over it, and beaten down with the brush. If one sheet does not cover it, another is laid on to overlap the first by about an inch, and so on till the whole is covered. Then a second layer is laid on in the same way, keeping the edges well off the joinings in the first layer. These sheets are also carefully beaten down into every letter. When fully half dry a dabber is dipped in a little lamp-black ground up with water and a drop of gum, and, taking care that the surface of the dabber is only moist (not wet) with this black ink, the whole inscription is daubed over with it. This is then allowed to dry thoroughly, and when dry it is carefully peeled off and rolled up. If the least moisture is in it when taken off, the chances are it will tear or be spoilt. If it does not peel off easily and entire, it is because the soap has not been equally rubbed over from the brush. [11]

The estampages emerge as black with the lettering white. This method, however, was not easy to apply. To take the estampages, elaborate scaffolding sometimes had to be erected and water, needed to remove moss and soak the paper, often had to be brought a mile or more over the rocks. If the sun were too hot the paper might dry too quickly before inking; if it were too cloudy the wet pulp might blur the letters.

The need for training to make effective squeezes was recognised by Bell, and in 1894 he reported that a native trained under Dr. E.Hultzsch had been borrowed from the Madras

Government. He taught Bell's Head Overseer, A.P.Siriwardhana, and over 200 impressions were taken, with more the following year, of inscriptions from the North-Central Province.[12]

The next stage of the quest was decipherment. When examining for the first time inscribed stones, drawings and symbols might catch the eye. On tour in the Eastern Province in September 1897, Bell explored a large cave at Aran-goda-gala. In an article written in 1918 he quoted his own diary in full:

> Inside, the back of the rock is covered with many quaint figures and designs, drawn in white ashes by Veddas who have sheltered in the cave. Among these, are rough delineations, most primitively executed, of man, woman, monkey, deer, lotus or sun, centipede or leaf, bow with arrow fitted; besides 'geometrical patterns', flowers, and a large unintelligible drawing, possibly intended to represent a tract of paddy fields with *nerawal* (ridges) and water-channels. These unique 'pictographs' of unsophisticated art - *ars casum simulat* - were photographed.[13]

Sinhalese incised figures regularly carried meaning and in September 1891 Bell writes of Ella-vewa temple:

> On the rock surface near the dagaba are carved a diagram, and in a row from right to left, a sword or a *deketta* (sickle), swastika, a prong, *ankusa* (elephant goad), a conch-shell and a fish - emblematic of certain privileges to the temple.[14]

Actually to read and interpret inscriptions required considerable knowledge of ancient languages and scripts. D.T.Devendra gives a simple introduction:

> The earliest script used is Brahmi, but shows certain variations or peculiarities; the probable origins of the language itself have been tolerably well located. It has also been shown that the language which directly evolved into Sinhalese, as we phonologically recognise it today, could be traced to the 8th century, with the appearance of the sound *a* (as in *hat*) as an example.
>
> The inscriptions are not all of them in the Sinhalese language or script. A few in Sanskrit, Pali, Tamil and Grantha, are known in the relevant scripts. A unique trilingual record where Tamil is accompanied by Chinese and Persian has also been found.[15]

Paranavitana writes of the early Brahmi script used in cave epigraphs that it is usually the same as that of the edicts of Asoka in India. He adds, 'Palaeographically, therefore, the inscriptions contained in Section I of this Volume may be taken as ranging in date between the last quarter of the third century B.C. and the middle of the first century A.C.'. A small number of these were written from right to left, which might have been the original direction.[16]

Wickremasinghe in 1901, writing on the inscriptions in the earliest Brahmi script, paid tribute to 'the indefatigable Archaeological Commissioner, Mr. H.C.P.Bell' for suggesting a right to left reading of an epigraph. He also told the 13th Congress of Orientalists of a rare Sanskrit inscription unearthed near the 'Twin-Ponds' in Anuradhapura.[17]

The lithic quest

Bell found early cave records on circuit; in a cave at Kotakanda in 1891 was one 'in the oldest form of cave character'. He especially indicates Mihintale as a fruitful locality. Of an early visit there with Ievers he wrote:

> The hills are honey-combed with countless cave dwellings of recluse priests, and rock-inscriptions abound. Many of these have a distinct palaeographic value, exhibiting the gradual transition from the Asoka character to a less ancient type, and are not without historical record of royal donors by whom these saintly habitations were prepared and bestowed on the priesthood.[18]

A difficulty faced by translators was incorrect spelling by illiterate monks. This was exemplified by an inscription at Puliyan-kulan, containing similar errors in spelling in four copies. Bell commented: 'If many people had been scholars, the odds are enormous against all four inscriptions being completed before the error was detected, and corrected in at least the last copy'.[19]

Tamil inscriptions form a special category. The problem throughout was of a paucity of Tamil scholarship to interpret them. Bell noted these as they were discovered, and listed the total of 48 in Appendix E to the Annual Report of 1911-12. None of them was from the South or East, and the majority were from Anuradhapura, Padaviya and Polonnaruwa. In 1911-12 Bell also recorded his gratitude for the help over the years of Epigraphists attached to the Archaeological Survey of India, saying, 'without their kindly aid these old inscriptions must have remained virtually a closed book'.[20]

He had some help from Dr. Hultzsch, and later from H.Krishna Sastri, Assistant Epigraphist of the Madras Archaeological Survey Department. He was indebted to him in 1908 for translations of epigraphs in mediaeval Tamil script on pillars and a bronze bell at the Mandapam near Yoda-ela, inscriptions which gave names of donors; also for details about the arrangement and purposes of rooms in Dravidian Hindu temples. The endowing of lamps to temples recurs; in a slab inscription at Siva Devale No. 2 at Polonnaruwa in 1909, the ghee to be supplied was ordered always to be from 'sacred cows never dying and never growing old'.

H.Krishna Sastri also translated an inscription on a pillar at the Monastery near the North Gate of the City. The dating was in the 15th year of Gaja Bahu II, also the 38th year of Jaya Bahu; later therefore than Vijaya Bahu I (1065-1120 A.D.), and apparently ignoring the intervening reign of Vikrama Bahu I. For Bell the inscription was especially interesting, because of its link with one he had found in a cave on the slopes of Dimbula-gala, referring to Queen Sundari, mother of Gaja Bahu II. This we shall give an account of later.[21]

A Tamil-Grantha epigraph which in 1903 had presented difficulty was found by Krishna Sastri to record an order by Vijaya Bahu I to a chief called Deva Sena to construct a relic temple for the Sacred Tooth of Jina, and a shrine for a beautiful large stone image of Buddha.[22]

In his Annual Reports Bell often recorded the numbers of inscriptions found in a year, and their location. In 1900 he summarised the findings to date as nearly 700, and classified inscriptions as from Caves 316, Rocks 170, Pillars 127, Slabs 78, besides many Sannas on copper plates. After 1900 the circuits were largely conducted by Bell's assistants. John Still in 1905 toured the Eastern Wanni of the Northern Province. A.P.Siriwardhana made copying tours from 1906 to 1912. [23]

In his Report of 1911-12 Bell finally summed up the epigraphical work of the Department to that date, again giving totals of inscriptions collected and indicating types, and localities covered. In Appendix B he listed, transcribed and translated inscriptions at Mihintale, and in Appendix C said that about fifty records belonged to Polonnaruwa. These he characterised, giving text, transliteration and translation of a selection of those previously unpublished. [24]

Similarly, Appendix D dealt with Sigiriya: Cave, Pillar and Gallery Wall inscriptions. In the Introduction to this we read:

> The glories of Sigiri Nuvara, during the occupation in the 5th century of the 'Lion Rock' as his citadel fortress by the parricide ruler Kasyapa I (479-497 A.D.), naturally diverts attention from any older archaeological interest in Sigiriya. Yet the exploration of caves existing beneath the numerous massive boulders which lie off Sigiri-gala on the west, proves, as was, indeed, to be expected, that the site, almost up to its conversion into a stronghold, had been the abode of forest eremites, some of whose names may be read to this day below the brows of the rock habitations which once gave them shelter.

Bell gives examples of these, e.g. an ancient inscription in Cave No. 10, 'Cave of Abajhi, son of the Chief Tiri'. He also translates some pillar-inscriptions, including a square pillar inscribed on four sides, dated 'on the tenth day of the bright half (waxing moon) of Vesak'. This indication, or the alternative 'dark half', is quite usual. The epigraph names Kasyapa IV (912-929 A.D.); it also contains the names of his nephew and successor, of the monastery, and instructions as to the property of the monastery and the protection of its monks. [25]

Appendix E to this Report described and listed the Tamil records. Finally, Appendix F tabulated all the inscriptions examined from 1906 to 1912 inclusive. These total 286, and a note on page 116 reads:

> For previous lists see Annual Reports 1890 to 1897, 1900, 1905. In all nearly 900 inscriptions have been examined, and copied by the Archaeological Survey in the period 1890 to 1912. [26]

Besides all the copying and recording of epigraphs, something was done to preserve original material. Some slabs and pillars were not left *in situ*. A ward of the former Anuradhapura Hospital had been in 1900 partially converted into a temporary local museum. In his Annual Report of 1906 Bell wrote:

> A large number of inscribed slabs and pillars are collected at Anuradhapura ready for transfer to Colombo as soon as room can be found for them in the Museum. Many more can be sent from Polonnaruwa. [27]

Though from 1906 sculptures and smaller artefacts were transferred to Colombo, in 1911-12 many lithic inscriptions remained at Anuradhapura. Bell listed forty-three pillars and slabs displayed there, and wrote:

The lithic quest

In this connection the better preservation of all inscribed stones recovered from various sites in the North-Central Province (Nuwarakalawiya and Tamankaduwa) has engaged attention.

The more southerly of the two ex-hospital wards at Anuradhapura (with open verandah all round), handed over to the Archaeological Survey Department as the local Museum, was doored and wired in to safeguard as many slabs and pillars as possible. Nearly all the lithic inscriptions collected from Nuwarakalawiya, which have had for years to lie out in the premises for want of adequate shelter, have now been arranged, and fixed in the verandahs and half-walled room of the building...

In 1912 about fifty inscribed slabs and pillars were carted into Anuradhapura from Polonnaruwa, where they cannot be properly protected. Until permanent shelter can be provided, these Tamankaduwa stones have to be kept in the open verandah of the northern ward. [28]

The material once available, it became possible for it to appear in print with facsimile, transliteration, translation and interpretation by scholars. Bell and his assistants achieved some detailed treatment of interesting epigraphs soon after they were found. The Seventh Progress Report, Appendix E, deals with many inscriptions; the transcripts made by Bell, with tentative translations by Gunasekera and Wickremasinghe. John Still gave transliterations and transcriptions of his findings in the Annual Report of 1905.

We have seen more examples of detailed treatment by Bell himself in the Appendices of his final Report. However, he had repeatedly stressed that such fullness was not often possible. From time to time he classified the discoveries of a period, or in a locality, in tables. The headings for these are listed by T. Vimalananda as I. Serial Number. II. Korale. III. Village. IV. Site. V. Class (i.e. Cave, Rock, Pillar or Slab). VI. Sovereign. VII. Year. VIII. Remarks. The final Index to all Bell's Reports has a full list of the sites where epigraphs had been found. [29]

Scholarly treatment of inscriptions often had to include comparisons with earlier work, and with the statements found in the Sinhalese chronicles. Henry Parker published work on very early inscriptions in *Ancient Ceylon* in 1909. On Parker as discoverer and scholar Paranavitana writes:

Henry Parker, an Irrigation Engineer in the employ of the Government of Ceylon, has brought several dozens of cave inscriptions to light for the first time, and published his readings and translations of them. Particular mention should be made of his discoveries at Periya Puliyankulama in the Vavuniya District. A cave inscription from this site which he published was regarded for over four decades as the earliest epigraph in Ceylon containing the name of a king who can be definitely identified. [30]

An instance of unfavourable comment by Bell on a predecessor occurs in the Seventh Progress Report. He describes a pillar lying prone among the 'Moragoda' ruins at Padaviya, discovered by Parker, and complains that Parker did not give the text of the inscription, though Bell himself does so. Consequently he dissents from Parker's identification of the king, who was regulating the use of a water-supply, as Kasyapa V, and prefers his uncle, Kasyapa IV, from a reference on the stone to the elder brother of the latter, Udaya I. Moreover Bell found his own identification confirmed by the *Mahawansa*. [31]

Also in the Seventh Progress Report and also at Padaviya, we see Bell differing from another epigraphist, H.Nevill, Acting Government Agent. This time the find was a pillar slab and situated on the bund of Padaviya tank, and the inscription concerned Parakrama Bahu I. It was notable in that the two panels were in different languages. Bell dealt with them in Appendix E of the Report, and described the first panel as beginning with an unalloyed Sanskrit sentence, headed by 'Swasti', and translatable as 'this was caused to be made for the benefit of the whole world by Sri Parakrama Bahu, Supreme Lord of Lanka, minded of what was fit to be done'. The second part, in Sinhalese characters of the twelfth or thirteenth centuries, translates as 'Having dammed up smaller streams, rivers [and constructed] tanks in Sri Lanka [and] caused fields to be cultivated [and] all the water to be retained [in the tanks] King Parakrama Bahu made this'.

Though Bell's account was written in late 1891, the Report was not printed till 1896, and meanwhile in the MLRC in February 1894 H.Nevill wrote a brief account of 'The slab at Padaviya Tank'. In April, in the same publication, Bell criticised this note, his own article closely resembling the description eventually found in the Report.

Nevill, who thought the first panel was in Prakrit allied to Sanskrit, translated it as 'Hail! Various writings were made by Sri Parakrama Bahu, the glorious chief Lord of Lanka - protect them as your own property'. His version of the lines in the second panel ('in Prakrit') was 'Having caused to be repaired all fields, bunded rivers, tanks in Sri Lanka, having held up all waters, King Parakrama Bahu made this'. Bell (in the MLRC only) remarked that Nevill 'must, I fear, be relegated to his own category of the "many enquirers" whose "ingenuity" the inscription "has baffled"', and said that this 'ripe scholar' had produced 'a travesty'.[32]

Bell's confidence in the interpretation of epigraphs by Muller varied. In the Annual Report of 1891 he said:

> The examination of these inscriptions had resulted in a distinct advance towards definitely reconciling the nomenclature, applied to sovereigns, ministers, etc. in the Pali and Sinhalese chronicles of Ceylon, with that of lithic records dating from that time. Dr. Muller's identification of the king 'Siri Naka' with Maha Sena is confirmed, that of one 'Malu Tisa' with Kanittha Tisa at least strengthened.[33]

On the other hand, when considering the cave inscriptions at Mihintale which Muller included in his *Ancient Inscriptions of Ceylon*, Bell described as 'regrettable' his failure to secure and print a better collection.[34]

It was desirable to resolve upon a vehicle for publication, other than the Annual Reports, which should be officially supported. In 1890 Bell wrote of the difficulty 'in editing these ancient records, which greatly tax the erudition of the most learned Oriental scholars'. In 1894 he defined his aim:

> It should be possible ultimately to publish an *Epigraphia Zeylanica* on the lines of the *Epigraphia Indica* issued under the authority of the Indian Government.[35]

The lithic quest

The first step had come in 1893 when B.Gunasekera, Mudaliyar, chief translator to Government, was appointed as Epigraphist to the Survey. Bell began to send him tracings of eye-copies, proposed readings and photographs, and wrote, 'The aid of so sound a scholar cannot but prove very advantageous to the Epigraphical Branch of the Archaeological Survey'. [36]

Articles by Gunasekera himself appeared in the JRASCB; in 1882 on inscriptions at the Ruwanweli Dagaba and in 1887 on some at the Lankatilaka. In his preface to *Epigraphia Zeylanica*, first volume, Wickremasinghe wrote of his colleague, after his death, that 'Ceylon has been bereft of a scholar as sound as he was modest, who had done much unostentatiously to elucidate the ancient history and literature of the Sinhalese'.

Professor W.Geiger, writing in the JRAS in 1898 on the work already done on inscriptions in Ceylon, was satisfied neither with the unorganised nature of the study nor with the inclusion of epigraphy in Annual Reports, though he was far from underrating Bell's work. He would like, he said, to see both new discoveries and epigraphs already treated, like Muller's, re-edited in what he called an *Epigraphia Ceylonica*. It should contain good facsimiles, not mere transliterations, and be entrusted to a man who combined practical knowledge and scientific method; a native scholar such as those whom Bell had already found useful and warmly acknowledged. [37]

The project was indeed to be launched. Bell in his Annual Report of 1899 reprinted the relevant section of the *Report of a Committee... upon the Archaeological Survey of Ceylon*, produced that year:

> The Archaeological Commissioner considers an *Epigraphia Zeylanica* (the publication in full with facsimiles and translations of a large selection of the inscriptions) to be a branch of the Archaeological Survey extremely important, and urges that it ought, as in India, to be carried out *pari passu* with the work of survey and excavation.
>
> The Committee advise the undertaking, provided that the expense can be kept within the limits of the Vote. The Committee adopts Mr. Bell's suggestion that Mr. Don M.de Zilva Wickremasinghe be appointed to do the Epigraphical work in England, and that B.Gunasekera, Mudaliyar, Chief Translator to Government, be instructed to verify, or revise, Mr. Wickremasinghe's conclusions. [38]

Wickremasinghe was appointed on April 4, 1899, and material for *Epigraphia Zeylanica* began to be sent to him. In 1906 the Government promised Rs. 1,000 yearly for the cost of collecting eye-copies and 'squeezes' and photographing them (for estampages were liable to be damaged by damp and vermin). [39]

In 1911 Bell arranged for the whole set of 287 'squeezes' to be photographed, the negatives retained, and the estampages to be shipped to England. He commented:

> Mr. Wickremasinghe has from first to last received some 380 estampages, a supply sufficient to provide ample material for many volumes of the *Epigraphia Zeylanica*. No question, therefore, as to lack of suitable 'straw' for making epigraphical 'bricks' should arise for several years to come. [40]

H. C. P. Bell

Year by year in the Annual Reports Bell had noted the publication of the Parts of *Epigraphia Zeylanica*, from Part I in 1904, in its 'neat and scholarly form'. Up to 1907 he was the supervisor of the enterprise, and in other Reports of those years he noted with a certain severity the fact that an expected Part had not in fact appeared. This may strike a note of warning as we approach the detailed account of Wickremasinghe's productions. [41]

19

Epigraphia Zeylanica

To the history of Epigraphical Research in Sri Lanka, the association of Dr. Wickremasinghe and H.C.P.Bell contributes a chapter both chequered and fruitful.

D.M.de Zilva Wickremasinghe (1865-1937) was educated at Richmond College, Galle. When Bell was stationed there from 1884 to 1885 he knew him as a young and zealous pandit, and in 1889 he joined the RASCB. His career from 1891 to 1893 had been as Native Assistant to Bell, and he developed expertise on inscriptions. Previously, from 1887, he had been Assistant Librarian working on the catalogue at the Colombo Museum under F.H.M.Corbet. Corbet was to be his constant friend, and in 1893 promoted the further education of his protégé, by inducing him to go to Germany on a scholarship to study Archaeology and Philology. An account of his career appears in *Recollections* by A.C.G.Wijeyekoon, who writes:

> Although he did not know a word of German when he went there, in six months he picked up the language so well that he was able to follow lectures in German, and converse freely in German. He studied at the Universities of Erlangen, Munich and Berlin, winning the Muir Prize at Berlin in 1895. In 1894 the RASCB had deputed him to search the Libraries and Archives of Holland for certain Sinhalese Mss. believed to have been removed from Ceylon by the Dutch during the occupation of the maritime provinces.[1]

Wickremasinghe then came over to London, and was cataloguing Sinhalese material in the British Museum Library between 1895 and 1900. His leave from the Colombo Museum had been extended; in 1900 he retired from his position there but asked to be reconsidered later. Instead, from April 1, 1899 he was appointed Epigraphist to the Ceylon Government in connection with its Archaeological Survey. The procedure was that the 'estampages' or 'squeezes' were despatched to England for his use in the projected scientific publication *Epigraphia Zeylanica*. For in London facilities and help were available for the literary treatment of inscriptions.[2]

Eventually in January 1908 Wickremasinghe was appointed to a lectureship at Jesus College, Oxford. His attainments appear in his serving for several Universities as Examiner in Sinhalese, Pali and Sanskrit. He later returned to London as Professor of Sanskrit and Pali at the University School of Oriental and Asiatic Studies. His numerous publications included books of *Sinhalese Self-taught* and *Tamil Self-taught*. Above all 'it can truly be said that he laid the foundation of the scientific study of Ceylon epigraphy on a firm basis… he edited and published between 1903 and 1927 thirteen parts of *Epigraphia Zeylanica* consisting solely of his own contributions'.[3]

In 1902 Wickremasinghe contributed to the thirteenth Congress of Orientalists a summary of the progress of archaeological research in Ceylon from 1890 to the date of writing. This concluded with his announcement that important inscriptions discovered would in due course appear in *Epigraphia Zeylanica* with facsimile plates, and that the first part was ready for the press. This was published in 1904 and included the Sanskrit inscription found in the precincts of the Abhayagiriya monastery (at that time described as the Jetawanarama). The second part appeared in 1907. [4]

Between 1903 and 1905 letters from Bell as Archaeological Commissioner appear in correspondence in the files of the Colonial Office, London, involving his subordinate and the Ceylon Government. The first theme was the payment to Wickremasinghe, and was related to the slowness of his production of *Epigraphia Zeylanica*, of which he had initially promised two parts a year; but already in 1903 Bell was so dissatisfied with the progress as to threaten to suggest the dismissal of Wickremasinghe. The latter in response pointed out his difficulties, including the death of B.Gunasekera in Ceylon, who had assisted him; and enlisted the Boden Professor of Sanskrit, Arthur A.Macdonell, to testify to his abilities and support his claims. In spite of Bell's uncompromising attitude, Wickremasinghe's request for £200 a year, for two numbers of *Epigraphia Zeylanica* of forty-eight pages each, was granted in January 1905. He was then hoping to have Parts III and IV ready in the year, but they did not appear till 1907 and 1909 respectively. [5]

The progress of the work was of course a good deal dependent on the supply by Bell of epigraphical material. In 1905 A.B.Keith, Secretary to the Crown Agents to the Colonies, was warning a colleague at the Colonial Office:

> I would suggest that instructions should be laid down as to the importance of the Archaeological Commissioner's supplying Mr. Wickremasinghe with material, and returning answers to any questions which may be referred to him with the least possible delay. It is quite clear from the correspondence that the Archaeological Commissioner is an extremely poor correspondent. At present the second part is being delayed by the fact that the Archaeological Commissioner has not sent copies of two inscriptions which he ought to have sent back long ago. [6]

Correspondence in 1907 over the production of *Epigraphia Zeylanica* Part III, and over the approach to Part IV, took on the character of a contest by mail over thousands of miles between the Lion in the Anuradhapura jungle and the Unicorn in the Indian Institute, Oxford. Part III was very productive of strife. A Memorandum by Bell sent in May 1907 recalled his instructions for a full list of the inscriptions, to be edited in each part, to be submitted to him ahead for sanction. Of a list for Part III sent to him in April, Bell had approved five items, but only one of these had been included, a Slab Inscription of Mahinda IV near the 'Stone Canoe'. Though Wickremasinghe had excused himself on grounds of shortage of time for not having submitted proofs to Bell, the latter's Memorandum concluded with severe criticism:

> The Introduction to this inscription (no proof of which has ever been submitted to the Archaeological Commissioner) is greatly marred by errors and omissions which could, and ought to have been avoided by timely reference to the A.C. [7]

The irate Bell also pointed out that his instructions back in March 1905 that each part should, as a rule, contain one example each of the classes of cave, rock, slab and pillar inscriptions, with occasionally other records (e.g. clay tablets, sannas, etc.) so as to cover as far as possible all periods, had not been followed. In Part III Wickremasinghe had merely dealt with two slab records of Mahinda IV, though in Part I he had already published two inscriptions from this king. Bell called Part III 'in many respects an unsatisfactory number', which had been rushed through the press 'in the hope of escaping further censure from the Government for your long-continued and inexcusable laches'. [8]

He enclosed a copy of another Memorandum to Government, complaining of the delays of Wickremasinghe 'whose working hours are likely to be taken up of late with private ventures, e.g. his recently published *Tamil Self-taught*, bringing in pecuniary profit at less expenditure of time and trouble than the *Epigraphia Zeylanica* involves'. [9]

To these roars of the Lion, the Unicorn on June 21, 1907 replied with some dignity, enclosing approving letters on Part III from seven 'ripe scholars of worldwide reputation':

> Allow me to submit respectfully my protest against the antagonistic attitude you continually take towards my work in spite of all my endeavours to work with you harmoniously, paying due regard to your official position as Head of the Department. It seems I can in no way please you now and I note with regret the want of that consideration which you showed me when I was your Assistant about fifteen years ago. [10]

On the same day he wrote to the Colonial Office a full defence of his practices, with a detailed reply to Bell's criticism of the Introduction to the Slab Inscription. He complained generally of harassments by the A.C., though admitting the value of the material from the man on the spot with his chances of verification. While accepting 'all legitimate emendations that he is good enough to make in proofs', Wickremasinghe felt he was himself capable of editing. On the next day he again wrote to the Colonial Office, to call attention to the respect of scholars for his work. He stressed the fundamental importance of accuracy and declared:

> The only criticisms offered by the A.C. refer to matter supplied to me from Ceylon over which I have no control. No exceptions are taken to the actual work of deciphering, translating, and explaining the inscriptions. [11]

Meanwhile the work on Part IV had to go forward. On April 26 Wickremasinghe had proposed to Bell that all the Cave and Rock inscriptions discovered by the latter at Ritigala in 1893 should be treated therein (this was, he wrote later, to attempt a chronological order) and he asked for material to supplement what he had. Bell on May 23 called the proposals 'discreditable', for they went against plans made in 1905; also he had already sent all the records he could muster. On June 22, Wickremasinghe traced his constantly being at variance with Bell to the anomalous position in which he stood to him. The A.C. had the responsibility for *Epigraphia Zeylanica*, but the text had to be studied by himself with Western methods of scholarship, then finally revised by one 'who is not a professional expert in Epigraphy'. He suggested that the Archaeological Department in Ceylon should supply him with plenty of material and useful information. He himself should be responsible for *Epigraphia Zeylanica*, while willing to submit the last proof to a leading English or European epigraphist or scholar. [12]

It had already begun to be realised by the authorities that the two uneasy yoke-fellows might have to be disentangled. Opinions on the two men emerge from a file of June 22, 1907. A.J.Harding, 2nd Class Clerk at the Colonial Office, told Sir Charles Lucas, Assistant Under Secretary:

> Whatever the abstract merits of the controversy, it seems to me clear that with so offensive a Commissioner as Mr. Bell no qualified person can be expected to work as his subordinate officer.

The Secretary of State, the Earl of Elgin, had strongly disapproved of the tone of Mr. Bell's correspondence, and epithets in his letters were described by G.V.Fiddes, a Principal Clerk, as 'monstrous' and 'studiously offensive', and his editorial corrections as 'unnecessarily minute and irritating', and even as 'piffle'. These comments are somewhat counterbalanced by Lucas's remark, 'I know this little Wickremasinghe slightly and he is rather tiresome and persistent. I do not feel clear as to the rights of the case'. [13]

However, high-level decisions were being taken. The Governor, McCallum, wrote from Ceylon on September 4, 1907 to the Earl of Elgin. He had decided, if this were approved, that in future Bell should only select material and forward it to Wickremasinghe periodically, supplying lists of the sendings to the Colonial Office.

> This will have the effect of preventing any recurrence of the friction between Mr. Bell and Mr. Wickremasinghe, and will enable the former gentleman to devote more of his time to the preparation of his own Annual Reports, which, I regret to find, are some years in arrear. [14]

There would also no longer be the delay caused by the passage to and fro of proof sheets; but the problem remained that though Wickremasinghe was well equipped for his task, he was probably not to be trusted to perform it without supervision. The *Epigraphia Zeylanica* must be a careful and scholarly production, so McCallum felt that the proof sheets should be submitted to 'some European savant of unquestioned repute' who must be fairly remunerated. The choice of a supervisor was pursued. A.J.Harding suggested A.A.Macdonell, whose residence at Oxford (he was Boden Professor of Sanskrit and Keeper of the Indian Institute where Wickremasinghe worked) would be an advantage. Keith told Harding that Macdonell, as well as Dr. Fleet (the most distinguished Indian epigraphist living) highly commended Wickremasinghe's work, and he should not be penalised for delay whenever it was not his fault. [15]

Arthur Berriedale Keith (1879-1944) was a man of parts, a constitutional lawyer of the Inner Temple, who served as Secretary to the Crown Agents for the Colonies 1901-14, having passed the Civil Service Examination with 1,000 marks more than any competitor of his year or previous ones. Among his three first-class degrees from Oxford was one in Oriental Languages, and from 1914 to 1944 he was Regius Professor of Sanskrit and Comparative Philology at Edinburgh. Keith volunteered to undertake the supervision of Wickremasinghe unless an outsider were preferred, and Lord Elgin accepted his offer but thought he should be paid a fee. In November 1907 therefore the plan was settled for *Epigraphia Zeylanica* to be produced in parts of forty-eight pages at £100 each, with a £10 penalty for each month taken over nine. Keith was to supervise; and Wickremasinghe and Bell were informed. [16]

The implementing of the new arrangement evoked some correspondence in Ceylon. Bell's friend Ievers wrote to the Governor, 'I personally can see no objection to the proposal beyond the fact that it will undoubtedly break Mr. Bell's heart'. The dry comment of McCallum was:

> *Angina Pectoris* must not act as a deterrent to a change of system. Mr. Wickremasinghe is an expert, Mr. Bell is not. The best course will be to put a stop to unnecessary squabbling.

He realised that Mr. Wickremasinghe was irreplaceable, and did not find his 'laches' unforgivable; he thought that Bell was perhaps somewhat jealous of his superior knowledge. 'Mr. Bell's correspondence is a series of examples of the countercheck quarrelsome'. [17]

Wickremasinghe's appointment to Jesus College, Oxford, came in January 1908. Perhaps this delayed production of Part IV; in November 1908 Bell had reported its non-appearance to McCallum. Keith, who believed that Bell deserved at least part of the blame, had seen proofs in December, containing an interesting theory of the date of the Buddha's death; and the complete Part IV was sent to Bell in March 1909. [18]

Wickremasinghe had been telling Keith of his future requirements from Bell of estampages or clear photographs and, if convenient, eye-copies or transfers, all grouped by locality, if possible chronologically, with details of the position where the material had been found. Specifically in January he was asking through Keith for some squeezes of Dambulla rock inscriptions and a list of material for Parts V and VI. Bell responded through the Ceylon Government that he had sent all except some photographs and enclosed a list; he suggested to 'the authorities in England responsible for controlling Mr. Wickremasinghe' that in future only inscriptions not yet published should be edited. This was more urgent than re-editing those already published by Goldschmidt and Muller, Gunasekera and the learned Buddhist monk, Volivitya Dhumaratne Totunnanse, as hitherto Wickremasinghe had mostly done.

Here was a promising new cause of controversy; so to minimise friction Keith, although he realised that re-editing was a necessary practice, suggested that Wickremasinghe should as far as possible follow the views of the A.C. 'with whom we must all sympathise'. The rather more at arms' length relationship of the supplier of material and the editor bore some fruit. Though in May 1909 Bell could only send squeezes, not photographs, of Ruwanweli and Pankuliya, on July 5 Wickremasinghe acknowledged these and some earlier packets, commenting:

> The care taken by Mr. Bell in despatching this material is very satisfactory, as is, on the whole, the material itself. There are, however, some important points to be cleared up, and as I am about to visit Ceylon, I should like to take advantage of the opportunity to collect on the spot the information I require. [19]

Wickremasinghe did go to Ceylon in September 1909, and revisited the North-Central Province where he had worked under Bell. In an address to the RASCB he praised the progress of the Archaeological Survey since his own time, particularly the excavations at Polonnaruwa. [20]

In 1909 Wickremasinghe treated, as he had desired, Ritigala inscriptions in *Epigraphia Zeylanica* Part IV. Though he and Bell were now less often in conflict, the authorities had to some extent to hold the ring. Bell still wanted to influence which inscriptions were published, and in April had pressed for them to be the new 'pabulum' of which he had enough and to spare, and not 'rechauffés' of work done by Gunasekera and R.Sewall. Keith in June defended the re-editing of inscriptions which had already been published, saying that this was in fact more demanding than producing the first version. Wickremasinghe wrote to Bell in July, defending his own practice. It was valuable to check defective readings of important inscriptions with the originals. Reliable texts thus produced could then be referred to when interpreting such newly-found epigraphs as were reasonably legible. [21]

Eventually the authorities told Wickremasinghe to prefer to use newly discovered material where possible. This he apparently did in *Epigraphia Zeylanica* Part V, published in 1911 and reviewed by E.Muller in the JRAS in 1912. Of the seven inscriptions edited, one in the Southern Brahmi alphabet of the 2nd century A.D. had appeared in Muller's *Ancient Inscriptions of Ceylon*, and Muller noted Wickremasinghe's discovery that the grant of a tank mentioned was to the priests of the Thuparama at Anuradhapura. The other inscriptions had been discovered by Bell and Wickremasinghe, and Muller detailed their characters. He quarrelled with the translation of 'mahavar' as meaning 'chief artisans, or fishers, or butchers', for the sense 'high roads' was preferable in an inscription warning rascally travellers from approaching a temple. Muller, though, concluded with thanks to Wickremasinghe for his great care and with hopes for more of his valuable work. [22]

Wickremasinghe had been getting into trouble with the authorities by being a year late with Part V. By November 1912, however, Part VI had been achieved, and the complete Volume I of *Epigraphia Zeylanica* had been published by the Oxford University Press, with the author described as Epigraphist to the Ceylon Government and Lecturer in Tamil and Telegu at the University of Oxford. The volume dealt with twenty-two inscriptions. Among them were included the Brahmi inscriptions at Vessagiriya and Ritigala, the Perumiyankulan rock inscriptions of Vasabha, the Anuradhapura slab inscription of Kassapa V, and the Vevalkatiya slab inscriptions of Mahinda IV. Keith could now be congratulatory on both the quality and greater speed of the work. [23]

This year, which marked a minor climax in the Epigraphist's achievement, was also the year of Bell's retirement from the post of Archaeological Commissioner. He was succeeded by E.R.Ayrton, whose tenure of office was unhappily brief, for he was drowned in May 1914. In this year, it appeared that the problem of the provision of good material for *Epigraphia Zeylanica* remained, for Wickremasinghe declared that his supply was exhausted and applied unsuccessfully for leave to revisit Ceylon in quest of more. Keith supported him, for, in spite of Wickremasinghe's procrastination, he thought him capable of actually being Archaeological Commissioner, the post being now vacant. He thought that it was 'better to have a man who does first-class work

Epigraphia Zeylanica

than to have one who scamps things'. While admitting that an archaeologist must always be a very busy man, Keith declared that Bell had been 'absolutely useless' as a supplier of proper material and deplored the untimely death of Ayrton, who might have set matters right. [24]

The 1914-18 war handicapped the progress of Wickremasinghe's work. By April 1915 he had only completed Vol.II, Part 3 of *Epigraphia Zeylanica* (he was not allowed to send copies to Germany), and Professor Keith referred to the exigencies of the conflict as increasing delays. In November 1915 the Governor of Ceylon, Sir Robert Chalmers, promised Bonar Law, Secretary of State, that he would 'send the stock of estampages of unpublished inscriptions from the collection in the possession of the Archaeological Survey Department when, after the war, cargo space in steamers is less valuable and costly than at present'. [25]

By January 1919 the war was over and Wickremasinghe, who had been working for the Ministry of Information, was again asking for a passage to Ceylon. He specified the work of collecting and checking which he would aim to do: making maps of Anuradhapura and Polonnaruwa, and perhaps extra eye-copies of inscriptions, in particular the Vessagiriya cave and rock inscriptions - he would need an experienced assistant. The request for these personal investigations was refused in spite of the advocacy of Keith. [26]

Wickremasinghe's complaints against Bell of inadequate supplies of epigraphs were now retrospective. They were intertwined with a scholarly contest between the two concerning an inscription in a cave at Dimbulagala, which recorded a benefaction to monks by a Queen, Sundari. Such a relationship between monks and monarchs had been frequent, and this instance will be discussed later.

20

Monks and Monarchs

What can be learned of past history from epigraphs was outlined by H.A.I.Goonetileke. They gave information on dynastic succession, taxation, land tenure, administration and place names. The donors belonged to all classes of society, from kings and royalty to the nobility, district and village chiefs, householders, soldiers, artisans, artists, craftsmen and lay devotees of both sexes. [1]

A few examples have been given, from names of forest eremites to those of kings. Those in the caves of Mihintale came from local chiefs or lay devotees. Of particular interest are some pillar and slab inscriptions, dealing with the life of monasteries, examined by D.M.de Z. Wickremasinghe in *Epigraphia Zeylanica*.

In Part I, when first published separately, and as the first epigraph in the collected Vol.I., Wickremasinghe treated the Sanskrit inscription from near the 'Twin Ponds' in Anuradhapura. It contained regulations for the guidance of monks and laymen living within the precincts of the vihares or in lands belonging to them. The quantities of food, milk, ghee, etc., allowed were listed, and revenues from two villages set apart for the renewal of monks' robes. Twenty-five monks from each of the four great fraternities were supported, but those coming from other vihares only if they had given up the food and raiment provided there. Monks must not themselves support anyone else except mother and father, and those 'whose conversation is coarse, who speak not the truth, and they also who commit wrong acts, shall not dwell in the Vihare, much less monks who carry clubs and weapons'. Among lay servants supported were clever stone-cutters and skilful carpenters. [2]

Wickremasinghe refers to inscriptions at Mihintale yielding similar insights into monastic life and administration; and in Part III of *Epigraphia Zeylanica* (No. 7 in the collected Vol.I) he wrote of certain tablets of Mahinda IV. One of them decreed that:

> Monks residing in this vihare shall rise at the time of early dawn and shall meditate on the four protective formulas, and having finished cleaning their teeth shall put on and cover themselves with their robes as prescribed in the *Sikakarani*...both ends equal, just as an elephant-keeper on his elephant... They shall then go to the 'check-room' at At-vehera, shall descend into the refectory, and exercising a spirit of benevolence and reciting *paritta* formulas, receive gruel and boiled rice.

Among actions prohibited were killing of animals and cutting of trees. Organisation of the vihare involved many officials; and lay-servants included cooks, thatchers, a physician, an astrologer, laundry-men and a 'keeper of blue water-lily'. [3]

To turn to secular matters, the frequent inscriptions from kings could help to identify ruined sites, or to confirm the genealogy of the monarchs. Their benefactions and concerns appear, their pleasures and sources of pride, and even personality. In his *Summary of Operations 1890-1900*

Bell says that 'grants of the following sovereigns of Ceylon have been assigned definitely or on strong grounds', and he subjoins a list of twenty-eight from Laja Tisa (119 B.C.) to Sri Vikkrama Raja Sinha (1798 A.D.).[4]

In 1893 at Andiyakanda, the east spur of Ritigala, he found many fine caves and wrote of an inscription:

> That of Cave No. 9 is historically valuable: it is among the few (like that at Dambulla) distinctly connected with a royal donor, one of the earliest kings. It runs: *Devanapiya Maha Rajha Gamani Tisaha puta Devanapiya Tisa A[baha] lene agata anagata chadu disa sagasa lene.* 'Cave of Tisa A[baya], beloved of the gods, nephew (*lit* son) of the great King, beloved of the gods, Gamini Tisa [is granted to] the monks from the four quarters, present and absent'. This record may well belong to Wattagamini Abaya (104 B.C.) and his uncle the great Dutthagamini (161 B.C.).

On the same tour, Cave No. 14 at Kuda-arambedda-hinna contained four important inscriptions of the early period - one of 'Lajaka Tisa'(Lajji Tisa, 119-109 B.C.) and one of 'Gamani Abaya' (Wattagamani Abaya - again). Bell notes specially that these confirm the *Mahawansa* record.[5]

That Wickremasinghe could differ from Bell on the interpretation of inscriptions appeared when in 1909 he dealt with Ritigala epigraphs in *Epigraphia Zeylanica*, Part IV. On the inscription found in 1893 in Cave No. 9 at Andiyakanda, he preferred to identify Devanapiya Tisa A[baha] with Lajji Tisa; and on the inscriptions in Cave No. 14 at Kuda-arambedda-hinna, he did not accept as certain Bell's identification of the monarchs. However, in Part V, he agreed with Bell's findings on the pillar of Kasyapa IV at Moragoda as against Parker's attribution to Kasyapa V.[6]

Not all inscriptions reflect piety, nor compassion for a king's subjects. Two very similar epigraphs, probably belonging to Mahinda IV, one of them shallowly cut on a slab at Kahata-gas-digiliya, 'are grimly significant as to lawlessness of the times', because they contain 'stringent regulations for the repression of crime and misdemeanours'. If murder and theft could not be punished by expulsion from a village or high communal fines, mutilations were in reserve, and even for killing or theft of cattle there were whippings and brandings.[7]

Records of interest found at Polonnaruwa were noted by Bell: an early cave inscription, of Parakrama Bahu I, at the 'Gal Vihare'; and at the 'Potgul Vihare' an early rock inscription referring to the above king's queens: the famous Lilavati who reigned alone later, and the pious and very beautiful Chandra or Rupavati.[8]

Information gathered from inscriptions could link kings and ruins. In the Annual Report of 1905 Bell wrote of a number of such examined between 1901 and 1905 at Polonnaruwa:

> Some of these lithic records have proved invaluable in enabling the names of several of the chief ruins and their constructors to be definitely fixed. Thus it is now known that (i) The *Wata-da-ge* or 'Circular Relic Shrine' is the *'Ratanagiriya'*, which King Nissanka Malla had erected for the enshrinement of the Tooth-Relic. (ii) The post-and-rail enclosure hard by was that ruler's *'Nissanka Lata Mandapaya'*. (iii) That once magnificent shrine Vihare No. 3 (*'Heta-da-ge'*) was probably built with the approval of Parakrama Bahu I, and subsequently re-named by his near successor *'Nissanka Dala-da-ge'*.

(iv) The ruin on the tank bund near the Hindu Devales on the road to Minneriya was one of Nissanka Malla's many 'Alms Halls', and styled *'Nissanka Dana Mandapaya'*. (v) The short record on the guardstone to the stairs at *'Jetawanarama'* (so-called) fixes that pre-eminent shrine - as its proportions and lavish design would alone sufficiently attest - as the *'Lankatilaka'* Vihare built by Parakrama Bahu I. [9]

Of King Nissanka Malla (1198-1207 A.D.) Bell writes in the Annual Report of 1903, 'His inscription on the front wall of Vihare No. 3 (*"Heta-da-ge"*) has a quaintly ostentatious reference, which may haply record the *ultra* rapid completion of this structure, by a ruler, among whose virtues modesty and respect for his predecessors cannot be counted'. The passage runs:

> Having beheld the *Maligawa*, which a former king had erected in seven years and seven months, [declaring] 'a monarch of Our Might (*lit* such as Ourselves) should be seated in a *Maligawa* worthy of Us,' he caused to be erected with incomparable magnificence, within five and forty days, the *Maligawa of Seven Storeys* and the *Satara balana Prasadaya*. [10]

Bell had been writing of the ostentatious style of the 'Seven-storeyed Shrine' or 'Sat-mahal Prasadaya', which was perhaps the result of Cambodian influence. The style may well match the monarch whom Bell elsewhere calls 'bombastic', 'egregious' or 'vainglorious'.

Wickremasinghe was more appreciative of Nissanka Malla. When treating, in Part IV of *Epigraphia Zeylanica* (No. 9 in Vol.I), a rock inscription about him at Dambulla, he said:

> There is no doubt that he did everything he could to pacify the unrest prevailing at the time, and to win his people over to his side. He relinquished the revenue for five years, remitted taxes, repaired tanks and other irrigation works, restored inheritances to their lawful heirs, and made various grants of lands, serfs, cattle and money.

A thoughtful touch was that no taxes were to be levied on those 'who laboured with the bill-hook in clearing thorny jungle'. [11]

To be sure, the king made every effort to commemorate his own bounties. Of his thirty or so self-advertisements, at Polonnaruwa, the longest - seventy-two lines - is engraved on the so-called Gal Pota, or 'Stone Book', described in the Annual Report of 1903. This huge monolith is also ornamented with *hansas* and by two figures of the goddess Lakshmi, whose flowers are being watered by pairs of elephants. A brief record on it claims that the granite block was transported all the way from Mihintale. [12]

Two other records, one incised on rock on some Hindu ruins on the Minneriya road, and the other on slabs of the portico to the Wata-da-ge, are largely duplicates. A portion of the rock inscription, originally translated by Gunasekera, runs thus:

> Accordingly, on receiving the kingdom by royal succession and attaining supreme sovereignty after coronation, His Majesty made good the assertion of his father, in as much as he dispersed his enemies as the Sun on the summit of the Rock where it rises dispels darkness: shining like Sakra in endless, royal prosperity, [he] lived like a Wish-conferring Tree (*kalpa vrksha*) produced by the merits of the

inhabitants of the world, and ruling with the ten royal virtues, promoted the welfare of the world and the [Buddhist] religion.

He lived in *Kalinga-pura*, named *Pulasti-pura*; remitted the taxes for five years for the benefit of the inhabitants of Lanka, who had become destitute by payment of heavy imposts in former times; and [moreover] gave them means of living, slaves, cattle, permanent holdings, clothes, ornaments, etc.: in this way he enriched the people. Thinking that thieves commit theft from greed of wealth, at the risk of their lives, he gave them whatever wealth and lands they desired: thus did he free the inhabitants from fear of thieves, by putting an end to theft.

The king also claimed to have been extremely generous to the Tooth Relic, and he was not unrewarded:

On his way his crown chanced to be blown off his head owing to the speed of the horse he rode, and the gods replaced it. On observing the divine aid thus vouchsafed to him, His Majesty declared: 'With my own eyes have I seen the reward of good deeds'.

As there does seem to be some foundation in fact for these eulogies, one is happy to record that Nissanka Malla also enjoyed his kingship:

His Majesty having partaken of such food as he desired, and drunk different kinds of delicious beverage, and eaten various sorts of cake and fruit, having washed his face, rubbed on his hands sweet-smelling powder, [and] chewed betel of five ingredients, [waited upon by] attendants who, their bodies smeared with fragrant ointment, performed manual or foot service; sleeping on different kinds of beds and sitting on different kinds of seats; constantly hearing many cries of joy [and] frequent '*sadhu*', etc.; bestowing provisions with great delight, he enjoyed the happiness of giving alms, and imparted the gift of religious doctrine, which is the noblest of all gifts. [13]

Differences between Bell and Wickremasinghe, which had originated during Bell's career as Archaeological Commissioner, continued after his retirement. The prolonged scholarly dispute about Dimbulagala between Bell and Wickremasinghe had its origin in 1897. In his Annual Report of this year Bell had recorded for September 3rd to 8th a camping at Kude Ulpota near a cool wooded spring, below the south-west side of Dimbulagala ('Gunner Quoin Hill'). Near the summit could be seen some caves with white plastered walls like the Sigiriya 'Gallery'. The cliff was known as 'Maravidiye' from an ancient road below it, and there were two caves. Number One had a high-up inscription in very large letters. By difficult ledges and tunnels Number Two was reached, which offered a fine view from the terrace of the Kandyan hills:

On the rock roof are two inscriptions - the older in a few cave letters, the second dated in the twenty-seventh year of 'Jaya Bahu' (Vijaya Bahu I, 1065-1120). This latter record of seven lines is cut on a smooth raised panel, and is of great interest. It proves the occupation in the eleventh century by monks, for whom the caves were prepared by Queen Sundari, wife of Wikrama Bahu I (1121-1142) and mother of Gaja Bahu II, the cousin and chief rival of Parakrama Bahu the Great. [14]

161

In 1909 Bell's reading of a Tamil inscription at Polonnaruwa produced a date for the brief reign of Jaya Bahu which made him no longer identify him with Vijaya Bahu I (1065-1120), his greater predecessor. [15]

Wickremasinghe treated Queen Sundari's inscription in *Epigraphia Zeylanica* Vol.II, Part 4 in 1917. He quoted Bell's 1897 account of the epigraph, and wrote that it 'seems to be complete, though the unusual ending suggests the possibility of its being continued on other panels in the rock roof which have escaped even the long-trained eye of an indefatigable explorer like Mr. Bell'. Wickremasinghe described the inscription thus:

> The contents tell us that Sundara Maha-Devi, the chief queen of Vikrama-Bahu and mother of Gaja Bahu, caused the construction of a road at Dimbula-gala between Sanda-maha-lena (the great Moon cave) and Hiri-maha-lena (the great Sun cave); that she had it paved with stone and had also cave temples built with statues, dagobas, and sacred bodhi-trees and that she further testifies to a certain benefaction which she had made to Demala-paha in the 27th year of the reign of Vijaya-Bahu.

Wickremasinghe accepted the identification of the Queen as the donor, partly from the form of the script and the phraseology, which were not later than the third quarter of the twelfth century. He placed the inscription after the accession of Sundara's husband in 1121 A.D. Reading the name of the king in whose reign the benefaction was confirmed as *Vijaya Bahu Vathimi*, he rejected Bell's original 'Jaya Bahu' interpretation. Working from a squeeze and a photograph of the inscription, Wickremasinghe interpreted 'Demala-paha' as a building linked with an important sect of Buddhist priests which later produced celebrated reformers. In his full translation of the text he referred to 500 members of 'the Great Community', and to sacred 'kusalan', possibly vessels, in which an offering of gruel was made. [16]

Bell had received *Epigraphia Zeylanica* Vol.II, Part 4 in May 1917. In an article in the *Ceylon Antiquary and Literary Register* in July, on Dimbula-gala, he paid tribute in the Appendix to Wickremasinghe's meticulous thoroughness and erudite scholarship, but offered a 'friendly criticism', confidently hoping that it would not be resented. He rebutted the charge that he had missed a continuation of the inscription, by stressing that the cave was exceptionally open and flooded with daylight. Wickremasinghe was, said Bell, a victim of unsupported estampages which had been earlier sent to him. These Bell describes as 'treacherous', although executed by A.P.Siriwardhana, who was well qualified. Bell's article contained plates of the caves and squeezes, photographs and eye-copies taken in 1897 and 1903. This account was much fuller than the 1897 version, containing descriptions of the setting, pools, ledges 'which troubled the Vedda escort as little as it would have monkeys', and of some images, also the inscriptions transcribed and translated. The Queen had improved the passageway for 'persons traversing with bent knees by the help of chains' and had endowed the monks with rice.

On Wickremasinghe's reading of the name on the inscription as *Vijaya Bahu Vathimi*, he accepted the third word of the name, but denied that the first word was 'Vijaya'. He was rejecting both his own 1897 identification of the ruler as Vijaya Bahu, and Wickremasinghe's choice of him. He was sure the monarch was Jaya Bahu I, who had disputed the succession with his nephew

Vikrama Bahu, Sundara's husband. Bell believed that the Queen was trying to make up for the sins of her relatives, who were hostile to Buddhism. [17]

Wickremasinghe wrote in 1919 a long comment on Bell's article, which he sent to the Colonial Office. It commenced with quite cordial references to the friendly spirit of Bell's criticisms and to 'my early days of apprenticeship when he and I had often to tackle many an inscription under most trying conditions in the malarial forests'. He proceeded, however, to complain that Bell 'comes down on me like an avalanche armed with a vast amount of inscriptional information which has been withheld from me'. In particular, out of the fifty-four inscriptions dealt with by Bell, Wickremasinghe possessed squeezes of only twenty-four, and no eye-copies nor photographs, nor any squeezes of Tamil inscriptions. [18]

However, he accepted some of Bell's points, and notably now the 'Jaya Bahu' identification. He thought that 'in the 27th year of "Jaya Bahu Vat-himiya"' was calculated from the coronation of Jaya Bahu, before his very brief reign, though he had died before the date of the inscription. Wickremasinghe clung to 'kusalan' as meaning vessels and not, as in Bell's view, villages. [19]

Bell's response was a Memorandum sent on March 15, 1920 to the Governor, Sir William Manning, and forwarded to England. He accounted for the discrepancy, noticed by Wickremasinghe, between the original notes from his own diary in the 1897 Report and his recent article by the fact that he had used, in the former, compressions from very rough field notes.

He dealt mainly now with Wickremasinghe's complaints of not having received adequate material; for example all the Tamil inscriptions had been sent to India. All estampages had been despatched by August 1911, and without knowing which epigraphs Wickremasinghe was going to treat, it would have been wasteful to supply photographs and eye-copies. The Epigraphist had not since 1907 sent a Programme of work, had only produced ten parts of *Epigraphia Zeylanica* in fifteen years, and was not entitled to resent this being supplemented by other scholars.

Bell was severe on the 1917 *Epigraphia Zeylanica* article, calling it a 'fiasco'; Wickremasinghe had depended on squeezes only, though he could, for any particular need, have appealed for help. It seems it was nearly impossible for the two men to see things the same way; but Bell's indignation may appear excessive, as when he commented:

> In such cases of mental aberration, it is always best to leave the 'possessed' alone to their own strangely balanced consciences. [20]

Governor Manning, who had licensed Wickremasinghe to acquire information from the Government Agent of North-Central Province, temporarily in charge of the Archaeological Department, also took a hand in the scholars' contest. Professor Keith had blamed Bell for only sending estampages to Wickremasinghe, but Manning pointed out that Bell had had other more pressing work, often lacked an Assistant, and had to take all photographs himself. Bell's present stocks of material post-1912, when not from the Archaeological Survey, had been built up at his own expense. To set his and Wickremasinghe's delays against one another was fruitless. As the oriental proverb said, 'Two black crows do not make one white pigeon'. [21]

The Dimbulagala controversy was wound up by two articles, in 1923 and 1924. In *Epigraphia*

Zeylanica Vol.II, Part 5, Wickremasinghe referred back to Bell's 'scholarly review in the CALR of July 1917'. Re-translating the inscription, he added the Queen's concern for 'hardship of people, who like old folk, hang onto chains and tread the path between' - not 'crawling on knees'. He criticised Bell's placing of 500 monks in the cave (they just resided locally). He agreed with more then half of the readings in dispute between them, but kept his own idea about 'kusalan'; and accepted, for the dating, Jaya Bahu, whom the Buddhist priesthood had favoured. [22]

Bell in the CALR Vol.10 in July 1924 summed up the controversy, still differing from Wickremasinghe on the exact dating of the inscription. He repeated a suggestion from his 1919 Memorandum that an impartial scholar should re-examine the inscription. [23]

Some other critiques by Bell of Wickremasinghe's *Epigraphia Zeylanica* work had earlier appeared, in which Bell was more complimentary. For example in CALR Vol.5 Bell praised Wickremasinghe's 'learned acumen and marked success' in his study of nineteen Polonnaruwa inscriptions in Vol.II, Parts 2, 3 and 4. [24]

In 1921 Wickremasinghe was writing to the new Archaeological Commissioner, A.M.Hocart, and suggesting a detailed scheme for registering inscriptions by serial numbers of the Provinces and areas of their discovery. Wickremasinghe also requested information from the Colombo Museum, especially of inscriptions at Vessagiriya. He ended with a friendly gesture:

> In *Epigraphia Zeylanica* Vol.I, Part 2 I have dealt with some of the inscriptions of this group but since then many more have been brought to light by the indefatigable labours of Mr. Bell, to whom all Ceylon students owe a profound debt of gratitude. [25]

Between 1921 and 1928 trouble constantly recurred for Wickremasinghe, because of delays in production of parts of *Epigraphia Zeylanica*. Hocart, to whom he had taught Pali, Sinhalese and Tamil, and who made excuses for him, was nevertheless obliged to complain, the Colonial Office to exert pressure, and Keith to defend him by reference to his work for the School of Oriental and African Studies. He was Lecturer there in Sinhalese and Head of the Dravidian Department, besides being Reader in Tamil and Telegu in the University of London. [26]

Two achievements came for Wickremasinghe in 1928. The *Cambridge History of India* Vol. III appeared, to which he had contributed the chapter on Ceylon from A.D. 1215 to 1527 - from the invader Kalinga Vijaya Bahu to the coming of the Portuguese. His own six-part Vol. II of *Epigraphia Zeylanica* was also published in the summer. The Preface contained thanks to Hocart for material and to Keith for revision and oversight. It is pleasing to note that after all their differences Wickremasinghe dedicated the volume to Harry Charles Purvis Bell 'as a small tribute of recognition of his eminent services to Ceylon Epigraphical and Historical Studies'. Most of the forty-two inscriptions included were those of King Nissanka Malla. Numbers 31 and 34, though, were reprints of the Dimbula-gala caves and Maravidye rock inscriptions articles. [27]

When Vol.III appeared in 1933, it was mainly the work of Paranavitana, then Epigraphical Assistant to the Archaeological Commissioner, and contained only two articles by Wickremasinghe (one a Chronology of Ceylon Kings). In the Preface the editor described how the *Epigraphia*

Zeylanica 'started about three decades ago through the initiative of Mr. Bell' and remained under Wickremasinghe's able editorship till the present, when he could not, owing to reasons of health and multifarious duties at the University of London, devote as much time to epigraphical research as the exacting nature of the work demanded. [28]

Our account of the career of Wickremasinghe has to end in a minor key. In December 1929 his appointment as Epigraphist to the Ceylon Government was finally terminated, and although he applied for a pension, it had not been granted by 1930. Wijeyekoon writes that owing to old age Wickremasinghe had to retire from SOAS, and return to Ceylon in 1935. W.S.Karuneratne in 'The history of epigraphical research' thus concludes the story:

> When this eminent scholar, who went blind in his old age, returned to Ceylon, the Government awarded him a pension in recognition of his services. Only very few comprehend his great contribution to linguistic and historical researches of Ceylon. It was Dr. Wickremasinghe who placed Ceylon Epigraphy on a firm footing, and Ceylonese owe him a great debt of gratitude. [29]

Since they both died in 1937, Wickremasinghe and Bell were not unnaturally linked in obituary notices. In the Annual Report of 1937 the Archaeological Commissioner, A.H.Longhurst, wrote:

> It is with deep regret that I record here the deaths during the year of Mr. H.C.P.Bell and Dr. M.de Z.Wickremasinghe, two scholars to whom the student of archaeology in Ceylon will always remain indebted... Dr. Wickremasinghe who, for some time, was Mr. Bell's Assistant, made the study of Ceylon Epigraphy his special field, and with the co-operation of Mr. Bell started the publication of *Epigraphia Zeylanica*, of which he brought out two volumes and the first part of the third. His work marked a great advance on that of his predecessors in the field of Ceylon Epigraphy and won for him international recognition as a first-class Orientalist. [30]

Paranavitana, in his Preface to *Epigraphia Zeylanica* Vol.IV, expressed his regret at the deaths between two years of one another of H.C.P.Bell, Professor A.M.Hocart and Wickremasinghe, writing of the last-named:

> Of Dr. Wickremasinghe, who predeceased his erstwhile chief by three months, it can truly be said that he laid the foundations of the scientific study of Ceylon epigraphy on a firm basis. In the midst of his multifarious duties, first at Oxford University and later at London University, he edited and published between 1903 and 1927 thirteen parts of this journal, consisting solely of his own contributions. The scholarly and able manner in which Dr. Wickremasinghe carried out this onerous task earned for him a first-class international reputation among Indianists; but it is sad to reflect on the indifference of his own countrymen towards the great services he has rendered his country by his researches into the history, language and culture of the Sinhalese people, incidentally bringing credit to Ceylon scholarship. [31]

The indifference here referred to seems confirmed in some degree by the comments of W.S.Karuneratne cited above, though to the tribute by Longhurst may be added that in the obituary in the JRASCB in 1937 which ran:

> He initiated and carried on the scientific publication of *Epigraphia Zeylanica* with scrupulous care and in patient investigation of doubtful letters and words. Issues of the *Epigraphia Zeylanica* edited by him are valued for accuracy and completeness. [32]

Nevertheless, D.T.Devendra, writing on Bell and Wickremasinghe in 1962 in the JRASCB, comments on Paranavitana's obituaries as follows:

> He seems to have written with special poignancy of the loss of Wickremasinghe, whose mantle had fallen on him, when he bemoaned the neglect into which his own countrymen had consigned the epigraphist who had done so much to interpret his country's contribution to the larger learned world. [33]

21

Bell and his Family

Eastern Service always entailed partings and separations. After going to Ceylon, Bell never saw his parents again. On his death in 1894 Bell's father, General H.W.B.Bell, left his son some keepsakes, including his godfather's ring and a signet with the device of a 'bell'; also various religious books. All the General's money went to his wife, but when she died in January 1900 Bell inherited £500 and Rs. 5,000 from a trust fund. In the same year his eldest daughter, Eva Laura, died; her grave is in Colombo beside those of her parents.

In those days of travel by steamship, the separation of parents from their children sent Home to school was not punctuated by holidays; and when they grew up their lives and careers were often in other countries than that of their birth. A certain detachment from the life of his family was thus imposed on Bell though perhaps it was also part of his temperament. None of his children shared his intellectual interests, though in one way or another they followed in his footsteps in sport.

His second daughter, Renée Isabel, always known as Daisy, no doubt because of the popular song of the period about Daisy Bell and the 'bicycle made for two', accompanied him in his climb on Sigiriya and sometimes went shooting with him in the jungle. By 1897, when the three 'children of Anuradhapura' began going to England to school, the elder ones had returned to Ceylon. Renée in 1903 in St. Paul's Church, Kandy, married Arthur Ashburner Prideaux, whose work was on a tea plantation and then as Acting Manager in the Colombo office of the Colombo Commercial Company.

Bell's first grandchildren were born in Colombo, Arthur Guyon in January 1904, Iris Renée in July 1907 and Laura Sabine in June 1910. Guyon recalls in this year seeing Halley's Comet. In 1912 the Prideaux moved; because of an illness Arthur was obliged to return to England and his family settled at Weybridge.

One colonial war and one international one were to separate members of Bell's family. His eldest son Harry Amelius, known in the family as 'Hal', was starting as a tea planter in 1899, but went off in January 1900 to the Boer War in South Africa with 130 others of the first Ceylon contingent of mounted infantry, and was among the representatives to visit England for the Coronation ceremony of Edward VII. Back in Ceylon he became an Assistant Railway Engineer on the Northern Railway Extension. Bell's Labour Assistant at that time, C.E.Dashwood, when going on sick leave, suggested Hal as a substitute; but his father dissented, apparently lacking confidence in his son.

After this he held a series of posts; in 1903 as an Assistant Irrigation Engineer, from 1904-5 as an Inspector of Police. He gradually passed examinations in Law and Languages, and in 1906 became an Assistant Collector of Customs and Police Magistrate, Trincomalee. From May 1908 he was a probationary Land Settlement Officer and the following year he married.[1]

Hal's bride, Ethel Howard, the daughter of a barrister who was also an R.A., had had an education like a boy's, with classics and mathematics, and had hoped to attend a university. Instead she had had an unusual career as a governess. In 1895 she was chosen as English governess to sons of Wilhelm II, the Kaiser or Emperor of Germany. Her three years in this post she later described in her very readable book *Potsdam Princes*. She draws sympathetic portraits of her three charges, Adelbert, August Wilhelm and Oscar; all were boisterous, affectionate and practical jokers. In her picture of Court life Ethel mingles homely details with those of exhausting formalities, ceremonial splendours, and the strongly militaristic orientation of society - and even of education. Serious illness led to her resignation in 1898, but she was from 1901 to 1907 employed in Japan to educate children of a noble family. [2]

Hal and Ethel were married on February 20, 1909. Trouble, however, followed shortly. His superior officers did not confirm his probationary appointment; he was reluctant to return to the Police unless promoted, and in April he resigned. He had formed an opinion, based on a now-lost letter to H.C.P.Bell, that the Governor, McCallum, was motivated by opposition to his marriage. It was more probable that he accepted the reports of Hal's inefficiency; and he passed them on to the Colonial Office in London. For when Hal went there in June to plead his cause, he made no headway. He made another vain approach to the English Government several years later, but although the former Governor of Ceylon, Sir West Ridgeway, won him the interview he was not re-employed. An official recorded, 'I find that he had been out in Canada and had there lost what money he had so that he and his wife were nearly at the end of their tether'. [3]

However, it appeared that Hal had some chance of going out to North Borneo with the British North Borneo Chartered Company. Sir West Ridgeway, the Chairman, would offer him an appointment. Family tradition has it that he was employed in the Police in North Borneo, but he died out there in 1915.

Ethel's *Potsdam Princes* was published first in America, then in England in 1916; inevitably it includes regretful references to the current war with Germany. Two years later she published her *Japanese Memories*, 'dedicated to the memory of my beloved husband'. This book, with its excellent photographs taken by a friend, gives a vivid impression of Japan between 1901 and 1908, when its traditional attitudes of loyalty to ancestors, to feudal superiors and to the Emperor were beginning to be affected by Western influences. The Anglo-Japanese Alliance concluded in 1902 was still in force in the First World War and Ethel was able to write with whole-hearted enthusiasm of 'this sweet land of laughter and lightheartedness', with its pervasive love of beauty. All the same, the 'brave spirit, patience and devotion' which she brought as English governess to Prince Shimadze and his four little brothers were qualities sufficiently tested. She faced great difficulties with language, customs and etiquette, and took long journeys by train or in dangerous carriages. Almost single-handed she took the three youngest of her devoted pupils on a visit to Korea and China. Besides the testimonial to her quoted above she received the gift of a black cloisonné vase which remains in the Prideaux family. [4]

To revert to Bell's younger children, Cyril and Malcolm were at Clarence School, Weston-super-Mare (Hal's former school), and spent holidays at Corston Lodge near Bristol, with a Mr. and Mrs. Bartlett and their children Amy and Fritz. Cyril was a promising sportsman, who shared the Champion Prize and Challenge Cup at the school athletics, was Captain of Football from 1900 to 1901, and in June of that year in a cricket match took eight wickets for two runs. For his entry to Cooper's Hill College for forestry training one requirement was German. In 1901, however, he failed the examination in the subject. It must have been decided to send him to Germany to get more practice in the language, for in January 1902 Amy Bartlett wrote to him in Hanover a glowing account of moonstones and other gifts received for Christmas from Ceylon. Malcolm was off back to school and Zoë to hers, the 'Beehive' at Worthing.

Cyril achieved Cooper's Hill that year, being one of the last Forest Officers to be trained there. During or after the course he had to see forestry work in practice, in France at Compiègne, and in the Black Forest in Germany. We next find him in 1906, posted to the Central Provinces in India, centred on Nagpur. One of his uncles, also a godparent, Frank Fyers, had been in the Forestry Service in Ceylon, which might have pointed him to his career. In any case he was particularly well suited to the work, was a keen shikari and a good shot like his father. Those were days when tiger shooting was still normal, and Cyril killed his first tiger at a Christmas camp, 1906. He continued to be a good player of cricket, also of tennis and golf, advanced steadily in his profession, and by 1915 was a Deputy Conservator of Forests, appointed to Jubbulpore, one of the best districts in the Province. Harry Hemingway of the I.C.S., a friend, saw this as a proof that he was good at his work, and also paid tribute to his character: 'He is one of the nicest men I know, and very steady and sensible, and what is almost more important, is always good-tempered.'

Hemingway was writing from Harold House, Pachmarhi, on October 26, 1915, to Mr. Charles Aitken of Totland Bay, Isle of Wight. The same day, to Mrs. Aitken, Mrs. Beryl Hemingway wrote of Cyril as 'all anyone could wish for as a son-in-law... good-looking... a fair-haired Viking sort of look' - and with no debts. Cyril himself wrote to Aitken, giving full particulars of his family and prospects, to ask for consent to his marriage to Phyllis Aitken; saying, 'I am an extremely lucky man to win a charming, capable and dear girl like your daughter'.

Phyllis was Beryl Hemingway's youngest sister. After some work as a V.A.D. in England at the beginning of the War, she had come out to stay with her sister in India. Phyllis was a talented and beautiful creature who had had many admirers. She made friends with Cyril in playing tennis, and after a four months' courtship they had become engaged on October 25. Family reactions came from Ceylon to Cyril, who told his fiancée that the ladies were 'delighted with your photo', and 'even the Old Bear is pleased and admires my taste and says you have good features and are very nice-looking'.

The Hemingways moved to Chindwara, where the marriage took place at St. Mary's Church on March 7, 1916 and was fully described by Beryl to her mother. It had been a considerable effort to arrange, for the place had been emptied by plague (which also killed squirrels) and supplies and workmen were very difficult to find. Somehow white flowers, the cake, and presents were achieved and the bridal attendants, Eric Hemingway, aged four, and a still younger Diana, 'looked perfectly sweet in their pale blue satin Dickens costumes', though they proved a good deal of a handful.

Cyril's mother (on paper black-edged for her son Hal's death) wrote welcoming letters and mentioned that Cyril had visited Kandy in 1912, and was 'the same dear, affectionate son'. Zoë, pleased to acquire a games-playing sister-in-law, also wrote from Richmond Villa, Kandy. Mrs. Bell was looking forward to seeing the couple between March and May at Nuwara Eliya, for this was where they were to spend the honeymoon.

This was one of the comparatively rare family reunions. Zoë and Malcolm, who during their education had sometimes stayed in Scotland with their Fyers relations at Camphill on Deeside, had by 1907 returned to Ceylon. Zoë, who lived with her parents, in her brief memoirs mentions her many prizes for golf and tennis, and wonders 'how I was so active in court in the dress of my youth':

> I wore vest, corsets, knickers, camisole, petticoat, blouse, and a heavy drill skirt almost to my ankles. As we played all day in the hot sun, one was in a dripping state at the end of a long match. [5]

Malcolm, starting in 1907 as a planting student, at Agra Ouvah, Agrapatana, became a planter there, remaining till 1911. This was the year of the Coronation at Westminster of King George V and Queen Mary. The event on Thursday, June 22 was also celebrated in Ceylon at a number of spots with processions and fireworks, but most spectacularly at Colombo, and brought together members of Bell's family.

The *Times of Ceylon* produced a special souvenir volume, with the programme, press reports and numerous photographs, which showed the gaily decorated public buildings, and streets innocent of any transport except rickshaws, bullock-carts and trams. On the day itself there were great crowds - 'Never has there been such a rush of traffic in Serpentine Road', said the *Times*, - but no accidents occurred, even though special trains arrived packed 'literally like sardine tins'.

The day's programme included a Church Service at St. Peter's, Fort, also a High Mass in St. Lucia's Cathedral and a United Service in Victoria Park. It was a crowded day for the Governor, Sir Henry McCallum, whom the photographs show involved in a State Procession from Queen's House to the Council Chamber. Here there was a Meeting of the Legislative Council, a brilliant spectacle of military uniforms, Judges of the Supreme Court, gorgeously dressed Kandyan Chiefs *et alia*. Addressing all these, His Excellency spoke of the King as 'Our Sailor Prince' who had visited Ceylon ten years ago; also of how the Queen would be wearing 'imperial robes emblematic of the mother and daughter nations, whose destinies are identical under the sheltering folds of the Union Jack'. The Governor also held a Levée and investiture, the numerous guests including A.A.Prideaux. Present was 'the Lascoreen Band, that relic of the past, which with its nondescript gorgeous uniform, and its music that is like nothing on land or sea, haunts all official functions in Ceylon'.

On the Havelock Racecourse from five p.m., besides gracing sports and a demonstration by Colombo school children - 'Miss Linda Modder, as Britannia, was particularly noticeable' - the Governor took the salute at a Ceremonial Military Parade. This was 'a magnificent display' with the colours of the uniforms of the Ceylon Light Infantry, the Royal Engineers, the Garrison Artillery, the 4th Rajputs, the Ceylon Planters' Rifle Corps, the Navy and Marines. The Ceylon Mounted Rifles at the gallop 'made a stirring picture as they flashed past in five troops'.

Bell and his family

The day concluded with a Fireworks Display on Galle Face, which gave pleasure to a tremendous crowd, though the *Times* frankly admitted that, for the money spent, it should have been more impressive. This, however, could not have been said of the Illuminations, thus described:

After dusk Colombo presented a scene of surpassing beauty. The usually sombre streets of the town were transformed into avenues of light and splendour, along which passed gaily decorated vehicles and crowds of enthusiastic people. Contrary to the expectations of many, and to the great relief, we may be sure, of the Electrical Company's engineers, the service proved adequate for the occasion and the buildings in the Fort and the Pettah were magnificently illuminated. The costumes of the natives harmonised with the gorgeous surroundings; and viewed from the top of one of the highest buildings in Colombo, the scene was one not to be forgotten. From the town rose one great blaze of vari-coloured light - red, blue, green, yellow and white all blending their hues - and in the streets the Japanese and Chinese lanterns suspended from countless conveyances slowly swayed when moving along the thoroughfares.

In the harbour the 'Highflyer' and the 'Proserpine', particularly helped by the 'Espiègle' and the 'Odin', looked like phantom vessels, the lines being studded with electric jets, and the funnels and masts similarly illuminated. The flagship was surmounted by a *gorgeous crown of light* which seemed suspended in the air. [6]

The extracts from newspapers quoted in the souvenir issue, elevated examples of loyal rhetoric, were simply summed up by the *Times of Ceylon*, which said of the Coronation, 'The tremendous interest which has been taken in the event all over the Empire was fully reflected in Ceylon and reached all classes of the people, without distinction of race or religious creed'. The celebrations concluded on Friday, June 23 with a State Ball at Queen's House for nearly a thousand guests. Among those invited on this occasion were Mr. and Mrs. Prideaux, and Mr. and Mrs. Bell and Miss Zoë Bell. The gardens were illuminated, and the Governor and Sir Hugh and Lady Clifford took part in a set of State Lancers.

From all this light the century moved into the shadows of the First World War, which brought tragedies to many. Of the Aitkens, Kenneth, Phyllis's elder brother, died some years later from its after-effects; Archie, the Royal Engineer, recipient of the M.C. and several other medals, was killed near Baghdad by a mad soldier in 1919.

The Government had had too much need of Forest Officers to let Cyril Bell go to the war, but the lives of others were touched. John Still, H.C.P.Bell's former Assistant, was a Second Lieutenant in the 6th East Yorkshires. In *The Jungle Tide*, after describing the nervous and wary behaviour of sambhur stags approaching water by night, he wrote:

When on Gallipoli we had to fill our water-bottles at springs measured and marked by snipers, we knew the sambhur's inner thoughts. [7]

Still became a prisoner of war in Turkey. Malcolm Bell from 1916 was a Second Lieutenant in the South Lancashire Regiment, served in France and became a Captain. Dorris Bell was to relate:

> He had been knocked out of the actual trench warfare by dysentery and colitis, but then had lectured and taught bombing all round the south of England. [8]

His leaves had been spent with the Prideaux, and when the girls had influenza in the epidemic that followed the war, Guyon stayed with his uncle at Weston-super-Mare. On Malcolm's return to Ceylon in 1919 he became Superintendent on the Binoya tea estate.

With peace renewed Bell would see something of his other children and also his grandchildren.

22

Polonnaruwa: The Promontory, Quadrangle and Citadel

Bell's last years as Archaeological Commissioner were mainly occupied by his excavations and restorations at Polonnaruwa. He had visited the ruins briefly in 1893, spending two days there, and reporting as follows:

> 1) The extent of the ruins of Polonnaruwa can be but approximately gauged, jungle having been cleared only round individual structures or groups of ruins. Felling and burning of a wide area of jungle undergrowth is essential.
> 2) The large Dagabas and main buildings should be freed of destructive vegetation, which is steadily penetrating them more deeply year by year.
> 3) Many of the ruined buildings being constructed of brick and hard mortar with walls of great thickness, the time and labour spent on clearing the debris must exceed the tale for similar work at the older and less massive ruins of Anuradhapura.
> 4) The most characteristic examples of Polonnaruwa architecture should be preserved from further decay and ruin, and restoration undertaken where justified - not a difficult undertaking with proper appliances - without delay.
> 5) Impressions of all known inscriptions should be obtained as soon as possible. [1]

Again in 1897 he spent a few days at Topavewa, re-examining and photographing the ruins, but it was not until 1900 that, with an increased Archaeological Vote and the appointment of a Labour Assistant, he felt free to start work.

Polonnaruwa succeeded Anuradhapura as a capital city in the middle ages; the period of its dominance was between 1017 and 1235. It differed as a site from Anuradhapura in several ways. It had not been built over to the same extent and, as the jungle was cleared, the plan of the main streets and buildings was laid bare. More secular buildings remained standing; there were more Hindu temples; decorative detail was more florid; more buildings were constructed wholly of brick. When Bell visited the ruins in 1893 he had remarked that, 'the contrast between the massive brick and mortar buildings of Polonnaruwa and the endless stone pillars at Anuradhapura is exceedingly marked'. [2]

It will be noticed that at Polonnaruwa Bell devoted much more time and energy to restoration than he had in the first ten years at Anuradhapura. This may be partly because the magnificent brick buildings such as the Thuparama were in immediate danger of collapse, but also because from 1904 there was a regular special grant for the purpose.

The main areas excavated at Polonnaruwa were listed as follows in the summary given by Bell in the *Ceylon Manual* of 1912-13:

1900-1901	Ruins on Promontory.
1902	Hindu Dewales (Minneriya-Topavewa Road).
1903	Ruins on raised quadrangle near Topavewa.
1905	'Raja Maligawa' (so-called).
1906	'Potgul Vihare' Monastery, and Siva Dewale No.2.
1907	Gal Vihare and Siva Dewale No. 1.
1908	Hindu Dewales (Topavewa-Divulankaduvala Road and in City).
1909	Demala Maha Seya, Maligawa and dagaba (in the tank), Monastery near North Gate of the City and Dewales.
1910-11	Jetawanarama Vihare, Kiribat Vehera. [3]

Bell began his excavations on the promontory overlooking the Topavewa tank, and after a diversion to undertake a 'rescue dig' of Hindu ruins exposed by road works about a mile away, systematically explored the area eastward and to the south and north.

The 'secular' ruins on the Promontory were listed as follows by Bell in his summary report of work achieved in 1900:

(a) The 'Council Chamber', a building with massive stone pillars standing upon a lofty platform stone-faced.
(b) The 'Audience Hall', or 'Court of Justice', a large building of brick and mortar, stucco-plastered, and one-storied at its western end.
(c) A 'Mausoleum' (?), storied, brick-built, and ornamented with stucco-mouldings picked out in colours.
(d) A 'Pavilion', partially walled, and floored in plaster, with short stone piers, from which an upper wooden storey may have risen. This building stood on an artificially constructed mound within the tank, but was formerly joined to the promontory bund and the buildings clustered west of (a), (b), (c) by a bridge.
(e) The walls of buildings connected with some irrigation work lying immediately below the tank, and once fed from it by a sluice now blocked.
(f) A pillared building, and brick-strewn mound, close to the Irrigation Bungalow on the tank bund. The form and object of the ruins at these last-named sites (e,f) have yet to be ascertained by excavation. [4]

When these areas were excavated in 1901 Bell found a large pokuna, fed from the Topavewa tank by a sluice, and with an ornamental shower bath at one end. In his Report for 1901 Bell draws attention to the manner in which modern excavation had confirmed the details of the *Mahavansa*:

The 'Council Chamber' bears its identification on its massive columns. The 'Audience (or Banqueting) Hall' is quite probably fixed by an inscription of King Nissanka Malla (1208 A.D.). And of the date and construction of the magnificently designed *pokuna*, baths, and park, the *Mahavansa* furnishes quaint record. These were among the 'many mighty works' of the most famed of Sinhalese rulers, Parakrama Bahu the Great (1154-1197 A.D.), though manifestly repaired by some of his successors.

Polonnaruwa : The promontory, quadrangle and citadel

55Here at least is sure ground, testifying at once to the genius of the sovereign and the veracity of the *Mahavansa*:

> The chief of kings and lord of the country (Parakrama Bahu I) caused also a park (*uyana*) to be made nigh unto the royal palace. And they called it *Nandana*, because that it displayed the splendour of *Nandana*, the 'garden of heaven', and pleased the eyes of the people and gave them delight. It had trees entwined with creepers of jasmine.
>
> And the air was filled with swarms of bees, roused with the enjoyment of the honey of divers flowers… Divers fruit-bearing trees of their kind were found there, such as charm the people. And it was made delightful by the cries of the peacock and the sweet and deep tones of the *kokila* that charm the world and always give pleasure.
>
> It was interspersed also with sheets of water ornamented with fine banks, and made pleasant by the abundant growth of the lotus and the lily, and the musical tones of the *seras*. It was railed also with pillars decorated with rows of images made of ivory.
>
> And it was ornamented with a bathing-hall that dazzled the eyes of the beholder, from the which issued forth sprays of water that was conducted through pipes by means of machines, making the place to look as if the clouds poured down rain without ceasing - a bathing-hall, large and splendid, and bearing, as it were, a likeness to the knot of braided hair that adorned the head of the beautiful park-nymph.
>
> It also glittered with a mansion of great splendour and brightness such as was not to be compared, and displayed the beauty of many pillars of sandalwood carved gracefully, and was like an ornament on the face of the earth. [5]

Later, in 1909, Bell records the discovery, which was made by John Still, further north, of the Lotus Bath which the *Mahawansa* had spoken of as being among the many pokunu constructed by Parakrama Bahu the Great:

> The artistic conception of this beautiful stone bath is worthy of all praise. Imagine a gigantic lotus flower of granite, full blown, 24 ft. 9 in. in diameter, with five concentric lamina (all single course stones except the topmost, which has three courses) of eight petals, gradually diminishing to a stamen 5 ft. 4 in. across. Then decide to reverse nature's order, and instead of the convex shape depress the petal rings into a concavity 4 ft. 6 in. in depth - and we have the granite 'lotus bath' as it exists in all its shapeliness to this day.
>
> The stepped descending 'petals' are flat in tread and vertical for riser, except the uppermost, which has an ovulo moulding at foot. The similarity to a lotus is still further carried out by rounding up the outer edges of the uppermost cusps, carving on their faces faint imitation of eight lotus petals, and giving to the interspaces a further eight. [6]

After devoting 1902 to the outlying Hindu shrines on the Minneriya-Topavewa road Bell turned to the outstanding collection of buildings standing on a raised platform which is known as the

Quadrangle. He described them as follows:

> The cluster of ruins excavated during the season of 1903 is situated directly east of Topavewa tank, and north of the Citadel and the isolated Hindu temple hitherto miscalled *'Dalada Maligawa'*. This is the most varied and important group at Polonnaruwa. It comprises in all more than a dozen ruined structures, exhibiting different types of architecture, in which Aryan, Dravidian, Kambodian, and may be, Burmese, forms are mingled with bizarre, but pleasing, effect.
>
> The chief buildings are:
> Vihare No. 1.   Nissanka Lata Mandapaya.
> Vihare No. 2.   Pilima-ge.
> Vihare No. 3 ('Heta-da-ge').   Wata-da-ge.
> 'Sat-Mahal-Prasadaya'.   'Thuparama'. [7]

The curious seven-storyed Sat-Mahal-Prasadaya had been cleared of debris by Mr. Burrows, and Bell did no work on it until 1910, when the tunnel dug into the centre by treasure-hunters was filled in and the outside stairs strengthened. Bell thought that they had once led up as far as the third storey. [8]

Various theories have been advanced as to the origin and purpose of this stepped building. Bell held 'that the solution of the puzzle is to be found in Kambodia'. When he has described the building in the Annual Report for 1903 he continues:

> These 'seven-tiered pyramidal structures' known as *Prasat*, are met with commonly amid the ruins of that once important kingdom of the Further East.
>
> The '*Sat-Mahal Prasadaya*' offers an analogy well nigh perfect with the less ornate Khmer pyramidal edifices. It stands as an architectural link between the simplest form of rectangular pyramid such as Ka Keo, with plain vertical walls and straight steep staircases up the middle of each side, and the elaborate towers at Mi-Baume and other similar shrines.
>
> The true significance of these stepped edifices is still open to doubt. They have been supposed to symbolize Mount Kailasa, and likened to Kailasari and Bur Budur in Java. Of late, the theory of intended comparison with Mount Meru and its seven surrounding mountain ranges has found favour, in as much as similar buildings are to be seen in every Siamese capital, under the name of *P' hu Khan Thong*, 'the golden mountain'. [9]

Bell draws attention to the close relations existing between Ceylon and Cambodia in the 12th century and suggests that the Ceylon kings may have employed Cambodian masons. He continues:

> Khmer architectural forms are apparent, not alone in the design of the *Sat-Mahal Prasadaya*, but by other proof among these ruins, though not to the degree of superseding the simpler crystalized mouldings, etc., of Ceylon's pure Buddhistic shrines by the extravagant and overpoweringly lavish

ornamentation which renders staircases, façades, and roofs of Kambodian temples marvels of sculptured detail carried to excess. [10]

Nissanka Malla had claimed to have built three of the edifices on the Quadrangle, though Bell believed that he had merely added 'a fringe of further adornment' to the Heta-da-ge, the Tooth Shrine built by Parakrama Bahu I. [11]

Bell was always chary of giving too much credit to 'Nissanka Malla the self-satisfied', but nevertheless devoted considerable effort to restoring two of the buildings which may be fairly attributed to him. Of the Wata-da-ge, or Circular Image House, Bell states simply that 'it is unrivalled as the most beautiful specimen of Buddhist stone architecture existing in Ceylon'. [12]

He gives the following brief description in his summary for the RASCB of work achieved in 1904:

> Upon a circular *maluwa*, or platform, (4 ft. 8 in. in height and about 370 ft. in circumference), granite-faced and paved throughout, stands a structure, also circular and 75 ft. in diameter, as bold in conception as chaste in its execution. The stylobate, or basement, (5ft. 6 in. high), is faced with moulded plinth, 'bull nose', and coping, relieved by broad bands separated by a bold double cyma torus. These block dados bear figured panels in low relief - the lower, lions passant guardant, the upper, dwarfs in ever-varying posture, etc., both alternating with pilasters.
>
> The coping surface has a narrow gangway, upon which rises a parapet wall of stone slabs, ornamented in flower and trellis work patterns joining up a ring of 32 slender octagonal pillars with spreading capitals, 8 ft. 6 in. in height. To each quadrant formed by the four cardinal doorways into the interior part of the shrine are eight of these short columns. Close behind this parapet is a tall brick wall. The only entrance to the lower *maluwa* of the *'Wata-da-ge'* was through a rectangular portico, bayed and recessed, projecting on the north. Within the brick wall (which mars much of the picturesqueness of the structure, and may be of later addition) at the centre of the inner paved *maluwa* is a small dagaba (28 ft. in diameter) surrounded by two concentric ranges of pillars (16 and 20 respectively, all broken) similar to those on the basement gang-way. To some degree these pillars recall the columns of 'Lankarama' Dagaba at Anuradhapura. They sustained a roof to shelter worshippers inside the shrine and round its basement.
>
> The shrine is entered on the four cardinal sides by granite stairs, 7 ft. in width, of which the steps, balustrades, terminals, and moonstones are freely ornamented with carved figures - dwarfs, makaras, lions, and *Naga dwarapalas*. Facing the doorways, on moulded *asana*, were once four large sedent Buddhas, also in granite. [13]

In the Annual Report for 1903 Bell had described the stairs and balustrades leading into the portico and the four at the cardinal points of the inner circular maluwa. He says that 'as typical examples of the handsomest form of granite staircase elaborated at Polonnaruwa this quartet at the *Wata-da-ge* stands unrivalled'. Although the pattern is similar, 'close examination reveals countless differences in detail, due doubtless to the individual idiosyncrasies of the respective stonemason responsible for each member'. Bell lists the figures on balustrades, guardstones and moonstones with loving care, but cannot help concluding that ornament at Polonnaruwa was in general carried to excess:

> The most finished form of Anuradhapura moonstone is ornamented by concentric belts of flower and trail work alternating with a band of *hansas* and another containing four beasts, always the same, and always moving from left to right in one invariable order - elephant, horse, lion, and bull - surrounding a central expanded lotus.
>
> At Polonnaruwa this single belt of combined animals gives place usually to two, separated by a narrow fillet, one entirely filled with horses, the other with elephants, neither having exclusive precedence in position. The *hansa* is retained; but in an outer band. The lion is generally omitted; the bull always, though retained on guardstones.
>
> This fondness for unduly augmenting figures on the moonstones is even more noticeable in the risers of the steps. The boldly cut trio of squatting dwarfs distributed evenly along the face of Anuradhapura steps, in broad panels flanked by pilasters, did not satisfy the depraved art ideal of a later age. Thus at Polonnaruwa the steps of shrines came to be overcrowded, and *pro tanto* disfigured, by an array of small full-figure *ganas*, between pilasters - ten, eleven, twelve, and even thirteen on one stone. These dwarfs are represented gesticulating and posing in various grotesque ways, starting from either end of the step and meeting towards the middle, where the confronting pair, in a single panel, for the most part join arms or embrace.
>
> This multiplication of massed carving, with its surfeit of detail, detracts inevitably from the beauty of these handsome stairways, which in Anuradhapura are exhibited at their best. [14]

Bell was determined, from the outset, that the Wata-da-ge should be fully restored. In the year of excavation, 1903, after the ruin had been cleared of debris, the outer slab wall was temporarily reset and one of the four broken Buddha images, which had been found around the central dagaba, pieced together and replaced facing the north entrance. As soon as he had secured a grant for restoration, major work was undertaken in 1904, and after the pause in operations decreed by Government in 1905, resumed in 1906.

The progress of the work in those two seasons was summarised as follows by Bell in his report to the RASCB:

> In 1904 the following progress was made in the restoration of this magnificent specimen of Buddhist stone architecture:-
> The north and east steps were relaid level. The latter had to be wholly taken down and reset, after filling in a deep tunnel which had been formed by the wash of years under the stone pavement of the upper floor round the central dagaba. Along the north-east quadrangle the entire moulded revetment of the handsome stone stylobate, and the slab wall above it, were reset in lime mortar pointed with cement. Vegetation had pierced the joints and displaced most of the stones. The broken octagonal shafts of the stone columns, between the slab wall and the inner high brick wall, were also joggled, cemented together, and replaced. Similarly, about two-thirds of the north-west quadrant was completed before the season of 1904 closed. A portion of the undulating stone pavement of the circular *maluwa* round

Polonnaruwa : The promontory, quadrangle and citadel

the stylobate required taking up and relaying in lime mortar. Near the dagaba within the circular wall two more of the four cardinally seated granite Buddhas, found broken into many pieces, were neatly cemented.

The past season (1906) witnessed material advance in the restoration of the 'Wata-da-ge'. The relaying of the pavement of the circular *maluwa* has been completed from the east to the west stairs on the north side; the west steps, and the unfinished portion of the north-west stylobate, with its slab wall and column shafts, reset; and the entire portico (walls, steps, pavement) on the north rebuilt. Many of the pavement slabs are very heavy, and every stone has had to be lifted and relaid, the levels being so arranged that the slope is outwards and inclined to the *pili*, or spouts, which project through the *maluwa* revetment wall at regular intervals.

The west stairs had suffered terribly from fire, probably when the trees covering the site, felled in 1885-86, were foolishly burnt instead of being cut up. Both balustrades - the left (north) one especially - are split and their surface ornament (lion and pilaster) greatly damaged. Fortunately the steps, 'moonstone' slab at foot, and both *Naga dwarpal* terminals, remain intact. A good deal of earth and vegetation, which had crept in behind the steps and balustrades, had to be removed. It was necessary to raise, re-level, and make a fresh bed for the steps which had sunk, and to straighten the guardstones. [15]

The south-west quadrant was completed in 1907; it proved to be the most damaged of the four and the stairs had to be completely dismantled and rebuilt. In 1907 drains were made to run from the centre through the surrounding brick wall, to prevent damage from standing water, and in 1911 the work was finished by repairs to the wall itself and to the central dagaba. Bell felt that he had left 'this magnificent granite ruin as well conserved as possible'. [16]

It was in 1910-11 and 1911-12 that the Nissanka-Lata-Mandapaya, or 'Nissanka's flower-scroll hall' was scrupulously restored. It is an unusual building, a square platform enclosed by a stone railing, imitating wooden posts and rails; on the platform is a miniature dagaba and also curious pillars fashioned as sinuous lotus stalks. Bell called it 'that gem of airy sculpture in granite' and said that the restoration was 'far the most difficult piece of renewal of battered and grossly maltreated stonework the Archaeological Survey has ever undertaken'. The whole ruin was dismantled and rebuilt. In the first year the post and rail fence was pieced together and reset, and the plinth and dado of the basement. Some of the pieces of the rail were missing, and casts were made, and the joints held together provisionally with iron collars, which Bell hoped to remove once the whole quadrangle was protected from the inroads of wandering cattle by the erection of a wire fence. In the second season the work was completed by reassembling and erecting the eight curving columns which represent the stalks of lotus, and which terminate in half-opened buds on which the original wooden roof was supported. Of the difficulty of the work and the satisfaction which he felt at its completion Bell wrote:

> After most tedious sorting, and resorting, of the countless fragments lying *perdu* far around, the scattered pieces of the coping of the basement, and many broken sections and lesser portions of the beautiful lotus-columns, were recovered: these *disjecta membra* were then fitted together, and the shrine restored almost as it stood of old, save for its roof.

Joggling and pointing in cement of the several pillar lengths, and of the many slices and flakes which had scaled off, taxed the skill of the blacksmiths and masons to the utmost. For long the task of resetting the pillars and coping appeared [a] hopeless waste of time; but patient perseverance has succeeded fully in the end.

The final re-assembling of the shattered rail, moulded members, and columns of this unique shrine is deemed by the Archaeological Survey, not unjustifiably, to be a *tour de force* - the happy renewal of a piece of work, extremely puzzling and delicate in places, which in a small way has proved the most intricate and aggravating that has so far fallen to the Department to handle. The difficulties surmounted may be partially realized by close inspection of the several parts of this choice structure as it stands at this day, with much of its pristine glory renewed. The accompanying Plates help to show that here 'love's labour' has not been 'lost'. [17]

Restorations were also carried out in the 'Citadel' area which lies between the Promontory and the Quadrangle. Here stood the so-called 'Raja Maligawa', which he described as 'an oblong basilica' and likened to the Council Chamber on the Promontory. He said that 'with its bold *makara* wings and lion-guarded staircase [it] is, among *Buddhistic* stone ruins of Polonnaruwa, second only in elegance and profusion of sculpture to the unique "Wata-da-ge"'.[18]

On the three rows of carved figures which ornamented the sides of the platform (elephants, lions and dwarfs) he commented critically:

The elephants (a few excepted) are carved with a stereotyped stiffness, strangely at variance with their life-like representation on moonstones; whilst the lions might well be stone bas-reliefs of indifferently stuffed specimens for all the animation they display. The dwarfs alone, by their ever varied poses and 'right merrie gestures', save the ornamentation of the elongated stylobate from that wearisome effect which monotonous repetition cannot fail to induce.

Of the main staircase he said:

The stairs when complete and undamaged must have nearly rivalled, in the massiveness and finish of their magnificent pair of granite balustrades, the imposing stairway at the main entrance on the east to the so-called *'Jetawanarama'* Vihare. These wing stones are of the most elaborate *makara*-headed type, with thick ornamental roll curling from the mouths of the saurians down to a bold volute at bottom. The exterior vertical face of the balustrades (which are 5 ft. 7 in. in height to the top of the monster's flat-curled trunk) bears the same sculpture seen on the wings of the staircases at the *Wata-da-ge*, namely, profile lion, preceding a pilaster with manifold spreading capitals. But here an additional figure is introduced - a *Doratupalaya*, facing full front, adorned with high *mukata* head-gear, heavy earrings, etc., who holds a staff across his body diagonally between both hands.

At the head of the stairs lay two lions:

The 'lord of beasts' is ludicrously travestied in these 'China dog' *sinhayo* so painfully conventionalized - semi-bull-dog in face, with humped forehead, scalloped ears, leafy tail, and unnatural claws.

Polonnaruwa : The promontory, quadrangle and citadel

Nathless, despite their grotesqueness, these fearsome janitors are imposing enough as placed to guard the portal.

There were two fine moonstones, one at the foot of the main stairs and the other at a point where stairs had disappeared. The first, unusually at Polonnaruwa, had thirty lions as well as fourteen elephants and twelve horses, moving from right to left with an inner belt of foliaged creeper and an outer band of forty hansas. The second had thirteen horses, thirteen elephants and two ducks.

Bell decided that the ruin was in danger of collapse and that he was justified in removing debris and the vegetation that tended to push out the walls. As all the carved slabs around the platform and most of the columns upon it remained unbroken, he pushed on with the restoration and declared that the result was 'exceedingly pleasing'. [19]

The 'Citadel' area in which stood the 'Raja Maligawa' contained only one other building above ground, although it was clear that the remains of other buildings, cross walls and bye streets lay buried below the surface. It was not until 1911 that this other building, a massive brick structure originally of three storeys, was excavated and identified as the actual 'Royal Palace'. Nearby was another beautiful pokuna, the Kumara Pokuna. Bell said that 'this pokuna is capable of neat restoration, and is worthy of it'. This has been achieved as part of the ever-continuing work at Polonnaruwa. [20]

23

Polonnaruwa : Hindu and Buddhist Shrines

In 1905 Bell was not supposed to undertake any fresh excavations. He had worked on the Raja Maligawa to prevent imminent collapse, but he otherwise confined himself chiefly to the clearing of vegetation on and around ruins, in particular the two great dagabas (Kiri Vehera and Rankot Vehera) and the tall, brick-built Jetawanarama. He wrote:

> Vegetation had laid a terrible grip on the magnificent ruins, and for years been surely working their certain, if slow, destruction. Drastic action was necessary; for serpentine roots of innumerable trees had penetrated deep into the masonry and caused yawning cracks, already lessening greatly their stability. From their height and conformation these structures cannot safely be scaled and cleaned during the prevalence of the strong south-west wind.
>
> The work of eradication proved heavy, and attended with no little risk. Some of the roots are as thick as a man's thigh, and the towering walls of the brick vihares too fragile at top to permit of strong blows with full-sized axes. Small 'Vedda axes' had to be used, and served well; but could only cope effectively with the countless massy roots by gentle and prolonged chopping. [1]

Further work on the Kiri Vehera did not begin until 1910, when scaffolding was set up round the bell and the many wide fissures cleaned out in preparation for re-filling. This was started in 1912, and although it was not possible to finish the repairs, Bell hoped that the work would be completed by his successor when the tee and pinnacle were tackled. He said, however, that 'all danger from water penetrating into the Dagaba had been prevented by the essential work carried out in 1911-12'. [2]

When first describing the Kiri Vehera in his 1910-11 Report Bell had remarked in a note 'that no dagaba of this magnitude has been so desperately attacked by treasure hunters', and he described the tunnel they had dug out in their search. [3]

In 1912 he describes how he cleared the tunnel in order to explore the central relic-chambers himself:

> In cleaning out the great fissure above the 'chapel' frontispiece on the north it was found that it was a veritable *ummagga*, or tunnel, driven centuries ago into the garbha high up by raiders, who had penetrated to the very bowels of the Dagaba, and reached the relic-chambers at its centre.
>
> This tortuous tunnel was choked with bats' dung, the removal of which was a dirty job, tedious and stifling owing to very cramped passage way available for penetrating along the horizontal shaft, and the need of air. Only by working 'time shifts' could the coolies face the undertaking, which filled their lungs with the light pungent powder, only removable slowly, in suffocating atmosphere, total darkness, and barest possible working space. [4]

Polonnaruwa : Hindu and Buddhist shrines

Bell found that the treasure seekers had reached the two topmost of the three chambers, and robbed them completely of any objects there placed. He presumed also that they had removed the central square-shafted stone symbolising Maha Meru, the mythical mountain at the centre of the earth. Bell assumed the existence of the third chamber beneath the others, and showed it in the plan and section of the tunnel and relic-chambers, made with great difficulty inside the Dagaba, and included among the Plans at the end of the 1911-12 Report. He writes:

> The existence of a third cella has been assumed and its position shown on the drawing, as there is room for it above the level of the Dagaba's *maluwa*. No attempt was made by the Archaeological Survey to penetrate below the second cella. The risk of deepening the shaft down the centre of this great Dagaba would have been serious had the two upper chambers, and cavern made by the treasure-hunters above them, been further weakened by additional loosening of the brickwork below. [5]

Bell had excavated the relic-chambers of two other dagabas, one at Polonnaruwa in 1909 and one at Sigiriya in 1910. Both had been breached and robbed, but careful re-excavation produced interesting results. In the Polonnaruwa dagaba he uncovered six cellas, and in the second, in some of the unbroken sections of the square brick *yantra-gala*, found a great variety of small bronze votive objects: gods, animals, reptiles and implements. Further down there was another *yantra-gala*, this time nine-holed, which 'produced a brood of cobras, [including] a mother and four young, in bronze, or 45 *nagas* in all'. There were also a few coins, some rare, scattered semi-precious jewels and a copper plate too corroded to be deciphered. But, said Bell, it was the third cella that 'contained the most important "find" of all - a squared pedestal of limestone (1 ft. 8 in. by 9 1/4 in.), with seven horizontal ribs (probably to represent Mount Maha Meru) and splayed at top pyramidically. This pedestal (of which three sides respectively still show traces of red, yellow, and white colouring - with blue, red, yellow, and white on the fourth side and top) stood on three small detached supports as tripod. It was crowned by a beautifully modelled *karanduwa* of beaten gold, 3 in. high, shaped like a diminutive dagaba. The *karanduwa* contained seventeen small gems of no intrinsic value'. [6]

The other dagaba where relic-chambers were investigated was in a monastic site three quarters of a mile from Sigariya on the road to Kimbissa. Three cellas were dug out, and in the third a fine example of the 'Maha Meru' stone was found. Bell said that although it was 'less true to type than the seven-ringed and four-coloured *Maha-Meru-gala* of the Polonnaruwa Dagaba, it makes up for these deficiencies in other respects. All four sides are incised elaborately in shallow sunk-relief, and each face differs from the others in its main motif; but otherwise the sides of the obelisk have a broad general resemblance'.

Each side is divided into three panels, separated by decorative bands, the top band 'shaped into *cyma reversa* bands of "cobra-leaf" acanthus'. Each of the bottom panels has six male figures in attitudes of adoration, and each of the top panels five figures moving to the right, but in different attitudes. Bell describes them as 'village scenes of a *genre* nature', with men, women, children and cows, but remains uncertain of their significance. Of the style of the work he says:

The whole carving of the stone has been executed more or less faintly in *intaglio*, and exhibits the stiffness and want of finish noticeable in some of the early Buddhistic bas-reliefs discovered in India.[7]

Roman coins found in the relic chamber dated this dagaba to the late 4th century A.D., and Bell said that the size of the bricks also suggested that it was considerably earlier than the dagabas at Polonnaruwa, which flourished from the 11th to the 13th century.[8]

In 1906 Bell had moved south of the Quadrangle to investigate the group of ruins near the huge statue once identified as that of King Parakrama Bahu I, but by Bell and others held to represent a guru or ascetic:

Of neither king, nor Buddhist abbot, is the rock figure the lithic representation. Clearly it is the presentment in granite, perhaps exactly twice life size, of some once famous Hindu *guru*. Clad only in a loin cloth and tall head dress, bare bodied, save for the *yupvita*, or Brahmin cord, wearing no ornaments, heavy in build and features, with beard long and grizzled, the statue possesses no single trait of that divinity which doth hedge a king. Moreover the palm leaf roll of the *veda*, held in both hands as though being studied, and the whole appearance and pose of the figure, stamp it unmistakably as a rock-hewn portrait of a revered religious teacher from the Indian continent...

The sculptor's skill in carving this 'statue from life' is specially exhibited by a side view of the figure. As a silhouette the elderly *guru* is seen not to hold himself fully erect, and to have developed the common tendency to obesity due to creeping old age. A true touch of naturalism is further quaintly brought out by the paunch being made to protrude beyond the tightly tied loin cloth and belt.[9]

1906 was also the year in which Bell started work on the Hindu temples lying within the city boundaries. Over the years Bell excavated a number of such temples at Polonnaruwa, both brick and stone. In the Annual Report of 1908 he tabulates the 'Hindu temples of Polonnaruwa', giving their names, the material of which they were built, measurements, and numbers of satellite fanes, and the Annual Report in which details may be found. He characterises them as follows:

All the devales agree in certain broad lines. Regarding their general features the following points may now be postulated:
(i) They stand within brick *prakara*, or enclosure walls, and are entered (with one solitary exception, Vishnu Devale No. 2) on the east.
(ii) Four, or possibly five, of the main shrines, in a total of thirteen Hindu temples so far discovered, were constructed of stone.
(iii) In plan, and exterior ornamentation, the devales follow almost slavishly one type:- basements of universal form, on which rose bare walls, relieved on three sides by a simple central niche (occasionally by more) flanked by pilasters (whole and dimidiated) with capitals more or less embellished and shapely, the whole crowned by well-defined curvilinear cornice.
(iv) Both inner vestibule and sanctuary of devales sacred to Siva were flat ceiled with stone slabs, and the latter chamber domed in stone or in brick.
(v) Saivite Devales at least were triple-storeyed *vimanas*, terminating in an ornate and graceful dome, circular or octagonal.

Polonnaruwa : Hindu and Buddhist shrines

(vi) The Saivite temples invariably possessed two or more subordinate fanes lying off the sides or angles of the main shrine: Vishnuvite temples none at all.
(vii) The Siva and Vishnu cults admitted each other at Polonnaruwa to a share in Hindu worship by countenancing the erection of shrines sacred to the god, or gods, of the rival persuasion adjoining the precincts of their respective devales.
(viii) No inscriptions have come to light in fixing the name and period of erection of any of the temples, except at Siva Devale No. 2. [10]

Bell selected this last for a full restoration, which was completed in 1911 when he concluded that 'this Saivite shrine, thus saved from further dilapidation, is the sole example existing in this Island of a mediaeval temple of Hindu cult, virtually complete as the "Thuparama" Vihare is of Buddhistic worship'.

Siva Devale No. 1 was excavated in 1907. Bell speculated on how it might have acquired its traditional misnomer:

> How did a shrine so manifestly self-declared a temple of uncompromising Hindu design and worship - that, moreover, of its most antagonistic cult, Saivism - ever acquire the appellation of *Dalada Maligawa*, 'the Shrine of the Tooth Relic of the Buddha'? Can the Devale, purged temporarily of its phallus and graven images of alien gods, have been for a season allowed to receive and shelter the sacred Tooth, pending its permanent lodgement in a Buddhist shrine worthy of its sanctity? If so - the hypothesis is just possible, but assuredly not more - the tradition may have clung to the structure and been handed on down to the present day unquestioned. [12]

In the course of the excavation, in a trench in front of the temple, were discovered the first of the splendid collection known as the 'Polonnaruwa bronzes'. Bell wrote:

> The bronzes are perfectly preserved, and as specimens of skilled art work in metal are magnificent, alike in the spirited action they exhibit and in finished detail. All relate to the worship of Siva. The most striking is the figure of Maha Deva (Siva), in a halo, dancing on the Daitiya, Tripurasura, whom he slew after a combat lasting ten days.
>
> A few unbroken stone figures of Hindu deities, both in *basso* and *alto relievo*, were also exhumed, besides many fragments. [13]

Further finds were made in 1908 and Bell lists statuary, slab reliefs and bronzes in Appendix C of the Report of that year. Of the reason for the burial of the bronzes Bell opines:

> These (doubtless cast in India), once housed in the Devale when Hindu worship held its own at Polonnaruwa, either exclusively or by sufferance side by side with Buddhism, must at a later period have been condemned and ejected. The active Buddhist revival under Parakrama Bahu II (1240-1275 A.D.) may not have scrupled to destroy these emblems of the dread Siva, the destroyer, alone of the Hindu Triad never admitted into Buddhist temples.

For the fate that befell the many stone images, now hopelessly wrecked, which lined the exterior walls of the Devale, and others within the temple, would doubtless have consigned these magnificent bronzes to the crucible, but for the reverence or superstitious awe of some non-fanatical Buddhist devotees. Or perchance they may have been rescued from destruction and buried temporarily by the Hindu priests, with intent - never fulfilled - to exhume and remove them elsewhere.

Be the explanation what it may, fortune has preserved to us in these bronze statuettes the most perfect specimens of aeroplastic art illustrative of the Saivite cult that has yet come to light in Ceylon, and perhaps not excelled on the Continent of India. [14]

A.K.Coomeraswamy, in an article written in 1910, agreed with Bell on the foreign origin of the figurines; he considered that of the boy saint, Sundara Marti Swami, unearthed in 1908, 'one of the great masterpieces of Indian sculpture', but from the first this provenance was queried. P.Arunchalam, who wrote an account of these and other finds in the Colombo Museum in 1909, declared that it was grotesque to claim them to be South Indian bronzes. 'Let it be asserted once and for all', he said, 'that they are Polonnaruwa bronzes'. Since Bell's time a further collection of bronzes was found at Polonnaruwa in 1960. C.E.Godakumbura, Archaeological Commissioner at the time, in his short pamphlet on the subject gives his opinion that all these bronzes were the work of Sinhalese artists, working for the Chola conquerors. [15]

In 1907, the same year in which Siva Devale No. 1, 'that chief of the Hindu shrines of Polonnaruwa' was excavated, Bell moved north to the Buddhist 'Gal Vihare'. He said:

Both these sites are characteristic of the semi-antagonistic faiths which ruled at Polonnaruwa, at times with that tacit rivalry and mutual toleration of broad-minded religionists, anon, when the tide of fanaticism rose beyond control, ousting each other's fanes and wrecking the images. [16]

Work on the Gal Vihare site was summed up as follows in the report to the RASCB:

The colossal figures and rock-hewn shrine of this picturesquely wooded site renders it probably the most impressive antiquity preserved in Ceylon.

Altogether four images exist carved from the live rock. Two are *ot-pilima* or sedent figures of the Buddha.

The largest, 15 ft. 3 in. by 14 ft. 8 in., is seated in the cross-legged meditative *mudra*, upon an elaborate *asanaya*, beneath an elaborately carved *torana* (arch) of *makara* design; the other, in similar attitude, is at the back of a rock-hewn shrine. The third, on the extreme right, is a recumbent image (*seta pilima*) 46 ft. 2 in. from head to foot. The figure is represented in orthodox fashion, lying on its right side, with right arm and hand on a pillow under the head, the left arm being straightened along the body.

But it is the solitary life-like figure, traditionally styled *Ananda*, the favourite disciple of the Buddha, standing erect with crossed arms on a lotus pedestal 24 ft. from the rock floor, which appeals specially to the imagination, from its sorrow-stricken expression and natural attitude of deep mourning. This

Polonnaruwa : Hindu and Buddhist shrines

statue is, *par excellence*, the most artistic and well conceived to be found anywhere in the Island.

Each of the four images was originally enclosed within its own massively walled brick shrine, and could thus be seen but darkly, in that 'dim religious light' which nearly all creeds seem to affect for their sanctuaries.

The superincumbent earth and debris which hid the basements of all these shrines has been wholly removed, and the ground between them cut down to the former level. [17]

In his Annual Report of 1907 Bell goes even further in his praise of this group of stone figures, describing them not only as 'the most impressive antiquity *par excellence*' to be seen in the Island of Ceylon, but declaring them 'possibly not rivalled throughout the Continent of India'. He writes thus:

The line of gigantic figures carved from the grey rock which forms their background, calm, immovable, majestic, amid the hush of the surrounding forest, gazing ever fixedly into space with the pensiveness of profound meditation, or wrapped in eternal slumber, must inspire in the thoughtful beholder wonder and admiration, mingled with an instinctive sense of silent awe. [18]

The standing figure is now generally held to be that of a Buddha, but Bell identified it unhesitatingly as the disciple. He wrote:

Yet tradition has unswervingly attached to it the name of Ananda, cousin and favourite disciple of the Buddha, construing instinctively the listless attitude and sorrow-stricken countenance as assuredly displaying, with no uncertainty, the grief of the mourner present at the death-bed of the Sage. And for once tradition is backed by evidence which, if not amounting to proof, supports the presumption very strongly indeed.

The close proximity of the figure to the head of the dead Buddha, the wearied posture of body, the reverential disposition of the crossed arms, the inexpressible sadness in the face - surely not accidental - all so eloquent of patient resignation, are strikingly confirmative of the popular belief.

'Insatiabiliter deflebimus, aeternumque
Nulla dies nobis moerorem e pectore demet.'

The unbiased gazer on this marvellously human statue, reflecting that deep personal bereavement to which philosophical consolation is but as wormwood, must needs feel that the great sculptor (whose very name has perished unknown), inspired by 'divine afflatus', has here visibly lived in his work - the *tour de force* of a man of sorrows and acquainted with grief himself. Obsessed with a vision of that memorable last scene on earth he has vitalized it in granite for the ages to come. [19]

Bell also admired the remains of paintings within the Cave Shrine. He writes:

> The walls and roof of the cave were once covered with old paintings worthy of the sculptures, until some modern dauber was enabled to work his direful will unbeknown to the Government. Then ancient paintings, rivalling in art those of Sigiriya, disappeared before distorted silhouettes and garish smearing in bright red, yellow, and green pigments, laid on with that meretricious lavishness and pitiable disregard - or may be, crass ignorance - of chastened canons, which disfigure the vast majority of present day Buddhist temples in Ceylon.
>
> This has been set right. Access to the ancient cave shrine at the 'Gal Vihare' has for some years been - *as it should ever be* - open to daylight, free access, and full view, unmarred by brick wall, closed door, and gaudy paint.[20]

In a note Bell relates how the Government in 1895 had allotted a sum from Archaeological Survey funds to the Government Agent (H.H.Cameron) for removing the modern painting. Under his enthusiastic direction the extremely hard lacquer was removed, and since then the Archaeological Survey had scraped and burnt off nearly every remaining trace.

The paintings thus revealed were of three rows of worshippers, divine Bodhisatvayo and human devotees, looking inward towards the seated Buddha. Faded though they were, Bell once more gave them unstinted praise:

> In the execution of the heads of the aged devotees the artist has reached the level of the Old Masters of Europe. For in dignity and repose of countenance these venerable Brahmin worshippers might be of the Apostles who appear in the 'Burial of the Virgin', by Duccio, or sit at the table in Leonardo da Vinci's 'The Last Supper'.[21]

In 1910 steps were taken to protect the Cave Shrine. It had first been suggested that the whole area should be closed off, but Bell persuaded the Governor to sanction a form of protection which would give limited access. He reports on how this was achieved:

> The blacksmiths party completed a neat screen of wire netting in iron framework round the sedent Buddha in the Cave Shrine. The two strips of mediaeval fresco painting at the sides of the cave will be wired in when copied. The netting (half inch mesh) does not interfere with sufficient view of the image, but effectually protects it from being damaged at the hands of over-zealous pilgrims by oil lights and candles thoughtlessly placed on the bare stone *asanaya*.
>
> The Kandyan village blacksmiths, being simple-minded Buddhists, have done this piece of merit-inducing work (Sin. *pin anumodanvenava*) with the greatest zest and very neatly. A stone altar for flower offerings has been fixed within the cave.
>
> It is of much satisfaction to feel assured that one at least of the choicest sculptures of Polonnaruwa is effectually safeguarded against the ignorant barbarism of unsophisticated Sinhalese pilgrims, whose persistent ruining of the altars at the Anuradhapura Dagabas (in charge of the Buddhist Atamasthana Committee) by *pan pujava* (offering of lights) at night has forced the Government in all interests - Crown and public - to begin to protect these well-intentioned and unwitting iconoclasts against themselves.[22]

Yapahuwa: sculptures on Third Staircase

The Kuttam Pokunas at Anuradhapura

Pankuliya Buddha at Anuradhapura

Bell at Ritigala forest monastery

'Resting and brooding'

Shooting bear with decoy buffalo

Polonnaruwa: the Wata-da-ge before 1890, by C.F. Gordon-Cumming

Polonnaruwa: the Wata-da-ge restored

Polonnaruwa: Rankot Vehera, uncleared

Cyril Bell and Phyllis with Bethia, Heather and the Forest Staff

John Still (1880-1941)

Edward Russell Ayrton (1882-1914)

H.C.P. Bell with Zoë, Malcolm and Dorris, Daphne and Kenneth

John Bell, Lourdette Lambert,
Tony, Marie, Christabel and Joe

H.C.P. Bell between Ahmad Didi and Abdul Majid Didi

Dorris and Malcolm Bell in Maldive dress

24

Polonnaruwa : The Brick 'Image Houses'

Most distinctive, perhaps, of all the buildings at Polonnaruwa are the three large brick-built vaulted image houses. In Bell's reports they are referred to throughout, albeit in inverted commas or with the qualification of 'so-called' or 'known as', as the Thuparama, the Jetawanarama and the Demala-Maha-Seya. Only the Thuparama is still so called. Bell had suggested that the Thuparama might be identified with the Tivanka Image House, built by Parakrama Bahu I, but this name is now given to the Demala-Maha-Seya. Bell had pointed out that this name properly belonged to the huge uncompleted dagaba, based on a hillock, then known as 'Unagala Vehera', now as the 'Damilathupa'. As for the Jetawanarama, Bell identified it as the Lanka-tilaka - 'Jewel of Lanka' - and puts that name after it in brackets; the latter name alone is now employed. Bell characterises the type of building as follows:

> In *'Thuparama'* is represented a class of sacred edifice distinct from all the rest of the group of shrines to which it belongs. Indeed, with the equally mis-called *'Jetawanarama'* and *'Demala-Maha-Seya'* Vihares (to both of which it has certain affinities as well as many points of differentiation), it forms a triplet of structures peculiar to Polonnaruwa. No building of the sort exists at Anuradhapura; nor, as far as is known, anywhere else in Ceylon...
>
> *'Thuparama'* combines in one structure, the regularly adopted ground plan of the largest type of Sinhalese Buddhist vihares at Anuradhapura and Polonnaruwa, with that style of Dravidian pyramidal roofing and wall ornamentation first found expressed in the stone *Rathas* and continued nearly unchanged to a very late period in Southern India. [1]

The three buildings, alike in form, square shrines for Buddha images, with massive stucco-decorated walls and vaulted roofs, yet were differentiated by Bell as follows:

> The three Polonnaruwan larger vihares in their sequence exhibit the gradual steps by which the simpler form of Buddhist orthodoxy asserted itself. At 'Demala-Maha-Seya' Buddhistic purity compromised with Hindu predilections; Siva and other alien gods were supplanted by miniature representations of Buddhist shrines, retaining a proportion of the Dravidian arched niches but with figures suited to the former cult: at 'Jetawanarama' a century later, the baldachinos have disappeared, leaving only *dwarapala* 'supporters' to the aediculae: at 'Thuparama' the final renunciation was made - the walls no longer know human adornment; what is countenanced is the simple facsimile presentment of Buddhist vihares, etc. [2]

Of the excess of surface ornament on the walls of the Demala-Maha-Seya Bell wrote:

> The architect of the 'Demala-Maha-Seya' has crowded the lower part of his edifice with a superabundance of pillarets and miniature presentments of shrines, etc., leaving little plain space to which the

eye can turn for rest. No other structure at Polonnaruwa - and *a fortiori* none whatever at Anuradhapura - fails so markedly in departure from that canon of pure art - *simplex munditiis*.

Dravidian influence in exterior ornamentation is plainly observable at the sister Vihares, 'Thuparama' and 'Jetawanarama'; but it is not pushed there, as it is at 'Demala-Maha-Seya', to that undesirable extent (carried to such egregious excess in certain temples of India and the Further East) destructive of the very artistic effect striven after. By revelling in undue prodigality of detail the sculptor, or moulder, defeats his own object. [3]

But, as always, he was not able to resist the appeal of the dwarfs that decorate the basement:

So crowded together are these merry little persons, in their *pradakshina* circumambulation of the building from left to right, that as many as 250 and upwards once 'joined the gay throng that goes laughing along' the foot of the temple's walls. For a more jovial band, male and female, it would be hard to find anywhere - jostling one another, jesting, and sporting the while, with all that exuberant good-natured conviviality which marks crowds on pleasure bent.

The ever-varied attitudes of these *ganas* are worthy of attentive study: they forcibly illustrate the breadth, power, and wondrous skill of the potter's hand which could fashion this engrossing procession of lifelike figurines - these jolly pigmies, bursting with the full joy of life. [4]

In his short account of work carried out here in 1909 Bell says:

The south and east walls stand in fair preservation, but the back (west) wall and much of the north have fallen, whilst the vaulted roof of vestibule and shrine has wholly collapsed. In 1885-86 the vestibule was unearthed, under the direction of Mr. S.M.Burrows, and disclosed remains of interesting frescoes (Buddhist legends, etc.) on its inner walls. Unfortunately no steps were taken to protect these paintings, and in the fifteen years' interval before the Archaeological Survey commenced work at Polonnaruwa, they had faded beyond recognition.

The first task of the past season's excavation was the removal of the debris which literally choked the entresol, leading on from the vestibule, as well as the shrine itself, up to the top of the walls, which are 25 feet high in places. The difficulty of dealing with this immense mass of caked brick and mortar *talus*, which filled the passage and shrine, rendered the work both slow and dangerous, in view of the crumbling state of the later built inner walls. Ultimately the whole space was cleared without damaging either the frescoes on these screen walls, or what remains of the colossal statue of Buddha (*hiti-pilima*) which stands erect against the back wall. This immense figure, formed of brick heavily plastered, is headless and had lost its right leg below the knee.

The frescoes are full of interest. They depict legendary episodes from the life of Gautama Buddha. The main piece on the south wall shows the 'Tathagata', stiffly posed in a boat with two rowers, who are admirably represented. Though not so well preserved as the paintings in the 'pockets' at Sigiri-gala, those found on the walls of 'Demala-Maha-Seya' yield nothing to the latter in variety and spirited execution. Many of the figures are larger than life-size.

Polonnaruwa : The brick 'image houses'

The extreme flimsiness of the screen walls (clay conglomerate packing, plaster coated) on which the frescoes are painted threatens their rapid disintegration, if not entire destruction. Every effort has, therefore, been made to preserve them for at least some time, in order to secure, before it is too late, copies in oil as far as the worn paintings can be reproduced.

A jungle stick roof, thatched with cadjans, has been thrown across the shrine to shelter it from the northeast monsoon rains. The Buddha has also been specially protected by temporarily trussing the figure in a stick 'crate' with *ramba* grass. But the image is tottering to its fall, and may not survive long. [5]

Bell pointed out that the pictures were systematically arranged, those in the vestibule and its entresol being devoted to the Jataka, or stories of the Buddha's former Births, while those in the passage leading to the sanctuary and in the shrine itself dealt with Buddha's life on earth. Bell attempted photographs; black and white sketches were drawn by P.G.Perera, the Third Draughtsman, and D.A.L.Perera made facsimiles of three of the shrine paintings. Controversy was to follow over the preservation of the whole series. [6]

The second in the series of image-houses, the Jetawanarama, the largest and most magnificent, was in a parlous state when excavation began in 1910. Bell wrote:

The roof had everywhere fallen in; the north and back (west) walls of the shrine stood to less than half their original height; the entresol between vestibule and shrine was badly ruined at the junction of the inner walls, leaving the side walls disconnected and unsupported where strength was most needed; the inner and outer faces of the vestibule's southern wall had flaked so badly that only a thin core remained, of dangerous flimsiness in proportion to its height; its northern wall had suffered equally inside, and hardly less externally in places; the towering piers at the entrance, no longer held by the side walls, were bowing inwards to certain fall; and serious cracks pierced the masonry everywhere. [7]

In two seasons of work, 1910 and 1912, Bell only succeeded in beginning the conservation. The piers which incline towards and flank the entrance had their cracks filled in, and channelettes were chiselled through the sills of the entrances to vestibule and shrine, to allow water to drain off. Some of the inner walls were rebuilt and strengthened and the front staircase relaid, but Bell in his final report said that the whole interior should be concreted, not only the entresol, which he had already treated in 1912. [8]

The restoration of the Thuparama had been on Bell's mind since he first saw the shrine in 1893, and he was particularly concerned because it still retained a large part of its roof, the only one of these buildings so to do. He described the situation as follows in his report to the RASCB:

This ancient vihare, built massively of brick and mortar, is one of the most striking structures remaining above ground at this old capital of Ceylon. It is unique in being (as far as known) the only ancient monument left with the roof almost intact. The vihare roof inside is in design an irregular stilted dome falsely arched. On the top of the structure the roof is flattish with a very heavy square-shaped tower rising at the centre.

The ruin is now in a very critical state. There are three vertical cracks in the back wall, and a part of this wall and of the roof it held up have fallen inwards. Two other vertical cracks run down the front

191

wall of the inner shrine, one on either side of the doorway, of which the stone lintels are both cracked through. There are further cracks in the vestibule.

The most ominous crack exists along the whole of the shrine roof at the apex of the dome. Owing to the wonderful strength of the ancient mortar this crack would not, perhaps in itself, give cause for immediate alarm. But the weight of the solid tower superstructure is so great that a sudden and total collapse of the entire roof over the shrine may occur at any moment. In any case it cannot be long before the roof falls in bodily, unless prompt and effective action is taken to support, and otherwise strengthen, the roof and walls of the building. [9]

Bell first approached the Government in 1903, asking that the Public Works Department should make an inspection. However, their recommendations, which suggested rebuilding, shoring up and tying the walls together with channel irons, did not meet with his approval. He objected 'to any pulling down or rebuilding, or additional incongruous support to the walls'. He had already, on his own responsibility, started to remove vegetation from roof and walls, and to fill in some of the large cracks in the back wall. He also began to build this up, so that it should be united to the remaining part of the roof to hold it in place. This he regarded as legitimate restoration. [10]

In 1905 there was the general stoppage of work, but Bell continued to fight off the Public Works Department proposals. In a letter written on April 24, 1905 he reiterated:

The one great essential to the preservation of *'Thuparama'* Vihare is to *once more unite its half unsupported roof with the back wall.* This junction again effected in strong masonry (brick and cement), and the several cracks duly filled in from bottom to top, the ruin will continue to stand for years to come. No iron supports will be needed to brace walls, which albeit cracked, neglected, and root pierced, have not opened in the least degree in modern days.

The less this magnificent structure is 'modernized' into execrable smugness by premature demolition and rebuilding of existing walls and resort to hideous iron adjuncts, the better in every way.

Despite the fact that Bell was still in bad odour because of his delayed Reports, he managed to win over the Governor, Sir H.A.Blake, to his point of view. Blake visited Polonnaruwa in July 1905 and after inspecting the ruins himself, gave the following ruling:

I have examined the *'Thuparama'* ruin very carefully with the Archaeological Commissioner. It is evident that a portion of the building added to the interior at a later date has sunk about 1/2 inch owing to the giving way of the foundation.

The various sections of the walls partly divided by cracks may be regarded as so many solid masses, the old mortar being as hard as stone. If the cracks are all filled, the old wall continued until it supports the roof at the western end, the gangways on the top being cemented so as to exclude water, and gargoyles so arranged as to discharge beyond the foundation - as proposed by the Archaeological Commissioner - I see no reason why the building should not stand for centuries in this climate.

Polonnaruwa : The brick 'image houses'

In this, as in other buildings, the keynote of the work should be preservation, not restoration, except where all original brick and stone work are simply displaced. [11]

Bell thereafter continued the work according to his own plans. After the back wall had been joined to the roof, he reported every year on the progressive stabilisation of the Thuparama by widening out of cracks on walls and tower and then refilling them with a conglomerate of lime cement and pebbles. Cracks in the roof were also filled in and the whole cemented over, while 'weep holes' were made to carry away the run off of water and discharge it away from the walls. An internal lintel was strengthened, an internal stairway rebuilt with added guard rails, and the floor was relaid in concrete. Finally the brick and stucco work on the outer walls, the bas-reliefs of miniature shrines, were carefully retouched and, where worn away, renewed. Eight damaged images of the Buddha, four erect and four seated, were replaced on pedestals and asana.[12]

Finally, in his Annual Report for 1911-12, Bell concluded with satisfaction:

The 'restoration' - so far as that term is applicable - of 'Thuparama' Vihare began in 1904, and has occupied eight seasons, the nature of the work being such as to render rapid completion impossible, with a limited yearly sub-vote intended to cover all work throughout the Island in the nature of restoration and conservation undertaken by the Archaeological Survey Department.

Finis coronat opus. The 'Thuparama' Vihare, unique in the possession once more of its old vaulted roof, tower, and walls now well repaired, deservedly attracts special attention from visitors to Polonnaruwa, hardly less from its massive boldness as a structure than owing to the chaste ornamentation of its wall façades.[13]

Finis coronat opus - the end crowns the work. The restoration of the Thuparama had been one of Bell's major aims at Polonnaruwa, and that was achieved. But he gave up his work reluctantly. He kept a jealous eye on his old stamping grounds, and did not fail to incorporate into his Reports, as they were published, his disappointment when operations he had started were not continued.

Bell showed particular concern for the ruins at Polonnaruwa. He made an inspection of the Demala-Maha-Seya Vihare in July 1918 at the request of the Government, and it appears that he then also became alarmed at the condition of the Jetawanarama. Some responsibility for the maintenance of the excavated remains had devolved on the Public Works Department, but it was not their primary concern, and moreover Bell never approved of their methods. On June 24, 1919 Bell wrote to Government saying that he would be prepared to take full charge of necessary repairs to the Jetawanarama, but although he was given supervisory authority in December 1919, he was obliged to work with and through the Public Works Department.

In January and February 1920 Bell was out of Ceylon, paying his second visit to the Maldive Islands, but just before setting sail, on January 19, he wrote to Government asking for pay for a peon, with an allowance of Rs. 1,000 for transport, which might rise to Rs. 1,500. This was presumably because Bell was now living in Kandy. He was temporarily restored to full pay and waived the right to his pension for the time. He was glad to obtain the services of W.M.Fernando, experienced in the work of restoration, but again found himself in conflict with A.Rothwell,

Provincial Engineer, North-Central Province, who not only had different views on the extent of restoration desirable, but did not send Bell his plans until he had already embarked on the work on his own account. Bell moreover complained in a letter of May 26, 1920 that he felt isolated and lonely, 'no longer surrounded by my "merrie men"' - the old 'Bell party'. [14]

Finally on July 28, 1920 Bell wrote to the Acting Colonial Secretary, B.Horsburgh, summarising his differences with the Public Works Department and the difficulties of a dual control. For the remaining months of the year it appears that Bell was given a free hand. He hoped to be left in charge even when Hocart, the new Archaeological Commissioner, arrived in Ceylon. He wrote to Collins on November 17, 'Unless Hocart is the "seven times fool" which I am sure he is not, he will like to depute the job'. But this was not to be. Hocart took charge on January 24, 1921, and the very same day wrote to Bell saying that he wished to 'learn by trying', and apologising for assuming responsibility for the work on the Jetawanarama. Fernando continued to direct the operations. [15]

In his first Annual Report, for 1920-21, Hocart acknowledges Bell's work as follows:

Fortunately Mr. Bell had called the attention of the Government to the dangerous condition of the Lankatilaka, commonly known as the Jetawanarama at Polonnaruwa. The work was begun by the Public Works Department, then by Mr. Bell in 1920, and a further sum of Rs. 19,150 was voted to continue the work this year. We were thus enabled to enter on a campaign of conservation less than a month after my arrival.

Splayed brickwork had previously been put in on the South side. Last year the ruined parts of the South wall were re-faced and rebuilt. The same work was carried on on the North side and on the jams of the main porch. In order to avoid blank wall, the outlines of the old mouldings were carried along the face of the new work.

The work was continued this year mainly along the lines proposed by Mr. Bell, with certain modifications; the amount of rebuilding was cut down to a minimum with the double purpose of putting in no more new work than could be helped and of relieving the foundations. [16]

Much later, at the end of Bell's life, the then Archaeological Commissioner, Longhurst, paid tribute to Bell's 'rescue work' at two of the Polonnaruwa sites. Writing of the Thuparama:

He repaired the roof and restored the ornamental parapet above the cornice, rebuilt the front entrance and executed repairs to the decayed brick and plaster walls of the exterior. But for these timely and well executed restorations, the state of the Thuparama would have been truly similar to that of the Lankatilaka. [17]

Of the latter he wrote:

But for the prompt measures taken by the late Mr. Bell for the restoration of this valuable ancient monument, it would certainly have collapsed and been past all repair today. Since then his successors have carried out repairs from time to time. [18]

25

Successors

The question of Bell's successor was first officially broached in 1908. It was in February 1908 that Bell had submitted the Memorandum on staffing which resulted in the reorganisation of the Department after the resignation of John Still. On July 23, 1908, he sent in another Memorandum, and this was on the subject of the most suitable type of man to appoint when he himself retired, now that the most obvious successor, John Still, was no longer available. The Governor, H.E.McCallum, had already applied to Sir John Marshall, of the Indian Archaeological Survey, to ask if he could recommend any of his own staff. Marshall replied, on May 4, 1908, that he could not spare anyone, and suggested that Ceylon either find an experienced archaeologist and provide him with training in the languages of the country, or a linguist, and send him for archaeological training.

Bell did not think much of either idea, as he felt very strongly that the first requirement for his job was a knowledge of local conditions. He said that an archaeologist trained to work in a different culture would not have the necessary qualifications to enable him 'to overcome the difficulties of working smoothly and profitably with a mixed oriental labour force (Tamil, Moor and Sinhalese), whose vagaries and nature are only to be understood by some years of experience as a Ceylon Government official or a planter'. It would be better, he thought, to send someone from the Island to get an archaeological training; and suggested H.W.Codrington, a Civil Servant, who later became an authority on numismatics, as a suitable candidate. Bell said that he did not know if Codrington would wish to take on the job, and that if he did so, he should be given a guarantee of promotion and a special allowance 'to compensate for the many disadvantages which the life of the Government Archaeologist naturally entails'. [1]

McCallum agreed with Bell that the candidate should be a man with Ceylon experience, and on August 5, 1908 wrote to Lord Crewe, the Secretary of State for the Colonies, suggesting that a successor to Bell should be immediately selected, sent for training in archaeology at the British School in Athens, read Sanskrit and Pali at Oxford, and follow this up with further practical training with the Archaeological Survey in India. He should then serve for six months under Bell before taking over charge of the Department. He proposed H.W.Codrington for the post, saying that he was studious by nature and had an extensive knowledge of Kandyan history, and had passed his examinations in Sinhalese. [2]

Colonial Office officials were, however, quite determined that the next Archaeological Commissioner of Ceylon should be 'a professional archaeologist'. In 1890, when Bell started work, there was no such animal; there was no professional training, and in India alone was there any official post. In Britain, the Mediterranean and the Near East the field was dominated by the inspired amateur. Such men worked on their own account or were supported by voluntary societies. [3]

By the first decade of the twentieth century things were changing. Excavation techniques had been gradually developed, and men like Petrie were passing on their expertise to others working with them. Yet such institutional training as existed was still only in the field of classical archaeology. This was true of the courses provided at Cambridge and London Universities and at the British School at Athens, founded in 1886, and the British School at Rome, opened in 1901. It was therefore among classical archaeologists that the first candidates were sought.

One reason that the Colonial Office was so determined that the next Archaeological Commissioner of Ceylon should be appointed from outside was that they held a very low opinion of Bell himself. Their chief advisers, Keith and Macdonell, had ranged themselves on the side of Wickremasinghe in the conflict already recorded and had formed the fixed notion that Bell, because he had received no formal training, was incompetent both as an epigraphist and as an archaeologist. With more justice the Colonial Office had come to the conclusion that Bell could be thoroughly pig-headed, and that it would be extremely difficult for anyone to take over from him, for 'no competent archaeologist will consent to serve under Mr. Bell for an indefinite period (and in view of the character of Mr. Bell as shown in the Wickremasinghe correspondence it is not to be expected that anyone should)'. [4]

Professor Macdonell strenuously opposed the appointment of Codrington, saying that it would mean that 'the archaeological conditions of the last thirty years in Ceylon are practically certain to be repeated', and stressing that the appointee must be a scholar and a trained archaeologist, not a Civil Servant. R.E.Stubbs, one of the First Class Clerks of the Colonial Office and always hostile to Bell, commented that 'in view of Professor Macdonell's opinion, fortified by the equally high authority of Professor Gardiner, we cannot possibly accept the Governor's proposals, unless we mean to make the Ceylon Archaeological Department ridiculous in the eyes of all competent judges'. A letter was therefore sent to McCallum which agreed with the type of training suggested by Ceylon but reserved the right to find candidates in England. It said:

> It is a matter of great importance that the person chosen shall be thoroughly qualified for the appointment, since the progress of Ceylon archaeology for years to come will depend almost wholly upon him. The future head of the Archaeological Department ought to be a first-rate archaeologist and an accurate Sanskrit, Pali and Sinhalese scholar, and these qualifications cannot be acquired by everybody, but anybody would be able to acquire the necessary knowledge of the vernacular and of local conditions in a very short time. I am sure you will agree and I will look for suitable candidates. [5]

The man chosen by the Colonial Office was Guy Dickins, a classical scholar trained at the British School in Athens, but his candidature was not to prove successful. McCallum first objected to him on the grounds that he was married, and then laid down that as a condition of his service he should undertake all the extra duties performed by Bell. In a letter of January 29, 1909, he said:

> Mr. Bell has in the past given valuable assistance in connection with land claims, by reporting on sannas and other documents, and it is equally necessary that the gentleman appointed should understand that

he is required, in addition to ordinary archaeological duties, to assist Government in all matters in which his advice may be sought.[6]

Under these conditions the post was offered to Dickins on March 11, 1909, but then a further difficulty arose. Dickins had apparently been unaware that the headquarters of the Archaeological Survey was at Anuradhapura. When he realised this he wrote a long and carefully considered letter on May 9, 1909, saying that he could only accept the post if headquarters were transferred to Kandy. He had come to the conclusion, from the information that he had received, that Anuradhapura was 'at once too enervating and too remote', i.e. that the climate was too trying and that work could be better organised from a more central position in the Island. He wrote:

> I am told that sixty or seventy miles of good road connect Kandy with Anuradhapura and with Polonnaruwa. With a motor-car, therefore, the Commissioner is within easy distance of either place at any time of year and, if a European or other assistant be appointed, it would be natural that he should be stationed at Anuradhapura itself...

> The Archaeological Commissioner, with Headquarters at Kandy, could spend 3 or 4 months of *continuous* residence at Anuradhapura during the best season (January to March); and another 3 or 4 months at Polonnaruwa (May to July). Another period, later in the year, could be spent in journeys of exploration, but the headquarters for the bad season, and for intervals in the work of the department would, to my mind, be more profitably fixed at Kandy.[7]

This proposal, which the Colonial Office regarded as eminently sensible, aroused the wrath of Bell. McCallum had asked for his opinion and he submitted a long and highly characteristic Memorandum, outlining his own methods of work and maintaining that they were the only possible ones. He wrote:

> I was appointed by Sir A.H.Gordon to take charge of the Archaeological Survey, when, as Governor, His Excellency initiated it in 1890. Since then up to date - a period of 19 years - with the exception of a short time in 1892, 1894, and 1906 when I was ill or temporarily detached for other duty, I have been, from first to last, in immediate touch with the Archaeological Survey operations wherever conducted, whether at Anuradhapura, at Sigiriya, at Polonnaruwa, or on tours. I have, therefore, I presume, fair claim to some right to express an authoritative opinion as to the conditions under which the Archaeological Survey should be conducted, if it is to be carried on to the best advantage.

> Whatever measure of success the Archaeological Survey may have been able to attain during my administration of the Department, I attribute (I say it with all humbleness, but without fear of contradiction) to the incessant close personal supervision which I have studiously devoted to its various operations, ever keeping the threads of the countless details of work in my own hands, so as to control every branch directly, as far as practicable...

> Hardly a day passes without the Archaeological Commissioner being called upon personally to decide questions cropping up regarding excavation of ruins, their restoration or due preservation referred to

him on the spot by his Assistant. To leave important work of this kind, constantly varying in its phase, to the tender mercies of subordinates not fully trained, however zealous, is to subject it inevitably to damage, often irretrievable...

In truth, the combined responsibilities falling upon the Archaeological Commissioner and his Assistants are such that my two Native Assistants, Messrs. D.A.L.Perera and W.M.Fernando, both men of exceptional experience and intelligence, make no secret of their unwillingness to remain longer in the Department, even in their honourable posts, unless the Archaeological Commissioner continues, as he has done hitherto, to strengthen their hands, and to generally 'stiffen' the Department throughout from top to bottom, by remaining in close and continuous touch with the staff and labour force.

He pointed out that the Government had built a house for the Archaeological Commissioner at Anuradhapura, with a special room for his library, and storage for finds; and that the ex-hospital buildings had been converted into offices for the staff, with a tool store and photographic studio. He concluded:

Taking all the above circumstances into consideration, it is difficult to understand how any person appointed as Archaeological Commissioner can even profess to work the Archaeological Survey properly from Kandy, with Clerks, Draughtsmen, library, and labour force at Anuradhapura, and needing his personal presence on the spot, to ensure the work of the office and field operations being adequately supervised, and the whole machinery of the Department made to run smoothly without incessant hitch and most undesirable delays.[8]

Bell also stressed that the Archaeological Commissioner was officially allowed two months recess at Kandy to write his reports, although he personally had never availed himself of these, nor even taken his regular allotment of 'furlough'. Bell never tired of pointing out his extraordinary attachment to duty and the fact that he had never taken 'furlough', i.e. home leave; he even included it in the entry which he supplied to *Who's Who*. In a letter to Government on May 14, accompanying his Memorandum, he added plaintively that 'for his own and his family's ease and comfort the Archaeological Commissioner would doubtless have preferred any time during the past nineteen (19) years to "lotus-eat" at Kandy "bordered with palms and many a winding vale", instead of putting up with the isolation and malaria of the North-Central Province'.[9]

Once again the Ceylon Government supported Bell, and before sailing for leave in Europe McCallum sent a telegram on May 21, saying:

Your telegram of 11 May   Anuradhapura is centre of archaeological work   Essential that Commissioner and staff should reside there   Bachelor preferred   Date not fixed for Bell's retirement.[10]

This was followed up by a letter dated June 8 from Hugh Clifford, the Colonial Secretary acting for the Governor, in which a copy of Bell's Memorandum was enclosed and its opinion endorsed as follows:

Successors

> I regard it as essentially necessary that the head of the Archaeological Department, in common with every other officer in the Service, should reside close to the work with which he is entrusted. I consider that in his case it is even peculiarly necessary because the Department is not manned by European subordinates, or even by natives who can lay any claim to sound expert knowledge, and because a mistake made through ignorance or lack of proper supervision may, in archaeological work, result in irreparable injury being done to ancient monuments, or loss, no less irreparable, to scientific knowledge. I am also strongly of opinion that visits of inspection, paid to the scene of the Archaeological Commissioner's work by means of a motor-car and from a distance, would be a substitute altogether inadequate for personal and daily supervision of excavations and restorations. No matter how highly qualified a man might be, his appointment as successor to Mr. Bell would be of doubtful utility to this Government unless he were prepared to devote to the work, over which no large measure of supervision can be exercised by the Secretariat, the same close, personal attention which it has always received from the present occupant of the post of Archaeological Commissioner.

The Colonial Office regarded the existence of a Government house at Anuradhapura as a valid argument, but were clearly surprised at the weight which the Ceylon Government were prepared to give to Bell's opinions, commenting that it was 'an astonishing despatch - apparently they really think that Mr. Bell is an archaeologist'. They were forced to accept the position and withdraw the offer to Dickins, but the opposition would not be forgiven, for 'Mr. Bell's reports are four years in arrears, and this will not be lost sight of when opportunity offers'. [11]

R.E.Stubbs had a last fling at Bell, suggesting that a letter should be sent to the Governor to say that:

> ...he has lost the best man Ceylon is ever likely to have a chance of: to say that we will take steps to find somebody else, but that before doing so it is necessary to have the date of Mr. Bell's retirement finally settled, as it will be impossible to get a qualified man to accept the job unless he knows definitely how long he will be required to serve under Mr. Bell.

> Mr. Bell will be 60 in September 1911, but the rule making retirement compulsory at that age is recent, and Mr. Bell is just the sort of person to make the point that the rule was not in force when he joined the service, and that he was being brutally treated if he was made to go at 60. I think we ought to get rid of him, if he won't go on his own initiative. He has earned his full pension - I mean he is eligible for the grant of it. I have never heard it suggested that he knew anything about archaeology, and it is high time the department was put on a proper footing. I would therefore suggest that if Mr. Bell is not able to give a definite date himself, one must be fixed for him, and that it must not be later than the end of June 1912. [12]

Bell had already suggested that he should retire at the end of 1911, so the search for a successor was resumed, this time with success. The choice fell on Edward Russell Ayrton. Ayrton, who was born in China, and was educated at St. Paul's School, had not been to the university, but had already had seven years experience of excavation in Egypt. Professor Petrie wrote to support Ayrton's application, saying:

> He worked with me for two years, and has done practically all the work for the Fund (under Naville) for four years. He has a fair knowledge of Egyptian things, is a diligent reader, quick at languages, and was born in China and clings to the East. He is absolutely straight. [13]

Ayrton's Egyptian experience was obviously rather more relevant than classical qualifications, and this time the appointment went through almost without a hitch. Ayrton was unmarried and agreed to all the conditions laid down by the Ceylon Government, including a new requirement that he should study Tamil as well as Sinhalese.

Bell's retirement was postponed for a year, and it was arranged that Ayrton should study Pali and Sanskrit, as well as Sinhalese and Tamil, and also Indian and Ceylonese Epigraphy. In the event he studied for two years in Oxford and in Germany and with the Archaeological Survey of India, and joined the Archaeological Survey of Ceylon as Assistant to Bell on March 8, 1912. He took on acting charge of the Department in September, and succeeded as Archaeological Commissioner on December 8, 1912. [14] As it turned out, his period of service was disastrously short. He was drowned when out shooting on the tank near Tissamaharama on May 18, 1914, and was buried near by in the old Dutch cemetery.

A full account of his life, with details of his early career, appeared in the *Journal of Egyptian Archaeology* in 1915. The writer noted:

> Characteristic of Ayrton's modesty was the fact that when he died nobody in Ceylon seemed to know anything much about his Egyptian record, except that he had worked with Professor Petrie. He never blew his own trumpet. The first notice of his death published in England dated him merely from his arrival in India, as if he had been any ordinary competition-wallah. [15]

When Hocart eventually took over as the next Archaeological Commissioner in 1921 he wrote:

> The untimely death of Mr. E.R.Ayrton, the late Commissioner, on May 18, 1914, was a great blow to archaeology in Ceylon; his career was too short to leave the mark of his experience, abilities, and intense activity so deeply impressed as to survive so long an interruption. The fragments of his work remain as ruinous as the monuments he was appointed to look after. [16]

Of his relations with Bell we know little for certain. Bell and John Still very properly proposed Ayrton as a member of the RASCB at a meeting held on April 18, 1912, and some official letters survive in the Colombo Archives in which Ayrton asks for and obtains information and plans from Bell. But although Ayrton followed up and confirmed Bell's work on the Western Monasteries, Bell seems to have felt that other projects he had started were neglected. There is a comment in a Colonial Office file to the effect that 'Mr. Bell has spent his time since his retirement writing up his very belated reports and constantly interfering with and complaining of Mr. Ayrton to the Secretariat'. [17]

Bell's only recorded comment on Ayrton was in his Annual Report of 1911-12, which was not published till 1915:

Successors

Mr. Ayrton's tragic death on May 18, 1914, cut short a most promising career in the line for which he had so well fitted himself. [18]

The English Government was too occupied with the war against Germany to search for a successor to Ayrton; and despite pressure from the RASCB the work of the Department was left in the charge of D.A.L.Perera, under the nominal supervision of the Government Agent of the North-Central Province. The interregnum lasted until the arrival of A.M.Hocart in 1921. [19]

And what of Bell? He continued to keep a watchful eye on 'his ruins', and he was also occupied in catching up on his belated Reports. In a Memorandum sent to the Colonial Office in 1919 he claimed credit for this:

> It suffices Mr. Bell to feel that his humble services of over 20 years as Archaeological Commissioner were graciously recognised by a Motion unanimously passed in the Legislative Council of Ceylon, and that unable to 'fulfil his full contract' in the matter of his Reports before his retirement (with the loss of an eye) in December 1912, he made all honorable amends in his power, by sacrificing himself conscientiously and going into 'self-elected banishment' for 18 months (1913-1914) at Anuradhapura (instead of seeking, on pension, badly needed rest and health with his family at Kandy), solely in order to discharge a *moral* obligation to the Ceylon Government, by bringing his Archaeological Reports up to date. [20]

There is a glimpse to be had of him in this period, taken from a travel book published in 1923, but based on articles that had appeared in earlier years, with the romantic title of *Cinnamon and Frangipani*. The author, Ashley Gibson, writes:

> I could no more draw you a map of the buried cities of Ceylon than I could fly, yet to Anuradhapura have I made my pilgrimage, by fortune meeting at the journey's end with an incomparable cicerone, who knows more of the lost cities than any other living man will ever know..... A tithe, perhaps, of the harvest of this very labour of love has been garnered and docketed - dry bones of facts only - in the official chronicles. The rest, I take it, dies with him, for he is an old man now, and a blight seems to rest on the labours of those who have picked up the spade where he dropped it. But what he told me as I sat open-eared on the verandah of his jungle bungalow, as he piloted me from stone to stone in the nearby forest, from tumbled monkish vihara to massy palace of dead kings and queens, from rock-hewn bath to bosky tumulus beneath whose verdure are traced the broken outlines of a thupa of brick and stone the size of Primrose Hill, was so much magic...... and what he showed me of these dead bones mouldering beneath their green shroud of forest was a wonder that thrills me whenever memory lingers on it, and will still thrill me when I am as old a man (if ever) as that kind and learned scholar who strove out of the kindness of his heart to lighten the outer fringes of my ignorance. [21]

We have here, to balance the hostile comments on Bell which emanated from the Colonial Office, a pleasant picture of the friendly savant welcoming the foreign traveller to his lonely retreat and giving him the benefit of his long experience and wisdom.

But was his retreat so lonely? His wife and children had not always stayed with him, but for shorter or longer periods moved to houses rented in Kandy or Nuwara Eliya. After his retirement from 1913 Bell is listed in directories as resident in Kandy, in a series of different houses of which Lake View was the first. Bell probably divided his time between Kandy and Anuradhapura, and even when residing with them remained curiously detached from the life of his family.

If not a very loving family man, he was yet not a man to do without women, and never had been. It was a period when extra-marital relations were both utterly accepted and utterly ignored. This attitude is strikingly represented in a curious little correspondence from the archives of the Colonial Office. It begins with a letter from Governor McCallum to the Earl of Crewe, dated February 4, 1909, acknowledging a circular despatch dated January 11, 1909. This despatch is not included in the file, but from McCallum's response, it must have been a request to circulate all Civil Servants with a warning against what it terms 'living in concubinage with native girls and women'. McCallum did not wish to send out this letter, giving as his reasons: a) that such customs no longer existed in Ceylon, and b) that if the circular were sent round, even confidentially, its contents would soon be leaked to the Press and cause scandal. The Colonial Office accepted the second argument, although the outspoken R.E.Stubbs commented as follows:

> If para. 5 is accurate, things are better than they were a few years ago. You will remember the case of the Engineer who was considered 'socially impossible' because he used to play cricket with his bastards - the objection taken being not that they were bastards or altogether that he played cricket with them, but that he did so on ground adjoining the Lawn Tennis Club's courts. [22]

So the official attitude was, at that time, that it did not happen, and if it did it must not be noticed. We know, at least, that Bell's reputation in this matter was and is still legendary in the Island. The authors were told that it was common knowledge that one of the comfortable bullock carts which accompanied Bell on his circuits was specially fitted out for the accommodation of his female companion.

In *Return to Kandy* by Vesak Nanayakkara we catch a glimpse of local folklore on the subject. At Attapitya the author was looking for the remains of Fort King, scene of events in the 1815 conquest of Kandy. Bell had found a portion of the wall intact in 1892, and this was pointed out by an ancient villager, Siriya of Palle Pamunuwa:

> A smile wreathed the old gentleman's face as he recalled a more recent and interesting tit-bit associated with his village, in that Bell chose a beauteous Sinhala belle as his mistress from his own Bathgama clan in the village. [23]

Does this date back to the time when Bell was completing his report on the Kegalla District?

There were two more lasting connections, at Anuradhapura and later at Kandy, and of each a child was born. The elder, Lourdette, was born in Anuradhapura on March 14, 1908, and baptised 'Lourdanna' at St. Joseph's church.

A child's view of Anuradhapura in the old days comes from the son of one of Bell's staff:

Successors

> I still have faint recollections of Abhayagiri stupa, the outcrops of stone pillars, some inclined, others fallen down broken and scattered; the sound of the tom-tom and the peal of temple bells; the Malwatu Oya, and last but not least the Holy Family Convent where I began my schooling. [24]

It was to the same convent that Lourdette was brought at the age of five, and entrusted to the nuns for her upbringing. Her eldest son, Tony Lambert, continues the story:

> She was supposed to be an orphan, but her needs were provided for by her father, H.C.P.Bell. I know very little of her early life, but I gather that she did a bit of teaching after finishing school, and then took up a job as a telephone operator, while still making the convent her home, till she married in November 1936.... A nun who knew my mother as a child once told me of the fine house H.C.P.Bell lived in at Anuradhapura and of the horse and carriage he used to have. [25]

Her daughters also remember how fond the nuns were of Lourdette and how her affectionate links with them were continued until the end of her life. To this day she is remembered in Anuradhapura by Asoka Mahadiulwewa. As a motherless boy he was placed in her care at the convent and she taught him to read.

Though Bell was not given as Lourdette's father on her baptismal certificate, nor on her certificate of marriage to Benedict Lambert at St. Joseph's, she was named on the latter document as Lourdette Bell. Also the Notification of Marriage, to the Diocese of Jaffna, from the parish priest, describes her as daughter of Mr. H.C.P.Bell, and of Saveri Amma. There is moreover a series of letters of the year 1935, that show Bell continuing to send money orders monthly to Lourdette through Father J.Majorel, O.M.I. The priest annotated the letters and sent them on to her with cordial notes. He once suggested that she should acknowledge receipt of the money directly, but it looks as if she preferred to maintain the impersonal relationship set by her father. She had five children, who all survive in Canada or Sri Lanka, but herself died on December 5, 1970.

The story of John, the youngest and only surviving child of H.C.P.Bell, begins in Kandy, where he was born in December 1916. His birth certificate, also, did not show Bell as father; his mother's name was Perumal Akka. Here again we see the pattern of Bell's affording support, but not encouraging personal contact. A Mr. Robert A.Clerk was appointed guardian of John, and the money sent to him to be deposited in the Post Office Savings Bank included pocket money for the boy. John was educated in Colombo, boarded at the Boys' Industrial Home and Orphanage, Wellawatte, and was sent to Nuwara Eliya for holidays. He met his father certainly once, playing truant from school and travelling up to Kandy on his own. He remembers that the old man 'sat there shaking his head'. Was this in reproof or a sign of refusal? For it appears John was not authorized to use 'Bell' as his surname till he was twenty-one, when his father died in September 1937. He bore the name, therefore, during his career in the Police, from which he has now retired. John twice visited Zoë Bell, but she did not encourage the acquaintance. It seems, though, that his mother inherited from Bell the house where she lived.

One sad result of the secretiveness maintained about Bell's children, was that for many years

Lourdette and John were unaware of each other's existence. John reports how about 1944, when he was attached to the Foreshore Police in Colombo, he had a friend and neighbour, Denzil Sela, whom he often visited. One day John saw a lady standing outside Denzil's door and asked who she was:

> She said she was Lourdette Lambert, née Bell. That amazed me, so I asked her across the wall who her father was. She said, 'H.C.P.Bell'.

John then identified himself and next day brought to show her the documents which 'confirmed that she was my sister whom I met for the first time after about twenty-seven years'. By this time Lourdette already had four children.

Old sins have long shadows, though gradually it is possible to work clear of them. Both brother and sister had, as it were, to create for themselves the family life they had missed. John married Noeline in 1955 and their very united family are grown up - Rebecca, Jerome, Clifford and Anton. Lourdette's husband had a career in the British Consulate at Saigon, for which he was awarded the M.B.E. Wars in the East brought trials for the young family, for Tony, Marie and Christabel were very young when the Japanese invasion of Indo-China in 1941 involved them in a long sea journey back to Ceylon. Although they returned to Saigon after the war, the situation in Vietnam sent them back again to base, the family now including the younger children, Joe and Cecilia. Benedict continued working in Saigon on his own, but now with the U.S. aid programme till he died in 1973. Nowadays Tony, Joe and Cecilia are resident in Canada, and the other two established with their families in Sri Lanka.

Though the Lamberts and Bells were friends, it was only very recently that their existence became known to the family in England. In 1981 the authors visited Sri Lanka. In the Island we were cordially entertained and in particular invited to give a talk on our grandfather to the Royal Asiatic Society. This was entitled, with more appropriateness than we then realised, 'Roots in Sri Lanka'. Our relatives in Colombo read the press report and tried to make contact, but we had already left and it was not until early in 1987 that we all became known to one another. That autumn, while researching in Colombo, we met many of our cousins and were most kindly welcomed. Cecilia later visited us in London, and there were further meetings in July 1990 at the Centenary in Sri Lanka of the commencement of the Archaeological Survey.

Thus out of old endings have come new and better beginnings.

26

Active Retirement

Bell never seems to have contemplated retiring to England, but was happy to make his permanent home in the Island; but not to 'lotus-eat'. Doing and writing, he filled his days.

He continued as Honorary Secretary and Editor of the JRASCB until 1914, and in 1913 and 1914 attended meetings with fair regularity. He served on the Committee of Management of the Colombo Museum until 1922. From 1915 to 1916 he was co-editor, with John M.Senaveratne, of a new journal, the *Ceylon Antiquary and Literary Register*. Together they issued the four parts of Volume 1, and Bell thereafter contributed a number of articles and notes, as well as encouraging others so to do. In 1923 he is reported as being engaged 'in one of his periodic squabbles' with the then editor, but he supported the latter's application to Government for a subsidy. This was not granted, and the journal came to an abrupt end in 1924 with Part 2 of Volume 10. [1]

His first energies were devoted to the completion of his official publications. He had, indeed, much leeway to make up. He had published his Annual Reports up to 1907, but those from 1892 to 1902 had been published without any plans or plates. The plans and plates for 1890 and 1891 had been published with the seven Progress Reports which covered those years. The reports for 1903 to 1907 had included plates. What he did, therefore, was gradually to publish the outstanding Annual Reports: 1908 in 1913, 1909 and 1910-11 in 1914, and 1911-12 in 1915, together with an Index which covers all the Annual Reports, but *not* the Progress Reports. Separate collections of Plans and Plates for the years 1892 to 1902 were issued in 1914, and finally, in 1916, appeared Supplementary Plates for Annual Reports 1903, and for 1905 to 1911-12.

Unfortunately Bell never drew together his findings into an over-view of Ceylon archaeology. The raw material is there, and he provided an index for the period 1890 to 1900 and an overall one for 1890-1912. However, his insights and conclusions remain scattered through the pages, and may be fitly compared with his own description of the ruins he explored as *disjecta membra*.

He also concerned himself with the publication of the Tamil inscriptions, which had not been sent to Wickremasinghe, but in 1911 to M. Krishna Sastri in Madras. Unfortunately the Madras epigraphists were no more speedy in the work than Wickremasinghe had proved to be. By 1918 nothing had been published and Gopinatha Rao of the Travancore Archaeological Department offered to edit them for the *Ceylon Antiquary*. But Gopinatha Rao died in 1919 with nothing accomplished, and Bell recommended that the work should be left to M.Krishna Sastri, 'the most competent scholar living in regard to Tamil inscriptions'. Eventually they were included in Volume IV of the *South Indian Inscriptions*, and in 1924 a free copy of this volume was sent by Madras to the Ceylon Government. [2]

Bell continued to be available to Government for the authentication of sannas, royal grants which could be of great importance in matters of land ownership. He was called upon to testify in court cases, usually on behalf of the Government. Exceptionally, in 1923, he gave evidence in a dispute between two private parties. After critically examining the document in question, he concluded in typical style as follows:

> In the above Report the several points *pro* and *contra* bearing on the merits and demerits of Talpata No. 2,932, have been set down *seriatim*, with patient endeavour to throw all possible light upon the document so as to aid, *pro tanto*, the impartial adjudication of the Court regarding its claim to be held a genuine *sannasa*. [3]

Bell's own publications often dealt with sannas, whether engraved on stone or copper plates, or written upon a *talpata*, or leaf of the palmyra palm. They were valuable for providing information on the sources of revenue and methods of administration of Buddhist temples. They often concluded with warnings against infringement of the contract such as, 'If any person causes to be taken land given by himself or another, he will be born a worm in faeces (and so continue) for a period of 600 years'. [4]

Sannas were too often forgeries. In 1920 Bell discredited a whole group of copper-plate sannas. Having disposed of the first three on the grounds of incorrect symbols, spelling mistakes, modern writing and flimsy copper plate only lightly engraved, he proceeded to denounce the remaining three with gusto:

> If the three *sannas* already dealt with be - and in very truth, they are - barefaced forgeries, these other efforts may be said to 'out-Herod Herod' in atrocity. This much at least can be said for the first batch of three 'fakes': they at any rate kept within bounds of chronological possibility. Not so the other trio, which have thrown all discretion to the winds, and brazenly put Time's clock back three centuries...

> These extraordinarily fatuous forgeries do not possess a single redeeming feature - plate, writing, style and professed date, all combine to damn them utterly. Even the veriest tyro in forging 'royal grants' should have known better than to antedate by three hundred years a king whose reign is conclusively fixed by lithic record at a well-known site. [5]

In 1925 he had reported on the Kuttapitiya Sannasa, which was important for it concerned the right to appoint the Nayaka Incumbent of Adam's Peak; and the priests of the Malwatta Vihare, believing the report to be favourable to their claim, published it in Colombo. Bell sent a copy to C.H.Collins, then Secretary of the RASCB, and in an accompanying letter on May 28, 1926, suggested that it might be published in the JRASCB as a guide for others to follow. He wrote:

> The admitted lamentable ignorance - to put it frankly - of Civil Servants generally in regard to these interesting old-time documents (Sannas, Tudapat, etc.), which may come up for decision before them at any time is appalling. It is hardly an exaggeration to say that the Members of the Civil Service at present capable of tackling these not-infrequently difficult documents do not number the fingers of one hand...

> Now, what I am venturing to suggest, with all diffidence, is that the Ceylon Asiatic Society might confer a really useful permanent boon on Civil Servants by publishing this *Kuttapitiya Report* in its

Journal. I need only add that to me it would be a source of greatest satisfaction to feel that I have, in a humble way, been able to *leave on record* some guide, in an out-of-the-way line, to aid my ex-brothers of the Civil Service, who may be called on to grapple with Sannas etc. [6]

It does not appear that Collins availed himself of this opportunity. We learn that the original manuscript of this Report is held by Senarath Panawatta, Curator of the Kandy National Museum. Bell himself had a considerable personal collection of these old grants, and advised his daughter Zoë that after his death she should offer them to the Government and ask a good price for them, as valuable both as historical documents and for their present legal importance.

Other work for Government included his continued repairs to the Jetawanarama at Polonnaruwa. He was also asked to report on the state of the Demala-Maha-Seya murals. Interest had been aroused in them in 1917 by a request for copies from the Director General of Archaeology, India, Sir John Marshall. The Acting Director of the Colombo Museum, G.A.Joseph, had taken the opportunity to raise money by an appeal enabling him to send W.M.Fernando to Polonnaruwa, to supplement the painted copies made by D.A.L.Perera. Joseph wrote of this in the JRASCB and Bell added a Memorandum, which contained the following last passage of praise for the work of the former members of his staff:

> The Ceylon Government has been very fortunate in the three draughtsmen attached to the Archaeological Survey, to whose joint efforts - each in his degree and line - demanding much patience, perseverance, and a talent beyond the ordinary, the Island is indebted for the possession of a perfect series, in worthy reproduction, of these unique paintings of a bygone day - now, alas, fast disappearing - which in beauty of execution, in wealth of colour, and skilful technique, originally approached - though possibly they did not quite rival - the magnificent Indian frescoes at Ajanta.
>
> In their mutual, and highly successful collaboration, Messrs. D.A.Perera, W.M.Fernando and P.G.Perera have done real honour no less to themselves than to the Archaeological Survey Department and to the Government which they served so well. To all interested in Ceylon Art of a past day, who care to visit the Colombo Museum, full and easy opportunity is at length afforded of studying closely the finest examples of ancient and mediaeval painting still surviving in the Island. [7]

In a further Note on the subject he described his own visit to the site, and his views on the state of the paintings and the great difficulty there would be in preserving them.

> The (a) exposed position, and (b) present state of the paintings, popularly styled 'frescoes', are such that their permanent preservation, is, so far as one can judge, out of the question as a profitable undertaking *qua* the interests of Art. Once unique, in all the glory of beautiful execution and rich colouring, these mediaeval paintings have badly deteriorated, owing to lengthy exposure to tropical atmospheric elements - for a period of over 30 years in the case of the Portico and Vestibule Paintings (laid bare by Mr. S.M.Burrows in 1885-6), and nearly 10 years for those within the Inner Entresol and Shrine, excavated in 1910. Their condition at the present time is little short of parlous...
>
> The writer yields to no one in unfeigned admiration for these unique paintings of a bygone day -

'frescoes', so called, but strictly speaking paintings *in tempera*. It follows, therefore, that, both as erstwhile Archaeological Commissioner and personally from love of Oriental Art, he should be out and out in favour of preserving them, did not stern facts emphatically point to the uselessness - nay, from the architectural point of speaking, the clear undesirability - of taking any special steps (beyond ordinary and regular care of what still remains) for their protection in the future...

Even as they stand, weather-beaten, faded, and incomplete, were it possible to protect whilst exhibiting duly what remains of the paintings, in such manner as not hopelessly to disfigure the architectural lines of the Vihare itself - a marked feature of which is its peculiarly open internal arrangement - and to do this at comparatively small cost, some expenditure towards this end might fairly commend itself to the Government. [8]

Some conservation work was attempted by A.M.Hocart when he was Archaeological Commissioner in the 1920s. He renewed Bell's jungle-stick roofing and, on the advice of the Archaeological Survey of India, washed some of the paintings with spirits of turpentine and bees' wax. [9]

Some chemical treatment was given to the paintings by Khan Bahadur Mohammad Sana Ullah in the 1940s, and he removed some of the salts and fungi which had obscured the paintings. A full-scale restoration was put in hand by Luciano Maranzi, the Unesco expert, in 1972 and 1975. On the new approach to the treatment of ancient paintings, R.H.de Silva writes as follows in his account of rock painting in Sri Lanka for the Stockholm congress on conservation in 1975:

One guiding principle in the preservation of rock painting that has been followed here in the recent past should be set down. Whereas the aim of measures taken to preserve rock paintings was formerly limited to their conservation, we have recently introduced an acceptable minimal measure of restoration in the treatment of rock paintings. [10]

R.H.de Silva, himself Archaeological Commissioner at this time, sprang to the defence of H.C.P.Bell when he was accused of being responsible for the decay of the murals, by uncovering them and exposing them to sun and rain. As Bell himself had constantly pointed out, it was Burrows who had first uncovered some of the murals in 1885, and he had then reported that the paintings were in a very fair state of preservation. When Bell excavated the entire building he had written that, 'As no steps had been taken to protect the paintings, many had faded beyond recognition'. Bell, as we have seen, made some effort to protect the remaining frescoes from further damage. It was perhaps a good thing that actual restoration was left to a later date, when more advanced techniques became available. [11]

Most of Bell's activity in the first ten years of his retirement was literary. Despite the loss of an eye (thereafter he had a startlingly blue glass eye) his output was extensive. He had always been ready to correct and criticise the discoveries and views of other scholars and now found new opponents. On April 2, 1912 P.E.Pieris gave the RASCB a paper on 'The date of King Bhuwaneka Bahu VII', and Bell's Appendix C was among several printed in the journal. [12]

Pieris' contention was that the king reigned not from 1534 to 1542 A.D., as given in Turnour's

Epitome of the History of Ceylon, but from 1521 to 1551 A.D. The death-date was accepted by the audience and the Appendix writers, on the authority of Diogo de Couto in his *O Thesauro do Rei de Ceylao*. He had recorded that 'this unhappy king was shot by the Mulatto servant of the Viceroy Dom Affonco de Noronha, the eminent nobleman who subsequently stole the deceased king's spittoons of gold'. Bell reproved Pieris for nowhere acknowledging that the Portuguese chronicles were 'virtually a sealed book' till, in 1908, Donald Ferguson published his translations. Bell called Ferguson 'a "Gamaliel" at whose feet Mr. Pieris might have been proud to sit'.

Pieris' authority for the accession date of 1521 A.D. was a certain Father Fernao de Queiroz, S.J. Later, in 1916, the Ceylon Government was to print his *Conquista temporel e espirituel de Ceylao*, and the Rev. S.G.Perera, S.J. in the CALR, 1916-17, praised the wealth of information in this, the author's candour about Portuguese misdoings, his missionary fervour, and his respect for the Sinhalese, a people whom he called 'noble, cultured and by no means barbarous'.[13]

In 1912, however, J.M.Senaveratne in the discussion said that practically nothing was known of de Queiroz, and Bell described him as 'a mysterious "dark horse" (the tip only of whose nose we have been so far privileged to see)'. Moreover, he had written about fifty years later than de Couto, who was in close touch with the records at Goa.

Bell was engaged in other controversies, with Simon de Silva. This scholar, in a paper for the RASCB in 1912 on 'Vijaya Bahu VI', was opposing the traditional view (expressed by Bell in the Kegalla Report) that in 1408 A.D. a Chinese invasion carried off the king, Vijaya Bahu VI, and an interregnum followed till the accession of his son, Parakrama Bahu VI. Simon de Silva conceded that a Sinhalese Prince was carried off at the date in question, for this appeared in a Chinese chronicle which called the captive 'A-lee-ko-nae-wak'. This could be Sinhalese 'Alagakonara', whom de Silva believed to be no king (there was therefore no interregnum), but an insurgent prince or petty ruler, Vira Alagakonara or Alakeswara. In the chronicle *Suddhamaratnekurya* he found, as successor to Bhuwaneka Bahu V in 1391 A.D., one Vira Bahu, who had driven out his elder brother Vira Alagesvera. The latter, however, returned, reigned twelve years, and was then ensnared by the Chinese.[14]

One would think this gave us at least a captive of royal blood, but reading on one develops a sympathy with the Chairman of the meeting, Sir Hugh Clifford, who plaintively commented, 'I go away with my mind a howling wilderness, as to whether the king Vijaya Bahu VI lived at all, what happened to him, or who reigned in his stead'.

Bell said of Simon de Silva, 'with delightful cynicism the Mudaliyar styles his paper "Vijaya Bahu VI" and incontinently proceeds to contend that no such king reigned at that period'. Bell stood by his own 'interregnum' from 1408 to 1412, when the Chinese Emperor released captives who included the next ruler, Parakrama Bahu VI. A decisive piece of evidence, for Bell, was a stone slab found at Keragala Temple. On one side was a grant made in the 11th year of Parakrama Bahu VI; on the other, one in a very similar script, in the 11th year of 'Sri Sangabo Sri Vijaya Bahu Maha Raja'.

An epigraphical debate was started in the CALR in 1916 by Bell and A.Mendis Gunasekera, by their treatment of the inscriptions at Kelani Vihare. They gave first the religious and historical background, recalling periods of destruction and repair, occupation by the Portuguese and Dutch, and the revival of Buddhism. They described four inscriptions. No. 1, from the Kit-Siri-Mewan Vihare, was a slab inscription dated by the Buddhist equivalent of 1343-4 A.D. The authors queried this date, for the small type of script employed was typically 15th century, and a Minister and a Hierarch mentioned were more likely to have flourished at that time. There could have been an error by an illiterate stone-mason, for such were extremely frequent, though antedating by a century was unusual.

Simon de Silva, in 1917, opposed the idea that No.1, the Kit-Siri-Mewan epigraph, had been carelessly antedated. He compared Bell and Gunasekera's texts and translations with the copy he had obtained from the High Priest Dharmarama, Principal of Vidyelankera College, and defended the script as 14th rather than 15th century, with reference to two inscriptions published in Bell's Kegalla Report. [15]

Gunasekera was unwilling for controversy with a co-religionist and brother Government Official (De Silva being Chief Sinhalese Translator to the Ceylon Government), but Bell readily enough, in 1917, submitted a rejoinder. He credited the slab itself and its photographic reproduction rather than the High Priest's text. 'Deciphered in his younger days', Simon de Silva had said, and Bell remarked, 'Was it not of a certain Father William that Lewis Carroll wrote:

> "In my youth, said the sage, as he shook his old head,
> I kept all my wits very supple".'

Concluding, he urged de Silva to 'vary for a change the familiar role of critic' and undertake original work:

> 'A man must serve his turn to every trade
> Save censure - critics are all ready-made.'

It is not altogether surprising that Simon de Silva responded with acerbity, 'My language may not be as virile as that of my critic, and I cannot say I regret it, but I hope to make my meaning clear without invoking the aid of *English Bards and Scotch Reviewers*'. He was more seriously offended at Bell's undervaluing of the High Priest, and was somewhat sarcastic on textual readings by Bell and Gunasekera. On one in particular, 'Having had built seven walls round the great Bo-Tree', he commented:

> Seven walls around a Bo-Tree would have been a singular spectacle and certain to arrest attention, for nowhere else had a Bo-Tree received so conspicuous a mark of honour.

He offered as a more correct translation, 'Having built from the foundation an enclosure 79 cubits in circumference round the great Bo-Tree'. W.F.Gunawardhana concluded the discussion, mainly in favour of Simon de Silva, for he found it unlikely that the date should have been wrongly recorded by a century, and also thought the script of the epigraph distinctly archaic. [16]

Active retirement

Subsequent scholars could differ from Bell. In an article by Bell in July 1914, in the Notes and Queries section of the JRASCB, describing the Galapata Vihare near Bentota in the South Province, he gave Plates of photographs taken in 1893 of a fine door-frame of granite, carved with dancers. Other Plates showed a long rock-inscription of which Bell gave much of the text and its translation. It was dated in the 30th year of 'Parakrama Bahu', and Bell accepted him as the second monarch of that name. However, in *Epigraphia Zeylanica* in 1939, Paranavitana found the script more like that of a Parakrama Bahu I epigraph. Also the benefactions described in the Galapata inscription were unlike those recorded in the chronicles of Parakrama II's minister. Paranavitana, while accepting Bell's identification of various geographical names with modern versions, improved on him by recording seven omitted lines which were the names of temple slaves. [17]

In other less controversial articles Bell drew on his own old diaries, notes and discoveries, and the information he had collected from the Dutch archives. He also found new sources. In the Memorandum sent to Government in 1919, he describes how he obtained further material either by applying to the Government Agent acting as Archaeological Commissioner after Ayrton's death, or by 'himself taking, or employing others to take for him, at his own expense, photographs of inscriptions not discovered by the Archaeological Survey, which have since come to light'. [18]

Bell's interest in the history of Ceylon extended to all periods. In 1915 he gave an account of the 'Tula-bhara' ceremony. This Indian custom, by which a king was weighed against gold to be given in alms, was adopted by King Nissanka Malla. His records claimed that he performed this most generous action not once but many times, either alone or with other members of the royal family also in the scales. Bell doubted the frequency of these occasions, but took the opportunity for a last reluctant tribute to this monarch, whose ostentation he had so often deplored. He noted his wide travels through 'the rough places of his kingdom', including a pilgrimage to Adam's Peak; his care for agriculture and irrigation, measures for the suppression of crime and the recording of grants of land on copper plates. Together with his lavish building projects and distribution of alms to the poor these achievements, said Bell, clearly reflect 'regal administration of a high order'. [19]

When writing of the 'Maha Saman Devale and its Sannasa' he turned aside to deal with an historical event sculpted on a slab outside the temple. It portrays a Portuguese soldier with sword raised, about to give the *coup de grace* to a Sinhalese warrior. Drawing on a paper by D.W.Ferguson, Bell tells the story of a Portuguese *fidalgo*, Simao Pinhao, who came out to India in 1590 and then served in the army of occupation in Ceylon, dying about 1617, having taken part in many campaigns and married a Sinhalese princess. The identity of the Sinhalese warrior is uncertain, Sinhalese tradition naming Kuruwita Bandara, 'a dreaded enemy of the Portuguese', although Ferguson believed that he long outlived Simao Pinhao. Bell concludes this section with a quotation from his favourite Sir Walter Scott:

> Be the truth what it may, the fine bas-relief will hardly fail to conjure up vision of that stern combat to the death, immortalised by the Poet, between 'Scotland's dauntless King' (James V) and the stalwart

H. C. P. Bell

Chieftain, Roderigh Vich Alpine Dhu, 'in close fight a champion grim,' when

'Foot, and point, and eye opposed,
In dubious strife they darkly closed'. [20]

Bell drew on the Dutch records to elucidate the story of one Andreas Amabert, a native of Grenoble, who had served in the Dutch army at Pitigala and had died on July 18, 1764. His death was recorded in Dutch on a granite slab within an old building, near Bentota, once used as a store room, but in Bell's time as the local Government Anglo-Vernacular School. Bell had found letters referring to Amabert and he printed translations which had been supplied by R.G.Anthonisz, the Government Archivist. They were all from Amabert's superior officer, Abraham Samlant. Bell said:

> The letters, interesting despite their matter-of-fact contents, are models of a high standard of official correspondence - clear, courteous, and decided; missing no point raised or likely to arise; offering help in every way possible whilst condemning, in no uncertain terms, all irregularities and slackness.

The last letter, sent to 'The Valiant Lieutenant Amabert, Commanding the Military Detachment at *Pittigelle*' and beginning 'Good Friend', regretted Amabert's 'indisposition' and his need to retire to 'Bentotte' to seek recovery. From these official letters Bell deduced the characters of the strict and businesslike Dutch Superior and the more casual French Lieutenant - inexperienced, with no knowledge of Sinhalese and little even of Dutch, an easy victim of an unscrupulous Mudaliyar and rascally coolies, and with neither medical officer nor medicines to help him in his illness.

Bell's sympathy with the long-dead young Commandant led him to urge that his gravestone should be in some way protected. Once the dumping place for bags of salt, it was now trampled upon by 'the heedless feet of merry, irresponsible, schoolchildren'. Should it not now be enclosed, as a mark of solidarity when Britain and France were at war, as Allies? [21]

Bell acquired information for papers from those still out in the field. He communicated to the CALR in 1916 in 'Some ancient ruins in Uva' an account of discoveries in a Province which was 'Virtually an unworked field for archaeological research'. C.A.Baumgartner, the Government Agent, had in July 1897 sent a letter about a ruin at Maliga-wela in the heart of the forest, containing a colossal Buddha nearly as large as those of Awkana or Seseruwa. Mr. B.Stork of the Survey Department reported finding, in 1907, an old Rock Temple near Ulgala, the cave floored with pungent bat dung, as soft underfoot 'as the finest toilet-powder'. A never-failing pool was now used by wild animals, but 'Centuries ago this little rock-basin of sweet water must have supplied the Cave Temple, which now lies hidden and unknown in the solitary forest'. [22]

It was D.A.L.Perera who in 1918 provided an account of an inscribed pillar found within a quarter of a mile of the Abhayagiriya dagaba. In his Foreword to this article Bell gave a general account of the development of scripts, from the archaic forms of the ninth and tenth centuries and as far as Mahinda IV, to those of the late twelfth and thirteenth centuries beginning under

Parakrama Bahu I, and again to the type of the fourteenth and fifteenth centuries. Perera had sent Bell the text of the pillar, with transliteration, translation and an introduction, and both of them commented on the unusual inverted engraving, the lines running from right to left and from bottom to top of each side. This and other 'freak pillars' pointed to the reign of Sena II, here inscribed as *Sri Sang Abaya*, whom Bell dated from 866 to 891 A.D., though Perera, following Wickremasinghe, preferred 917 to 952 A.D. This *gal sannasa* bestowed a garden on monks of the Mangale Pirivena, near the Abhayagiriya Dagaba; and the location of the pillar confirmed its more recent identification. [23]

Bell drew on his own long-past experience when describing the surviving lower half of a pillar slab at Nuwara Eliya. It had been a suprising discovery when he first copied it in June 1891 on the bank of Telegala-oya. The high plateau had been even in 1828 a wild tract frequented by grove elephants. So the characters of this lithic record 'fragmentary though it be' were 'of considerable interest, as proving the existence of a Buddhist Temple at Nuwara Eliya... nearly 1,000 years ago'. The tenth century characters of a royal decree to chiefs, yet surviving in what must then have been the wildest country, were 'a striking testimony to the zeal of the Tapowani, forest-dwelling monks'. [24]

Perhaps because research in the wild made it harder to write full accounts at the time, it was jungle experiences that he long after treated more expansively. It was in September 1897 that he had found the Maravidiye Caves containing Queen Sundari's inscription which initiated the Dimbulagala controversy with Wickremasinghe; but in 1917 that he treated this fully in the CALR. The 'Rock Elephant', found in the same month of 1897, he also described fully twenty years later. In 1918 'Archaeological research in the Egoda Pattuwa, Tamankaduwa' chronicled meetings with the jungle dwellers, the Veddas, in 1905. Bell also wrote of the 'Ahigunthikayo' or Ceylon gypsies without indicating dates of his encounters with them.

Bell had never ceased to take a particular interest in the Maldive Islands, and to hope that one day he could return there and conduct further investigations. From 1915 to 1918 he published in the CALR a series entitled 'The Maldive Islands, 1602 - 1607'. Here he printed, side by side, extracts from two accounts which were freely based on the descriptions given by Pyrard. His intention was to show how they compared, for accuracy and completeness, with the full text published by Albert Gray and himself. The two accounts were Captain Symson's *New Voyage to the East Indies*, 1715, and Harris's *Collection of Voyages*, vol. I, 1744. Bell showed that Symson gave more detail of clothes and customs, murders and punishments, while Harris gave a fuller account of justice and government. Of the two, Harris is the more 'mealy-mouthed', though even Symson omits the marital vagaries of a Sultan characterised by Bell as a mixture of the English Henry VIII and the Biblical King David, prepared to use violence to obtain the women he wanted. In contrast 'the garrulous and plain-spoken French captive did not mince matters'. [25]

Bell had also maintained his interest in the Maldive language, and undertook the editorship of 'Maldivian linguistic studies' by Wilhelm Geiger, when it appeared in 1919 in the JRASCB.

27

The Maldives : Return

Throughout his career Bell was held to be the great authority on the Maldive Islands. He was always referred to for information, and his 1881 report on the Maldives long remained the only detailed account extant. All visitors to the Islands, official and unofficial, took care to obtain copies. When W.T.Taylor, Acting Colonial Secretary, after a semi-formal visit in 1900, reported to the Governor, Sir J.West Ridgeway, he wrote:

> I do not think I need to dwell further on the subject of the general conditions and features of the islands. They have been exhaustively treated by Mr. Bell in the paper compiled by him and published in Sessional Paper No. 43 of 1881. What was true of the Maldives then and of their inhabitants is true now. [1]

Earlier, when Sultan Ibrahim Nur-ud-din died in 1892, and one of his younger sons was placed on the throne, Bell was asked to submit a Memorandum to Government on the law of succession in the Maldives, which he did in a letter sent from Anuradhapura on March 25, 1893. In it he quoted historical precedents to show that the Sultan had always had the power to nominate his successor, but that normally the throne would go to the eldest son, in the absence of any disability. The elder brother, Muhammad Shams-ud-din, was shortly afterwards raised to the throne, and though displaced temporarily by his cousin, Muhammad Imad-ud-din, who had been acting as Regent, he returned to power in 1903. [2]

Documents concerning this period of history collected from the Colombo Secretariat were published under the title of *Papers Relating to the Maldive Islands 1887-1910*. No editor nor compiler appears on the publication itself, but it is entered in the catalogue of the Library of the Foreign and Commonwealth Office (old Colonial Office) in London as being compiled by H.C.P.Bell, and he draws on it extensively in the historical portion of his own final work on the Maldive Islands, published in 1940. The history of the Islands during this period was one of confused revolution and counter-revolution, with the guiding thread the alternation of influence between two Maldive noblemen, Ibrahim Didi and Muhammad Didi, Prime Ministers of successive Sultans. Bell writes of it as 'the in-and-out political ascendancy, as of alternating barometer puppets, of these two able chiefs - heads of rival factions (Atiri-ge, Kaka-ge), but themselves interconnected by marriage, and at times quite friendly, if more often antipathetic, which persisted for many years'. Bell had known Ibrahim Didi during one of his periods of exile at Galle, and they continued as friends throughout their lives. Ibrahim Didi, who finally returned to power in 1903, remained as the Prime Minister until his death in 1925. In the Maldive report of 1940 Bell gives an account of his life with the following obituary tribute:

The Maldives : Return

A.Haji Ibrahim Didi, *Bodu Dorimena Kilegefanu*. On Tuesday, March 31, 1925, at the age of 80, there passed away in Male, during the month of Ramazan, holy to Muslims, quite the most able Servant of the Crown in the Island's history. *Multis ille flebilis occidit*. Fitly, in truth, did this truly great, and justly beloved, Maldivian gentleman, earn *par excellence* the noble appellation of 'the Grand Old Man of the Maldives'.[3]

Bell's friendship with Ibrahim Didi is probably the reason for his having been picked out, along with other high-ranking officials, as a target for accusations of accepting bribes from the Maldive Government. This emerges from a correspondence between Mr. Stanley Gardiner, of Gonville and Caius College, Cambridge, and the Colonial Office in London. Stanley Gardiner went on a scientific expedition to the Maldives in 1899. He was there from October 22, 1899 to April 1900, at a time when Muhammad Didi had succeeded in ousting Ibrahim Didi, and when charges and counter-charges were being laid concerning the large debt owed by the Maldive Government to Carimjee Jafferjee and Co., a firm of Indian Merchants. Gardiner was informed, both by members of this company and by Maldive officials of the new government, that a large part of the money had in fact been paid as bribes 'to white officials'.

In a Memorandum to the Colonial Office, which he asked should be treated as confidential, he gave details of the various stories that he had heard. One such came from Hassan Didi, *Velana Manikufanu*, who accompanied him on his cruise in the Northern Atols, and of whom he noted that 'this gentleman is not a total abstainer', adding, however, that 'drunk or sober, alone or in company, Hassan Didi never contradicted himself on the matter in any way'.

Hassan Didi told tales of money passing to the various Colonial Secretaries and even to the Governor, Sir West Ridgeway. There were stories of Rs. 50,000 in silver rupees taken from the Treasurer by Ibrahim Didi, and taken to Sir Noel Walker 'in a *single* box' when he was visiting Male; and of money going through a jeweller in Kandy - though this was not supposed to have reached the Governor. Gardiner added, 'The only other white man about whom definite statements were made was Mr. Bell of Anuradhapura' - but he gave no details of the accusation.[4]

Gardiner was at pains to stress that he did not believe that any money had ever been paid to white officials, but he believed that it had been retained by Carimjee Jafferjee and by Ibrahim Didi. The Colonial Office, having no doubt of the integrity of its officials, passed the matter to the Ceylon Government. There the rumours of Ibrahim Didi's involvement were also discounted, for he had always been found both efficient and friendly. When Sultan Muhammad Shams-ud-din was restored to power in 1903, and Ibrahim was recalled from exile, Mr. E.F.im Thurn, who had been sent on an exploratory mission, reported as follows:

> The Maldivians appear to realize that Ibrahim Didi is the cleverest of their nation; that, though he formerly was somewhat too advanced in his views, he had paid for this; and that there is now no reason why he should not return, should he wish to do so, to Male. Even Muhammad Didi, the rival Prime Minister, would, I believe, be in favour of this. A very strong and united Maldivian party would thus be formed, and one which would be entirely in our (British) interests.[5]

When Bell returned to the Maldives in 1920 and 1922 Sultan Muhammad Shams-ud-din was still reigning and Ibrahim Didi was his Prime Minister, aided, says Bell, 'by a trio of brilliant sons, each, like their father, eminently fitted from sound British education in Ceylon for his respective career'. Ahmad Didi, son of his first wife, was Private Secretary to the Sultan and in charge of Customs and the Post Office; Abdul Majid Didi and Abdul Hamid Didi, sons of his second wife, were Treasurer and Controller of the Revenue, and Maldivian Representative at Colombo, respectively. The family continued to occupy many important posts in the Government of the Maldives, and their sons after them. Bell had friends in high places to welcome him. [6]

On January 20, 1920, H.M.S. 'Comus' (Capt. C.Wason) of the East Indies Squadron left Colombo for Male with the Hon. Mr. B.Horsburgh and the Hon. R.Trefusis, who were to confer the Order of St. Michael and St. George upon His Highness the Sultan, and also to deal with the Census of 1921, and with the serious shortage of rice, caused by the prices charged by Indian middlemen and by the lack of Maldive Government ships. Bell went with the mission to collect material to update his report of 1881; to examine the *Tarikh*, or chronicle of the Maldives since the Mohammedan Conversion; and to make enquiries regarding Buddhist remains on the Islands. When his going became probable in 1919 he requested from Sir William Manning, the Governor, the necessary status and a grant comparable to that for his post-retirement work at Polonnaruwa. To Horsburgh he wrote, 'Hope you won't be scared to death by "old Bell" and his senile ways', and also described the large Admiralty charts he had obtained. He told Trefusis he regretted that 'Comus' would not call at an island, visited by Ibn Batuta, 'the wholly isolated and mysterious island Fua Mulaku'. [7]

The whole visit lasted only from January 20 to February 21, 1920 and was confined to Male Island. Bell did, however, obtain a sight of the *Tarikh* and, with great difficulty, a translated summary. The *Tarikh* had been compiled, said Bell, 'by three members of one erudite family, father, nephew and grandson, each in due course *Kazi* [Chief Justice]- who flourished during the reigns of thirteen Sultans, from the end of the Seventeenth Century to well into the Nineteenth'. It covers the period from Sultan Muhammad-ul-Adil, converted to Islam in 1153, to Sultan Muhammad Mu'in-ud-din who reigned until 1835.

After the *Tarikh* had been formally inspected by Bell and Trefusis, and a double spread photographed, Bell got down to the work of translating the Arabic text with the aid of Ahmad Didi, Private Secretary to the Sultan, and Husain Didi, the acting Kazi. Of Ahmad Didi, friend since his student days at Richmond College, Galle, Bell wrote that he 'retains the same winning personality'. The two Arabic scholars did their best to complete the task despite frequent official calls on their time. 'Nevertheless', said Bell, 'by devoting such mornings as could be spared - and finally part of one night - the whole of the present copy of the *Tarikh*, as it exists at this day, was closely scrutinized from page 1 to page 59 (the last written) before Mr. Bell's stay of three weeks at Male terminated'.

The *Tarikh* begins with exhortations to righteous conduct to all rulers, and a brief chronicle of world history from Adam to the Prophet Muhammad and the Khalifas as far as the twelfth century. It then relates the conversion of the Maldives by the Shaikh Yusuf Shams-ud-din of Tabriz and gives an account of his miracles. It proceeds to chronicle the reigns of seventy-six

The Maldives : Return

Sultans, with several interpolations praising or blaming them.

In his 1920 report Bell included 'Brief Notes on Maldivian History under the Sultans', giving information from the *Tarikh* on selected rulers, and a revised list of all ninety-one Sultans. He further printed a provisional list of Kazis of the Maldive Islands, who were the Chief Justices, Civil, Criminal and Ecclesiastical, styled in Maldivian *Fadiyaru*.

Bell's diary of his stay began with the arrival at Male. He wrote:

> Steaming slowly into the Atol the aquamarine of the lagoon, in beautiful contrast to the deep blue of the sea outside, added to the Island's rich greenery, exhibited, under a cloudless sky, the most vivid of pictures.

Among the Ministers who came on board the 'Comus' was another old acquaintance from 1884, Ismail Didi, 'the sprightly young Ambassador to Ceylon in the 80s, as smiling as ever'. After their landing Horsburgh presented the Order to His Highness, seated in the State Chair. While the Mission's messages were discussed (translated from Maldivian through Hindustani and Tamil to English, and vice versa), Bell had leisure to observe the Sultan and the Durbar Hall. His Highness, with a face clean-shaven save for a short moustache, placid in expression but brightening when interested, 'was today dressed in a rich under-garment, covered *modo Arabico* by a long robe of rose-flowered silk, bordered in heavy gold lace', and had a white turban 'terminating in a small spike-ornament of gold'. The next day the Sultan paid a State visit to the 'Comus', where he told Bell he was pleased that he had been present in 1879 at the Sports in honour of his own birth. The 'Comus' left on January 24 with the Mission, but Bell remained.

Ahmad Didi, who had been interpreting, gave other help to Bell. He arranged for a Survey and Plan of Male, and Bell included the Plan in his 1920 report. He also wrote his own connected account of Male; of Harbour and Bazaar, Mosques, Fortifications, Palace, streets and buildings, giving a tour of the four quarters, and describing the calm inhabitants.

Ahmad and his brother Abdul Majid also showed Bell an elaborate and complex Genealogical Table giving the pedigrees of Sultans and nobility back to the seventeenth century. This belonged to their father Ibrahim, now seventy-five years old. Bell several times visited the 'fine old man', though he was not in good health; a pleasant resumption of the intercourse which had been close in the Eighties, when Ibrahim was living in Galle almost as an exile. Bell always felt he had been badly treated.

For his stay in Male, Bell was lent by Abdul Majid an excellent well-built house, with its own garden and a bathroom with a bathing-pool. It was not far from a mosque, the Hukuru Miskit, whence he heard the *Mudin's* call to prayer, 'so impressive in its plaintive, drawn-out pleading'. During his stay he viewed many mosques, the Kaluwakura Miskit the most picturesque, as others had modern corrugated metal roofing; also tombs of Sultans. Writing about gravestones, he noted those with pointed tops denoting males, and the round-headed, females. He admired their ornamentation, saying:

> This is nearly always chaste, and often really beautiful, by virtue of its manifold variation of arabesques

and other flowery designs... their superscription is usually in Arabic, less frequently in Maldivian *gabuli tana*, though now and then stones may be noticed (e.g. that of *'Bodu Rasgefanu'*) cut, in sunk relief, in the bold rounded *dives akuru*, the ancient character of the Islands.

The Maldives lie close to the Equator. Though Bell admired the main street of Male, fifty feet wide, straight from sea to sea, East to West, and kept beautifully clean and white, he could not but admit that there were disadvantages:

Weather gloriously fine; but a tropical sun in a brazen sky, beating down on blinding white streets...renders the heat and glare, untempered by shade trees or breeze, very trying in the day time. A plague of most aggressive mosquitoes, which cease not from troubling day nor night, is an added amenity.

However, he was greatly impressed by Male as 'A Capital of Silences'. Not only was there the total absence of all vehicles but 'the uncanny silence of wayfarers is equally noticeable'. Voices were never raised in anger, and at night the perfect stillness became almost eerie; not even a 'cry of child or fretful babe; no irrepressible dog (these animals being *anathema* to Muslims) bays the moon'. He continued:

All is peace. During the glorious nights, as now, when the moon is at full - and what a moon, in its intense preternatural brightness reflected from gleaming white coral underfoot! - very occasional 'serenaders' passing along break the weird calm by pleasing native songs.

Bell was shown, or happened upon, various sights of interest: the old ordnance at the Bastion, which included a cannon bearing Portuguese Royal Arms, and a Dutch one made in 1600 at Amsterdam. Near the Munnaru Tower was a curious oblong 'sun-dial' slab which helped time the Muslim hours of prayer. He watched fine lacquer work being done by the only skilled workman in Male. In particular he was taken over the Henveru Gaduvaru, the fine New Palace whose garden had even a small white rose in bloom, intended for the young Prince, the Heir Apparent, due to arrive from Ceylon. Prince Hasan Izz-ud-din, eighteen years old, had been away seven years for education, partly at the Royal College, Colombo, and to welcome him a 'Sea Pageant' was being prepared, organised by Ismail Didi as Harbour Master. The jetty was decorated in perfect taste with fruit, foliage, streamers, and 'Welcome' placards. Bell declared, 'The Maldivian Islander - *simplex munditiis*, "plain in his neatness", is an exceedingly artistic person'.

On February 14 the 'Lady McCallum' arrived with the Prince and some young cousins and Abdul Hamid Didi; also with 8,000 greatly welcomed bags of rice. Mrs. Lawson Robins, wife of the Captain of the 'Lady McCallum', in a booklet *English Lady's Visit to the Maldives*, described the excitement of the homecoming Prince on the voyage - he had balloons hung out and a firework display. A Royal party came on board to greet him, and she photographed the group of the Sultan and others. She brought out the intense exhilaration of the day for a people

The Maldives : Return

'whose pleasures are simple and unusual'.

With her husband and the Chief Engineer, Mrs. Robins went ashore and was shown by Bell the main sights of Male; she admired the streets and trees and noticed the women peeping from entrances. 'Their faces were not lacking in beauty,' she wrote, 'their eyes being full and soft and their teeth good'. Only when her male escorts had assured the women of her harmlessness (she was the only white woman they had ever seen except for one American lady) did they dare to be photographed with their children. On February 15 Mrs. Robins was rowed to Fonadu Island, less than a mile north of Male. It was uninhabited and jungle-clothed - she saw birds, including a lonely hen - but what she was to remember most vividly was the sight of the coral reef:

> The coral stood out as in a kaleidoscope, brown and branching like a fir-tree, or like deer's antlers, now spongelike, now like a giant fungus or a cluster of begonia leaves - and sometimes extending in green-grey branches as if a monstrous lichen - usually drab or brown in colour, but with frequently recurring masses of bright pink, purple, green and blue. The sea floor below was of white coral sand. In and out of the tiny grottos and caves formed by the coral darted fish, of colour unimaginable and passing description - bright orange or flame-colour, soft pinks, vivid greens and peacock blue, silver, dull grey with a belt of purest green between back and tail - all displayed against the subdued background of coral and irradiated by sunlight gleaming through the clear blue water. [8]

The island itself had more melancholy associations, for it was reserved as a cemetery where all foreigners who chanced to die at Male were buried. Mrs. Robins saw the carved coral head-and-foot stones of two graves of Englishmen, Captain Overend and Private Luckham. Bell gave a full account of these in 1927 in one of his 'Excerpta Maldiviana'. Private Luckham had been drowned on a picnic with a naval party on September 9, 1909, while bathing off the neighbouring island, Hulule, and had been buried with full military honours. When Bell visited Fonadu in 1922, he saw the stones and recorded Luckham's epitaph; he was 'Private Victor Luckham, R.M.L.I., H.M.S.Proserpine, aged 24'.

The grave of Captain J.C.Overend presented more of a problem. Bell related:

> The 'Ketch of Tranquebar', freighted with piece-goods for Colombo by her recent purchasers Captain J.C.Overend and Mr. George Fischer, sailed from 'the Island of Veypar near Tuticoryn' on January 6, 1797, under command of J.H.Thuring, Lieutenant, Marine Survey, Netherlands' East India Company. [9]

Bad weather drove them to take refuge in the Maldives, where the vessel stranded. Some Islanders pilfered most of the cargo, and the officers and crew were taken to Male. On March 16 Captain Overend died there of fever. In his Notes Bell gives records of the ravages of 'Maldive Fever'. He said:

> Male is very subject to recurrent waves of this pestilence - apparently a virulent form of what is nowadays termed 'Influenza'. One such epidemic (300 deaths) struck Male in the autumn of 1922... All three members of the Archaeological expedition of 1922 continued to suffer periodically for two or three years after their return to Ceylon.

H. C. P. Bell

Letters published in the *Ceylon Times* and *Ceylon Observer* on April 14 and 16, 1887, above the initials F.C.H. of an employee in the Basses and Minicoy Lights Office, Colombo, had recorded a headstone on which appeared:

HERE LYETH THE BODY OF CAPTAIN J.C. OVERAND, LATE OF H.M.S. 36TH RGT,
WHO DEPARTED THIS LIFE THE 16TH MARCH, 1797

Apart from the spelling of the name, this accorded with the facts, Overend having presumably left the Army and become a merchant captain. However, when Bell in 1922 examined the grave on Fonadu, he read on a board affixed to an entirely plain headstone:

CAPTAIN OVEREND R.N. / H.M.S. 'DORIS' / 1797

In his article in 1927 Bell wondered how the original gravestone had vanished, and how and why Overend had received his 'posthumous promotion to the Senior Service'. [10]

Mrs. Robins visited Hulule as well as Fonadu, and there pleasantly improved her acquaintance with Maldive women. She admired their collars of braid, woven by themselves in silver, gold and coloured threads. They showed her their best dresses and were proud of a green striped silk. She continued:

> They dressed my ears in long chains of gold ornament, as recorded by François Pyrard the French captive, and hung a necklace round my neck - then ran for an old hand mirror for me to view myself in all my new charms.

However, she resisted having her hair done like theirs in a round flat chignon on the right side of the head, covered with cloth and resembling an over-turned flat-bottomed saucer. [11]

Bell was not able to follow up his intention of looking personally for Buddhist remains. His section 'Some Notes on Buddhism in the Maldives' contains mostly reports from Maldivians themselves or from foreign visitors, much of the material being repeated in the 1940 report. He gave more detail here about Fua Mulaku Island, describing the visit there of the Frenchmen, Jean and Raoul Parmentier, in the 'Pensée' and the 'Sacré' in 1529. In September they landed on the island, whose Chief Priest called it *Moluque*, and saw an ancient stone 'Temple or Mosque'. Frederick de Houtman in 'The Lioness' (with his brother Cornelis in 'The Lion') landed there on June 1, 1599. He described in detail many 'Temples and altars' including a 'crumbled Pyramid'.

Bell himself examined the largest and probably oldest bathing tank on Male Island, called 'Ma-Veyo'. In spite of its close proximity to a Mosque, this almost square tank reminded him of the Kuttam Pokuna, or ancient Buddhist 'Twin Baths' at Anuradhapura, and he was sure it was of Buddhistic execution.

On February 16, Bell had a farewell interview with the Sultan, who invited him to return, and informed him that he had already despatched an expedition to the Southern Atols to investigate

The Maldives : Return

Buddhist Archaeology. On this occasion, when invited to speak in Maldivian, Bell asked after the health of the Sultan, but used too unceremonious a phrase. However, 'with delightful tact, but undisguised merriment' His Highness declared the expression quite correct.

The 'Lady McCallum' conveyed Bell back to Ceylon, from February 18, 1920 to February 21, together with Royal Pilgrims on their way to Mecca, and noblemen, including Ahmad Didi's only son, Muhammad Amin, on his way to school in Colombo. There was a pathetic parting with Ibrahim Didi, who had 'helped to steer the Ship of State through fair winds and foul' for seventeen years. Bell recalled:

> As with tears in his eyes, he wrung both my hands, he said, 'I am now too old to come Ceylon again before I die, but I never forget, *never* forget'.

28

The Maldives : Dream Fulfilled

Between 1920 and 1922 Bell was preparing his own study on his recent visit to the Maldives and collecting Trade and Tonnage returns. In January 1922 special copies of this report were sent to the Government and to the Sultan and his son. This report (Sessional Paper XV, 1921), based on so brief a trip, was not the thorough updating of his original work which Bell had wished for, but a proper expedition to the Maldives was bound to cost money. The Archaeological Survey in 1921-22, in spite of rising prices, spent little more than in 1912-13, but A.M.Hocart in the Annual Report complained of 'the transfer of all the money voted for scholarships and Rs. 3,000 of the conservation vote to an expedition to the Maldives'.[1] To Bell, however, this grant was most welcome; at New Year, 1922, he told Trefusis of how he longed for one more visit, 'before I go forward to be no more seen'.[2]

This heart's desire was to be fulfilled. Captain R.S.Sneyd, D.S.O., in H.M.S.'Comus', sailed for Male on February 2, carrying Bell, his clerk W.L.de Silva, a young, active and intelligent Sinhalese, and a very capable Malay Peon. The Sultan accorded an audience and received from the Captain an invitation for the Crown Prince to attend the reception at Colombo in March for His Royal Highness the Prince of Wales.

Bell was able to go on two expeditions to the Southern Atols in search of reported Buddhist remains. Both are fully described in his Diary printed in the Monograph of 1940. The first trip, from February 9 to 18 in 'Comus', had to be short as the ship was due to convey the Prince to Colombo before March 23. Captain Sneyd carried Bell's party, with Ismail Didi as Interpreter, down to the very far southern Addu Atol, where the ship had Admiralty work to do. Bell described the islands strung along the 'horse-shoe' of coral reefs, surrounding the 'sapphire lagoon bordered by beach of pure white sand'. The evergreen islands were 'thickly wooded by slim graceful coconut, massive bread-fruit and many another tropical tree'.

He went ashore on Gan to examine the ruined Dagaba mound (Maldivian: *Ustubu*) and its connected monastic site. The official, Elage Don Manikku, 'an elderly grave-faced man, quiet, gentle of speech and charmingly courteous in manners', had assembled from the islands more than a hundred men, 'a veritable glut of raw labour in face of our hopeless shortage of tools', to dig into the mound. Despite the 'delightful keenness' of the workers, 'each stepping where his comrade stood the moment that he fell', little could be done in the three days available. For the next day had to be given to Hitadu Island, and the 'dilapidated shell of an old coral-built Fort' with Portuguese connections. This was strenuous, Bell writing that as the ruin was absolutely shadeless, and lay but forty miles south of the Equator, 'the intense heat and glare proved almost intolerable, though the kindly natives plied us liberally with *Kurumbas* (young coconuts) to drink'. They then rested in the pleasant house of one Ali Didi, surrounded by flowering shrubs, and were given a good meal.

The Maldives : Dreams fulfilled

'Comus' then steamed on to Fua Mulaku where there was a somewhat hurried examination of an ancient coral-built Dagaba called *Havitta*. For Bell, though, there was great satisfaction in landing at an island so isolated that of Europeans only the brothers Parmentier in 1529, the brothers de Houtman in 1599, and some Surveyors for the Indian Navy, had set foot there. In spite of a 'treadmill' climb up loose coral shingle, Bell found the walk to the ruins by a perfectly shaded and well-kept thoroughfare a 'matter of ceaseless wonder and delight'. The old *Goiveri*, another Ali Didi, entertained them on his verandah with a rare treat of pineapples and oranges. At their departure Bell wrote, 'Isle of beauty, fare thee well. *Ave atque vale*'. To this site he was not to return, and the ship headed northward for Male and sailed with the Prince for Colombo on February 19.

On this first trip Bell had met and talked with islanders and seen a little of their life; on Hitadu he watched men hand-weaving and on Fua Mulaku saw some of its products, besides receiving 'the quaint present of half-a-dozen most creditable cakes of *stamped* soap, also made locally'. The soap was made from ashes, coral-lime, and coconut oil, and the cakes came in three colours - cream, mauve, pink; the shapes oblong or oval. The island and sometimes the owner were named in Arabic on one side, and in English on the other was stamped 'Best soap' and 'Mulaku'. Bell noted the dress of the women, their long upper bodices being not only in the familiar blue or terracotta, but in scarlet, ochre and brown. Both on Gan and on Fua Mulaku they were much less shy and unwilling to be photographed than on Male; they exhibited 'the unsophisticated simplicity and natural fearless bearing of animals in a "Game Sanctuary"; rarely or never having seen alien man, they have not yet learnt to doubt him'.

The unavoidable sketchiness of the investigations on the first trip to the Southern Atols was made good by the generosity of the Sultan, who placed at Bell's disposal the small Maldivian Government schooner 'Fath-ul-Majid' and the services again of Ismail Didi. It sailed on March 7 down to an area less southerly than the Addu Atol and Fua Mulaku, and north of the one and half degree Channel. This was the Haddummati Atol. Bell described the two-masted schooner, 68 ft. 2 in. long, with a small cabin. The *Malim* or Captain, Ali Koya Fulu, had a boatswain and eleven sailors. Bell praised the smaller fishing boats (Maldivian: *Mas-doni*), the graceful sweep of their lines. 'Maldive Islanders', he wrote, 'love their boats (each piece of which has its distinct name) and take just pride in their shapeliness and sea-worthy qualities'.

Some short squalls helped them on their way, 'rocked in the cradle of the deep', and from Kolumadulu Atol onwards Ismail 'commandeered' as escort a boat-owner Adam *Kalegefanu*. They entered the Haddummati Atol on March 10. There was here another island called Gan with Buddhist remains, and ten days were devoted to excavating a larger group of ruins, and a smaller coterie to the south, known as Kuruhinna. The main group near the village comprised what Bell concluded to be a large 'Dagaba', a 'Wata-da-ge', a 'Vihare' or 'Pilimage', a spacious 'Pirivena' and some wells. Each of these had to be cleared of all except coconut trees. The 'Dagaba', called *Hat-teli* by the Islanders, was investigated by trenching in. Bell first allowed their head to the zealous Maldivian Chiefs, then organised them on his well-tried lines into parties, each to break in and to carry earth away; he later arranged the work in shifts. The 'Dagaba' no longer had a 'tee', but an old man remembered it 'like a room open to the sky' in which he and other boys once played. The resourceful *Atoluveri* (headman) procured poles for shoring up, against the danger of falling lumps of coral. Here on March 16 occurred the three 'glorious finds', of a Bodhisatva's headdress, a small damaged sedent image of the Buddha and, as Bell wrote:

> The chief is the face of a colossal Buddha, showing part of the forehead and skull covered with short orthodox curls.

This was the final nail to clinch the connection of the remains with Buddhism. All three objects would have been buried as 'accursed things' by the Muslim converts eight centuries ago, but now, said Bell:

> It falls to a votary of a creed alien to both religions to 'grasp the skirts of happy chance' and expose the truth! *Veritas vincit.*

Of the wells on the site the most promising was excavated. They cut down through coral to a well-made floor, supporting centrally a fine jar of old-time pottery in white porcelain. The 'Wata-dage' was also attacked by 'a virtual rabble of good-natured raw recruits', very obedient, however, to their 'overseers' Ismail Didi, and the *Atoluveri* (old Ali Fulu Koya), also to Adam *Kalegefanu* and leading men of the other islands. Half of a cylindrical pedestal, well carved from white coral, Bell thought had been the supporter of an image. A raised oblong ruin, when cleared of stones, showed mouldings and emerged as a 'Vihare' with Portico, moonstone and steps. A large stone structure, belatedly cleared of jungle - the workers showing 'no slackness, no skimping', urged on by cries of 'Shabash' (pronounced by Maldivians as a long-drawn-out 'Savas') - was revealed as a 'Pirivena'. It had been once adapted as a mosque, then abandoned and overgrown.

When the ruin at Kuruhinna first caught Bell's eye, it looked like a temple with much of its dome, resembling Siva Devale No. 2 at Polonnaruwa. On Friday, March 17, when the Mohammedans could not be expected to work, till noon at least, the crew of the 'Fath-ul-Majid' volunteered, so long as they could have a recess for the noon meal and prayers. They were joined by the crew of the *Mas-doni* that had been ferrying the party ashore. The 'temple' was in fact a small Dagaba on a plinth with 'Greek cross' bays standing on a circular platform. It yielded a square 'Relic-casket' containing tiny coloured beads, which was later shown to the Sultan. Bell regretted the absence of coins, which could have indicated date. The sailors also helped finally at the main Gan ruins, to pack up the 'finds' and make a Compass and Tape Survey.

On the journey north to Mundu in the Atol began the absence of wind which was to entail the schooner's frequently needing to be towed by rowing boats. Bell much appreciated the 'merry light-hearted rowers; boat challenging boat to show its metal, cheered the while by lusty chanties of very "variegated" character, seemly and otherwise, well adapted to raise yells of delight'. In a different tone Bell paid tribute to the beauty of the lagoons:

> See a Maldive Atol, and die. ''Tis beauty truly blent.' Each day the lagoon at dawn has lain spread out like an endless sheet of opal glass, with not the faintest shimmer to ruffle its mirrored surface.

The Maldives : Dreams fulfilled

Of evenings, in the unbroken spell of dead calm which has ruled since our advent, the sun has sunk daily in the full glory of its brilliance, a ball of fire lighting the few fleecy clouds with manifold, ever-varying tints - gold and crimson, pink and mauve, fading to softest shades of chrome and grey.

No less entrancing have been the stilly nights - 'clad in the beauty of a thousand stars' above, and below in silvery phosphorescence lambent round the vessel's sides - with naught to break 'the serene of heaven' in the all-pervading peace of an Atol's lagoon when darkness reigns.

Mundu had a low dagaba mound which yielded one solitary white bead, and then began the frustrating voyage of return. With so little wind, two attempts to cross the *Veimandu Kadu* channel, unhelped by boats, failed, the schooner being drifted back by currents. Bell fretted, 'Like frightened "rats" we have twice now "bolted back" to the protection of our "hole"', - the Haddummati lagoon. He got tough, and insisted on the help of towing boats the very next day, and the *Atoluveri*, Ali Fulu Koya, rose to the occasion. He even did what the schooner's Captain should have done before, called up boats from Guraidu Island. So this *'homo antiqua virtute ac fide'* got them into Kolumadulu Atol.

During the rest of the voyage, from March 31 to April 9, when traversing Mulaku Atol, sixty miles south of Male, Bell wished to land on Kolufuri Island. The extensive shallows on the lagoon side meant that a *Mas-doni* could not approach near. So they used *Kadufati*, light rafts almost awash in the water, propelled by poles, and much used for hunting the shell-bearing turtle. Of his visit Bell recorded:

At the 'Khutba' Mosque are religiously preserved certain 'relics' (not improbably genuine) of Sultan Muhammad *Bodu Takurufanu*, its builder, the great Sixteenth Century hero of Maldive history, and deliverer of the Islands from the Portuguese yoke; whose famous *Odi*, '*Kaluwoffumi*', of legend and ballad, was finally wrecked off Kolufuri where he oft lurked in safety.

The *Khatib* of the Mosque was reluctant to show the relics, owing to their great sanctity in the eyes of Maldivians, but was overpersuaded by Ismail Didi. The antiques comprised a very corroded Portuguese sword, most carefully wrapped; part of a boat's pennon staff, and a choice silk head-kerchief, brilliant red with chocolate, black, and white stripes at each end.

The voyage continued slow because of well-nigh windless days, the Maldivians' dread 'King of the Winds' being asleep. Consequently some men of the Digguru Island, called in to drag the schooner, performed a weird ceremony, called 'Ahmad Rafaigefanuge Ratibu', to invoke a favourable wind. Bell described this:

There were ten performers in all, dressed in white shirts with red sashes and white caps. The ceremony, under the dim light of the ship's lanterns, in which were chanted *Zikuru* led by their *Khatib* and three or four others, took somewhat the form of a Muslim 'Mawlud'. Ranged in line on the deck the men seemed to suffer from great mental and physical excitement - anon kneeling, rocking, swaying with intermittent groans and gasps, anon bowing heads to floor and beating palms on the sail-covered deck, anon rising to throw hands forward and back - in short, displaying every presumed sign of great emotional grief...

Ismail Didi considered that these Islanders made 'a poor job of it', contending that this semi-'Mawlud' is well performed properly at Male only. Certainly the appropriate solemnity was greatly marred by bandied jokes, and light laughter, indulged in between spells of posturing and chanting. Ginger and sugar were handed round to strengthen the leaders' voices; and at the end of the performance jaggery, coconut milk and rice provided for all by the Schooner's caterers.

The next day there was a slight North-West breeze, and three days later they reached Male.

Though recording warm thanks to the Sultan, officials and ordinary Islanders, Bell wrote to Horsburgh on April 12 that he was dog-tired from the crawl back, which 'took the stuffing out of me for the time' though that 'kick in the old dog yet' would soon rejuvenate him. [3]

For the archaeological discoveries had been conclusive. Plans and drawings had been made by W.L.de Silva, photographs taken, and finds from the sites despatched to the Colombo Museum. The trip had also secured epigraphical material. In his diaries Bell describes being shown, on the Islands, inscriptions and documents. One example was on Hitadu on February 14, of which he wrote:

> Ibrahim Didi, son of the absentee *Atoluveri* Ahmad Didi who lives in Male, produced for inspection three interesting old paper documents (carefully preserved in an old brass telescope tube) all *Fat-Kolu*, or grants by Sultans of the 17th and 18th centuries, two written in *Dives Akuru*.

During the summer Bell was studying similar old documents, and inscriptions on gravestones and slabs, and on copper plate. He also revised and filled out his hasty summary of the *Tarikh* made in 1920, besides copying three manuscripts, secured with some difficulty (one in *Dives Akuru*, two in *Tana*) of a *Radivali* (Sinhalese: *Rajavaliya*), or brief history of Maldive Sultans from the twelfth to the eighteenth century.

He also witnessed days of ceremonies, with processions for prayers from one Mosque to another, or the paying of respects to the Sultan, bowing to touch His Highness' feet in 'the salutation to the sandals'. Bell called April 20 *Dies infaustus*, for the necessary annual scouring of the bathing tanks, one of which adjoined his lodging, raised most offensive smells. This was done in preparation for *Ramazan*, throughout which month a gun was fired at sunset to mark when each day's fast might be broken.

The *Hiti Duvas* Festivals were performed between May 20 and 26 in remembrance of certain saintly personages; for example Sultan Ali VI, who fell defending Male against the Portuguese in A.D. 1558, and Shaikh Yusuf Shams-ud-din of Tabriz, Apostle of Islam to the Maldives. The most notable one, the *Henveru Bodu Hiti*, was carried out at the *Lonu Ziyarat*, a promontory to the South-East, on the night of the 22nd of Ramazan, which was on May 20. [4]

Bell witnessed the *Henveru Bodu Hiti*, guided by Ismail Didi. All day the streets, freshly strewn with dazzling white coral sand, were alive with wayfarers, the younger men well dressed and 'the whole air felt charged with social electricity'. At Government expense, foods were provided, the caterer spreading out some forty dishes including boiled rice, fish puffs and sweetmeats, 'some in triangular slices made from edible seaweed resembling to sight Turkish delight'. These were carried in wicker-work cages to the *Ziyarat*, where were a cadjan hut for the Sultan's band, a banqueting hall, a shed for recitation of the *Quran* and the *Hiti-ge*, a tent reserved for Royalty. This was lined with felt, the ceiling of rich orange, the inner walls rich green with façades of Mosques portrayed. [5]

At 9.30 p.m. the Sultan and his nephew advanced along a vista of kerosine lamps, flanked by torch-bearers and escorted by the State Band, the Militia and the Body Guard in scarlet and blue. The Royal Insignia - State Umbrella, Fan, Sword and Shield and Palanquins - were borne in the procession. Royalty had prayed at Ziyarats on the way and again recited the *Fatiha* etc. within the shrine. Then the Band, of drums, trumpets and flageolets, played, reinforced by an old noble, Kakkage Maniffulu, who was a brilliant performer on the *beru*, a drum. Shortly afterwards Bell was invited to an interview within the *Hiti-ge*. [6]

Bell's time was also occupied in achieving, from interviews with Maldivian officials, 'for the most part as short as sporadic', all he could gather about the Administration. Though in April Horsburgh wrote to Bell, 'I do not suppose that any other than yourself could have established their good will and sympathy in the way you have', and in May, 'You have been a loss to the Diplomatic Service', Bell did not find it easy to extract information from his helpers. That same month he reported an impasse because things were left to drift; declared that 'the worm had to turn', and threatened to write to the Government of Ceylon. The officials, alarmed, asked him to draft the letter they would need to reply to the complaint, a 'Gilbertian situation' which tickled him. The Sultan impressed on his Ministers 'the permanent necessity of aiding me daily' from the end of May. [7]

In April Bell was writing to Horsburgh that his wife and daughter were going to England for six months, on a pressing invitation from his daughter, Renée, and her husband, Arthur Prideaux. In July he had received a letter written by his *'placens uxor'* on the voyage. While they were at sea, he was himself delayed in the Maldives. The Maldivian Government Schooner 'Mary' had been expected from India for *Ramazan* (April to May) and could have taken him to Ceylon before the close of July. She was, however, held up for three months by adverse winds. Bell told Horsburgh in July that any *bagalas* or dhows available were unsafe, 'vilely dirty' and fish-smelling. [8]

This was not unreasonable. In *The Two Thousand Isles* by T.W.Hockly, the author described a visit to Male in 1926 by *buggelow* both ways. On the return voyage the 'Nirani' carried a cargo of Maldivian fish which had 'a most pungent and penetrating odour' like that of a long-uncleared stable plus a strong fishy smell. 'I found', he wrote, 'the only thing to do was to smoke incessantly'. Moreover ants, two kinds of cockroach, copra beetles and black maggots abounded, and storms with mountainous seas made the crew deeply thankful to sight the Colombo light. [9]

No wonder that Bell, since a hoped-for Astronomical Expedition steamer had not materialised, thought he might be held up till the 'Fath-ul-Majid' went with the annual Missives in October or November. He feared to tire even the 'ungrudging Eastern hospitality' and longed for a cruiser, *'Sic fata volebant'*. Horsburgh, while hoping to send a Government trawler, wrote, 'Thought you were settling down like a second Ibn Batuta'. [10]

Early in August Bell reported that he was fairly well, eating mainly vegetables and farinaceous foods, and collecting small Maldive objects - measures, games and toys - for the Museum. Meanwhile coconuts were pouring in from the Atols to go by the 'Mary' to Calcutta. She arrived at last on August 20 and Bell sailed with her on September 17. He had paid a parting visit to Ibrahim Didi, and with Ahmad and Abdul Majid had a farewell interview with the Sultan, respectfully tendering thanks for his extreme kindness, unfailing hospitality, and indispensable assistance. [11]

The 'Mary' reached Colombo on September 22 after an exceedingly rough and precarious voyage. Though the Astronomical Expedition had not, after all, gone to the Maldives to view the Eclipse of the Sun, Bell got a hazy view of this at sea on September 21. It was his birthday, and his diary records:

> *Natalis*. Three score years and ten plus one. *Eheu fugaces, Postume, Postume, labuntur anni*!

29

Maldive Studies : Anthropology, History and Archaeology

Bell came back from the Maldives with a mass of material and spent the rest of his life, until he died at the age of eighty-five, sorting and revising it for his monumental work *The Maldive Islands: Monograph on the History, Archaeology and Epigraphy.* This was not, in fact, published until 1940, three years after his death, having been completed by his clerk, W.L.de Silva, who had accompanied him in 1922. In the Preface De Silva describes some of the difficulties which had prevented Bell from completing the section on 'Epigraphy', and records Bell's special indebtedness for help in translations to the various members of Ibrahim Didi's family, and to the Qazi M.Husain Didi Salah-ud-din.

The sources for Bell's work on the Maldives are to be found in the Colombo Archives, and are listed in the Catalogue of the H.C.P.Bell Collection, Lot 25/16. They include the proofs of the Monograph, as well as separate collections of documents and notes on various aspects of Maldivian history and administration, language, life and customs, fishing and flora. There are photostat copies of letters and inscriptions, maps, drawings, photographs and boxes of beads. There are also newspaper cuttings relating to the Maldives, correspondence with Maldive friends and officials, and the diaries and notes compiled by Bell during his visits. [1]

These working tools for the final Maldive report were presumably handed over to Government by De Silva when he had finished his task. Thus Bell's collection on the Maldives was preserved, though unfortunately most of his papers relating to Ceylon were not. Among the files of correspondence there are some letters relating to his personal affairs and to his official career.

While working on the final report Bell also used his material for a series of articles in the JRASCB, from 1922 to 1935, with the running title of 'Excerpta Maldiviana'. In these he either gave short accounts of aspects of the history and life of the Islands, which he did not see his way to incorporate in the main report, or published in detail some supplementary sources. Every scrap of Maldive information was gold to Bell.

Thus in 'Excerpta Maldiviana. No. 1.' he reproduced a Maldivian Government permit to build a trading vessel, or *Furedda Odi*, cutting down one hundred and fifty coconut trees according to the customary methods. This had been given to him by a Maldive captain when he had been in the Customs Office at Galle in 1885. [2]

And in 'Excerpta Maldiviana. No. 4.' he reproduced a description of the Maldive Islands written by an English captain at the end of the seventeenth century, found by D.W.Ferguson in the records of the old East India Company, and originally published in the *Ceylon Monthly Register* in 1895. [3]

Bell also printed two selections of the 'Sultans' Missives', the letters sent with the annual embassy from the Maldive Islands to the occupying power in Ceylon, first the Dutch and then the English. Bell had found one hundred and twenty of the original Missives and their translations among the Dutch Records and had them photographed, but he only printed a small selection.

'Excerpta Maldiviana. No. 2' included the first extant example, sent to the Dutch Governor in 1713 and written in Tana, and also one in English of 1819 concerning the wreck of a British ship on the Maldives. Bell took the opportunity once more to praise the Maldivians for their kindness to shipwrecked sailors. He wrote:

> The Maldivians may lay claim to the proud distinction of being probably the only race, similarly situated on the face of the globe, who have not required to be taught by special contract, or legal enactment, the duty they owe their fellow men who have fallen into 'troubles by shipwreck' on their 'tempest-haunted' Atols. [4]

The other selection from Sultans' Missives, 'Excerpta Maldiviana. No. 13. Some polyglot Missives of Sultan Ibrahim Iskandar II', first gave a general account of the normal content of the Missives - appeals for friendship and protection against enemies, requests for aid for Maldivian subjects chancing to be wrecked on the coasts of Ceylon, or for the arrest of Maldive rebels and their deportation to Male, together with flowery compliments and lists of presents sent - and then printed a selection of Missives not in the usual Maldivian languages; one in Arabic, one in Portuguese, one in French. [5]

The 1940 Maldive Islands Monograph itself contained three main sections: History, Archaeology and Epigraphy, with a short introductory section on Physical Features and Inhabitants. When dealing with 'Archaeology' Bell gave fuller details on the physical features, inhabitants and occupations of the three areas he had visited personally: Addu Atol, Fua Mulaku Island, Haddummati Atol. Apart from this Bell did not include in the Monograph much detail on the physical and cultural anthropology of the Islands, and C.Moloney in his study of the *People of the Maldive Islands* regretfully concluded that 'Bell had an antiquarian rather than an anthropological perspective'. [6]

In fact Bell did collect material in this field. There are many glimpses to be obtained in the descriptive passages of the Monograph, and particularly in the diary extracts which he includes. The full diaries are available in the 'H.C.P.Bell Collection', which also contains a diary written by De Silva, and a number of note-books filled with observations. Some of these are systematically crossed through as he included them in his published work, but there is much unworked material, a quarry for the mining. There are notes on sowing ceremonies, boat-launching ceremonies, fishing and household customs, songs, charms and mantras. Some, such as the Charm for the King of the Sea, seem to relate to pre-Islamic and probably pre-Buddhist magical religion. There is a special charm for catching tortoises.

Three of the 'Excerpta Maldiviana' are mainly anthropological in content. No. 7. on '"Lonu Ziyarat": Male', which gives a detailed account of religious ceremonies, has already been mentioned. 'Excerpta Maldiviana. No. 12.' deals with Maldive Proverbs. In this paper Bell printed fifty Maldivian proverbs, with similar ones drawn from other languages; he gave Sinhalese equivalents in almost every instance, but also included like sayings in Arabic, English,

French, Greek, Hebrew, Italian, Latin, Scotch, Sanskrit and even West African. Bell was amused by proverbs and proverbial sayings and his library contained a number of such collections. He drew conclusions as to the similarity of race of the Maldive and Sinhalese peoples from the marked similarity of their proverbs, but also stressed the predominance of sea-faring and fishing metaphors in the proverbs of an ocean-orientated civilisation. Thus we find 'Like baiting two hooks on one line' with the English equivalent of 'killing two birds with one stone'. [7]

'Excerpta Maldiviana. No. 5.' deals with the physical traits and general characteristics of the Maldive Islanders and includes some photographs of the inhabitants from the Northern and Southern Atols not found in the 1940 Monograph. It was written to supplement the Maldive section of the 1921 *Census Report*, which Bell had revised for the press, and as well as describing the varied racial types to be found in the Islands, it gave details of dress, occupations, trade, language and scripts. [8]

The paper stressed the rarity of 'crimes of a heinous character', the humane and generous nature of the Islanders and their far-ranging voyages 'from the "tempest-haunted" Atols, in their small, light-built but most seaworthy vessels, as far as Aden, Calcutta, Penang, Sumatra, etc., braving the storms which sweep round the Indian Ocean and elsewhere'. [9]

On the predominant racial origin of the Maldive Islanders Bell was of the opinion that 'at this day it is not open to doubt that the whole archipelago - including Maliku (Minicoy) now grouped with the Lakkadives and no longer owing allegiance to the Sultans of the Maldive Islands - was occupied, either directly from Ceylon, or alternatively, about the same time as the B.C. immigration into that island, by people of Aryan stock and language. This supposition is supported greatly by the close kinship between the Maldive and Sinhalese languages'. [10]

Later writers have deduced the existence of other racial stock in the islands from traces of pre-Aryan religion and from words in *Divehi* which may stem from early North-Indian Prakrits and Tamil-Malayalam roots but, as Maloney says, 'There is no question that the principal cultural affinities of the Maldives are with the Sinhalese'. [11]

Bell's account of the history of the Maldives in the 1940 Monograph falls into three sections. Up to the Conversion he draws on the same scattered references in the writings of foreigners which had formed the basis of his 1881 Report; for the period A.D. 1237 to 1821 he draws mainly on the *Tarikh*, the Arabic chronicle, with supplementary material from the *Radavali*, brief histories in Maldivian scripts; for the British period he draws on his own collection of *Papers Relating to the Maldive Islands, 1887-1910*, picking his way delicately through Maldive intrigues and revolutions, but making no attempt to carry the story further than his own visit in 1922. [12]

Fuller details of the earlier relations between the Maldivians and European powers in the sixteenth to eighteenth centuries he relegates to supplementary articles. 'Excerpta Maldiviana. No. 10.' is a detailed comparison of Portuguese and Maldive sources, for three periods of history: A.D. 1500-1550, 1550-1700 and 1700-1930. It draws on material in the Portuguese Archives as well as on published histories, and gives detail of the history of the Maldive Sultan who defected to the Portuguese and was converted to Christianity in 1552. 'Excerpta Maldiviana. No. 11.' moves on to the period of the Dutch connection with the Maldives, which was primarily a matter of trade, particularly in cowries, for which the Dutch had 'an insatiable greed'. [13]

H. C. P. Bell

The section in the Monograph which is headed 'Tarikh Chronicle' is not a full translation. Bell describes it as 'epitomised details of Maldivian history', and it is indeed a summary, only occasionally quoting verbatim, as when he writes of a period of Portuguese rule when 'the sea grew red with Muslim blood'. It was then, in 1573, that the famous event took place when the 'freedom-fighter' Muhammad Khatib Takurufanu recaptured Male from the Portuguese under the renegade Captain Adiri Adiri. In the Monograph he deals with it briefly:

> They reached Male the night before the day fixed by the Portuguese garrison for the forcible conversion of the inhabitants, on penalty of death for non-compliance. The Maldivians, determined to die for their Faith, assembled with arms at the house of the Qazi Abu Bakr, son of Qazi Don Kurali Takurufanu, and prepared to fight to the last.
>
> The Expeditionary force, under Muhammad Bodu Takurufanu, made secret landing when the night was two-thirds spent (i.e. 3 a.m.). Adiri Adiri was killed by a musket shot fired by Bodu Muhammad himself; and the whole Portuguese garrison slain.
>
> This recapture of Male took place on 1st Rabi-ul-Awwal A.H. 981 (A.C. 1573). The Portuguese had held the Maldives for 17 years - a period of 'rule and power transient as sunbeams'. [14]

In 'Excerpta Maldiviana. No. 10. The Portuguese at the Maldives', however, more colourful details are given:

> That very night the (Male) Islanders held a meeting at which they agreed to die in their Faith. They assembled in the house of the *Qazi* Abu Bakr, son of Don Kurali Fadiyaru Takurufanu, son of Sharaf-ud-din Ismail Famuderi Fadiyaru Takurufanu; and vowed not to obey Adiri Adiri's command to embrace his religion, but to fight to the death against those sent to compel them. They then collected knives, swords, lances, bows and arrows, and even clubs, and prepared to meet their enemies.
>
> Then Muhammad Khatib made a vow that, if they succeeded in retaking Male from the Christians, he would recite the *Maulud* to the Prophet every year near the shrine of Shaikh Yussuf of Tabriz.
>
> The same night, after offering prayers to the Omniscient God, when two-thirds of the night had passed, Muhammad Khatib Takurufanu anchored off Male, and landed when the Christians were making merry with song and carousal. Adiri Adiri's supporters then emerged and began to fire on the Muslims, who returned the fire. The fusillade of the Christians was unavailing but the Muslims' fire began to take effect. The fighting continued until God weakened the Christians, and they offered to surrender. Many had already died, and the survivors were mortally wounded.
>
> The calamity, fear and sorrow, which they (the Portuguese) suffered, were sympathised in neither by Heaven nor Earth, which wept not for them. Their rule and power proved as transient as sunbeams. Their name was detested by the people, and their might had departed for ever. They had been masters of the Maldives for seventeen years...

> The long-suffering Muslims, their faces radiating happiness, assembled before the Great Takurufanu, who came to meet them, his broad brow bright with light sufficient to fill the four corners of the world. They kissed his hands and offered prayers that his rule might long continue. He, in turn, offered prayers for the prosperity and health of his subjects. They (the Islanders) then took the oath of allegiance to him as Sultan. [15]

Bell always hoped that his friend Abdul Hamid Didi would produce a full translation of the *Tarikh*, but this never seems to have been completed. A manuscript copy of the *Tarikh* was presented to the Ceylon Government by Sultan Muhammad Shams-ud-din, but appears to have been mislaid. H.Yajima, who is editing an Arabic edition, says:

> Recently, Mr. Andrew D.W.Forbes and some other scholars exerted all possible efforts to find out the lost MS of 'Ta'rikh' from any archives, libraries and museums in Sri Lanka and the Maldive Islands, but their efforts were not crowned with success.

But when Hikoichi Yajima visited Male in 1981 he found three Arabic copies of the *Tarikh* and two copies in *Divehi* script, and from these he has edited a text. These manuscripts are now kept in libraries and archives at Male. [16]

When Bell turned to 'Archaeology' in the Monograph he was primarily concerned to establish without doubt that there had been a Buddhist civilisation in the Islands before the Islamic Conversion. He began his triumphant description of his finds by setting out the evidence that had been gathered by previous visitors to the Islands. He said that the first hint of the former existence of the Buddhist cult on the Maldives was furnished in the 'Memoir' of Lieutenants I.A.Young, and W.Christopher, at the time of the Survey in 1834-5. They amounted only to vague rumours of two Buddhist temples, the existence of a Bo-tree near a mosque, the Maldivian burial posture, and the inhabitants' dread of taking animal life. [17]

Bell himself in 1879 had found nothing conclusive, but thought it interesting that the first Maldive Sultan bore the Buddhistic title *Darumavanta* (religious or just), that some Island names approximated to 'Lanka City', 'Buddha's City', etc., and that the Maldivian names applied to ruins were recognisable as those used in Ceylon. Thus *Ustuba* corresponded to the Sinhalese *Sthupa*, *Havitta* to *Chaitya* and *Vire* to *Vehera*.

Between Bell's visit of 1879 and his return in 1922 two scientific expeditions to the Maldives provided further clues. C.W.Rosset in 1886 mentioned that he had been told of 'a Dagaba, called *Havida* on Fua Mulaku and the ruins of a temple called *Ustumba* on Hitadu Island in Addu Atol'. J. Stanley Gardiner in 1900 reported 'mounds' in various atolls, one with a kind of pit formed by square blocks in which had been found gold discs. This Bell felt to be a good description of a dagaba with a relic chamber. [18]

In 1920 Bell was not able to visit any island except Male, but he collected accounts of possible ruins from natives of different atols. As well as those on Fua Mulaku and Hitadu, ruins with suggestive names such as *Budu-ge* (Shrine of Buddha), were reported on Gan Island in Addu Atol, Gan Island and Mundu Island in Haddummati Atol, and Landu and Miladu Islands in Miladummadulu Atol.

In 1922 Bell was able to make two archaeological expeditions to the Southern Atols and explored four islands. He believed that he had found remains of all the various elements of the orthodox Buddhist complex: the Dagaba with its relic-chamber, the Vihare or image house, the Pirivena or monks' residence, and even one example of the Wata-da-ge or circular relic house. That the remains were sparse and in great disrepair was easily accounted for by the determined onslaught on an 'Infidel' creed by the Muslim converts. Of those described, shortage of time and lack of any skilled labour rendered investigation necessarily superficial. Nevertheless Bell concluded:

> Despite all disabilities, such remains as have been discovered - albeit comparatively few, greatly wrecked, and sadly ravaged almost beyond recognition in places, as they necessarily are - suffice, by surprisingly good fortune, absolutely to establish past shadow of doubt the irrefutable former existence of pronounced Buddhism at the Maldives - if not *passim* throughout the Archipelago, at least sporadically - up to the full acceptance of Muhammadanism by all the Islanders throughout the Atols, possibly not complete for some time subsequent to the traditional date of the Muslim Conversion in A.C. 1151. [19]

The islands investigated were: Gan (or Gamu) in Addu Atol; Fua Mulaku; Gan (or Gamu) and Mundu in Haddummati Atol.

On Gan in Addu Atol he found 'sorry remains of what was once a Buddhist Monastery of no special pretensions'; a miniature hillock less than 30 feet in height and the foundations of an oblong site. Bell identified the first, called 'Ustuba' by the inhabitants, as a 'sthupa' or dagaba, and the second as a pirivena or monks' dwelling. Rapid trenching revealed no relic chamber in the dagaba and Bell said that 'the total antiquarian yield - *"ridiculus mus"* - from the hillock's two days "labouring" was two ancient beads'. Nevertheless Bell would have protested strongly when the remains of the dagaba were razed by the British in constructing an air-strip on the island. [20]

Little was left also of the dagaba on Mundu island in Haddummati Atol. Known as the *Buda-ge*, it was but twelve feet in height and about fifty yards in circumference. Bell discovered traces of a stairway on the North side and the remains of curling balustrades, the only example he found of this common feature of Ceylon architecture. A single pear-shaped milky white bead was unearthed. [21]

It was on Fua Mulaku and on Gan island of the Haddummati Atol that Bell found the most conclusive evidence. In the 'Havitta' of Fua Mulaku Bell found 'the assured certainty, beyond any possibility of question, of the survival of at least one structure still manifesting unmistakably exclusive association with the Buddhist cult'. He described it as follows:

> On the North-East, East, and South faces a fair proportion of the coral casing of the Dagaba, immediately above the once existing *pesaval*, or 'circular basal platforms' remains in position as originally built, though the stones are much off the straight.
>
> The entire *hatares kotuwa* (square 'tee') and *kota* (spire or pinnacle) which surmounted the *garbha*

(dome or bell) - to use the Sinhalese terms employed in Ceylon archaeology - and most of the basement, have disappeared - no doubt to serve utilitarian purposes - but much of the vertical lines of cylindrical neck drum, moulded capping, with plinth and contour stones of the bellying *garbha*, besides a little of the Dagaba's tholobate platforms, stand more or less clearly visible, and in good preservation on the whole.

Sans its superstructure, the present height of the Dagaba is only some 25 feet; the circumference, at ground level (naturally now much larger than the true original periphery), as taped round the bottom of the fallen debris, measured 200 feet more or less.

The top, nearly 2 feet wide, of the upper stage of a probable double tholobate stands now 7 feet, or so, above ground level; its coping, where left, confidently shows ogee moulding. Of the width of the lower platform tier, or tiers, nothing can be postulated, as a mass of fallen masonry overlies it, or them; and, being easiest to remove, doubtless afforded most of the worked ashlar freely exploited by the Islanders.

From the repeated basement staging the neck shafting rose, plinth-less, 5 feet perpendicularly in four plain horizontal courses capped by a heavy cornice, 1 foot 6 inches high by 12 foot projection, partly in ogee, partly rectangular; this supported the dome's plinth, also 18 inches in height by 9 inches horizontal. Of this bell some 8 feet is the maximum height surviving. [22]

When excavating in the 'Hat-teli' Sthupa on Gan, Haddummati Atol, where Bell heard rumours of the existence, within living memory, of a square tee on the top of the dagaba mound, he also made some conclusive finds:

With little hope of finding the Dagaba's 'Relic-Chamber' unrifled, a deep trench was run into its bare Northern, or opposite face, where the mound slope seemed most suitable. No trace of such a cell was disclosed.

A few feet directly under the hillock's summit was unearthed a flattish circular coral slab, 4 feet in diameter, with 4 'ear-like knops', presumed to be the *Indra-kila-gala*, or centring stone; 5 feet lower came to light - an astounding and portentous discovery - in two sections, and those not perfect, a huge face of a colossal Buddha, probably a Standing Figure (Sin. *Hiti Pilima*), carved from coral; and further down still, at 15 feet or more, a small image of a Sedent Buddha (Sin. *Ot Pilima*), also of coral, with traces of colouring, bereft of head, hands and lower half of the legs; besides part of the ornamental head-dress of a Bodhisatva.

A day or two previously, amid the debris at the foot of the mound had been found, by great good fortune, a 'cushion-shaped ring' really a *sat* or *Chatra* ('umbrella') of the Dagaba's missing pinnacle - the only one recovered of seven reputed members once existing, which have given the traditional name, *Hat-teli* ('Seven Cauldrons') to this Sthupa. [23]

The 'Mumbaru' Sthupa at Kuruhinna, which lies at the South end of Gan island, was erected on a double platform, the lower circular and the upper in the form of a Greek cross. Both were well preserved and the coral casing of the bell had survived in reasonable condition:

A trench, run into the ruin through this detritus to below ground level, confirmed definitely the former-day rifling of the Dagaba. Further, that a 'Relic-Chamber' once existed, and had been denuded of its contents was placed beyond doubt by the recovery amid the debris from the Dagaba of a square coral 'Relic-Casket' (Sin. *Karanduwa*) with semi-bevelled lid detached.

The only yield of the *Karanduwa* left by the despoilers was a handful or two of tiny glass beads of assorted colours (in no way dissimilar to many exhumed by the Archaeological Survey of Ceylon from time to time); with a couple of small precious stones of no value. [24]

On Gan Island, Haddummati Atol, he thought that he had found a Wata-da-ge or Circular Shrine, and he described the ruins as follows:

When first examined, this ruin presented the appearance of a small irregular mound, 10 to 12 feet in height and about 40 feet in circumference, covered with jungle growth and littered by a fair crop, dislodged and much broken, of sculptured monoliths (pillar and pointed post fragments, and capitals) besides a varied assortment of other moulded stones, all of coral. These evidently formed the *disjecta membra* of a colonnade and railing, which must originally have encircled whatever once occupied the centre of the Shrine.

After removal of all loose carved stonework, the mound was very thoroughly exploited by trenching. In the middle was struck a line of foundation-stones once footing a probable square central dais; and, hard by, first the broken half of a beautiful moulded image pedestal, cylindrical in shape; with at a little distance the other half, cleft further in two by the iconoclastic wreckers.

This pedestal (Sin. *gal-asana*), carved from hardest madrepore (M. *hiri-ga*), is 2 feet 2 inches in diameter by 1 foot 6 inches high and morticed at top, 4 1/2 inches by 7 1/2 inches. The torus member of its chaste plinth bears a string of well-recognized *pala peti* (Bo leaf) ornamentation.

In its circular plan and ring of pillars surrounding the Shrine of a Buddhist image, this ruin may well have borne resemblance to the *Wata-da-ge* of Toluvila Monastery at Anuradhapura, with the probable addition of post-and-rail fence immediately shutting in the dais and image.

Of the Vihare on this Island he wrote:

The low oblong and flat mound at this site, when divested of jungle growth and ruined debris, and dug to test its conformation, disclosed the ruins of a rectangular building, erected upon a neatly moulded podium with wide gangway, and preceded by a Portico on the East which was entered by broad stairs starting from a plain 'moonstone' slab of unusual size at foot. Accordingly the structure thus declared itself to be of the *Vihare* type very familiar at Ceylon's ancient ruins *passim*...

The unique 'moonstone' (Sin. *sanda-kada-pahana*), 10 feet by 6 feet 3 inches - the sole example seen at the Maldives - in its total bareness, follows the simplest type found at Anuradhapura and elsewhere (notably among the Toluvila ruins) in Ceylon.

Of the Pirivena he opined:

> This, the largest ruin in the group forming the *Sangharama*, and justifiably presumed to have been the *Priory* of the Buddhist monks, is situated to South-West. The edifice stands, centrally placed, within a *prakara* extending 184 feet East and West by 146 feet North and South. This stout enclosing wall, 8 feet in width, is at this day pierced by two openings - one 10 feet in breadth towards the East angle of the North wall, the other only 3 feet 6 inches near the North end of the West wall.
>
> The original outline plan of the *Pirivena* structure would appear to have been oblong, 67 feet in full length from East to West by 55 feet crossways as recorded above. In all probability it was served by three staircases, 13 feet in width, with seven steps (riser, 9 1/2 inches; tread, 1 foot 9 inches) projecting some 12 feet from the middle of the North, East, and South faces, but leaving the West face to run unbroken.
>
> The building stood on a handsome stylobate with a duplicated revetment of 5 feet 6 inches full height (lower part 3 feet, upper 2 feet 6 inches) moulded in almost exact accord with that of the Vihare platform. This fine basement is still in excellent preservation at its South-East corner; and, here only, are yet standing three plain courses (2 feet 6 inches high in all) of the buildings' wall, for a lateral extent of not more than 15 feet...
>
> As there are no remains, either here or at the Vihare, of masonry pillars to support the interior superstructure, it may be taken for granted that these were of wood; but no clue is afforded at either site of their columniation. A few of the flat roof-tiles somewhat similar in form to Kandyan *peti ulu* were collected. [25]

From the photographs and measurements taken at each site sections and plans were prepared. Bell admitted that in many cases so little remained that 'only the veriest tentative venture can be made, and that with pardonable diffidence, towards reconstructing, however imperfectly, a reasonable conception of the Sthupa's erstwhile lines and dimensions'. [26]

Nevertheless he felt sufficiently confident to use the existence and type of the ruins he had excavated to pronounce on the probable date of the introduction of Buddhism into the Maldives. He wrote:

> In the light now shed archaeologically by recent research, it seems highly probable that, whatever degree of Buddhistic belief and worship may have filtered to the Islands sporadically by prior fitful waves of Sinhalese emigration, the full establishment of recognized Buddhism, in the orthodox ecclesiastical organization of its cult, was delayed, and – *pace* the silence, not surprising, of Ceylon 'Chronicles' amply absorbed ever in the far more stirring internal events of 'Lanka' and Southern India - not definitely implanted with firm roots at the Maldives until the Christian era was more than a century or two old.
>
> For all the evidence supplied by such Buddhist ruins as still survive on the Group lead but to one conclusion, viz., that the architectural forms exhibited, in their broad structural lines, in lesser

functional members, as well as in moulded design and ornament, speak loudly to a period of execution late rather than early, which continued to enjoy the hey-day of vigour contemporaneously even with Ceylon Monasteries of the advanced period dealt with by the Archaeological Survey at Anuradhapura (Toluvila, Puliyankulama, Vijayarama Monasteries) and Mihintale ('Indi-katu Vehara'). [27]

In 1983-4 the Norwegian expedition to the Maldives has found further examples of Buddhist remains and has conducted test-excavations in two islands. In the island of Nilandu the party was able to obtain two radio-carbon datings from two layers of a trench through the outer wall of a temple area. These gave calibrated readings of A.D. 540-670 and A.D. 660-740. The second excavation was of the Havitta on Gan island in Gaaf Atol, named Gaaf Gan to distinguish it from the Gan in Addu Atol and that in Haddummati Atol, between which it lies. Its ground plan is similar to, but not identical with, that of the cruciform based dagaba excavated by Bell at Kuruhinna on Gan in the Haddummati Atol. From the style of the decoration of its facing slabs the tentative conclusion was reached that the building might date back to the first centuries A.D., being thus of an earlier period than those described by Bell, which he equated with those of the early tenth century in Ceylon.

Bell, however, had postulated the first settlement of the Sinhalese in the islands at the beginning of the Christian era and the introduction of Buddhism to date from a similar time. [28]

30

Maldive Studies : Language and Epigraphy

Bell never provided a systematic treatment of the Maldive language, ancient and modern. Instead, we shall see that his writings arose from the work of other men, which he was moved to draw on, to criticise, to edit. When the most complete treatment of Maldivian, 'Maldivian linguistic studies' by Wilhelm Geiger, was published in 1919, as an extra volume of the JRASCB, Bell edited this. He added, of his own composition, four Appendices, and some of the Plates of Maldive characters.

Also he constantly turned to the language for the light it threw on history, and valued and studied all the written records he could find. Thus in the 1881 report, in the Early Period section of his Historical Sketch, he had taken the affinity between Maldivian and *Elu*, the oldest form of Sinhalese, as evidence of common Aryan racial origins. There could have been a colonisation of the Islands at a date 'synchronic with that of Ceylon itself', or subsequent immigration. Geiger, going on the evidence of sounds in Maldivian and Sinhalese, thought they diverged about A.D. 900.[1]

Bell referred in the 1881 report to Gray's early article on the Maldives for the JRAS, which drew on Pyrard's vocabulary of the language, but at this time went into little detail himself. Gray, in his review of the 1881 report, wrote that 'Bell reserves for the learned societies his examination of the Maldive grammar and vocabulary'.[2]

Bell in 1881 did briefly contrast the modern Maldivian script, *gabuli tana*, written from right to left, with the older script, *Dives Akuru*. The latter was still used at the time of Lieutenant Christopher's visit, for orders to the Southern Atols. Bell said that it contained twenty-five letters, was syllabic, capable of some hundreds of vowel mutations and was written from left to right. He added:

> The letters bear some resemblance to old Sinhalese, as Mr. Gray has shown, but would seem rather to be modifications of the old Vatteluttu character, once used throughout the South Tamil and Malayalam districts of India.[3]

For light on *Dives Akuru* from an earlier source than Gray, Bell looked to Lieutenant Wilmott Christopher, on whom he wrote an interesting footnote in his edition of Geiger:

> Lieutenant Christopher met the travelled French savant, M. Antoine d'Abbadie, at Tagarrah in 1841. D'Abbadie later wrote: 'I never *saw* Christopher, for I was blinded by ophthalmia when he called on me. He promised to send me a copy of the Old Maldive syllabary, and I thanked his messenger warmly the following day, a few hours before Christopher set sail to receive his death-wound by the Indus (1848). When I recovered my eyesight, I saw with regret that he had sent me a list of consonants (34) vocalised only in A, followed by a tantalising "etc.". I boarded the Indian Navy warship, but Christopher was then gone.'

The correspondence from which this note is drawn survives in the Colombo Archives. [4]

Fortunately, that same year, characters of the syllabary were communicated to Dr. John Wilson, and they appeared in a Plate in Geiger's article. Bell called Christopher's characters 'valuable but incomplete' as they comprised eighteen letters only of the Alphabet; and therefore treated them fully. In the Appendix A to Geiger he set out Christopher's *descriptions* of each character. On Plate II in columns he gave for each the name, value, *tana* character, Christopher's *Dives Akuru* equivalent and a corresponding Sinhalese twelfth century character. [5]

Bell's own most complete treatment of *Dives Akuru* was in his Appendix C to Geiger, 'The Old and Modern Maldivian Alphabets'. He followed Gray and Christopher, though differing from the latter on the effect of vowels on consonants. Some years later, in 'Excerpta Maldiviana. No.3.' he summarised this, saying that he had:

> ...supplied a Table (Plates VI and VII) in which are set out the basal forms - 26 in all, inclusive of the *sukun* as nasal and reduplicator - a) of the letters ('vowel consonants') commencing with H and ending at Y and the *sukun*; b) some variants; supplemented by c) the five initial vowels, short and long, and d) their medial signs; with the addition of e) the consonant H, as modified by all its vowel inflections, as well as f) a few compound letters.
>
> The *aksharas* were given both in i) the purer form ruling in the Southern Atols, and ii) as now modified in Male. Short specimens iii) of the *Dives Akuru* writing, by modern hands, were also offered (Plates VII and IX).

He had derived material on the dialect of the Southern Atols from Ahmad of Fua Mulaku, and for Male language from Ibrahim Didi. [6]

Some terms in the above were elucidated in Bell's last treatment of the old script, in the Appendix to 'Excerpta Maldiviana. No. 9.'. He recalled its affinity, in the older *Evela Akuru* form, with mediaeval Sinhalese, and with the yet older *Ariya Eluttu* of Malabar, South India. He referred to additions he had made to Geiger's study in 1919; the Syllabary, the Plates VI and VII, and explanations. He added that his own researches in Male in 1922 had suggested some amendments. He therefore briefly tabulated a fresh alphabet, and in his comments defined the *akshara* ('a vowel-consonant') and the *sukun* (an undulating stroke drawn diagonally upwards to right above the *akshara*, which has three uses). He drew distinctions between the vowel signs of Male and those of the Southern Atols. He also called attention to likenesses to Sinhalese symbols. This was Bell's last account of the ancient script. [7]

Geiger's research for his 'Maldivian linguistic studies' had been assisted in January 1896, when he was unable to visit the Islands, by Ibrahim Didi, then living in Colombo. Geiger acknowledged the nobleman's kindness in giving him information during three intensive mornings. Geiger believed:

> I not only acquired a fairly extensive Maldivian vocabulary, but also examined in some detail the grammar, inflection of nouns and verbs, and so on. I wrote down a number of sentences too. [8]

Bell regarded Geiger's work as full and valuable, but questioned one of his sources for Maldive vocabulary. This was 'The London Vocabulary' of Persian, Hindustani and Maldive words from the library of its author John Casper Leyden, which had been printed in Calcutta in 1808. Bell had seen this back in 1890, and both he and Ahmad Didi, son of Ibrahim, and Abdul Hamid Didi, believed the characters to be pure inventions of Leyden's Maldive source, Hasan-bin-Adam of Hamiti. [9]

Geiger thought the Maldivians who wrote off 'The London Vocabulary' did not possess the necessary knowledge of Persian and Hindustani, and that they took no pains to consult Bell. On these points Bell commented in Appendix B that Ahmad Didi knew Hindustani and had a travelled friend who knew Persian. As for the consultation, Bell was at Anuradhapura from 1890 onwards, so that the 'pleasant walk and pleasant talk' required of a dweller in Colombo 'would have met with success equally that of the cynical introduction by a certain Walrus and Carpenter to the luckless oysters, when "answer came there none!"' [10]

Bell's critical, almost hostile, attitude arose partly from his warm regard for his Maldivian friends. Geiger was not, he said, sufficiently grateful to Ibrahim Didi, whom he had bombarded for three days with wearying linguistic questions. Still, Geiger and Bell shared a romantic feeling for the Maldives. Geiger wrote that every student had, within his field, a special province to which he always returned:

> Such a province to me, at this time, are the distant Maldive Islands, surrounded by the blue waves of the Indian Ocean. [11]

While Bell quoted lines in which the island-dwellers might express their destiny:

> 'Green Earth has her sons and her daughters,
> And these have their guardians, but we
> Are the wind's and the skies' and waters'
> Elect of the Sea.' [12]

Ibn Batuta, visiting the Maldives in 1343-4, is the first source of our knowledge of their vocabulary. In Bell's Appendix A to Geiger's article, he noted that the Traveller used about forty Maldivian words, rather disguised as Arabic. He quoted Gray's comment, in his 1878 study of Pyrard's vocabulary, to the effect that the Frenchman's spelling of Maldivian words sometimes indicated his own pronunciation. [13]

In this early treatment Gray had compared Pyrard's vocabulary with Christopher's much fuller and more recent one of nearly 1,100 words. Both sources provided the Dictionary in the last volume of Gray and Bell's edition of Pyrard's travels, and in the list Bell compared old and new Maldive words. [14]

A country's language grows out of its social and economic life. As dried fish was one of the most important exports of the Maldives, its name interested Bell. In 1882 in the *Indian Antiquary* he wrote on *Cobily-mash*, the Maldive term for the boiled and dried *bonito*. *Mash* in its variants clearly meant fish. Donald Ferguson, following Louis De Zoysa, had regarded *Cobily-mash* as *Kebali-mas*, 'piece-fish', from the cutting up of the bonito. However, Pyrard's translation had been 'poisson noir', accepted by Albert Gray, and Bell derived the term from *'Kalu bili mas'*. For *Kalu* meant 'black' in Maldivian and Sinhalese alike; *bili* (the *balaiya* of the Sinhalese) was the bonito. [15]

In his report of 1881, Bell noted the borrowing in Male of Hindustani words from Indian traders. It was religion that had promoted the importance of Arabic, which since 1830 had been used for Sultans' Missives. The influence of Arabic was also responsible for the change in the mode of writing, from the older left to right, to the right to left method of *gabuli tana*. These newer characters had been in use for more than two and a half centuries. The first nine letters were merely the Arabic numerals from 1 to 9, the last nine probably simplifications of the corresponding letters in the old alphabet. Bell treated the *gabuli* (the 'composed') *tana* more fully in Appendix C to Geiger, considering its origin, and in a Postscript wrote of its evolution even during the last two hundred years. [16]

In Bell's work on Maldivian Epigraphy in the Monograph of 1940 and in articles for the JRASCB, he dealt with inscriptions on stones, particularly gravestones; with grants on Copper Plates, and with Board and Paper Grants. He was interested in the languages and scripts used, and found value in the epigraphs as footnotes to history, political and religious. In 'Excerpta Maldiviana. No. 3.' he noted that Male had had a multitude of burial grounds, attached to the twenty-nine Mosques. He described the shapes of the mainly grey headstones and their pattern of a tall central arched panel, the border often covered with beautiful, varied and perfectly carved arabesques. Though since the beginning of the eighteenth century epitaphs had been incised in *tana*, about thirty gravestones and other slab records survived in Male in *Dives Akuru*, with some Arabic characters; others were wholly in Arabic. [17]

Bell chose to consider one old gravestone in Arabic from the graveyard of the Bandara Miskit. Like all, it was dated in Muslim chronology. The date of this one corresponded to A.C. 1692, and it commemorated an attendant on Sultan Iskandar Ibrahim I (A.C. 1648-87). For this and the other stones Bell supplied text, transcript, translation and a photographic plate. [18] The other headstones he dealt with were inscribed in *Dives Akuru*. Two undated ones were at the Etere-Kolu Miskit, and recorded the burial of princesses. The epitaphs praised, however, not the ladies but their fathers, for example:

> Be it remembered that (Sanfa) Rendi Kabafanu, born to the Great King, a Kshatriya, Sultan Ibrahim Iskandar, endowed with beauty, of the great glorious race (of the Moon and Sun), rich in gold and great elephants, strong as a lion, famed like the nine gems, accomplished (in arts and sciences)... Mighty Monarch of the Universe, passed away on...

This Sultan reigned A.C. 1721-50. [19]

When thanking the Government for the services of Husain Takurufanu (Khatib of Hitadu, Addu Atol) Bell noted that his intelligent copying of three inscriptions had showed that two, never before verified, were not what had been supposed. The discoveries were naturally accepted reluctantly, and only when the Acting Qazi, Husain Didi, had personally examined the stones. Husain Takurufanu had discovered that a slab in *Dives Akuru* at the Hukuru Miskit, honoured by the descendants of Sultan Hasan Izz-ud-din, actually belonged to his half-brother. The real grave of the Sultan was eventually traced, with its original beautifully worded Memorial Brass Plate, which, having deteriorated, was later replaced by a copy.

Husain Takurufanu, the copyist, had also discovered that one of the slabs at the Etere-Kolu Miskit was not a gravestone at all, but a record of events in A.C. 1752. It was very similar to two at the Palace entrance and one near a gateway of the Fort. Bell outlined these in his 'Excerpta Maldiviana. No. 3.':

> These record the capture of Male in A.C. 1752 by Malabars, the deportation of the Sultan Muhammad Imad-ud-din III, the nominal regency of his daughter Amina Rani Kilegefanu, and the administration of the realm by Hasan Manikufanu, raised later to be *Masnad* as Sultan Hasan Izz-ud-din (A.C. 1759-67).

Of the other versions the Palace doorway ones show that Male was actually recaptured by Hasan Manikufanu, the hero whose tomb was lost and found. [20]

'The appalling redundancy of graveyards' induced in Bell a melancholy scarcely consoled by lines from Thomas Hardy, 'They've a way of whispering to me - fellow-wight who yet abide... Fear of death has even bygone us: death gave all that we possess.' [21]

Bell called attention to how the Maldivians, like other nations, softened on their gravestones the bald word for 'died' (*maruvejye*) with euphemisms: *niau-vi*, 'extinguished'; *avahara-vi*, '(life) abandoned'; *filara-midi*, 'released from the body'; *fura-uttara-vi*, 'coming out, crossing, landing'. [22]

In the Monograph of 1940 Bell began his Section on 'Epigraphy' with Inscriptions and Grave Epitaphs, and described twelve such. Only two had been seen outside Male. One example he saw was on April 8, 1922, on Guraidu Island in South Male Atol, at the *Ziyarat* of Sultan Husain II, who died there A.C. 1620; the successor of Ibrahim III who had been killed in an Indian raid recorded by Pyrard. The stones in Arabic also bore the Muslim *kalima*. [23]

The most archaic writing met with, called *Evela Akuru* rather than *Dives Akuru*, was on a slab near the Ma Vego tank in Male. The word *Fashiyama* was followed by a few syllables, probably numbers to aid the masons. A more recent wall-slab, in Arabic, in the wall of a North-West Bastion of the Old Fort, recorded its being built by Sultan Ibrahim I, 'as a defence to repel the accursed Portuguese', probably in 1686-7. [24]

Arabic was also the language of most of the six inscriptions at the Hukuru Miskit, the most striking being in blue, all round the white Minnaru, or Minaret Tower, the call to prayer, 'that impassioned heart-searching appeal... indescribably impressive when heard in night's stillness or the silence of dawn'. Others recorded good works: the pilgrimage to Mecca and Medina, establishment of a religious school, donating provision for reciting the Quran at royal tombs, or the construction of a Mosque. There was also a typical denunciation: 'If any Muslim takes but the weight of a grain of corn from the property of the Mosque theftuously, his prayers will prove futile even were he a Prophet of God.' [25]

Epigraphs of a second type were grants on Copper Plates, issued by Sultans. In the Introduction to the 1940 report Bell wrote of the objects attained on his visit in 1922:

> Photographs were taken, and provisional Roman transcripts (so far as the text survives) made of four sets of ancient Copper-Plate Grants (M. *Lomafanu*) long laid aside in the Islands as quite illegible, owing to the want of knowledge by any Maldivian of the particular archaic form of script (M. *Evela Akuru*) in which these plates are inscribed.

Bell, however, could decipher them, tentatively, from his acquaintance with not very dissimilar characters in old-time Sinhalese lithic inscriptions. The epigraphs were taken down from his dictation in modern Maldivian *tana*, and the copies entrusted to the Acting Qazi in the hope that he might be able to work out so much of their phraseology as resembled modern Maldivian. However, apart from the help he gave in 1922, M.Husain Didi could not assist. Because of this and other handicaps, Bell never completed his work on these *Lomafanu*, but it was accomplished after his death by his assistant of many years, W.L.de Silva, who faithfully rendered Bell's own translations and spelling of Maldivian texts. [26]

In the 'Epigraphy' Section of the Monograph, under 'Copper-Plate Grants' are ranged in a table the four main sets of *Lomafanu* studied. Three of these were in the most ancient script, *Evela Akuru*. Some plates were missing from each set, and only one set retained the uniting ring to go through holes on the left of each plate. The datings and/or namings of Sultans placed a set from Haddummati Atol at A.C. 1195-6, one found in Male at 1196-7, and another from Haddummati after 1232-3. Muslim chronology was of course used in the dates.

The characters gradually developed towards the less archaic *Dives Akuru*, and it was in an early phase of this that the fourth *Lomafanu* was inscribed. This *Bodugala Miskit Lomafanu* bore on its front cover the record of the erection of the Mosque, the date A.H. 758 (A.C. 1356-7), and the Arabic seal of Sultan Uma Vira Jalal-ud-din. He was the father of the Queen, Rehendi Khadijah, who made the grant in the 16th year of her reign. Her identity was confirmed by the *Tarikh* and by the narrative of Ibn Batuta; Isa, the Qazi whom he replaced, was named on one plate. Many usual features of *Lomafanu* were present: the list of former rulers, praise of the Queen, details of the sources and purposes of the income granted to the Mosque, and the religious benefits or evils accruing to those who upheld, or interfered with the grant. [27]

When Bell in 1930 wrote on *Lomafanu* in 'Excerpta Maldiviana. No. 9.' he showed in a note how the meaning of the term, 'metal-made leaf', could be traced back to Pali and Sanskrit. He also thanked M.Husain Didi, Abdul Hamid Didi, Ahmad Didi and his son, A.Muhammad Amin, for revising the translations, for he felt himself 'a pioneer ploughman of a lonely furrow in a fallow field'. He was not now writing on the sets of Copper-Plate Grants, but on certain 'singleton' stragglers. [28]

No. 1 of these had some connection with the *Bodugala Miskit Lomafanu*. Besides other links, a high post of *Henevi Ras Kinage* (or *Kilage*) was named in both, and the learned *Fadiyaru* or Qazi mentioned on the single plate *could* have been Ibn Batuta himself, or the venal Isa whom he was asked to replace. In this paper Bell fully transcribed and translated the texts on the plates.[29]

The second single plate studied was strung with the Bodugala Miskit set, but was an interloper. It granted revenue from twelve islands to a Mosque. The inscription also spoke of certain islands as being the Sultan's own property. This *Janman* or proprietary right no longer held in the Maldives, for they were a Constitutional Monarchy:

> 'Broad-based upon (the) people's will,
> And compassed by the inviolate sea.'

So Sultans could not claim *de jure* personal as distinct from Government right to land or produce, though in the past they had sometimes *de facto* acquired it.[30]

The third solo Copper-Plate was presented to Bell by his friend Ismail Didi, the Harbour Master and his Interpreter on his 1922 voyages to the Atols. Bell deduced, with the help of the Chronicles, that it emanated from Muhammad Shuj-ai Imad-ud-din I (A.C. 1620-48) who built the Fort and breakwater at Male, for on the plate his great-uncle Al Ghazi Ibrahim Farina, who died in A.C. 1609 fighting against the Malabars, was named as martyred. Pyrard gave lively detail of this galley fight, and the event also appears in an old *Fat-Kolu*.[31]

Some of Bell's extra insights into *Dives Akuru* came from his study, in 1922 at Male, of *Fat-Kolu*, Board and Paper Grants. Of eleven seen, one from the sixteenth century, four from the seventeenth and six from the eighteenth, only one was in *tana*. Of this type of Grant Bell wrote in the Monograph of 1940:

> When *Fat-Kolu* (pronounced *'Fai-Kolu'*) Grants made under the Sultan's Seal, written usually on Paper but occasionally on Parchment, e.g. *Kuda Huvadu, South Nilande Atol* (A.H. 1164) or even Wooden Board, e.g. *Gan, Addu Atol* (A.H. 1063) - first superseded *'Lomafanu'*, Copper-Plate Grants, at the Maldive Islands is unknown.

> But, with much probability, the period may be assigned to the late 16th century, and the reign of Sultan Ghazi Muhammad Bodu Takurufanu (A.C. 1573-85), that resuscitator of Muslim religious zeal and learning; after the Portuguese had been finally expelled from the Maldives mainly by his action, and the Realm settled down to nearly a quarter century of peace and order.

Almost all the *Fat-Kolu* studied came originally from islands outside Male, as appeared in a Table provided, showing origin, grantor, grantee, date and script. Bell chose three for study as fairly representative.

The first selected, preserved at Male, was claimed to be the oldest extant, from between A.H. 981 and 993 (A.C. 1573-85). It was a donation to the Hukuru Miskit on Kolofuri Island in Mulaku Atol from the hero whose relics were exhibited there, the above-mentioned expeller of the Portuguese. He had rebuilt the Mosque and assigned for its upkeep three islands as *Waqf* (benefaction granted, bequest for religious or charitable purposes). Bell was rather doubtful of this document as the original, though the Maldivian authorities accepted it.

Three seventeenth century grants came from Addu Atol: one from Gan and two from Hitadu Islands (all from Sultan Ibrahim Iskandar I); and a late seventeenth century one from Funadu Island in Haddummati Atol, from whence also one in the late eighteenth century.

The second *Fat-Kolu* studied, found on Gan Island on February 13, 1922, was the unique *Fila Fat-Kolu* or Board Grant, 5 ft. 7 in. by 1 ft. 9 in., sawn from a bread-fruit tree. Dated A.C. 1652, it made arrangements for the upkeep of the Mosque just erected by the Sultan (not named, but receiving a stream of honorifics). The Mosque must receive cadjans for thatching, oil for lights, mortar for repairs, sweepers for the floor, ladles for drawing from the wells; and the Five-Period Services of Prayer be observed.

The finest of the others was that from Kuda Huvadu, which had fifty-nine lines on fine goatskin parchment. The islanders, 'approaching (His Majesty's) most compassionate auspicious feet', had petitioned to have an older grant renewed. Besides the Seal of the Grantor, Sultan Muhammad Mukarram Imad-ud-din (III), (A.C. 1750-2), there were five seals of later Sultans, including that of Hasan Izz-ud-din, the recapturer of Male in 1759; also seals of Qazis. One of these officials later betrayed the grantor Sultan to the Malabars. Among the provisions for the Mosque appeared a tax (in cowries) for gathering cowries. [32]

An interesting footnote to Bell's researches on the Maldives may be found in the files of the Colonial Office. When the 1940 Monograph was published in Ceylon, copies were sent to England, only to be put away in 'the confidential cupboard' for the duration of the war as being of potential 'interest to the enemy'. At first, in 1941, it was accepted as a conspicuous contribution to knowledge of the Islands, and plans were made to send copies to learned societies and libraries. One was accepted with appreciation by the Naval Intelligence Division of the Admiralty.

Then doubts arose as to whether the detailed maps would not give away information to an enemy, and although it was known that the report had already been published in Ceylon, it was decided not to distribute copies in England, and to request that the Ceylon Government should withdraw copies from sale and prevent the exportation of any already on the market.

At this point a clerk notes:

File reverently buried. [33]

As soon as the war was over the Ceylon Government wrote on October 31, 1945 asking if the book could be released for sale; and on November 24, 1945 the Colonial Office readily agreed. [34]

No one seems to have noticed that the maps in the 1940 Monograph were identical with those included long ago in the 1881 Report.

31

The Old Man

Insights into Bell's life in his old age may be drawn from his writings. We have also three series of letters in the Colombo Archives, and there are records of visits from his children and grandchildren.

Cyril Bell had advanced in his career, to Conservator and eventually to Chief Conservator of his Province. The life of Forest Officers demanded plenty of hard work and organisation, for about half the time was spent out in camp, travelling on elephants, shooting for the pot; and for Phyllis, doctoring the forest dwellers. Bethia Bell was born at Jubbulpore in March 1918, and in 1919 mother and child returned to England, with father following. Heather was born at Southsea, Hampshire, in December 1920. All were in India from 1921 to 1923, and then, as the All-India Forest Service covered Burma, they were stationed there till 1925 with a home in pleasant Maymyo. Then the need to send the daughters to school involved a voyage home, which made possible a short stay in Ceylon on the way. The authors can just remember seeing buffaloes from the train to Kandy; the verandah of The Grange and the view of the Lake; the Old Man's box of spare glass eyes, and his aviary.

Malcolm Bell, in Ceylon from 1919, was Superintendent on the Binoya tea estate, and so came to meet Dorris Murray-Clarke. She was a lively young woman with a love of dancing and acting, who had come out to stay with her brother Murray, Superintendent on the adjoining Templestone estate. From her autobiography, written for her children, we learn of her meeting with Zoë Bell, 'tall, with lovely waving hair and a charming manner', who invited Dorris to the New Year Ball at the Queen's Hotel, Kandy. She encountered her hosts:

> I found I was in the bedroom adjoining Zoë Bell's and I received a very warm welcome from her and her mother, a delightful old lady with very blue eyes, pink cheeks and masses of white hair. She did not look as if she had lived in a hot tropical climate for years.

Renée Sabine Bell had, in fact, lived all her life out of England, and had many friends and relations in Ceylon. She was greatly loved by her children, who called her 'Mater', while the Old Man was addressed as 'Pater'. Dorris relates of this first visit:

> An amusing incident happened during tea. There was a double closed door leading from the dining room to the other half of the bungalow, which Mr. Bell lived in most of the time, attended by his own boy, and only appearing for main meals... Well, as we were sitting at tea, I suddenly looked towards the closed door and I distinctly saw an eye peering at me through the keyhole. It seemed to be looking straight at me, and I wondered if Mr. Bell could be sufficiently interested in a stray guest to take this most peculiar action. However, later in the evening, I met him and he appeared very affable. He was a big man, good-looking, with a grey beard and hair.

H. C. P. Bell

After H.C.P.Bell's brief Maldive visit, Dorris was again invited to Kandy and recalls:

> Old Mr. Bell greeted me very affably, although I did not feel as much at ease with him as I did with Zoë and Mrs. Bell. He took me over the Temple of the Tooth and calmly took a little figure of Buddha off an altar.
>
> 'You did not mind?' said he to the Buddhist priest in his saffron robe.
>
> 'Oh no,' was the reply. 'Master may take anything he wishes. Master does so much for us translating our Olas.'
>
> I still have the little Buddha on my mantelpiece in the dining room. I have always treated him with respect and given him a prominent place in our home.

Malcolm and Dorris bcame engaged during 1920 and the wedding was arranged for the Tuesday after Easter in 1921, March 30, in Nuwara Eliya. The Kandy Choir came up, and the men as well as the bride wore white or cream.

Malcolm's tactful handling of the labour force at Binoya and on another estate led to his being transferred to a more remote one, Calsay, where there had been labour trouble. However, in 1923 they went on leave, and for the next ten years Malcolm was employed on tea estates in Kenya and Tanganyka.

In the years following his long stay in 1922, Bell kept in touch with his Maldive friends. Letters survive in the Colombo Archives from between 1928 and 1931, to and from himself and Abdul Hamid, Maldivian Government representative in Colombo; his half-brother Ahmad, the Sultan's Private Secretary; and *his* son, A.Muhammad Amin. Abdul Hamid corresponded with Bell about his move in 1929 from The Grange to Florence Villa and about a visit in 1930 from Renée Prideaux. Bell visited Abdul Hamid that year in Colombo.

Bell is still remembered by Mohamed Ibrahim Loutfi, now Special Advisor to the National Centre for Linguistic and Historical Research in Male. Long ago Bell had correctly predicted the birth of a son to his father, and when the young man came to Ceylon on his way to be educated in Egypt, Bell invited him to Kandy and showed him his collections.

We had met young Muhammad Amin sailing to Colombo in 1920 to be educated in Ceylon. By June 1929 he had proceeded to Aligarh University in India, and letters between him and Bell were frequent and cordial. The young man wrote of a Test Match:

> I am sure, to a grand old Cricketer like you, the splendid success of Chapman and his men 'down under' must be most heartening. [1]

Muhammad Amin received from Bell a set of the JRASCB, with his own Maldive articles and Albert Gray's translation of Ibn Batuta. On his part Muhammad Amin translated for Bell some Maldive proverbs and was also helpful to Bell in preparing 'Excerpta Maldiviana. No. 14. Maldivian taboo of free English education'.

The old man

This paper recorded a letter of November 6, 1838 to Sultan Muhammad Imad-ud-din IV, in which the Governor of Ceylon, Sir J.A.Mackenzie, offered free education in English to two Maldive boys. The extant reply was in Arabic, and the English translation, though polite, was cool, rejecting the offer on religious grounds. In Muhammad Amin's correct translation for Bell, which he included in the article, the letter was more friendly, and rejected the offer, not on religious grounds, but merely as 'not suitable'.

Bell's paper also recorded the growing tendency for Maldivian nobles and royal scions to receive education in India and Ceylon. On his own Maldive visits he had noted that children, besides reading the *Quran*, learnt to write *Tana* and Arabic. Some further education was available in navigation, and in the Arabic, Urdu and English languages.

Bell also gave instances of the earlier resistance in the Maldives to foreign influences. Under Sultan Muhammad Mu'in-ud-din (1799-1835) there had been objection to the British Survey of the Maldive Islands in 1834. The Indian Navy Memoir of 1836 also recorded that an attempt in Bengal to translate the New Testament into Maldivian failed, because the man engaged in the work was recalled by the Sultan before the Gospel of St. Matthew was completed. For the unknown fate of the translation, Bell refers in a note to the Ceylon *Times* and *Observer* of January 14, 1925.[2]

However, letters of 1934 in the Colombo Archives suggest that the translation and the printing press were probably destroyed in a fire at Serampore on March 11, 1842. The British and Foreign Bible Society, besides vainly trying to trace the Gospel, approached H.C.P.Bell in hope of finding someone to make a new translation. Bell returned some dusty answers. He pointed out that the Ceylon Government, in process of trying out a new Constitution in the Maldives, wanted no grievance nor protest to be stirred up. On August 27, 1934 Bell wrote to P.A.Krishnaswamy, Secretary of the Society at Colombo:

You are evidently unaware of the rigid opposition to all attempt to force Christian doctrine on the suspicious and stubborn Maldive race in any way. Their slogan has been, since the 12th century:

'Lead, O God, the Maldive race
Along the Prophet's way,
Ever staunch to Muslim Faith
Until the Judgement Day.'

In October Bell wrote again, that no translator would be both able and willing. 'The "consummation devoutly to be wished" by the Bible Society will, I am afraid, be very far to seek'. He also made, though did not send, the comment:

The 'Island Kingdom' has plenty of *ordinary* 'fish to fry', with no taste for *Biblical* 'loaves and fishes', I trow, for a while.[3]

To return to Bell's correspondent Muhammad Amin: the young man congratulated his elder on

249

his seventy-eighth birthday, and described a letter from him as 'full of the unselfishness and consideration for others which are such marked characteristics of an Englishman'. He confided his wish to become Postmaster at Male, and in fact did become Assistant Postmaster and Assistant Principal Collector of Customs, and married the youngest daughter of Husain Didi, the Qazi.

The position of Ahmad Didi makes it unsurprising that in 1931 he was engaged in Constitution-drafting for the Maldives; but he was also concerned to supply Bell with material for his Monograph, and was sure it would be characterised 'by the same thoroughness, patience and skill that distinguish all your noble invaluable "efforts" on the Maldive Islands'. Bell exerted himself to obtain for his friend a copy of *Pyrard*. He thought there should be a more up-to-date edition, and Ahmad (who had also been trying to have the *Tarikh* translated in Male) agreed; but would Bell edit it?

Bell said that the Monograph must come first; and the effort to complete this is apparent in a correspondence in the Colombo Archives with the Government Publisher, Cottle, between 1927 and 1933. He was to sum up his difficulties in a letter of November 10, 1933, but their gradual emergence can be traced. He was indeed receiving proofs, and in September 1929 acquitted the Government Printing Office of committing 'laches', but he made so many corrections and annotations that he had to request that amended proofs should pass to and fro up to six times. This was particularly necessary when in January 1931 they were proofs of the especially heart-breaking Section IV, 'Epigraphy'. When Cottle on January 7 allowed him more proofs, 'it is the finest tonic pick-me-up I could possibly have been given'.

Bell had distractions in the form of Government requests to translate ancient *sannas*. In September 1927 he was doing work on some, concerning a land claim, before the District Court at Kandy. In the letter of 1933 he wrote of the urgent call to 'tedious and difficult research' on grants by Kandyan kings involving claims to valuable Crown lands. Moreover, in September 1928, the Governor had asked for details on 'Revenue and Expenditure' to take with him on a visit to the Maldives.

The checking by Maldivian officials of what Bell had written was a needful part of the process of publication, and not to be rapidly achieved. For example, in January 1931 the Monograph's Appendix E, 'Tenures and Taxation' had been sent to Ahmad Didi 'to ensure that the statements should conform strictly to the truth as well as in no way to infringe any Maldivian state etiquette'. Bell wrote to Cottle of the 'inborn procrastination of my otherwise excellent Maldivian friends among the Male authorities', and called them 'ever willing but (*more Maldivico*) ever procrastinating'.

Difficulties and lack of help came to a head in the work on Epigraphy. In January 1929 Bell's valuable assistant, W.L.de Silva, got a fixed clerkship in the Kandy Kachcheri and could only help him on Sundays. So in May 1930 Bell wrote that the Epigraphy proofs were 'extremely "hard nuts" to deal with as I have to, virtually single-handed, in an entirely new language, but I am plodding on stubbornly to a conclusion'. He expanded on this the next January, pointing out that he was dealing with three written characters all unfamiliar to him, two of them virtually still unknown to scholars, i.e. Arabic, *Dives Akuru* and *Tana*, and the language, archaic Maldivian, equally unfamiliar. The aid of Maldivian scholars, promised for years, had only reached him in the autumn of 1932, and even then was limited.

In spite of these hindrances Bell now and then showed a confidence, which was to be justified, in the ultimate value of his work. In January 1931 he declared to the publisher, Cottle:

> This Monograph (*quantum valeat*) will not be an ephemeral report but (as far as the writer's knowledge covers the subject) a *standard opuscule*, reliable *pro tanto* and not likely to be capable of revision (even if desirable) for many years to come perhaps, the author being unfortunately (*pace* any unintentional egotism in the assertion) the *only European living* in a position to carry through this exceptional undertaking, self-imposed when on pension in the closing evening of his days, after serving the Ceylon Government for thirty-nine years continuously. [4]

Bell advised his Maldive friends on eye troubles. He recommended to Abdul Hamid a lotion of boric acid, rose water and water of sea salt; and directed Muhammad Amin to his own highly qualified oculist in Kandy, Dr. A.F.Senaviratne. In his correspondence with Cottle, Bell's own poor eyesight recurs as a reasonable excuse for his delays in preparing the Monograph. In January 1930 'in a very despondent state', for 'the stars in their courses' seemed to have fought against the Monograph, he wrote of '*my own* sad "cross", diminution of my one eye's sight'. Dr. Senaviratne had told him that he ought to give his remaining eye a quarter of an hour's rest in every hour's continuous use. But how could he rest with the Epigraphy Section giving him so much mental distress?

> It is (as you will understand) quite useless issuing it in a garbled half-completed state to be 'the laughing stock' of Oriental savants. Either *whole hog* or *none* fits the case. [5]

Anxiety and distress about his family were also there to prey on Bell. He wrote to Cottle in February 1930:

> Owing to the serious illness of my daughter and my wife - the former lying for a while at death's very door - and their prolonged detention at the Kandy Nursing Home for the past three months, I have been quite unfit physically and mentally to give any attention to matters outside my own sad domestic affairs.

Worse was to follow. Mrs. Bell was in fact suffering from cancer and in the apology of November 1933 Bell was obliged to write:

> The continued, and increasing, serious illness of Mrs. Bell in 1932 (after a dangerous operation at the General Hospital, Colombo), culminating in her death in March of the present year - combined with a flood of other untoward aftermath circumstances, quite unhinged my mind from all futile attempts at calm literary work for the first six months of the year. [6]

Looking back fifty-seven years, to before the marriage of Harry Charles Purvis and

Renée Sabine, we find an incident preserved in family tradition. Bell had attended a ball at which Miss Fyers was expected, but she did not appear. Everyone carried a programme in which to enter the names of promised partners. Harry's programme still exists, in which he wrote, 'Renée, where art thou?'

In spite of all the causes which Bell detailed finally to Cottle for the 'unconscionable delay' in completing the Monograph, he declared 'it is my plain, honest duty not to shirk entire responsibility' and to 'tender the fullest apology'. Besides his duty to do so, he felt 'intense eagerness to place my Monograph in the hands of the Ceylon Government before, at Death's call, "I go hence and be no more seen"'. As we know, this was not to be.[7]

However, Bell could continue in his final years to enjoy the pleasures of a friendship closely linked with another branch of his work, some 'Excerpta Maldiviana' connected with the later history of the Islands. In the Colombo Archives is the Vossen Correspondence which covers the years 1932 to 1936. Father L.Vossen S.J. of the Papal Seminary, Kandy, translated for Bell, or found seminarians to do so, Maldive papers in Dutch and Portuguese. When sending to Vossen in March 1933 a copy of 'Excerpta Maldiviana. No. 10. The Portuguese at the Maldives' Bell referred to a Portuguese letter translated by one of the Father's students. A note to 'Excerpta Maldiviana. No. 11. Dutch intercourse with the Maldives: Seventeenth Century' records Vossen's valuable aid towards translation of Dutch extracts quoted therein.[8]

Early in 1934 Bell was asking for English translations of Dutch documents, and when thanking for these he forecast a second instalment on the Dutch period, this time on the Eighteenth Century:

> Whether I shall live to tackle that formidable period (with such kind and most generous friends like your good self) rests with a Merciful God sparing *health* and *sight*.

He began to see that the undertaking, drawing on two volumes of Sultans' Missives and Dutch replies, could only be done with paid assistance. An agreement was made and a clerk engaged and paid, to whom Vossen would dictate translations, and the volumes were sent to him. In November 1934, welcoming an instalment, he wrote to the Father:

> It is no empty compliment, believe me, when I say with *absolute truth* that your command of *virile English* specially displayed in the rendering of the important *Institutions* fairly *astonishes and delights* me. O! if we 'Britishers' could but rise to the level *of other European nations*, like your noble country.[9]

Bell thought the English 'linguistically deficient, due to crass self-opiniated laziness'. When Vossen feared his versions 'smacked very badly of the stiff 18th century Dutch', Bell reassured him. The Father was in fact not Dutch but Belgian, so in March 1934 we find Bell expressing to him his 'sincere regret at the loss not to Belgium alone but to the whole world of that noble sovereign, the late King of Belgium. *Date manibus lilia plenis*'.

Bell commented also on what emerged from the Missives of Dutch influence in the reign of

The old man

the masterful Sultan Ibrahim Iskandar II (1721-1750): 'That which persistently drained "Maldive life-blood" - the mercenary demand for more and more *cowries*'.

When there appeared 'Excerpta Maldiviana. No. 13. Some polyglot Missives of Sultan Ibrahim Iskandar II', Bell again paid tribute to Vossen's help, and to the translation of Portuguese Missives 'made through the agency of obliging Goanese students of the College'. [10]

In June 1936 Father Vossen was telling Bell, 'Your "Excerpta" has by now reached the development of a history of the Islands'; but the full eighteenth century instalment was never to materialise.

Bell's appreciation of the help he received was privately as well as publicly expressed; the letters abound in almost flowery thanks for Vossen's unselfishness, thoroughness and perseverance:

> You overpower me with your ever kind and generous response to my incessant worrying. Verily you are a 'William Deloraine', 'very good at need'. [11]

In October 1933 he wrote, 'May I come and see you at the Seminary? I should much like to have a pleasant pow-wow'. Invitations to tea also recur. Bell despatched a present to the boy clerk, who may also have been Vossen's 'amanuensis, the Eurasian lad' who was helped to a post by money from Bell. In his turn Bell recommended to Vossen the petition of 'Charles Croos, my cook' who 'has served me loyally and with much satisfaction for many years'. In his petition Croos recorded gratitude to Bell for paying for urgent medical treatment for two of his children, and to Miss Bell for the fees for a son, John, at present attending the Seminary school. He was asking for free education there for Aloysius, another boy; and had in fact himself, and his father before him, worked nearly fourteen years as cook in the Seminary.

No letter from Bell about his wife's death appears in this series, but he repeatedly confided to Vossen his own state of health, sometimes to account for long silences. So in December 1932 we learn of his worst attack to date of influenza, 'accompanied by that torturing ailment lumbago'. In October 1933, living as a 'positive hermit' he had avoided the worst of the same 'dread insidious fiend' thanks to Dr. Spaar's careful treatment and effective injections, and though 'not without a bit of a tussle and prolonged aftermath' achieved 'as full and rapid a recovery as an All Merciful God working through human medical agents will vouchsafe in His never failing loving kindness'.

November 1934 saw Bell 'suddenly gripped by the annual North-East Monsoon season attack of flu' which led him to contrast, as we have recorded, the treacherous cool nights of Kandy with his preferred dry heat of Anuradhapura. This 'flu' may have been recurring bouts of the 'Maldive fever' of which he had often written. In October 1935 he had avoided this 'persistent enemy flu' for he wrote of being:

> ...temporarily free from all physical 'snags' except the frequent concomitants of Old Age (84 last month), dwindling sight, increasing deafness, annoying low blood pressure preventing all hill climbing. No matter... by the Mercy of an ever loving God it is no more than I have a right to grouse about. [12]

In June 1936 Vossen expressed his 'joy to see your fine clear hand again. I was wondering how you are'. Bell's letter was 'proof of your keeping well and of your wondrous activity', and in the last letter of the series, on June 27, Bell was hoping to arrange a meeting.

After her mother's death Zoë kept house for her father. When Dorris Murray-Clarke first met Zoë, she had noticed her voluntary work:

> Not only did she clean the church brass weekly, no mean feat in the humid heat of Kandy. She interested herself in the school for Anglo-Indian boys.

She had a keen concern for maternity and child welfare, such as was provided by the Milk Centre of the Social Services League. Early in 1935 Father Vossen wrote to Bell of his anxiety about sick children, 'I hear Miss Zoë Bell has had her hands full with the poor people round about'. This was in consequence of a severe outbreak of malaria in Kandy and the surrounding villages. Bell wrote of Zoë's efforts to 'do her bit in this terrible visitation', saying:

> 'Dorwin' has automatically become a 'semi-outdoor dispensary' for the preparation and distribution of *Fever Mixture*. [13]

Zoë's manuscript memoir supplies details. There were not enough dispensaries in the villages, and those existing were apt to keep money for themselves instead of spending it on food for patients. So people flocked into the towns for treatment. Quinine was hard to obtain, but Zoë as Head of the District Nurse Association got a certain amount. She wrote:

> My father had a wonderful Moslem personal servant. He opened a little dispensary in our garden where this servant, Allan by name, treated patients. I had much to do keeping my nurses busy. People would be lying in the streets. It was a very terrible time, but we came through in the end.

It was not till after her father's death that Zoë, in the middle of a fête in aid of social work, was notified that she had been awarded the M.B.E.; and received it at Queen's House, Colombo.

To return to Bell: late in 1935 he described the past year to Father Vossen as *Annus Miserabilis*, perhaps for the epidemic, or that once again he had been called on for a Special Report for the Land Settlement Department on the genuineness of grants by Kandy chieftains. Moreover he had written in February of that year:

> Also there is, I regret to say, much private worry (sickness and *res angusta domi*) about certain members of my family in England and Africa. [14]

This points us back to Malcolm Bell and his family. The vivid illustrated autobiography by Dorris describes their years in Africa, and the birth of children: Daphne in 1928, Kenneth in 1930. There was a brief visit to Ceylon in 1931, for a last glimpse of Mrs. Bell, and in England they had met Cyril's family and the Prideaux, and had lived some time in Putney. It became necessary for them

The old man

to seek work in Ceylon once more, and they arrived in Colombo at the end of June 1935. Dorris writes:

> Malcolm purchased several lovely little birds in tiny little cages, bought by a member of the crew at an East African port, to take to his Father for his very fine aviary.

They went up to stay with Bell and Zoë in Kandy at 'Dorwin', 'a fine house but without the attraction of being as near the Lake as had been The Grange, where they had formerly lived'. These two houses can still be seen, though the latter has been altered. The name 'Dorwin' was derived from Doris and Winston, children of A.G.C.Wijeyekoon, from whom Bell rented it. Dorris Bell describes it as:

> …set high up in a rubber estate and was readily divided into two portions, which suited old Mr. Bell. He had his own side of the house, with library, sitting-room and bedroom, and his own two servants, one a very nice Malay who was very good at mending Ken's toys, and was called by him 'the magician'.

This would have been Allan, who is also remembered by the children as once bringing in a snake on a plate. Bell may have had something of a menagerie, for animals were sometimes sent to him, besides keeping an aviary. A bird in this was called by him 'Thomas Arthur' after a local Government Agent. As he disliked the bird, it can be concluded that the naming was no compliment.

The child point of view is quite likely to include food. Daphne and Kenneth were to remember that Madeira cake was especially baked and cut into squares to feed the birds, for they stole pieces of it. Bell only sustained meals with the family for a fortnight, though for some time more he wanted the children to visit him before they went to bed, and amused them by showing them how to draw houses. The roofs must always overlap the walls to carry off rain. A little is remembered about the Old Man's simple tastes in music. He was fond of Strauss waltzes, and of the bagpipe tune of the Gordon Highlanders; also of a song called 'Barren rocks of Aden'.

The young Bells moved away when Malcolm was employed, at Sydney Hill and then Hindugalla, in spite of illnesses; and Daphne went back to England to Zoë's old school 'The Beehive'. In 1937 Iris and Laura Prideaux came out to stay. There was a Mynah bird in the aviary that used to say, 'Hello, Laura', in the voice of 'Mater', presumably once taught by her. Bell was friendly enough to his nieces, but once remarked to one, who had just had her hair done, 'Laura, you look like a Vedda!'

His relatives remember that at 'Dorwin' everything was paid by postal order. Also that against the 'chilly' climate of Kandy Bell wore two pairs of woollen socks. He liked to sleep in a chair rather than in bed; his wife had done this too, before Sundays, in order to rouse early to attend church. During their stay the Prideaux attended St. Paul's Church. Because of its proximity to the Temple of the Tooth, processions of monks could be seen outside, and Bell used to ask his returning family, 'Did you have a Perahera this morning?'

H. C. P. Bell

H.C.P.Bell died on September 6, 1937. The next day his funeral, at Kanatta Cemetery, Colombo, took the form of cremation. Iris and Laura, Dorris and Malcolm were present, all wearing white, and it fell to Malcolm to light the pyre. Among others present were two nephews on the Fyers side, various friends and Government representatives, W.L.de Silva, Bell's personal clerk, and his servant Allan, who had been with him for twenty-seven years and to his last hour. [15]

Bell had left detailed instructions about his funeral and his monument. It is placed between those of his wife and of his daughter, Eva Laura, on each of which is carved a recumbent cross. Bell's has the cross erect at the head, for, as he stipulated, 'I must predominate'.

32

Bell as a Collector

The record of Bell's career would be incomplete without an account of his activities as a collector. These ranged over a varied field, and included his private collections and his contributions to the growth of those in the Colombo National Museum. Mr. C.J.de Saram is the author of a thesis in which he sets the role of H.C.P.Bell in the context of the emergence of the British official as a collector of antiquities in the colonial period of Ceylon. He traces the changes in the situation; at first that of the loss, neglect or re-structuring of traditional Sinhalese items, on account of the influence of British social dominance and European imports. There followed the growth of interest, on the part of travellers and officials, in Oriental works of art. Collectors of antiquities, even when fascinated by the Sinhalese cultural heritage, began mainly as amassers of objects, who were prepared to profit by their collections or remove them from the country.

Nevertheless, the nineteenth century saw the growth of the scholar-connoisseur among the Civil Servants. These were beginning 'to consider the cultural pattern of the country on its own terms rather than as a mere extension of the British Empire'. Their analytical minds and close association as Government Officials 'with people of all walks of life and localities' made them intelligent collectors; and of such was H.C.P.Bell.

Bell's studies on the Maldive Islands involved a close scrutiny of the cultural and ethnological objects there found. In April 1882 he told Albert Gray, 'My coins and the Seals in the Sultans' letters have been invaluable as fixing names and dates not otherwise get-at-able'.[1]

Maldivian objects were his earliest gifts to the Colombo National Museum. De Saram notes in his Annexure A an interesting collection given in 1879 and others in 1881 and 1882; and in the text gives a receipt to Bell on November 17, 1881 for a fishing-rod, a waist knife, etc. When after Bell's death the Museum bought his private collection, at least seventy-one items were Maldivian, including clothes, games boards, objects of shell, lacquer, coconut and coral, and a tortoise-catcher.[2]

No Maldive coins are recorded in this donation. We know that Bell collected them, but he was slow in publishing his findings. *The Maldive Islands* of 1881 drew on *Pyrard* to describe the Maldivian 'larin' of silver, 'long as the finger, but doubled back' and stamped with Arabic characters, of which Bell obtained a single specimen. In Gray and Bell's edition of *Pyrard* is a drawing of the Maldive 'larin', and the notes show that there was a similar fish-hook-shaped coin in Ceylon, which is also illustrated in *Pyrard*, together with pictures of the copper *bodu lari* and *kuda lari*. Gray said that Bell had specimens dating from 1716 to 1877.[3]

The early letters between Bell and correspondents in England are frequently concerned with Maldivian coins. He obtained in November 1883 a *digu lari* from his friend Hassan Didi. In 1881 he had asked Gray to see what specimens the British Museum held, in case exchanges with his own items were possible. Gray, perhaps the more interested of the two, frequently asked for

257

drawings and photographs, which Bell despatched, and for actual coins which might be presented to the Numismatic Society. [4]

Bell wished to add to his Maldivian coin collection, and attempted to obtain some coins from Rosset, who had been to Male. Rosset's, however, were sold to Sir H.W.Peek, M.P. for Mid-Surrey, of Wimbledon House, Wimbledon. Bell obtained from him an impression of a 'fish-hook', and two coins. In spite of promises to Gray in 1884 and 1885, Bell produced no early monograph on Maldive coins. A.Haly, the Director of the Colombo Museum, was still hoping for this in 1899, and referred to Bell's own 'complete and unique collection'. [5]

Bell's only extended study of the Maldive coinage is in the 1940 Monograph. He refers there to the 'pioneer work already done by Mr. J.Allan in contributing a Paper to *The Numismatic Chronicle* (Fourth Series, No. 47, Article XIV, 1912) on "The coinage of the Maldive Islands, with some Notes on the Cowrie and Larin"'. Bell reproduces the list of coins given by Allan, of which he had illustrated twenty-four, from the reign of Sultan Muzaffar Muhammad Imad-ud-din II (A.C. 1704-1721) to that of Sultan Muhammad Imad-ud-din VI (A.C. 1893-1903). There were seventeen listed but not illustrated.

Bell then gives a survey of Maldivian coinage: the use of cowries for exchange; the *digu lari* or long larin, of which he possessed an example, possibly of the reign of Sultan Ibrahim III (A.C. 1585-1609); the circular larins introduced by Sultan Iskandar Ibrahim I (A.C. 1648-1687); and the seventy issues in three denominations from A.C. 1664 to 1913. Bell has four plates of coins, Plates Q to T, which illustrate sixty-four items, including one cowrie and four *digu lari*. These are described in a 'Tabulated List of Maldive Coins', and he gives translations of legends on obverse and reverse. He says that they include all issues of coins up to date, but he does not indicate which ones come from his own collection. [6]

Bell does not seem ever to have presented any Maldive coins to the Museum, but De Saram in Annexure A records some gifts; thirty-two Ceylon challies in 1887 and in 1894 a Friesland ducat coin. The Museum gained coins by exchanges with Bell. In 1883 it acquired twenty, including two Ceylon modern silver larins and a number of stuiver pieces and challies dating between 1730 and 1812. To Bell in 1883 went a silver-gilt Sri Vijaya Bahu coin and in 1888 a Tissamaharama coin that had been nailed to a Moor boat as a charm.

Bell's special knowledge was called on to identify coins and assess their genuineness. In 1882 a gold coin of Sri Mat Sahasa Malle emerged as merely gilt, after Bell had declared that no gold coins of that reign were known. In 1883 he was able to assure Haly that a Sri Raja Raja coin, the type from which Parakrama Bahu took the design of his coinage, was not only a South Indian coin, as he had several authentic Ceylon specimens in his collection. He also identified, in spite of its very imperfect obverse, a rare Lion coin of Sri Parakrama Bahu. Haly paid Bell a tribute in his *First Report on the Exhibited Coins in the Colombo Museum*:

> When there was no reference in any work in the Museum Library I have endeavoured to describe it... In this I have been given Mr. H.C.P.Bell's invaluable assistance, which I take the opportunity to gratefully acknowledge. [7]

Bell was consulted by other experts. B.Lowsley in the *Numismatic Chronicle* compared a good silver coin of Parakrama Bahu (1153-1181) with one of Bell's which the latter had previously judged to be either silvered over or made of an alloy. He got from Bell a description of a rare coin of the eleventh or twelfth century which Bell felt unable to date more closely.[8]

John Still in the JRASCB in 1907 spoke of 'Bell's fine private collection' of Roman coins. He had eighty-eight of an issue struck in imitation of fourth and fifth century Roman coins, and two hundred and fifty of genuine ones from 306 A.D. to 423 A.D. Speaking of some early copper coins of Ceylon, Still added, 'I desire here to record my indebtedness to Mr. Bell, who not only put his collection of notes at my disposal, but also assisted me much by his great knowledge of the bibliography of the subject'.[9]

De Saram exonerates Bell from any charge of taking articles of exceptional value out of the country. He had found no definite evidence that Bell had followed other collectors in doing so:

> That he was resident in this country, after his retirement, seems to imply that he had his permanent interests here. The only recorded items of Bell's collection, that I have been able to locate as having been sold abroad, are those classified under the Numismatic Collection of the British Museum.

De Saram's Annexure H records that Miss Zoë Bell sent to the British Museum eleven coins, six of them gold.[10] In 1939 she also sent two Maldivian coins, one 'bodu lari' of A.H. 1182, and one 'kuda lari' of A.H. 1318. We have to assume that the rest of his holdings were sold privately after Bell's death to collectors in the Island.

One other 'collection' originating from H.C.P.Bell is in the India Office Library, London. His grandson, Guyon Prideaux, in 1972 donated a Sinhalese manuscript. Within brown paper covers are three sections. First comes *Eighteen Sanni Yakun*. Ten pages contain sixty-two verses on the eighteen yaksas who cause disease, plus three verses headed 'Epilogue'. The names of the Sanni Yaksas are given as: Kola, Bita, Amukku, Gulma, Vedi, Kana, Kora, Golu, Bihiri, Vata, Pit, Murttu, Naga, Demala, Abuta, Buta, Ginijal, Deva. Enclosed in the Ms. is a note reading, 'Will Mr. W.A.de Silva undertake to translate and edit this with notes for the *Ceylon Antiquary*? For purposes of illustrating the article Mr. Bell will supply a coloured drawing of each of the "Yakun". (Signed) John M.Senaveratne'.[11]

The projected article does not appear to have been published, although the drawings referred to had been executed in watercolour (10 x 8.2 inches) by B.M.Armstrong at Galle in 1885 and are in the Prints and Drawings section of the India Office Library (WD 3139 - 3157). The drawings cover eighteen Yaksas, but instead of Bita, Pit and Murttu they display Andiri, Maru and Unajal. These vivid paintings have labels indicating the diseases caused by each Yaksa. The Sinhalese manuscript continues with four pages of a corrupt Sanskrit verse, followed by seven stanzas concerning the flag of the Four Korales, with English translation. The third section contains a list of captions for illustrations of Buddhist legends.

The authors own a Maldivian object, not remarkable as such but a 'family heirloom' and known as 'the Sultan's teapot'. This is a large china teapot with all-over formalised fruit and flower designs in green, pink and gold. Circular panels on each side carry Arabic inscriptions;

such china was a normal nineteenth century export from China. The teapot was a gift to H.C.P.Bell, and was probably received in 1922 during his longest visit to the Islands.

Besides those from the Maldives, archaeological finds from Ceylon began to enter the Museum, sent by Bell. De Saram's Annexure A reports in 1886 'a clay cap of a dagoba, a stone carved with feet of the Buddha, and a carved stone base'. When, however, Bell became Archaeological Commissioner in 1890, De Saram shows that he acquired increased authority and the power to forge links between his Department and the Museum, and from his excavations many discoveries became available for transfer. Normally the larger objects excavated were left *in situ*, but the very notable great sedent Buddha found at Toluvila in 1890 was despatched to Colombo and now benignly dominates the entrance hall of the Museum. In his Annexure B, De Saram records for 1895 a collection from Bell from the site of the Buddhist railing at Anuradhapura, and very ancient chatties from a tank at Sigiriya. Most of the small objects at Anuradhapura were at first roughly collected together there and then kept in the temporary museum in the old hospital. But De Saram writes:

> Effective steps of a more binding nature, however, were taken in 1906, when Dr. A.Willey, then the Director of the Colombo Museum, with the strong support of Mr. Bell, prevailed upon the Government to permit the transfer of the finds of the Archaeological Survey to the Colombo Museum. [12]

In Annexure C of his paper De Saram notes a series of such transfers: in December 1906 one hundred and eighteen packages arrived of beads, bronzes, iron implements, pottery, stones such as statuettes, carved granite stonework and small carved woodwork. John Still was seconded to see to the labelling, arranging and storing. In 1907 a large stone figure of the goddess Kali, its stand, and a plain stone lingam were sent. In the same year, the important finds from Polonnaruwa were forwarded, including twenty-five bronze images, besides a miniature Gold Bull, a miniature Gold Lingam, etc. De Saram includes photographs of two of the bronzes, which had aroused much interest; being, as Bell pointed out, 'illustrative of the Hindu cult of the twelfth to thirteenth centuries A.D.'. The bronze images included ten of Siva and Parvati, singly or together, dancing or seated, and figures of devotees. One image was of the Maha Deva (Siva), in a halo, dancing on the Daiteya, Tripurasura, whom he slew after a combat lasting ten days. In 1908 more bronze finds were transferred, figures of animals, e.g. cobras, and stone carvings. In 1909 Bell sent the seven-tiered stone pedestal, each side of a different colour, excavated from the centre of a dagaba at Polonnaruwa, which he identified as the representation of the mystic Mount Maha Meru, the world centre. The year 1911-1912 saw acquisitions from Anuradhapura and Polonnaruwa of stone items - dolphin, elephant, lotus, lion, bull; and from the latter site figures of Vishnu as well as of the Buddha. [13]

'With his usual thoroughness' Bell ensured the careful cataloguing of finds and of their original location, which was immensely useful for research and comparison with other collections. De Saram's Annexure F is an extract from Bell's contribution on 'Archaeology' to the Annual Report for 1905 of the RASCB, outlining his plan for a catalogue of finds with illustrations, so that the items could be compared with those in other museums. John Still prepared the catalogue, which was compiled in 1906-7. De Saram's Annexure G reproduces its first page. [14]

Bell as a collector

After his retirement Bell continued to give objects to the Museum; in 1918 in particular 'one unique Buddhist crystal seal' described by the Director Dr. P.H.D.H.de Silva as 'a most outstanding donation'. Bell had given a full account of this in 1917 in the CALR. It had probably been unearthed, before the Archaeological Survey commenced operations, by a cultivator at Alankulama, two miles from Anuradhapura, not far from the Vessagiriya Rocks, where there had once been a Buddhist monastery. It was a small cone of semi-transparent crystal, pierced for hanging. On one flattened side was engraved 'a well-drawn, if stilted, bo-tree... with three boughs on either side'. On the other side of the seal was a dagaba, correctly shown with its triple-ringed drum base, its bell, square tee and pinnacle. Both were deeply and excellently engraved, much better than on a double-die Buddhist Copper Coin which had been described by Still in 1907.

Bell's article also dealt with a bronze object, perhaps a seal, found in 1893 during excavations to the North-East of the Jetawanarama Dagaba. It partly resembled *Sri-pada* stone slabs, but the toes were more raised, the feet more rounded, and the 'stiff *chatra* sometimes carved to overshadow the feet' on *Sri-patul* offering slabs, softened into graceful foliated arabesques which cover the sole. Bell's Plate VII showed both seals in actual size. [15]

In 1922, after his successful excavations in the Maldive Islands, Bell arranged for a presentation which:

> ...consisted of 39 archaeological objects from Gan (Haddummati Atol), Maldive Islands, which included finials, a Buddha face, a sedent image of the Buddha, ornamental carvings, pillar capitals, a teli, one of the flattened orbs of a dagaba pinnacle (Gan Island dagaba) and a Bodhisattva crown ornamental piece. [16]

De Saram reproduces illustrations of some of these from Bell's Monograph of 1940.

Finally, after Bell's death at Kandy in 1937, his daughter, Miss Zoë Bell, sold his personal collection of antiquities to the National Museum. De Saram's Annexure J gives the full list from the Register of the Colombo Museum, 1938. The items from the Maldives were listed at the beginning of this chapter. Those from Ceylon covered an even wider range of materials: bronze, brassware, stone and pottery, china and glass, wood, cloth, ivory and silver. Their purposes were as varied: weapons (Veddah, Portuguese, Dutch, Kandyan, Malay, Devale), Devale masks, betel-chewing instruments, jewellery, locks, writing instruments, coins (not many), images of Buddha, relic cases, tobacco boxes, pill boxes, flags, drums, flutes and bells, and household items that included a string-hopper machine.

De Saram records that the collection was purchased in May 1938 for Rs. 2,000. The *Sunday Observer* of September 28, 1980 printed a story that the valuation was conducted by Dr. Andreas Nell and Mr. Loker Bandaranayake. Miss Zoë Bell gave them tea, and when alone with Dr. Nell confided that she would have difficulty in paying her intended passage to England. Dr. Nell generously asked Mr. Bandaranayake (the first Curator of the Kandy Museum) to double the valuation on each item seen and also on those yet to be seen in 'recognition of the noble services' of Miss Bell's father.

De Saram feels that more could be done in the Museum to identify and display, and supplement with photographs, the material of which Bell was the source. He himself includes a number of photographs of the items.

De Saram describes Bell's collecting of data on antiquities as a systematic activity, 'in the same way as a zoologist or botanist might have collected relevant specimens for study'. Some of Bell's notes to *Pyrard*, and much detail in his first Maldive report, sufficiently show his interest in Natural History. Indeed in 1905 he presented to the Natural History section of the Museum two snakes and a caterpillar of the Death's Head moth. After Rosset's visit to the Maldives in 1885 we find Ferguson replying to Bell's queries about plants brought to him from the Islands. In the *Annals of the Royal Botanic Gardens, Peradeniya* J.C.Willis and J.Stanley Gardiner wrote that, in 1896, one hundred and seventy-four plants were presented to the herbarium of Henry Trimen, Director of the Peradeniya Gardens in Kandy. These came through Bell from the herb garden in Male of the Prime Minister, Ibrahim Didi, but were possibly not all indigenous to the Maldives. In 1889 Trimen had sent to Ibrahim Didi advice on plant collecting, requests for indigenous specimens, and even Government drying paper. [17]

In 1938 the Colombo National Museum Library acquired Bell's collection of books and manuscripts, comprising, as De Saram writes, 'approximately 840 volumes of books, 78 annuals and 46 ola manuscripts'. [18] The books have been recently fumigated and are housed together in controlled temperature in the Rare Books section. The catalogue of the collection is alphabetical of authors, titles and subjects.

An examination of the books reveals the nature and variety of Bell's interests; in the following the numbers are approximate. There are thirty-six Greek and Latin classics, a life-long interest, as his writings attest. The only gift ever received by one of the authors from her grandfather was a small translation of the poems of Catullus, sent to her when she was studying Latin on her own. His interest in other languages is shown by the thirty-seven dictionaries and grammars of French, Dutch, Portuguese, Latin, Turki, Arabic, Syriac, Hindi, Malayalam, Kanarese and Telegu, Malay, Sanskrit, Pali, Elu, Sinhalese and Tamil. Works of Sinhalese literature run to nearly a hundred volumes. The thirty-five books of geography and maps are mainly of the Ceylon area, as are over fifty history books and periodicals, though these cover other parts of Asia. Of the books on religion over thirty are on Buddhism, with some on Hinduism, Jainism and Islam. Some of those on Christianity might have come from the collection of 'marked books' willed to him by his devout father.

The field of the Arts (Architecture, Sculpture, Painting) extends from Europe to India, Ceylon, Cambodia and Java, in over fifty volumes. Of archaeological works proper twelve were seen; besides those on Asia some are on Central America. Bell's own work appears in his Archaeological Survey Reports; and among the collection on the Maldives and Laccadives are his own Maldive Reports. The forty books of English literature, mediaeval and modern, classic and popular, include books of phrases and quotations, and collections of love poems. Among these are several by 'Laurence Hope'. This was the pseudonym of Adela Florence Nicolson, author of the words of the once-popular 'Indian Love Lyrics' of which the best-known is 'Pale hands I loved beside the Shalimar'.

Fifty scientific works cover Astronomy, Geology and the Natural History of India and Ceylon, including several books on snakes. A dozen works of Anthropology contain one on Caste, and the Library also holds the 'Caste Books', handwritten volumes of Bell's researches into castes and tribal families. This was an investigation, as far as is known, not followed up nor published. [19]

Among the papers in the Bell Collection in the Colombo Archives are to be found many cuttings which illustrate Bell's wide interests and squirrel-like propensities. They range from the historical and political (Pirates of the Indian Ocean, The Amir of Afghanistan, the visit of the Shah of Persia to England) to scientific research on the colour of the sea, and articles on the economics of the rope industry and the cutting of diamonds. [20]

The Museum records chronicle donations of books to the Library, and Bell made such gifts in 1890, 1894, 1904 and 1923. An article by J.Harwood, then President of the RASCB, on 'Fra Mauro's map', the Mappa Mundi in the Ducal Palace Museum at Venice, contains considerable detail on Bell's attempts to obtain a copy of this and another old map of Ceylon from Amsterdam. Harwood says:

> Mr. Bell has offered the map and other papers to the Museum at cost price, and I hope that the authorities will soon be in a position to accept this offer. [21]

De Saram thinks that other collectors were encouraged to make gifts or loans by Bell's example. He was also able to exert some pressure on those who undertook amateur excavations. The Annual Report of 1909 relates his success in inducing a landowner of Kotte (J.Fonseka, Muhandiram) to hand over some of his finds:

> The Museum has thus tardily acquired about a dozen broken sculptured pillars, etc., from Royal, or Temple, edifices of *Jayawardhana Kotte* of the 15th century. Not a single carved stone is perfect. Among the most beautiful, but all too fragmentary, carvings is part of a fine *kirtti mukha* face, with a lotus and buds depending from the mouth. This must once have formed the crown of a magnificent granite *makara torana* over the entrance to the Palace or some important Vihare. [22]

So closely were Bell's private collecting and his concern for the general preservation of antiquities intertwined, that it requires scrutiny to define which was dominant in each of various fields. When we turn to olas it seems that Bell did not make outright gifts, but De Saram writes:

> He lent many ola manuscripts from his collection to the Museum so that copies could be made of them and these were often transcribed under his personal supervision. [23]

In his Annexure A De Saram notes the loan in 1889 of a Sinhalese translation of a Pali history of the Buddha's Tooth Relic, and a Sinhalese version of the history of the Bodhi tree and its branches brought to Ceylon. From 1895 onwards Bell supplied the Museum Library with transcriptions, made under his supervision, of olas found by the Archaeological Survey during Circuits. He recorded the numbers of those made annually in his Reports, but for details referred readers to the Administration Reports of the Museum in each year. In all 131 olas were transcribed up to 1905.

Some olas in the Museum Library are of special interest; in 1901 one probably of the thirteenth century, lent by Parker, required great care in copying. It was a very old copy of the 'Vinaya Tike', with 240 leaves of twenty lines each closely written in archaic Sinhalese character. Of the olas transcribed in 1895 Bell said that they were very rare, if not unknown, in the low country, and not often met with in the Kandyan districts. The rates of pay for the copying by an intelligent and reliable ex-priest sent round to temples were above those normal in Colombo. [24]

The themes of the olas comprise the Buddha's biography, enumeration of the virtues of Buddha, beauties of Buddhism, a Buddhist catechism, themes of meditation, Buddhist sins and virtues, rules for the priesthood, rewards of merit and demerit, and crimes that defrock priests, 'Message from eight female pilgrims', religious rituals and purification, Buddhist preaching, how the sacred Bodhi tree came to Anuradhapura (expressed in poetry, as is not uncommon), how the Tooth Relic was brought, rules for making images of Buddha, demonology and exorcism.

Astrology also recurs, Pali grammar and an Elu vocabulary; some chronology of kings and queens and eulogies of them, even one of Don André, a Portuguese captain; medical works on pregnancy and on hydrophobia, and descriptions of dagabas. The 'Hastiyoga Sataki' dealt with the training of elephants and charms and prescriptions for their cure.

From 1905 onwards Bell is not recorded in connection with olas until 1924. Then, however, we find in the Museum Administration Report:

> A valuable collection of Sinhalese ola manuscripts was acquired... from Mr. H.C.P.Bell, late of the Ceylon Civil Service. This consists of 200 books comprising in all 418 works. The manuscripts with some exceptions have been copied from original books by an expert copyist, whose Sinhalese script seems exceptionally good. These works are confined to Buddhism, History, Poetry, Philology, Medicine, Astrology, Demonology and other local cults...
>
> Mr. A.E.Jayasinghe went up to Kandy in connection with the above, inspected the manuscripts, saw to the careful packing and brought them safely to the Library in person. [25]

Since H.M.Gunasekera, supervised by Bell in 1898, had catalogued the Library's collection of olas, the number had grown, by 1935, to over 2,000, swollen by collections from Parker, Bell, Nevill and W.A.de Silva. [26]

In 1937, after Bell's death, one of his olas which had previously been copied was acquired for Rs. 600. It was briefly noted in 1967 by K.D.L.Wickremaratne in 'Palm leaf manuscripts of Ceylon' in *Ceylon Today* as the oldest leaf manuscript available, written in the thirteenth century during the reign of King Parakrama Bahu II. [27]

The authority for these details was the Archaeological Commissioner, Paranavitana, who had written a full account of it for the Museum Administration Report of 1937. He reckoned that it was worth acquiring at any price and of the greatest value to the country, surpassing in age and value any other work in the Museum Library. It was a Ms. of the *Cullavagga*, a Pali text forming part of the *Vinaya-Pitaki*, written in thirteenth century characters with a Sinhalese colophon identifying the copyist. Paranavitana wrote:

> Judging from the script and the names of the *theras* mentioned therein, I would tentatively take the Parakrama Bahu mentioned in the colophon to be the 2nd of that name (1236-1271). [28]

As we have seen, another thirteenth century manuscript, that of the *Vinaya Tike*, had been copied for the Museum in 1901, but Parker's original manuscript was, in 1937, no longer traceable. Paranavitana described the size and good condition of Bell's valuable Ms. and of its boards, which were painted within and without. [29]

Throughout his life Bell was a keen amateur photographer, who reached a professional standard. He experimented successfully with the telephoto lens. His first publication was of his pictures of the Maldives and a selection also appeared in the Pyrard volumes. All the photographs of the Kegalla district which were collected in an album in the Colombo Museum Library were by him. [30] In the 1911-12 Annual Report he wrote:

> Since its commencement in 1890 the Archaeological Survey has secured upwards of 4,000 photographs, mostly whole plate. These comprise views of ancient structures and sites, sculpture and ornament, inscriptions and antiques. [31]

Many, though not all of these, were taken by him. There is a small collection of prints, mostly of Sigiriya in 1896 and 1897, in the possession of the authors, all described and annotated on the back in his distinctive handwriting. Some of these are identical with those held by the Archaeological Department today. There is also a collection of photographs of the finds sent to the Colombo Museum in 1906 and 1907. [32]

First and last C.J.de Saram stresses the value of the role of H.C.P.Bell in the growth of the collection in the National Museum. On Bell's personal collection of Ceylon antiquities and Maldivian objects purchased after his death, he writes:

> The collection itself is an obvious reflection of a broad and interested mind, which studied in reasonable depth and clarity the changing historical and cultural patterns of this island. [33]

Finally relating Bell to his theme of the British Official as a Collector of Antiquities in the Colonial Period of Ceylon, De Saram writes:

> The contribution made by Mr. H.C.P.Bell to Ceylon History, Archaeology, Maldivian subjects and the Royal Asiatic Society, Ceylon Branch was, indeed, formidable. It established him as a man of stature of the British Colonial period who succeeded in establishing strong personal links with this country. It was no easy task to fuse colonial objectives to National Goals, but he was successful in making his fields of study an area where the smooth functioning of such a paradox was amply demonstrated. To this extent, the objects in the Museum collections which he promoted, are not simply a collection of antiquities to be anonymously dissolved in the general pool of the Museum, but a means of reflecting and acknowledging the aura attached to the 'Bell' name. [34]

33

The Man and his Work

How does one obtain a true estimate of a man, his character and achievements? Surely not by a study of his obituaries, where the writer searches only for what can be praised. Yet a comparison of obituaries and tributes can tell something, by showing what characteristics are most often mentioned, and not less by revealing what fails to be praised. So even though obituaries may give a false rosy glow, and are often inaccurate in minor matters of fact, they afford interesting glimpses of how Bell appeared to his contemporaries.

Thus Dr. Andreas Nell writes of 'that virile and warm-hearted worker', and A.C.G.Wijeyekoon says, 'He had a fine sense of humour. He was a hard-hitting fighter with plenty of determination. He was a great intellectual force, and never spared Government whenever he got the opportunity'.[1]

A long, and rather less believable tribute by 'A.N.W.' appeared in the *Times of Ceylon* on September 8, 1937. In addition to a full account of his public career, we have the following personal appreciation:

With the death of Mr. H.C.P.Bell, at 'Dorwin', Kandy, Ceylon will mourn the loss of her pioneer archaeologist.

This grand old man passed away peacefully on Monday last at the ripe old age of 86, and I believe that the greatest invisible monument to his memory is the gratitude in the hearts of a host of friends who have profited by their contact with him.

His was a rugged, virile personality, tempered by a deep sentiment and a whimsical sense of humour, which endeared him to all who knew him. He was a clean, hard-hitting fighter and a sportsman to his finger-tips. At times there was a stately glint in his eyes, but this indicated determination, not venom, for he was always a generous adversary. He possessed a tenderness of heart and a hatred of cruelty which made him the champion of all wild life, but he was free of any maudlin sentimentality.

He was a great man possessed of the rare combination of greatness in stature and greatness of intellect; he also had a depth of character which held him to his ideals and would brook no compromise with expediency. The great charm of his personality was his sweetness and gentleness of nature accompanied by a sympathetic understanding. All honour to him...

After his retirement Mr.Bell settled down in Kandy, and his leisure was devoted to his literary work and to aviculture - a hobby that gave him a good deal of pleasure. He seemed to be never so happy as when he could spend a little time with his feathered friends, and his collection at 'Dorwin' was a remarkably interesting one. He was always delighted to take friends round, introduce them to his pets and discourse freely on his Golden Orioles, Indian Roller and the African birds brought by his son, Malcolm.

The man and his work

And now this wonderful old man, with his marvellous intellect and simple tastes, is no more, and we are left with a sense of great loss. [2]

Often it is the later additions to formal obituaries which are the most personal, and such was the letter from J.A.Will Perera which appeared in the *Times of Ceylon* on Sept. 23, 1937:

> As a friend and one who derived immense aid from the late Mr. H.C.P.Bell, please afford me a little space in your valued journal, to add my humble tribute to a great English pioneer just departed.
>
> Despite the great heights to which he had soared, Mr. Bell did not despise humble students like myself. Hours could be spent in his company. He never made me feel uneasy in any way whatsoever. There was no superiority complex. He was not a cynic. He gladly held out a helping hand to those in quest of knowledge. He withheld nothing from the earnest seeker...
>
> Notwithstanding his great age, his mind worked normally, his memory was excellent, his signature bold and legible, not betraying the faintest sign of infirmity. Ferreting out his letters to me, I perused them over once more. It is with a pang of sorrow and dimmed eyes that I replace them in my desk. Not a single letter shows any *hauteur*. He wrote to me as man to man, although I am a pigmy beside him. He wrote in vigorous style, laying emphasis here and there, sprinkling profusely wit and humour. [3]

We have seen that 'the old bear' was somewhat unapproachable and unsympathetic to his children, but it does appear that he had some gift for friendship. This is illustrated in the account given in A.C.G.Wijeyekoon's *Recollections*. He writes of visiting Bell in Kandy, of finding him uncomfortably lodged, and letting to him his own house 'Dorwin', the home in which Bell spent the last years of his life. Wijeyekoon continues:

> Whenever I went to Kandy I made a point of seeing him, as it was a great disappointment to him if I failed to visit him. It was indeed a most profitable half hour I, usually, spent with him in his library... One day, he told me, that when he was about to retire from service, the Colonial Secretary, at that time, asked him whether he would accept an I.S.O. His reply was that his neck was not strong enough to hold the I.S.O. medal. The then Colonial Secretary, who was afterwards Governor of Ceylon, used to visit him frequently at 'Dorwin', Kandy, and talk to him about the Civil Service and Archaeological matters. These were private visits, and hardly anybody knew that the Governor visited him so often at his house.
>
> He never failed to celebrate his birthday. His daughter was always anxious to observe this birthday anniversary, by affording him the pleasure of meeting his many friends, of whom he had a wide circle, and I was present at his last two birthdays. At one birthday he had two of his old friends of the Civil Service who came out with him as cadets. These two ex-Civil Servants were on a visit to Ceylon, as they found the climate in England too cold for them. [4]

Wijeyekoon says that Zoë told him of her father's death, knowing that 'I was one of his most intimate friends', but that he believed that Bell had wished for no public announcement. Indeed, in an unsigned paragraph in the *Ceylon Observer*, the writer said that Bell 'was extremely modest, an unmistakable mark of the real scholar. His death-bed request was that only the fact that he had died should be mentioned of him'. In fact he had carefully arranged that his funeral ceremony should be striking, and that his monument be simple but imposing, achieving for himself a memorial that should justly rate his own favourite phrase, *simplex munditiis*. [5]

Several writers call him 'virile' and 'a good sportsman'. That he enjoyed both games and sport appears throughout his life, and that he liked to give the bear 'a sporting chance' may be seen in his preferred method of hunting. He was strong and active. There in no doubt that an iron constitution stood him in good stead during his years in malarial jungles, living and travelling in conditions which often discouraged his assistants. Athleticism and a good head were needed for his work on the Sigiri Rock; in contrast, Hocart in his Annual Report for 1922-23 admitted that when the iron ladder to the frescoes had to be replaced by a temporary ladder of timber 'it made too great demands on my capacity for facing a void', so that he deferred his inspection. [6]

Perhaps the most penetrating comment on Bell's character, however, comes from a private communication to the authors from Dr. Urmila Phadnis of Delhi University. She had studied in depth Bell's writings on the Maldive Islands, although knowing little of his career in Ceylon, and concluded:

> If his writings are any indication, Bell should have been highly methodical, arrogant, punctilious and a difficult man to deal with. On the other hand one does feel that though it is difficult to grasp the nature of his interaction with his peers, he was an affectionate and liberal man towards his juniors - a father figure, a patriarch... His references to his servants and his junior Sinhalese colleagues have a degree of warmth which passes the 'correct' style of acknowledgement. [7]

It is from Bell's own writings, published and unpublished, that the fullest picture of his personality may be extracted. He jumps from the page - self-centred, irascible, meticulous, opinionative, but with a strong appreciation of good work and a love of beauty in nature and in art.

His life was self-centred, or perhaps it would be fairer to say that it was 'work-centred', for his work was his life. To it he devoted that pertinacity which won ever increasing funds for the Archaeological Survey, and enabled him to carry on with his monumental study of the Maldives despite very serious physical disability. But his dedication had its reverse side, an inability to share and a reluctance to delegate which was delicately expressed as follows by D.T.Devendra in his reappraisal in 1962:

> He was so deeply involved in his work that he tended to be a jealous guardian of it and hesitant to let others come in. But all that was not due so much to an esotericism as to his own devotion which required all of his concentration on it. [8]

He liked to have things both ways, to enjoy independence and to resent being left to do his work 'single-handed'. This phrase often occurs - even as early as 1881 he was complaining of correcting the proofs of the Library Catalogue of the RASCB 'single-handed', and it was one of his defences for delay in producing his Reports. But his remark that it was 'good to be Head Man even in Hell' shows his real pleasure in being able to take his own decisions. That official at the

Colonial Office was not far off the mark who wrote in 1909, 'Mr. Bell prefers Anuradhapura [as headquarters] because he is left more to himself, and nobody else in Ceylon is likely to know much about such matters'. [9]

He never lacked confidence in himself. Whether defending his record to the Legislative Council against accusations of the destruction of monuments, or laying down the law for his successors, he was perfectly satisfied that his own methods were the best 'in all humbleness, but without fear of contradiction'. [10]

Of the importance of his writings on the Maldives he was equally certain, although making the same bow to proper self-depreciation:

> It is obvious, that within its humble scope, this monograph is likely to have to be - with all its undoubted imperfections - the standard of reference *re* the history, archaeology and epigraphy of the Maldives for many years to come. [11]

This conviction of the correctness of his own judgement appears in the various scholarly controversies recorded, and most notably in the long, grumbling battle with Wickremasinghe. He may have had some right to be exasperated with Wickremasinghe's delays, but the acerbity of his language did him permanent harm with the officials of the Colonial Office. He told Mr. Wijeyekoon that he had been offered and had refused the Imperial Service Order, but family tradition has it that he expected, perhaps with some justification, to be awarded the more prestigious rank of Companion of the Order of St. Michael and St. George, and felt that it was the English Government that blocked the honour.

He did resent what he took to be slights. In moments of pique there were occasions when he threatened resignation from the Secretaryship of the RASCB, and had to be tactfully persuaded to remain; and he was only saved from giving up the work of the Archaeological Survey at an early date by the intervention of Ievers. On a lighter note we may remember Bell's annoyance when the clergyman at Kandy refused to deliver his offered sermon.

He could, on occasion, admit error. He had originally maintained, against Hugh Nevill, that the Eastern Dagaba at Anuradhapura should be called the Abhayagiriya, and the Northern the Jetawanarama, and had so named them in his Reports. He ridiculed Nevill's 'belief that the Abhayagiriya and Jetawanarama have, like the unfortunate "twins" of the story "got completely mixed"'. But when, in 1910, an inscription was found which confirmed Nevill's view, he made the following *amende honorable*:

> To the late Mr. H.Nevill, Ceylon Civil Service, belongs the real credit for urging, more than twenty years ago, that the names of the Abhayagiriya and Jetawanarama Dagabas had been wrongly transposed in the course of centuries. [12]

On many occasions he criticised the work of his predecessors - Muller, Williams and Burrows - but this may be balanced by his equal determination to give credit where it was due. He was punctilious in always quoting earlier accounts of the places he visited or monuments he excavated; and was critical of those who did not do so. He referred with particular commendation to the work of Smither at Anuradhapura. Moreover he was lavish in his praise to his subordinates, notably Perera, but also Fernando and Ambrose. This appreciation extended to the skill of the village blacksmiths who did such good work at Sigiriya, Polonnaruwa and Anuradhapura, and the courage of the lad who led the ascent to the inaccessible cave on the east face of Sigiriya. He cared for the health and well-being of his work-force, his 'merrie-men' whose absence he so regretted when attempting conservation work at Polonnaruwa after his retirement. He got on well with the villagers and hunters of the jungle tribes. He treasured among his papers the tribute given to him by his subordinates when District Judge at Kalutara, although he may have laughed a little at its superlatives.

Bell is credited with 'a whimsical sense of humour', a quality that is more ephemeral than most. We know that he collected jokes, for his daughter Zoë incinerated a book of these after his death, since she considered some of them unsuitable! There are touches of comedy in his descriptions of the more curious of the animals and dwarves which he unveiled in his excavations, and there is a certain bluff, knock-down humour in some of his literary controversies. He liked sending enigmatic telegrams. He recorded a safe arrival at the Maldives with the brief words 'Goat and Compasses', the English Inn sign derived from 'God encompasses us'. A Biblical reference was despatched to one of his sons whose fortunes were at a low ebb: 'Genesis, ch.49, v.4', which when searched out is Jacob's denunciation of his eldest son Reuben: 'Unstable as water, thou shalt not excel'. It would have amused the sender rather than the recipient. A somewhat obscure Latin/English pun was inscribed by him beneath the portrait of his daughter's beloved cat: *Micat inter omnes*, which may be translated : 'He shines among them all'.

The only 'humorous' writing that survives is the 'Anuradhapura Anthem', and the circumstances of its composition suggests that he then got on well with his contemporaries. His friendship with Albert Gray survived the difficulties of long-distance literary co-operation. Their correspondence continued, and many years later Bell cut out and preserved among his papers the report of the death in action of 2nd. Lt. Patrick Gray, only child of Albert Gray of the Ceylon Civil Service.

Government Agents at Anuradhapura - Cameron, Byrde and Booth - usually supported him warmly in his work, as did John Ferguson of the RASCB. Ievers, his greatest friend, even when exasperated with his insouciance and dilatoriness, tried to defend him to Government, and sympathised with him when his intransigence led to Wickremasinghe's being removed from his control. Bell's relations with those Governors who were particularly interested in archaeology, Gregory and Gordon, were friendly, and he generally won over later occupants of the office to his side of any controversy.

H.R.Freeman, whom Still called 'Knight-errant, and champion of the Jungle People's rights', was one of his friends in his later years; and we may include in this group H.W.Codrington, numismatist and historian, whom he proposed as his successor, and Father Vossen of the Papal Seminary. He was friends with Maldivians, old and young. His cordial relations with his Sinhalese staff continued during his retirement, and A.T.G.A.Wickramasuriya, in a letter to the authors, says that Bell was invited to the wedding of his eldest sister in Colombo in January 1937,

The man and his work

and that though Bell was unable to attend, in his reply he recalled his presence at the wedding, in Anuradhapura, many years before, of Wickramasuriya's father, Ambrose, to the daughter of W.M.Fernando.

Where he was interested, he was approachable. He encouraged young writers. In the CALR in 1916 J.G.C.Mendis published a 'Lay of Ancient Lanka' on the life of Dutu Gemunu, in the style of Sir Walter Scott; and in his introduction he says, 'The writer has been much encouraged in his effort by Mr. H.C.P.Bell, without whose liberal and valued help these halting lines would hardly have assumed the form in which they now appear'. [13]

Hockly, who went to the Maldives in 1926 and again in 1934, gives full credit to Bell's advice in his book *The Two Thousand Isles*. When it was published in 1936 he presented a copy to Bell, and the following is written on the fly-leaf:

> To H.C.P.Bell in grateful remembrance of all the assistance so freely given and without which I should have found the compilation of the book more than difficult. With the author's best wishes. 7.9.35.

So much for Bell as a man. He would probably have preferred to be judged for his work. He is indeed praised by those who have followed as a pioneer and for the sheer extent of his operations. His final Maldive Monograph was reprinted by the National Centre for Linguistic and Historical Research in Male in 1985. The Foreword declared it to be 'the most comprehensive work on Maldive history to date. It represents fifty-eight years of dedicated research, and is, undoubtedly, an invaluable guide and source of reference for every Maldivian as well as for all students of Maldivian history'.

R.H.de Silva, in his study of 'Archaeology' in the volume *Education in Ceylon*, says that 'Bell's Progress as well as Annual Reports were published as Sessional Papers, and they are essential reading material for any student who professes to conduct archaeological research in Ceylon'. The Kegalla and the Seventh Progress Reports are particularly praised and valued. R.H.de Silva writes of the Topographical Surveys of Anuradhapura, Sigiriya and Polonnaruwa, either initiated or actively carried through by Bell, and says that 'the preparation of archaeological survey plans was thus concomitant with the exploration of ancient sites, and these plans are still of immense service when work is undertaken in the areas initially explored and surveyed by Bell'. [14]

Bell's maps and plans are consulted by workers in the field, and measurements he took at remote jungle sites such as Ritigala are used when restoration is undertaken today. He planned his operations carefully in advance, laying down the sections to be systematically covered; his Reports may have been late, but they were detailed, thorough and well indexed. The previous chapter has considered Bell as a collector of objects; he collected facts with equal passion. We have seen his meticulous, even obsessive, enumeration of every dwarf and every animal on every staircase and façade. We have noted also his insistence on exact measurement of everything recorded - even the ship that carried him to the Southern Atols in the Maldives is put down as 68 ft. 2 in. in length. There are no measuring poles in his photographs, but a human figure always appears to indicate scale. He himself appears beside the great statue of the Buddha at Seseruwa in 1895.

He also collected historical facts, ethnographical details, records of natural history and observations on the great irrigation works of the past, and noted them down *pari passu*. It was in this determination that every survey should be comprehensive and exhaustive that lies much of the enduring value of his work.

From time to time articles in the press have accused Bell, with other colonial archaeologists, of looting their sites of valuable artifacts. The same accusation was levelled against Ievers when he dug a trench at the Abhayagiriya Dagaba. We have seen, in fact, the anger of Bell towards the 'fatuous treasure-hunter', and that what he collected, both as Archaeological Commissioner and as an individual, has remained as part of Ceylon's heritage. [15]

His interpretations and identifications have not always passed unchallenged. Other writers besides Wickremasinghe have differed from him over his translations of inscriptions; the 'ladies' of Sigiriya are not now generally held to be human princesses and their attendants; the Polonnaruwa bronzes may not be Indian; the mourning figure at the Gal Vihare may not be Ananda. Yet such changing views are common form in any developing study, not least in archaeology, where intuition often precedes proof. Devendra, in his account of Bell's career written to mark the twenty-fifth anniversary of his death and that of Wickremasinghe, says:

> Bell familiarised himself with the background of our culture so that he could express himself authoritatively, whether on Buddhist life, architecture and art, or inscriptions. It is to his credit that what he has written by and large stands up to modern tests. His interpretations are not often challenged - many of them, on the other hand, receive further confirmation. [16]

Paranavitana was one of the most generous of commentators on Bell. In his book, *Glimpses of Ceylon's Past*, which is drawn from his own Annual Reports, Paranavitana records the finding of a slab on the pavement of the so-called Tomb of Elara which proved it to be the Dakshina Vihara. So Bell had identified it in 1898, but his opinion had not then gained acceptance. Paranavitana writes:

> The discovery of this inscription, once a part of the monastery itself, labelling it, as it were, finally sets to rest all doubt with regard to Bell's identification, and it is a source of particular pleasure to the present writer that, in this matter, he has been able to justify the sagacity of one of his predecessors in office - the pioneer of Ceylon archaeology. [17]

A recent critique of Bell's work appears in the book on Ceylon in the popular series *Archaeologia Mundi*. Jean Boisselier accords him, despite his lack of training, 'a leading place among the archaeologists of the period'. He recognises that Bell worked without technical support and that scientific methods of excavation and conservation were in their infancy. He concedes that treasure hunters may have already destroyed much evidence. Nevertheless he believes that some of Bell's restoration work was hasty, and that information may have been lost through failure to make a systematic collection of small objects and potsherds. [18] Indeed we find Bell's successor Hocart complaining that he found objects in the spoil of old excavations, whose archaeological value was diminished in that their stratification had been lost. [19]

The man and his work

That Bell's methods of excavation were not those of today goes without saying, but they were not entirely slapdash. The description of the finding of the crystal eyeball and pupil of a Buddha image at Vihara No. 2 of the Pankuliya ruins at Anuradhapura suggests that, when possible, soil was carefully sifted. Such small finds as occurred were carefully listed.

Boisselier says that most of the conservation work at this period was carried out by the Public Works Department. It appears, however, from a detailed study of Bell's work, that he was more concerned with the problem of conservation generally than has been sometimes suggested, and that he played an active role in the preservation of the monuments he unearthed. Far from leaving it to the P.W.D., he was constantly at war with them and had very clear opinions as to the extent to which restoration was justified. His ideal was to restore an ancient monument to its original beauty, if it could be done without propping it up with intrusive iron or brick work, and when it was achieved to his satisfaction he called it 'a labour of love'.

For his love for his work went far beyond enjoyment of an independent command and a life of freedom. Although he occasionally characterises results as disappointing, far more often he rejoices that what has been discovered is of a 'chaste beauty', or the best specimen yet found. Thus the Toluvila Buddha, found in 1890, is 'the finest yet brought to light at Anuradhapura', and two years later the Pankuliya Buddha becomes 'undoubtedly the finest of the larger Buddhas yet discovered at Anuradhapura'.

At Polonnaruwa the Wata-da-ge 'is unrivalled as the most beautiful specimen of Buddhist stone architecture existing in Ceylon', and the Nissanka-Lata-Mandapaya, 'that gem of airy sculpture in granite'. We have quoted at some length his appreciation of the stone figures at the Gal Vihare site - 'the most impressive antiquity *par excellence*' to be seen in the Island of Ceylon and 'possibly not rivalled throughout the Continent of India'.

His imagination was caught by the sheer audacity of the building operations at Sigiriya, and the great lion staircase entrance; he waxed lyrical on the frescoes there and not less on those at Polonnaruwa. It is, though, to the description of sculptured animals that he devotes his hyperboles: the 'spirited and life-like' elephants disporting themselves at Pokuna A on the banks of the Tissavewa, the lion rampant on the bath at Mihintale, and all the varied decorative animals which adorned the steps and balustrades of temple and monastic building. His enthusiasm shines through. He loved what he found for what it was as well as because he had found it, and his appreciation spills over into his style. Even when describing the somewhat sparse remains unearthed in the Maldive Islands, the words 'beautiful' and 'handsome' and his favourite 'chaste' recur.

There is nothing bare about his writing, despite his disclaimer of the intention to indulge in 'delightful flowery "word-pictures" of ruins'. We have seen his most characteristic tendency to include quotations. The same Latin tags appear frequently, such as *pro tanto*, *me judice*, *quantum valeat* and *magnis componere parva*; but his range of English quotations is wider, from Shakespeare to Scott, from Butler's *Hudibras* to Thomas Hardy, with many others from lesser-known poets which could perhaps be traced by a careful study of the books in his library. Another feature of his style is his zest for the footnote - the footnote to identify a source, but also the footnote to pay off a score or to underline an argument. One may also note a proclivity for the dash in his punctuation, much used by those who tend to write as they speak, pouring out ideas with asides thrown in. Altogether his style is as individual as his 'fine, clear hand', with his elaborately curled signature, which yet is unmistakably 'H.C.P.Bell'.

Although his style cannot be compared with the limpid clarity which distinguishes John Still's book, yet there are passages which truly reflect his identification with the culture he studied and his deep appreciation of beauties of nature. The bright expanses of the Sri Lankan tanks, the beauty of evening on the lagoons of the Maldives, these bring out a response from the heart.

Among the few papers preserved by Bell's daughter Zoë, there is an appreciation of his work, a cutting from a newspaper, obviously written just before his retirement, but without a note of its provenance. The following extracts may show why he kept it:

> Mr. Bell's work lifts him permanently into the rank of one of the ablest men who ever handled the historical remains of an ancient Eastern land... His name stands in the Civil List without any of the decorations which grace younger and less permanent names. But the permanence of his name is higher honour than ribbons on his coat, and that honour the gratitude of the people and the recognition of historical students have conferred upon him...

> Apart from the light he has thrown upon the story of this Island, he has restored much that was forgotten in its religion, for he has laid the land under a lasting debt of gratitude by his sympathetic interest and his careful preservation of the relics of the ancient times. What he has recovered from the destructive grasp of time is not merely of historical interest: much of it is rated higher than history, for it is sacred and holy, and the object of reverence to a living religion. Here, good fortune favoured him, for it is seldom that an archaeologist dives into the dead past to retrieve what belongs to a living faith. The treasures of Egypt are concerned with a dead cult; of Greece with a discredited mythology; of Mexico and Yucatan with discarded heathen worship. But the religion which erected the monuments recovered by Mr. Bell is living and a power still. That placed him in a situation of unexampled delicacy, and called for qualities of tact, forbearance and patience such as no worker in the same field has ever had to exhibit. It is his distinction that, on the whole, he has emerged creditably from the unusual test.

> No man in his place could have avoided giving offence occasionally. Sometimes, the feelings roused have been extravagant; at other times, it is not improbable that there was good reason for resentment. But, taking his record as a whole, what is surprising is, not that he occasionally exposed himself to misunderstanding, but that he avoided causes for offence so carefully and consistently as he did...

> His real work it is for more competent students to appraise accurately. But an accurate estimate will scarcely come during his lifetime. A scientific man, especially an archaeologist, is notoriously not honoured as a prophet among his own group until a certain measure of distance intervenes between himself and the members of his cult. Time must place his record in perspective, must test its value, must mellow his memory, and then will come the correct verdict. But no man ever had better reason to anticipate that verdict with confidence and pride than Mr. H.C.P.Bell. [20]

Time also is beginning to place in perspective the whole period in which Bell lived, and it is possible to view with more detachment the phenomena of colonial rule and to consider whether

anything of permanent good remains. Bell probably never questioned his perfect right to make a career and a name in a country not his own. Yet even while he lived and worked, there were Englishmen who questioned the assumption. One of these was Leonard Woolf. In his book *Growing : an Autobiography 1904-1911*, he writes of his years in the Ceylon Civil Service. He mentions a dinner party at Anuradhapura at which the Archaeological Commissioner was present. He writes:

> We were all Civil Servants. They were all very friendly and wanting to put the new boy at ease. The conversation never flagged, but its loadstone was shop, sport or gossip, and if anyone or anything turned it for a moment in some other direction, it soon veered back to its permanent centre of attraction. But we were all rather grand, a good deal grander than we could have been at home in London or Edinburgh, Brighton or Oban. We were grand because we were a ruling caste in a strange Asiatic country; I did not realise this at the time, though I felt something in the atmosphere which was to me slightly strange and disconcerting. [21]

So might have pondered an unconventional official in a Villa of some Province of the Roman Empire in Europe. That dominion, however, left its permanent traces; for example, its road system, amphitheatres, and the 'Romance Languages'. Writers on the later centuries of Sri Lankan history have debated what parts of the Island's heritage derive from vanished colonial rule. John Still in *The Jungle Tide* considered:

> Fate has for some reason picked for survival religion, language and music from among the wisdom of the Portuguese; and law, household comfort and family pride from the customs of the Dutch; and some future observer will doubtless note what is selected for survival from among the manifold ways of the British. To hazard a prediction, I would give my vote to cricket. [22]

The authors, from their visits, would pick out tiny items: red post-boxes on lonely roads; and on hotel menus, alongside the country's delicious fruits, the 'nursery puddings' probably once demanded for English children.

A more sombre note was struck at an earlier date by the traveller, Jules Leclercq. He wrote:

> They will go tomorrow (said a resident who had observed them closely), leaving behind few remembrances and regrets; because they made little impression on the people, because they never made their way into any home, any spirit, any heart; because they were known only as a curious and unamiable people who bought land, cultivated it, and never forgave a fault. One day they will pack their bags and leave. [23]

Bell's own legacy is a lasting one. He is remembered not only for having laid the massive foundations of organised archaeology in Ceylon, but as a remarkable personality. Moreover, the love he had for the land, its culture and its people led him never to uproot himself from them.

Whoever else left, H.C.P.Bell remains.

Notes

1. Forebears

Main Sources
BELL, R. *Memoir of General Robert Bell, Madras Artillery 1779-1820.* Unpublished. (A copy is kept in the India Office Library)
POYNTER, H.M. 'Soldiering under John Company : an officer in the Madras Artillery 1779-1820, by one of his grand-daughters' *Journal of the Royal Artillery*, 48, 1921-2: 333-6, 391-4, 416-9.
East India Register.

Notes
1. SLNA 25/16/316.
2. POYNTER, H.M., op.cit.: 333.
3. Ibid.: 417-8.
4. POYNTER, H.M., op.cit.: 333-4.
5. *A Preliminary View of the Establishment of the Honorable East India Company in Hertfordshire for the Education of Young Persons Appointed to the Civil Service in India.* 1886: 1.
6. *Directions for the Guidance of the Students at the East India College.* 1814: 1-3.

2. Early Career

Main Sources
Ceylon Blue Book.
Ceylon Civil List.
Great Public Schools, by various authors. London, Arnold, 1893.
HUNTER, A.A. ed. *Cheltenham College Register*, 1841-1910. London, Bell, 1911.
MORGAN, M.C. *Cheltenham College: the First Hundred Years.* Chalfont St. Giles, Sadler for the Cheltenham Society, 1968.
STAUNTON, H. *The Great Schools of England.* London, Dalby, Isbiston and Co., 1865.
WRIGHT, A. *Twentieth Century Impressions of Ceylon.* London, Lloyds, 1907.

Notes
1. BELL, D. *Autobiography.* Unpublished.
2. BELL, R. *Memoir.* Unpublished.
3. *The Cheltenham College Magazine*, June 1872: 157-8.
4. SLNA 25/16/190.
5. LOWELL, A.L. *Colonial Civil Service: the Selection and Training of Colonial Officials in England, Holland and France.* New York, Macmillan, 1900: 66-7; CIVIL SERVICE COMMISSION. *Eighteenth Report of Her Majesty's Civil Service Commission.* London, Eyre and Spottiswode, 1874: 217.
6. *Ceylon Blue Book*: passim.
7. BELL, H.C.P. 'Andreas Amabert: 1764' CALR, 1916, 1/4: 250, note 24.
8. *Ceylon Civil List*, 1873: 142-3.
9. SLNA 25/16/41.
10. BREMER, M. *Memoirs of a Ceylon Planter's Travels, 1851-1921.* London, Rivingtons, 1930: 55.
11. DEP, A.C. *The History of the Ceylon Police. Vol.II. 1866-1913.* Colombo, Asoka Trading Co.,1969: 378.
12. SLNA 25/16/41.
13. SLNA 25/16/190.
14. SLNA 25/16/41.
15. TOUSSAINT, J.R. *Annals of the Ceylon Civil Service.* Colombo, Apothecaries Co., 1935.
16. SLNA 25/16/41.
17. Ibid.
18. JRASCB, 5, 1870-74, Proceedings 1871: xxxiii-xxxiv.
19. JRASCB, 7, 1881-2, Proceedings 1881: xxx.
20. JRASCB n.s. 14, 1970: 2-3.
21. JRASCB, 24(68), 1915: 2.

3. The Maldives : Pyrard and Other Visitors

Main Sources
BELL, H.C.P. *The Maldive Islands: an Account of the Physical Features, Climate, History, Inhabitants, Productions and Trade* (SP XLIII, 1881). Colombo, Frank Laker, 1883.
GRAY, A. ed. *The Voyage of François Pyrard of Laval to the East Indies, the Maldives, to the Moluccas and Brasil: translated into English from the third French edition of 1619, and edited with notes by Albert Gray assisted by H.C.P.Bell.* 3 vols. London, Hakluyt Society, 1887-90. SLNA 25/16/41.

Notes
1. BELL, H.C.P. *The Maldive Islands : Monograph on the History, Archaeology and Epigraphy.* Colombo, Government Printing Press, 1940: 1.
2. *The Athenaeum*, No. 2975, Nov. 1, 1884: 554.
3. Ibid.: 554-5.
4. SLNA 25/16/23.
5. BELL, H.C.P. *The Maldive Islands.* 1940: 48; SLNA 25/16/23.
6. SLNA 25/16/299.
7. SLNA 25/16/41.
8. JRASCB, 6, 1879-80, Proceedings 1880: xxiii.
9. CO 54/536.
10. CO 54/574.
11. JRAS n.s. 14, 1882: xxxiii; Ibid., 16, 1884: lxiii-iv.
12. *The Athenaeum*, No. 2975, Nov. 1, 1884: 554-5.
13. YULE, A.F. 'Memoir' in YULE, H. ed. *The Book of Ser Marco Polo.* 3rd. edn. London, Murray, 1903: xxvii-lxxii.
14. YULE, H. and BURNELL, A.C. *Hobson-Jobson:Being a Glossary of Anglo-Indian Colloquial Words and Phrases, and of Kindred Terms:Etymological,Historical, Geographical, and Discursive.* London, Murray, 1886: 'Coco-de-Mer, or Double Coco-nut': 176-8;   BELL, H.C.P. 'Fish-curing at the Maldives' *Indian Antiquary*, 11, 1882: 196-8.
15. SLNA 25/16/190.
16. BARTHOLOMEUS, O. *Minicoy and its People.* London, 1885; SLNA 25/16/41.

4. Archaeology before 1890 : The Collecting of Records

Main Sources
Administration Reports.
DE SILVA, R.H. 'Archaeology' in *Education in Ceylon : a Centenary Volume.* Vol.III. Colombo, Ministry of Education and Cultural Affairs, 1969.
DEVENDRA, D.T. 'Seventy years of Ceylon archaeology' *Artibus Asiae*, 22, 1959: 23-5.
GODAKUMBURA, C.E. 'History of archaeology in Ceylon' JRASCB n.s. 13, 1969: 1-38.
IEVERS, R.W. *Manual of the North-Central Province, Ceylon.* Colombo, Skeen, 1899.
[MULLER, E. ed.] *Papers on the Subject of Literary and Scientific Work in Ceylon* (SP I, 1878).
RUTNAM, J.T. 'Some aspects of the history of archaeology in Sri Lanka: Presidential Address by James T.Rutnam, 9 Nov., 1874' *Journal of the Jaffna Archaeological Society*, 1975: 1-6.

Notes
1. [MULLER, E. ed.], op. cit.: 3.
2. Ibid.: 6.
3. CUMMING, C.F.Gordon. *Two Happy Years in Ceylon.* Vol.I. Edinbugh and London, Blackwood, 1892: 288.
4. SLNA 30. Kandy Archives. Diaries of Assistant Government Agent.
5. JURRIAANSE, M.W. *Catalogue of the Archives of the Dutch Central Government of Coastal Ceylon, 1640-1796.* Colombo, Government Printing Press, 1943.

277

6. BELL, H.C.P. 'Letter from the Kandyan Court : 1726' CALR, 1/2, 1915: 118.
7. JRASCB, 10, 1887-1888, Proceedings 1888: cx-cxi, lxxxv-vi.
8. ANTHONISZ, R.G. 'Resolutions and sentences of the Council of the town of Galle, l640-41. Being the translation of volumes I and II of the Galle Dutch Records made by the Society in Holland' JRASCB, 17(53), 1902: 259-528.
9. GREGORY, Sir W. *An Autobiography*; edited by Lady Gregory. London, Murray, 1894: 314-5.
10. JRASCB, 5, 1870-1874, Proceedings 1872: xxvii-ix.
11. [MULLER, E. ed.], op. cit.: 29-30.
12. *Administration Report*, 1868 Part II: 22.
13. JRASCB, 5, 1870-1874, Proceedings 1870-1871: x-xi.
14. JRASCB, 5, 1870-1874, Proceedings 1870-1871: xxxv.
15. CAPPER, J. 'The dagobas of Anuradhapura' JRAS n.s. 20, 1888: 165.
16. *Administration Report*, 1871 Part II: 9. (Two volumes of Lawton's photographs may be seen in the Foreign and Commonwealth Office Library in London)
17. JRASCB, 5, 1870-1874, Proceedings 1872: xix-xx.(Godakumbera, in his 'History of archaeology in Ceylon' JRASCB n.s. 13, 1969 states that Lawton was a native of Jaffna by the name of Svaminathan Kanakaretnam Lawton. He was given this *incorrect* information by J.Rutnam, who in his 'Some aspects of the history of archaeology in Sri Lanka' *Journal of the Jaffna Archaeological Society*, 1975 confirms that J. Lawton was an Englishman. See also J.Falconer 'Nineteenth century photography in Ceylon' *The Photographic Collector*, 2/2, 1981: 39-54)
18. [MULLER, E. ed.], op. cit.: 20.

5. Archaeology before 1890 : Epigraphy and Monuments

Main Sources
Administration Reports.
CHAPMAN, J.K. *The Career of Arthur Hamilton Gordon, First Lord Stanmore 1829-1912.* Toronto, University of Toronto Press, 1964.
GODAKUMBERA, C.F. 'History of archaeology in Ceylon' JRASCB n.s. 13, 1969: 1-38.
IEVERS, R.W. *Manual of the North-Central Province.* Colombo, Skeen, 1899.
[MULLER, E. ed.] *Papers on the Subject of Literary and Scientific Work in Ceylon* (SP I, 1878).
VIMALANANDA, T. 'Two pioneers of epigraphy' *Ceylon Historical Journal*, I/4, 1952: 358-60.

Notes
1. [MULLER, E.ed.], op.cit.: 16-7.
2. GOLDSCHMIDT, P. *Report on the Inscriptions found in the North-Central Province* (SP IX, 1875). (Reprinted in *Indian Antiquary*, 5, 1876: 189-92); *Further Report on Inscriptions found in the North-Central Province* (SP XXIV, 1878); *Report on Inscriptions found in the North-Central Province and in Hambantota* (SP XI, 1876). (Reprinted in *Indian Antiquary*, 6, 1877: 318-29); 'Notes on ancient Sinhalese inscriptions' JRASCB, 6(20), 1879: 1-45.
3. [MULLER, E. ed.], op. cit.: 26.
4. CO 54/661.
5. MULLER, E. *Report on the Inscriptions in the Hambantota District* (SP XXV, 1878); *Report on Ancient Inscriptions in the North-Western Province* (SP XI, 1879); *Report on Ancient Inscriptions in the North-Western Province and the Districts of Matale and Trincomalee* (SP III, 1880). (Reprinted in *Indian Antiquary*, 9, 1880: 268-74); *Contributions to Sinhalese Grammar* (SP XXI, l880); 'Textual translation of the inscription of Mahinda III at

Mihintale' JRASCB, 6(21), 1880:5-36; 'Notes on ancient Sinhalese inscriptions' JRASCB, 8(26), 1880: 18-43; *Translation of Ancient Inscriptions in the Anuradhapura and Hambantota Districts now in the Colombo Museum* (SP XXV, 1881); *Ancient Inscriptions in Ceylon*. 2 vols. London, Trubner, 1883.
6. IEVERS, R.W. *Manual*, op.cit.: 234.
7. PARANAVITANA, S. *Inscriptions of Ceylon. Vol.I. Early Brahmi Inscriptions.* Ceylon, Department of Archaeology, 1970, Preface: i.
8. SLNA 6/41/1309 A.
9. IEVERS, R.W. *Manual*, op.cit.: 224.
10. WILLIAMS, A.E. *Report on the Restoration of the Dalada Maligawa at Yapawa* (SP LI, 1886); ASCAR, 1904: 8; SLNA 6/13547 B.
11. *Administration Report*, 1888 Part I: 217 A.
12. [MULLER, E. ed.], op. cit.: 30.
13. *Administration Report*, 1869 Part I: 107.
14. WICKREMERATNE, A. *Thomas William Rhys Davids and Buddhism in Sri Lanka*. Delhi, Motilal Banarsides, 1984: 107-8.
15. *Administration Report*, 1872 Part I: 117.
16. IEVERS, R.W. *Manual*, op.cit.: 227-32; BURROWS, S.M. *The Buried Cities of Ceylon.* Colombo, Ferguson, 1905: 46.
17. CO 54/566.
18. IEVERS, R.W. *Abhayagiri and Mirisawetiya Dagabas* (SP LVI, 1890): 2; *Administration Report*, 1886: 14; IEVERS, R.W. *Manual*, op. cit.: 237.
19. *Ceylon Legislative Coluncil Debates during the Session 1886 to 1887*: 80-1.
20. CO 54/578.
21. CEYLON LEGISLATIVE COUNCIL. *Addresses delivered in the Legislative Council of Ceylon by the Governors of the Colony. Vol.III. 1877-1890*. Colombo, Skeen, 1900: 353.

6. Kegalla

Main Source
BELL, H.C.P. *Archaeological Survey of Ceylon. Report on the Kegalla District of the Province of Sabaragamuwa* (SP XIX, 1892). Colombo, Skeen, 1892.

Notes
1. SLNA 25/16/41.
2. SLNA 30. Kandy Archives. Diaries of Assistant Government Agents.
3. *Administration Report*, 1889 Part I: J 31.
4. CO 54/715.
5. *Kegalla Report*, Preface: v.
6. SLNA 25/16/202.
7. *Administration Report*, 1890 Part I: J 32.
8. *Kegalla Report*, Preface: v-vi.
9. Ibid.: 16.
10. Ibid.: 17.
11. Ibid.: 18.
12. Ibid.: 68.
13. Ibid.
14. SLNA 30. Kandy Archives. Diaries of Assistant Government Agents.
15. Ibid. (Price compares the treasure hunters with those in Sir Walter Scott's *The Antiquary*)
16. SIMPSON, W. 'Review of the Kegalla Report' JRIBA n.s. 9, 16 Feb.1893: 198-202.
17. 'Archaeological Survey of Ceylon : the Kegalla Distict' MLRC, 1/5, May 1893: 105-9.

7. The Anuradhapura Establishment

Main Sources
Ceylon Blue Book.
SLNA 25/16/202.
TOUSSAINT, J.R. *Annals of the Ceylon Civil Service*. Colombo, Colombo Apothecaries Co., 1935.

Notes
1. SLNA 25/16/202.
2. Ibid.
3. SLNA PF/661.
4. *Administration Report*, 1891 Part I: H 9.
5. BELL, Z. *Memoir*. Unpublished.
6. SLNA 6/13432 B; SLNA 6/13255 D.
7. CO 54/716.
8. BELL, H.C.P. 'Dimbulagala : its caves, ruins and inscriptions' CALR, 3/1, 1917: 4, note 7.
9. CO 54/716.
10. ASCAR, 1893: 13.
11. *Report of a Committee Appointed to Consider and Report upon... the Archaeological Survey of Ceylon* (SP I, 1899): 2.
12. ASCAR, 1899: 9.
13. BELL, H.C.P. *Summary of Operations 1890-1900* (SP XLVI, 1904): 1.
14. SLNA 25/16/202.
15. Annual Report 1891, JRASCB, 12(43), 1892: 159.
16. FERGUSON, J. *Ceylon in 1893*. London, Haddon; Colombo, Ferguson, 1893: 346-51.
17. FERGUSON, J. *Ceylon in 1896 with its New Governor H.E. Sir West Ridgeway, K.C.B.* (Reprinted from *The Ceylon Observer*). Colombo, Observer Printing Works, 1896: 28.
18. TOUSSAINT, J.R., op.cit.: 167-8.
19. Ibid.: 157; NEVILL, H. CLR, 2, 1888: 294; 5, 1891: 356-7, 364-5, 389; BELL, H.C.P. 'Anuradhapura - identification of ruins' CLR, 5, 1891: 373.
20. *Administration Report*, 1872 Part I: 122.
21. TOUSSAINT, J.R., op.cit.: 155-6.
22. LECLERCQ, J. *Un séjour dans l'île de Ceylan*. Paris, 1900: 148-52. (Translation by H.Bell)
23. *The Times of Ceylon*, Christmas Number, 1917: 67.

8. From Exploration to Excavation

Main Sources
BELL, H.C.P. *First and Second Reports on the Archaeological Survey of Anuradhapura* (SP XLIV and SP L, 1890).
BELL, H.C.P. *Third, Fourth, Fifth, Sixth and Seventh Progress Reports on the Archaeological Survey of Anuradhapura* (SP XXXV, 1891; SP XVI, 1892; SP X, 1893; SP XII, 1896; SP XII, 1896).
BELL, H.C.P. *Summary of Operations 1890-1900* (SP XLVI, 1904). (Includes an Index for the *Annual Reports* 1890-1900)

Notes
1. *Kegalla Report*, Preface: v.
2. SLNA 25/16/202.
3. ASCAR, l890: 1.
4. *First Report on...Anuradhapura,* op.cit.: Frontispiece.
5. ASCAR, 1895: 1.
6. *First Report*: 1.
7. STILL, J. *The Jungle Tide*. Edinburgh and London, Blackwood, 1930: 104-8.
8. *Sixth Progress Report*: 1.
9. *Seventh Progress Report*: 14.
10. *Third Progress Report*: 9.
11. *Fourth Progress Report*: 14.
12. SLNA 25/16/202.
13. BELL, H.C.P. *Summary of Operations 1890-1900*: 2.
14. WICKREMASINGHE, D.M.de Z. 'On the progress of archaeological research in Ceylon' *Verhandlungen des XIII Internationalen Orientalisten-Kongresses, Hamburg, Sept. 1902*. Leiden, Brill, 1904. Sektion II A, Indien: 75.
15. ASCAR, 1891: 4.
16. *Fourth Progress Report*: 4-5.
17. *Seventh Progress Report*: 4.
18. SLNA 25/16/202.
19. *Second Report*: 3-4.
20. Proceedings JRASCB, 12(42), 1891: 30-1; JRASCB, 13(44), 1893: 12-7.

21. Proceedings JRASCB, 15(49), 1898: 147-50; 'Archaeology' JRASCB, 15(49), 1898: 140.
22. ASCAR, 1891: 4.
23. *Sixth Progress Report*: 12.
24. Ibid.: 7-8.
25. Ibid.: 16-7.
26. *Fifth Progress Report*: 4.
27. MLRC, 2/1, Jan. 1894: 19.
28. *Sixth Progress Report*: 9.
29. ASCAR, 1911-12: 80. (Plates LVII and LVIII are photographs of the restored figure)
30. *Seventh Progress Report*: 6-7.
31. Ibid.: 7.
32. BELL, H.C.P. *Summary of Operations 1890-1900*: 2.

13. ASCAR, 1895: 7.
14. Ibid.: 8.
15. ASCAR, 1893: 7; ASCAR, 1890: 7; ASCAR, 1895: 8.
16. ASCAR, 1905: 20.
17. ASCAR, 1897: 8; ASCAR, 1892: 6-7.
18. ASCAR, 1893: 9,8.
19. ASCAR, 1895: 12-3.
20. Ibid.: 6-7.
21. ASCAR, 1910-11: 47.
22. ASCAR, 1896: 7.
23. ASCAR, 1897: 6-7.
24. Ibid.: 11.
25. BELL, H.C.P. 'The "Gal Aliya" or "Rock Elephant" at Katupilana, Tamankaduwa' CALR, 3/2, 1917: 144-7.

9. Jungle Trails

Main Source
BELL, H.C.P. *Archaeological Survey of Ceylon. Anuradhapura and the North-Central Province. Seventh Progress Report October to December 1891*, Appendix B.

Notes
1. BELL, H.C.P. *Summary of Operations 1890-1900* : 3.
2. 'The Archaeological Survey of Ceylon (Seventh Progress Report)' MLRC, 4/11, Nov. 1896: 244.
3. *Seventh Progress Report*: 28.
4. Ibid.: 22.
5. Ibid.: 23.
6. Ibid.: 18.
7. Ibid.: 15.
8. Ibid.: 18.
9. LECLERCQ, J. *Un séjour dans l'île de Ceylan*. Paris, 1900: 116-23.
10. WICKRAMASURIYA, A.T.G.A. 'Are the toils of the archaeological pioneers forgotten?' *The Island,* Jan. 23, 1987: 7.
11. ASCAR, 1896: 6.
12. *Fourth Progress Report*: 7,6,9-10.

10. Jungle Dwellers

Main Sources
BELL, H.C.P. 'Archaeological research in the Egoda Pattuwa, Tamankaduwa' CALR, 3/3, 1918: 196-8.
STILL, J. *The Jungle Tide*. Edinburgh and London, Blackwood, 1930.

Notes
1. BELL, H.C.P. 'The "Ahigunthikayo" or Ceylon gypsies' CALR, 2/2, 1916: 111.
2. *Seventh Progress Report*: 28.
3. BELL, H.C.P. 'Egoda Pattuwa', op. cit.: 196.
4. Ibid.: 198.
5. BELL, H.C.P. 'Memorandum on the boundaries of Tamankaduva, July 28/30, 1903', BROHIER, R.L. *Land, Maps and Surveys : a Review of the Evidence of Land Surveys as Practised in Ceylon from Earliest known Periods and the Story of the Ceylon Survey Department from 1800 to 1950*. Colombo, Government Printing Press, 1950. Vol.I. Appendix I: 115-7; ASCAR, 1905: 19, 22-3.
6. BELL, H.C.P. 'Egoda Pattuwa', op. cit.: 197.

7. STILL, J., op. cit.: 216-8.
8. Ibid.: 132.
9. BELL, H.C.P. 'Egoda Pattuwa', op. cit.: 196, 198.
10. Ibid.: 197.
11. BELL, H.C.P. 'Bear shooting in Ceylon' *Times of Ceylon*, Christmas Number, 1917: 24-7, 76.
12. WALTERS, A. *Palms and Peaks, or Scenes in Ceylon*. London, Richard Bentley, 1892: 77.
13. CUMMING, C.F.Gordon. *Two Happy Years in Ceylon*; illustrated by the author. 2 vols. Edinburgh and London, Blackwood, 1892. Vol.I: 112.
14. MITTON, G.E. *The Lost Cities of Ceylon*. London, Murray, 1916: 48.
15. STILL, J., op. cit.: 111.
16. ASCAR, 1896: 6.

11. Sigiriya : The Ascents

Main Sources
BELL, H.C.P. 'Interim report on the operations of the Archaeological Survey at Sigiriya in 1895' JRASCB, 14(46), 1895: 44-56. Discussion: 56-8.
BELL, H.C.P. 'Interim report on the operations of the Archaeological Survey at Sigiriya (Second Season), 1896' JRASCB, 14(47), 1896: 242-60. Discussion: 260.
BELL, H.C.P. 'Interim report on the operations of the Archaeological Survey at Sigiriya, 1897' JRASCB, 15(48), 1897: 93-122. Discussion: 122-5.

Notes
1. *Interim Report*, 1897: 106-7.
2. ASCAR, 1905: 7-8.
3. FORBES, J. *Eleven Years in Ceylon.* 2 vols. London, Bentley, 1840; RHYS DAVIDS, T.W. 'Sigiri, the Lion Rock near Palastipura, Ceylon' JRAS n.s. 7, 1875: 191-220; BLAKESLEY, T.H. 'On the ruins of Sigiri in Ceylon' JRAS n.s. 8, 1876: 53-62; *Interim Report*, 1895: 57.

4. ASCAR, 1894: 8, note. (Bell is probably incorrect in his spelling of Bayley. See Wijeyekoon's account below)
5. MLRC, 2/6, June 1894: 144.
6. WIJEYEKOON, G. 'Ascent of Sigiri' MLRC, 3/9, Sept. 1895: 216.
7. RENTON, A.V. 'Ascent of Sigiri' CLR, 4, 1889: 38.
8. *Interim Report,* 1896: 247-9.
9. MURRAY, A. 'Rock paintings of Sigiriya' CLR, 6, 1891: 85-6.
10. ASCAR, 1905: 17-8, notes.
11. Editorial note. 'Sigiriya' MLRC, 3/9, Sept. 1895: 217.
12. *Interim Report,* 1895: 46.
13. *Interim Report,* 1896: 244.
14. *Interim Report,* 1897: 97.
15. *Interim Report*, 1895: 47.
16. *Interim Report*, 1896: 245.
17. *Interim Report*, 1897: 97.
18. Ibid.: 108.
19. *Interim Report*, 1896: 242-3.

12. Sigiriya : Glories Revealed

Main Sources
BELL, H.C.P. 'Interim report on the operations of the Archaeological Survey at Sigiriya in 1895' JRASCB, 14(46), 1895: 44-56. Discussion: 56-8.
BELL, H.C.P. 'Interim report on the operations of the Archaeological Survey at Sigiriya (Second Season), 1896' JRASCB, 14(47), 1896: 242-60. Discussion: 260.
BELL, H.C.P. 'Interim report on the operations of the Archaeological Survey at Sigiriya, 1897' JRASCB, 15(48), 1897: 93-122. Discussion: 122-5.

Notes
1. ASCAR, 1898: 6.
2. *Interim Report*, 1895: 50.
3. *Interim Report*, 1896: 250-1.
4. Ibid.: 252-3.

5. *Interim Report*, 1897: 101-2.
6. ASCAR, 1898: 9.
7. ASCAR, 1905: 7.
8. ASCAR, 1948: I 19.
9. Ibid.
10. ASCAR, 1905: 12.
11. Ibid.: 14, note.
12. Ibid.: 14.
13. *Interim Report*, 1896: 257.
14. Ibid.: 258.
15. ASCAR, 1905: 19.
16. Further restoration work has been undertaken by the Archaeological Survey and is briefly reported in DE SILVA, R.H. 'Rock painting in Sri Lanka' *Conservation in Archaeology and the Applied Arts* (Preprints of the contributions to the Stockholm Congress, 2-6 June, 1975). London, The International Institute for Conservation of Historic and Artistic Works, 1975: 69-73. See also: ULLAH, Mohammad Sana, Khan Bahadur. *Report on the Treatment of the Sigiriya Frescoes and Suggestions for the Preservation of Paintings in the Various Shrines and Monuments in Ceylon* (SP XXI, 1943).
17. DE SILVA, R.H. 'The evolution of the technique of Sinhalese wall painting and comparison with Indian painting methods' *Ancient Ceylon*, I, 1971: 90-104. The article has a useful bibliography.
18. Bell is quoting from 'Ajanta caves' *Indian Antiquary*, 2, 1873: 153.
19. *Interim Report*, 1897: 114.
20. BELL, H.C.P. *Interim Report*, 1897: 93-122. Discussion: 122-5. Appendix 'Sigiriya frescoes' by C.M.Fernando: 127-8; Reply by H.C.P.Bell: 128-31. Appendix reprinted in *The Buddhist*, n.s. 1(46), 1898: 2-3; BELL, H.C.P. 'Letter in reply to one from C.M.Fernando in the *Ceylon Standard*, 20 Jan., 1898', TA (LR Suppl), 17 April, 1898: 2-3.
21. UNESCO. *Ceylon Paintings from Temple, Shrine and Rock* (Unesco World Art Series 8, edited by P.Bellew and A. Schutz), Preface by W.G.Archer, Introduction by S. Paranavitana. Greenwich, Conn., published for Unesco by the New York Graphic Society, 1957: 13-14.
22. *Interim Report*, 1897: 119-20.
23. ASCAR, 1905: 16, note.
24. Ibid.: 17.
25. Ibid.: 53.
26. Ibid.: 54.
27. PARANAVITANA, S. *Sigiri Graffiti : Being Sinhalese Verses of the Eighth, Ninth and Tenth Centuries*. 2 vols. London, Published for the Government of Ceylon, London, Oxford University Press, 1956. Vol.I, Preface: iv.

13. Protection of the Heritage

Main Sources
HARISCHANDRA, W. *The Sacred City of Anuradhapura*. 2nd. edn. Colombo, The Author, 1908.
ROGERS, J.D. *Crime, Justice and Society in Colonial Sri Lanka* (London Studies in South Asia no. 5). London, Curzon Press, 1987.

Notes
1. SLNA 41/1301.
2. BELL, H.C.P. *Summary of Operations 1890-1900* (SP XLVI, 1904): 3.
3. ASCAR, 1903: 6; ASCAR, 1911-12: 76-7.
4. ASCAR, 1911-12: 91.
5. SLNA PF/942.
6. ASCAR, 1898: 10; SLNA 6/13347.
7. *An Ordinance relating to Treasure Trove* (Ordinance No. 17, 1887): 1.
8. JRASCB, 12(42), 1891, Proceedings 1890: 26-9.
9. *An Ordinance to amend the Law relating to Treasure Trove* (Ordinance No. 3, 1891).
10. *Sixth Progress Report*, Appendix C: 17.
11. *An Ordinance for the Better Preservation of the Antiquities of the Island* (Ordinance No. 15, 1900): 1.
12. ASCAR, 1909: 26.
13. ASCAR, 1910-11: 64.
14. ASCAR, 1911-12: 76.

15. ASCAR, 1909: 24.
16. HARISCHANDRA, W., op. cit.: passim; DEP, A.C. *The History of the Ceylon Police. Vol.II. 1866-1913.* Colombo, Asoka Trading Co. 1969: 396-7.
17. 'A BUDDHIST' 'Vandalism by the Archaeological Commissioner' *The Buddhist*, 7(19), 30 May, 1895: 151-2.
18. *Ceylon Legislative Council Debates*, October 23, 1901: 8-9.
19. WICKREMERATNE, L.A. 'The rulers and the ruled in British Ceylon : a study of the function of petitions in colonial government' *Modern Ceylon Studies*, I/2, 1970: 228-32; SLNA 41/497, Petition no. 1007, 1895.
20. Ibid., Petition no. 109, 1901.
21. ASCAR, 1910-11: 64.
22. Ibid.: 46.
23. SLNA 41/1305.
24. PARANAVITANA, S. *Glimpses of Ceylon's Past*. Colombo, Lake House Investments Ltd., 1972: 1-2.
25. SLNA 6/13660 D.

14. Restoration : the Great Dagabas

Main Sources
HARRIS, G. *Restoration of the Abhayagiriya and Mirisawetiya Dagabas* (SP VIII, 1900).
OERTEL, F.O. *Report on the Restoration of Ancient Monuments at Anuradhapura, Ceylon* (SP XX, 1903).
RIDGEWAY, Sir J.West. *Administration of the Affairs of Ceylon, 1891-1903: a Review*. Colombo, Skeen, 1903.

Notes
1. SLNA 41/1309 A; ASCAR, 1910-11: 63-4.
2. SLNA PF/164.
3. CO 54/647.
4. Ibid.
5. *Stanmore Papers* (Add. Mss. Brit. Mus.): 49, 207.

6. HARRIS, G., op. cit.: 1-2.
7. OERTEL, F.O., op. cit.: 4.
8. Ibid.: 6-7.
9. *Ceylon Legislative Council Debates*, Nov. 25, 1903: 15-8.
10. RIDGEWAY, Sir J. West, op. cit.: 121.
11. *Ceylon Legislative Council Debates*, Dec. 6, 1904: 21.
12. ASCAR, 1910-11: 63.
13. OERTEL, F.O., op.cit.: 9.
14. RIDGEWAY, Sir J.West, op. cit.: 120-1; 'Archaeological Survey' *Ceylon Manual 1912-13*; edited by E.B.F.Sueter. Colombo, Ferguson, 1914: 232.
15. OERTEL, F.O., op. cit.: 7-8.
16. ASCAR, 1910-11: 10-6.
17. SLNA 6/13347; ASCAR, 1910-11, Appendix B: 67-8.
18. ASCAR, 1911-12: 42-3; Private information.

15. Delay : Reasons and Remedies

Main Source
Ceylon Civil List.

Notes
1. SLNA 25/16/202.
2. SIMPSON, W. 'Review of First and Second Reports of the Archaeological Survey of Anuradhapura, Ceylon, by H.C.P.Bell' JRIBA n.s. 7, Aug. 27, 1891: 421-3.
3. SIMPSON, W. 'Review of Third and Fourth Reports of the Archaeological Survey of Anuradhapura, Ceylon, by H.C.P.Bell' JRIBA n.s. 8, Sept. 29, 1892: 421-2.
4. SIMPSON, W. 'Ancient Ceylon Architecture' MLRC, 1/7, July 1893: 163.
5. SIMPSON, W. 'Review of Fifth Report of the Archaeological Survey of Anuradhapura, Ceylon, by H.C.P.Bell' JRIBA 3rd. series 1, 1894: 267-8; 'The Archaeological Survey of Ceylon (Sixth Progress Report)' MLRC, 4/9, Sept. 1896: 197-202.

6. SLNA 25/16/41; SLNA 25/16/202; *Administration Report*, 1896 Part I: H 2; *Administration Report*, 1908, Part I: G 1; SLNA PF/661.
7. SLNA 25/16/41; SLNA 25/16/202.
8. SLNA 25/16/202.
9. SLNA 25/16/202; ASCAR, 1898: 10.
10. SLNA PF/661.
11. BELL, H.C.P. 'Archaeology' JRASCB, 16(50): 9.
12. SLNA PF/661.
13. *Report of a Committee Appointed to Consider and Report upon ....the Archaeological Survey of Ceylon* (SP I,1899): 1-3.
14. SLNA 6/13347.
15. Ibid.
16. Ibid.
17. Ibid.
18. Ibid.
19. Ibid.
20. CO 54/683.
21. SLNA 6/13547 B; CO 54/687.
22. ASCAR, 1905: 25; STILL, J. *Index to the Mahavansa, Together with Chronological Table of Wars and Genealogical Trees*. Colombo, Cottle, 1907.
23. SLNA 6/13347; SLNA 6/13432 B.
24. SLNA 6/13347.
25. Ibid.; BELL, H.C.P. 'Archaeology' JRASCB, 19(57), 1906: 10.
26. ASCAR, 1905: 29, 30.
27. Ibid.: 37.
28. BELL, H.C.P. 'Archaeology' JRASCB, 19(58), 1907: 128.
29. JRASCB, 21(61), 1908: 55.
30. ASCAR, 1907: 1.
31. CO 54/715.
32. CO 54/716; CO 54/717; ASCAR, 1908: 15.
33. CO 54/716.
34. JRASCB, 21(61), 1908: 55-6.
35. ASCAR, 1911-12: 40, note, 91.

16. Anuradhapaura and Mihintale

Notes
1. 'Archaeology' JRASCB, 18(55), 1904: 148.
2. 'Archaeology' JRASCB, 19(58), 1906: 127.
3. 'Archaeology' JRASCB, 17(53), 1901: 77-8.
4. ASCAR, 1901: 6.
5. Ibid.: 9.
6. ASCAR, 1910-11: 3.
7. 'Archaeology' JRASCB, 19(58), 1906: 128-9.
8. ASCAR, 1907: 6.
9. ASCAR, 1911-12: 2.
10. Ibid.: 16-7.
11. ASCAR, 1910-11: 18.
12. Ibid.: 25-6.
13. ASCAR, 1911-12: 47.
14. ASCAR, 1912-13: 5.
15. HOCART, A.M. ed. *Memoirs of the Archaeological Survey of Ceylon*. Vol.I. Colombo, Government Printing Press, 1924: 18-47.

17. Outlying Sites

Notes
1. ASCAR, 1896: 7-8.
2. ASCAR, 1907: 34.
3. STILL, J. 'Tantri Malai : some archaeological observations and deductions' JRASCB, 22(63), 1910: 73-88. Appendix C 'Accounts of Tantri Malai' and Appendix D 'Additional archaeological notes' by H.C.P.BELL: 89-96, 97-101.
4. ASCAR, 1897: 7.
5. ASCAR, 1907: 30-2.
6. PARANAVITANA, S. 'An ancient sanctuary newly revealed : discoveries and reconstruction in the Ceylon jungle' *Illustrated London News*, June 19, 1948: 698-700.
7. SLNA PF/942.
8. 'Archaeology' JRASCB, 22(65), 1912: 256.
9. ASCAR, 1910-11: 42-50.
10. ASCAR, 1911-12: 60.

11. PREMATILLEKE, P.L. *Nalanda : a Short Guide to the 'Gedige' Shrine.* Colombo, Central Cultural Fund, Ministry of Cultural Affairs, 1985.
12. [BAILEY, J.] 'Yapahoo' *Once a Week*, 11, June to December 1864: 225-8, 281-4.
13. ASCAR, 1910-11: 58-9.
14. Ibid.: 72.
15. Ibid.: 73.
16. ASCAR, 1911-12: 92-3.
17. Ibid.: 61.
18. DARTON, I. 'One of the last of the Sinhalese capitals : the rock citadel and granite portals of the little-known Yapahuwa' *Illustrated London News*, Dec. 20, 1952: 1046-7; FERNANDO, W.B. Marcus. *Yapahuwa*. Colombo, Archaeological Department, 1969.

18. The Lithic Quest

Main Sources
DEVENDRA, D.T. 'Seventy years of Ceylon archaeology' *Artibus Asiae*, 22, 1959: 33-9.
Epigraphia Zeylanica. Vol.I. 1904-1912; edited by D.M.de Z.Wickremasinghe. London, published for the Government of Ceylon by the Oxford University Press, 1912.
GOONETILEKE, H.A.I. 'Writings on Ceylon epigraphy' *Ceylon Historical Journal*, X/1-4, July 1960 - April 1961: 170-207.
PARANAVITANA, S. *Inscriptions of Ceylon. Vol.I. Early Brahmi Inscriptions.* Ceylon, Department of Archaeology, 1970.

Notes
1. GOONETILEKE, H.A.I., op. cit.: 171.
2. PARANAVITANA, S., op. cit., Preface: ii.
3. DEVENDRA, D.T., op. cit.: 39.
4. GOONETILEKE, H.A.I., op. cit.: 171-207.
5. Ibid.: 171.
6. PARANAVITANA, S., op. cit., Preface: vi.
7. Ibid.: iv.
8. Ibid.: ii.
9. ASCAR, 1905: 45.
10. *Fourth Progress Report*: 6-7.
11. BURGESS, J. 'Letter' JRASCB, Proceedings 1884: xxx; PARANAVITANA, S., op.cit., Preface: iv.
12. ASCAR, 1894: 7; ASCAR, 1895: 9.
13. BELL, H.C.P. 'Archaeological research in the Egoda Pattuwa, Tamankaduwa' CALR, 3/3, 1918: 197.
14. *Seventh Progress Report:* 14.
15. DEVENDRA, D.T., op. cit.: 34.
16. PARANAVITANA, S., op. cit., Preface: xvii, xxii.
17. WICKREMASINGHE, D.M.de Z. 'The Semitic origin of the Indian Alphabet' JRAS, April 1901: 301-5; WICKREMASINGHE, D.M.de Z. 'The progress of archaeological research in Ceylon' *Verhandlungen des XIII Internationalen Orientalisten- Kongresses, Hamburg, Sept. 1902.* Leiden, Brill, 1904. Sektion II A, Indien: 76.
18. ASCAR, 1891: 8; *Second Progress Report*: 6.
19. ASCAR, 1905: 48.
20. ASCAR, 1911-12: 113-5, 109.
21. ASCAR, 1908, Appendix A and B: 15-6; ASCAR, 1909: 26-7.
22. ASCAR, 1911-12: 110-2.
23. BELL, H.C.P. *Summary of Operations 1890-1900* : 4; ASCAR, 1911-12: 72.
24. ASCAR, 1911-12: 93-105.
25. Ibid.: 106-9.
26. Ibid.: 109-23.
27. ASCAR, 1906: 25.
28. ASCAR, 1911-12: 72.
29. VIMALANANDA, T. 'H.C.P.Bell and archaeology in Ceylon 1890-1912' *Ceylon Historical Journal,* II/1-2, January - October 1952: 87.
30. PARANAVITANA, S., op. cit., Preface: i.
31. *Seventh Progress Report*: 60.
32. *Seventh Progress Report*, Appendix E: 63; NEVILL, H. 'The slab at Padaviya tank' MLRC, 2/2, Feb. 1894: 46-7; BELL, H.C.P. 'Inscribed pillar at Padaviya' MLRC, 2/4, April 1894: 75-8.
33. ASCAR, 1891: 11.

34. ASCAR, 1911-12: 93.
35. ASCAR, 1890: 9; ASCAR, 1894: 7.
36. ASCAR, 1893: 12.
37. GEIGER, W. 'The Archaeological Survey of Ceylon and its work' JRAS, 1898: 13-4. Reprinted in TA(LR Suppl), April 1898: 1-2.
38. ASCAR, 1899: 10.
39. ASCAR, 1906: 25.
40. ASCAR, 1911-12: 72.
41. ASCAR, 1904: 3.

19. Epigraphia Zeylanica

Main Sources

Epigraphia Zeylanica. Vol.I. 1904-1912; edited by D.M.de Z. Wickremasinghe. London, published for the Government of Ceylon by the Oxford University Press, 1912.
Epigraphia Zeylanica. Vol.IV. 1934-1941; edited by S.Paranavitana. London, published for the Government of Ceylon by the Oxford University Press, 1943.
WIJEYEKOON, A.C.G. *Recollections*. Colombo, Associated Newspapers, 1951: 22-3.

Notes
1. WIJEYEKOON, A.C.G., op. cit.: 23.
2. *Report of a Committee Appointed to Consider and Report upon.. the Archaeological Survey of Ceylon* (SP I, 1899): 2.
3. EZ Vol.IV, Preface: iii.
4. WICKREMASINGHE, D.M. de Z. 'On the progress of archaeological research in Ceylon' *Verhandlungen des XIII Internationalen Orientalisten-Kongresses, Hamburg, Sept. 1902*. Leiden, Brill, 1904. Sektion II A, Indien: 75-6.
5. CO 54/696; CO 54/715.
6. CO 54/698.
7. CO 54/715.
8. Ibid.
9. CO 54/708.
10. CO 54/715.
11. Ibid.
12. Ibid.
13. Ibid.
14. CO 54/710.
15. Ibid.
16. *Dictionary of National Biography, 1941-50*. Oxford, Oxford University Press, 1959: 443-5; CO 54/712; CO 54/713.
17. SLNA PF/2229.
18. CO 54/719.
19. CO 54/724; CO 54/731.
20. WICKREMASINGHE, D.M.de Z. 'The antiquity of stone architecture in India and Ceylon' JRASCB, 21(62), 1909: 327-38.
21. CO 54/749; CO 54/743.
22. CO 54/745; MULLER, E. *'Epigraphia Zeylanica,* being lithic and other inscriptions of Ceylon, edited and translated by Don Martino de Zilva Wickremasinghe, Vol.I. Part V, London, 1911' JRAS, 1912: 514-7.
23. CO 54/753; CO 54/759.
24. CO 54/772; CO 54/779.
25. CO 54/791; CO 54/792; CO 54/795.
26. CO 54/828.

20. Monks and Monarchs

Main Sources

Epigraphia Zeylanica. Vol.I. 1904-1912; edited by D.M.de Z.Wickremasinghe. London, published for the Government of Ceylon by the Oxford University Press, 1912.
Epigraphia Zeylanica. Vol.II. 1912-1927; edited by D.M.de Z.Wickremasinghe. London, published for the the Government of Ceylon by the Oxford University Press, 1928.
Epigraphia Zeylanica. Vol.III. 1928-1933; edited by S.Paranavitana. London, published for the Government of Ceylon by the Oxford University Press, 1933.
Epigraphia Zeylanica. Vol.IV. 1934-1941; edited by S.Paranavitana. London, published for the Government of Ceylon by the Oxford University Press, 1943.

Notes
1. GOONETILEKE, H.A.I. 'Writings on Ceylon epigraphy' *Ceylon Historical Journal*, X/1-4, July 1960-April 1961: 171.
2. EZ Vol.I: 3-4, 6-9.
3. Ibid.: 99.
4. BELL, H.C.P. *Summary of Operations 1890-1900*: 4.
5. ASCAR, 1893: 9.
6. EZ Vol.I: 135-53, 210-7.
7. *Seventh Progress Report*: 51-2.
8. ASCAR, 1911-12, Appendix C: 99; ASCAR, 1906: 16.
9. ASCAR, 1905: 38.
10. ASCAR, 1903: 16.
11. EZ Vol.I: 126.
12. ASCAR, 1903: 7.
13. ASCAR, 1911-12: 105.
14. ASCAR, 1897: 9.
15. ASCAR, 1909: 26-7. (On these pages Bell partly followed the *Mahawansa* in indicating the sequence of rulers and their relationships. Vijaya Bahu I was succeeded by his brother, Jaya Bahu, who perhaps reigned for only one year. Then followed Vijaya Bahu I's son, Vikrama Bahu I (1121-1142). Sundari, his Queen, was mother of Gaja Bahu II, who then succeeded.)
16. WICKREMASINGHE, D.M.de Z. 'Dimbula-gala : Mara-Vidiye rock-inscription' EZ Vol.II: 184-9.
17. BELL, H.C.P. 'Dimbula-gala : its caves, ruins and inscriptions. Part I' CALR, 3/1, 1917, Appendix: 8-12.
18. CO 54/828.
19. Ibid.
20. CO 54/818.
21. CO 54/821.
22. WICKREMASINGHE, D.M.de Z. 'Dimbula-gala : Mara-Vidiye rock-inscription' EZ Vol.II: 194-202.
23. BELL, H.C.P. 'Dimbulagala : Maravidiye cave inscription' CALR, 10/1, 1924: 1-14.
24. BELL, H.C.P. 'Critical notes on the "Epigraphia Zeylanica No.9. Polonnaruwa inscriptions"' CALR, 5/1, 1919: 20-30.
25. CO 54/850.
26. ASCAR, 1920-21: 8; CO 54/878.
27. *Cambridge History of India*. Vol.III. Cambridge, Cambridge University Press, 1928; EZ Vol.II, Preface.
28. EZ Vol.III, Preface: v.
29. WIJEYEKOON, A.C.G. *Recollections*. Colombo, Associated Newspapers, 1951: 22-3; KARUNARATNE, W.S. 'Archaeology in Ceylon. No.II. The history of epigraphical research' *Ceylon Today*, IV/11, Nov. 1955: 13.
30. ASCAR, 1937: J 3.
31. EZ Vol.IV, Preface: iii.
32. Annual Report JRASCB, 34(90), 1937: 3-4.
33. DEVENDRA, D.T. 'H.C.P.Bell, C.C.S. (1851-1937)' JRASCB n.s. 8(1), 1962: 163.

21. Bell and his Family

Main Sources
Ceylon Civil List.
Family Letters.
General Directory of Addresses. Colombo, Ferguson, 1892-

Notes
1. CO 54/730.
2. HOWARD, E. *Potsdam Princes*. New York, Dutton, 1915; London, Methuen, 1916.
3. CO 54/730.
4. HOWARD, E. *Japanese Memories*. London, Hutchinson, 1918.
5. BELL, Z. *Memoir*. Unpublished.
6. *The Coronation Celebrations in Ceylon, 1911* (Illustrations supplied by F.Skeen & Co.). Colombo, "Times of Ceylon", 1911: 29.
7. STILL, J. *The Jungle Tide*. Edinburgh and London, Blackwood, 1930: 195.
8. BELL, D. *Autobiography*. Unpublished.

22. Polonnaruwa : Promontory, Quadrangle and Citadel

Notes
1. ASCAR, 1893: 11.
2. Ibid.
3. 'Archaeological Survey' *Ceylon Manual 1912-13*; edited by E.B.F.Sueter. Colombo, Ferguson, 1914: 231.
4. 'Archaeology' JRASCB, 17(52), 1901: 7.
5. ASCAR, 1901: 13.
6. ASCAR, 1909: 16.
7. ASCAR, 1903: 6-7.
8. ASCAR, 1910-11: 39.
9. ASCAR, 1903: 16.
10. Ibid.
11. ASCAR, 1903: 13-4.
12. ASCAR, 1904: 5.
13. 'Archaeology' JRASCB, 18(56), 1905: 341-2.
14. ASCAR, 1903: 23-4.
15. 'Archaeology' JRASCB, 19(58), 1907: 133-4.
16. ASCAR, 1904: 5-6; ASCAR, 1906: 23; ASCAR, 1907: 24; ASCAR, 1909: 19; ASCAR, 1911-12: 57.
17. ASCAR, 1910-11: 38-9; ASCAR, 1911-12: 58.
18. 'Archaeology' JRASCB, 19(57), 1906: 8-9.
19. ASCAR, 1905: 4-6.
20. ASCAR, 1911-12: 50-6.

23. Polonnaruwa : Hindu and Buddhist Shrines

Notes
1. 'Archaeology' JRASCB, 19(57), 1906: 7.
2. ASCAR, 1911-12: 89.
3. ASCAR, 1910-11: 29, note.
4. ASCAR, 1911-12: 89.
5. Ibid.: 90.
6. 'Archaeology' JRASCB, 22(63), 1910: 53-4.
7. ASCAR, 1910-11: 69.
8. Ibid.: 70.
9. ASCAR, 1906: 11.
10. ASCAR, 1908: 10-1.
11. ASCAR, 1910-11: 40.
12. ASCAR, 1907: 23.
13. Ibid.: 26.
14. Ibid.: 36-7.
15. COOMERASWAMY, A.K. 'Indian bronzes' *Burlington Magazine*, 19, 1910: 86-94; 'Ancient bronzes in the Colombo Museum : with descriptions of some of the Polonnaruwa bronzes by the Hon. Mr. P.Arunchalam, Registrar General : and remarks on inscriptions by D.M.de Z. Wickremasinghe, Government Epigraphist' *Spolia Zeylanica*, 6(22), Sept. 1909: 57-74; GODAKUMBURA, C.E. *Polonnaruwa Bronzes* (Art Series 5). Colombo, Archaeological Department, 1964.
16. ASCAR, 1907: 7.
17. 'Archaeology' JRASCB, 21(61), 1908: 49.
18. ASCAR, 1907: 7.
19. Ibid.: 13.
20. Ibid.: 12.
21. Ibid.: 34-5.
22. ASCAR, 1910-11: 40.

24. Polonnaruwa : the Brick 'Image Houses'

Notes
1. ASCAR, 1903: 28.
2. ASCAR, 1909: 16.
3. Ibid.: 12.
4. Ibid.: 11.
5. 'Archaeology' JRASCB, 22(63), 1910: 50-1.
6. ASCAR, 1909: Plates XXV - XXVII, LXXI (photographs), Plates A - M (line drawings).
7. ASCAR, 1910-11: 31.
8. Ibid.: 30-7, 40; ASCAR, 1911-12: 58-9, 90.
9. 'Archaeology' JRASCB, 18(56), 1905: 340.
10. ASCAR, 1904: 9-10.
11. ASCAR, 1905: 5-6.

12. ASCAR, 1906: 22-3; ASCAR, 1907: 24; ASCAR, 1908: 11; ASCAR, 1909: 19; ASCAR, 1910-11: 38.
13. ASCAR, 1911-12: 57.
14. SLNA PF/2835; SLNA 25/16/205.
15. SLNA PF/2835.
16. ASCAR, 1920-21: 6.
17. ASCAR, 1936: J 6.
18. ASCAR, 1937: J 5.

25. Successors

Notes
1. SLNA PF/2277.
2. CO 54/718.
3. LEVINE, P. *The Amateur and the Professional: Antiquarians, Historians and Archaeologists in Victorian England, 1838-1886.* Cambridge, Cambridge University Press, 1986.
4. CO 54/725.
5. CO 54/718.
6. CO 54/723.
7. CO 54/730.
8. CO 54/726.
9. SLNA PF/2277.
10. CO 54/725.
11. CO 54/726.
12. CO 54/725.
13. CO 54/731.
14. CO 54/728.
15. HALL, H.R. 'Edward Ayrton' *Journal of Egyptian Archaeology*, 2, 1915: 23.
16. ASCAR, 1920-21: 3.
17. SLNA 25/16/299; CO 54/779.
18. ASCAR, 1911-12: 91, note.
19. CO 54/774; CO 54/776; CO 54/779.
20. CO 54/821.
21. GIBSON, A. *Cinnamon and Frangipani.* London and Sydney, Chapman and Dodd, 1923: 126-7.
22. CO 54/723.
23. NANYAKKARA, V. *A Return to Kandy: Over Balena and Beyond.* Colombo, The Author, 1971: 120-1.
24. WICKRAMASURIYA, A.T.G.A. 'Are the toils of the archaeological pioneers forgotten?' *The Island,* Jan. 23, 1987: 7.
25. Private letter.

26. Active Retirement

Notes
1. CO 54/821.
2. SLNA PF/2229 A; KRISHNA SASTRI, H. ed. *South Indian Inscriptions (Texts). Vol.4. Miscellaneous Inscriptions from the Tamil, Telugu and Kannadu Countries and Ceylon* (Archaeological Survey of India, New Imperial Series 44). Madras, Government Press, 1923: 489-96.
3. BELL, H.C.P. *Report on Talpata No. 2,932* (D.C.Karunegala: Case No. 8,199). (Photocopy supplied by P. Jayasuriya)
4. BELL, H.C.P. 'Maha Saman Devale and its Sannasa' CALR, 2/1: 46.
5. BELL, H.C.P. 'Prince Taniyavalla Bahu of Madampe' JRASCB, 28(73):48-53.
6. Private letter.
7. JOSEPH, G.A. 'The Gal-Vihare and Demala-Maha-Seya paintings at Polonnaruwa' JRASCB, 26(71), 1918: 101-6; BELL, H.C.P. 'The "Demala-Maha-Seya" frescoes' Ibid.: 106-8.
8. BELL, H.C.P. '"Demala-Maha-Seya" paintings' JRASCB, 26(71), Notes and Queries, 1918: 199-201.
9. ASCAR, 1920-1: 7; ASCAR, 1921-2: 7.
10. GODAKUMBURA, C.F. *Murals at Tivanka Pilimage* (Art Series 7).Colombo, Archaeological Department, 1969; DE SILVA, R.H. 'Rock painting in Sri Lanka' *Conservation in Archaeology and the Applied Arts* (Preprints of the contributions to the Stockholm Congress, 2-6 June, 1975). London, The International Institute for Conservation of Historic and Artistic Works, 1975: 69-71.

11. DE SILVA, R.H. 'In defence of H.C.P.Bell' *Ceylon News*, Jan. 29, 1976.
12. PIERIS, P.E. 'The date of King Bhuwaneka Bahu VII' JRASCB, 22(65), 1912: 267-302. Appendices: A by A.E.Buultjens, 280-2; B by Simon de Silva, 282-3; C by H.C.P.Bell, 283-95; D by W.F.Gunawardhana, 295-7; E by P.E.Pieris, 297-8; F by W.F.Gunawardhana, 299-311; G by P.E.Pieris, 301-2; H by W.F.Gunawardhana, 302.
13. PERERA, S.G. 'The "Conquista de Ceylao" by Fernao de Queyroz, S.J.' CALR, 2/3, 1917: 158-66.
14. DE SILVA, S., Gate Mudaliyar. 'Vijaya Bahu VI' JRASCB, 22(65), 1912: 316-81. Appendices: A by C.E.Corea, 332-6; B by A.M.Gunasekera, 336-7; C by W.F.Gunawardhana, 338-40; D by H.C.P.Bell, 340-66; E by Simon de Silva, 367-72; F by E.W.Perera, 372-81.
15. BELL, H.C.P. and GUNASEKERA, A.M. 'Kelani Vihare and its inscriptions' CALR, 1/3, 1916: 145-61; DE SILVA, S. 'The inscription at Kit-Siri-Mevan Kelani Vihara' CALR, 2/3, 1917: 149-55.
16. BELL, H.C.P. 'Kit-Siri-Mewan Vihare inscription : rejoinder to paper of Simon de Silva' CALR, 2/3, 1917: 182-90; DE SILVA, S.'The inscription at Kitsirimewan Kelani Vihara. I' CALR, 3/2, 1917: 101-5; GUNAWARDHANA, W.F., Mudaliyar. 'The inscription at Kitsirimewan Kelani Vihara. II' CALR, 3/2, 1917: 105-9.
17. BELL, H.C.P. 'Galapata Vihare inscription' JRASCB (N & Q), Pt.4, No. 29, 1914: lxix-lxxvii; PARANAVITANA, S. 'Galapata Vihare' EZ, Vol.4, 1943: 196-211.
18. CO 54/821.
19. BELL, H.C.P. 'Kirtti Nissanka and the "Tula-bhara" ceremony' CALR, 1/2, 1915: 83-8.
20. BELL, H.C.P. 'Maha Saman Devale and its Sannasa' CALR, 2/1, 1916: 39-41.
21. BELL, H.C.P. 'Andreas Amabert : 1764' CALR, 1/4, 1916: 243-54.
22. BELL, H.C.P. 'Some ancient ruins in Uva' CALR, 1/4, 1916: 278-81.
23. BELL, H.C.P. 'Inscribed pillar at Anuradhapura' CALR, 4/2, 1918: 102-8.
24. BELL, H.C.P. 'Inscribed pillar slab at Nuwara Eliya' JRASCB, 26(71), Notes and Queries, 1918: 61-4.
25. BELL, H.C.P. ed. 'The Maldive Islands : 1602-1607' CALR, 1/2 - 4/2, 1915-1918.

27. The Maldives : Return

Main Source
BELL, H.C.P. *The Maldive Islands: Report on a Visit to Male, January 20 to February 21, 1920* (SP XV, 1921). Colombo, Government Printer, 1921. (This includes extracts from his Diary of 1920)

Notes
1. [BELL, H.C.P. ed.] *Papers Relating to the Maldive Islands, 1887-1910*. 3 parts in one volume. Colombo, Secretariat, 1910: 52.
2. Ibid.: 21-30.
3. BELL, H.C.P. *The Maldive Islands : Monograph on the History, Archaeology and Epigraphy*. Colombo, Government Printing Press, 1940: 65, note.
4. CO 54/668.
5. BELL, H.C.P. *The Maldive Islands*. Colombo, Government Printing Press, 1940: 54.
6. Ibid.: 65.
7. SLNA 25/16/205.
8. ROBINS, L. *English Lady's Visit to the Maldives*; revised by H.C.P.Bell. Colombo, 'Ceylon Observer' Press, 1920: 9-10.
9. BELL, H.C.P. 'Excerpta Maldiviana. No.6. Graves of Captain Overend and Private Luckham at the Maldives' JRASCB, 30(80), 1927: 439.
10. Ibid.: 445.
11. ROBINS, L., op. cit.: 18-20.

28. The Maldives : Dream Fulfilled

Main Source
BELL, H.C.P. *The Maldive Islands: Monograph on the History, Archaeology and Epigraphy.* Colombo, Government Printing Press, 1940. (This includes extracts from his Diary of 1922)

Notes
1. ASCAR, 1921-2: 3.
2. SLNA 25/16/205.
3. Ibid.
4. BELL, H.C.P. 'Excerpta Maldiviana. No. 7. "Lonu Ziyarat", Male' JRASCB, 31(81), 1928: 185.
5. Ibid.: 186-9.
6. Ibid.: 189-91, 195.
7. SLNA 25/16/205.
8. Ibid.
9. HOCKLY, T.W. *The Two Thousand Isles.* London, Witherby, 1935: 120-1, 134-5.
10. SLNA 25/16/205.
11. Ibid.

29. Maldive Studies : Anthropology, History and Archaeology

Main Source
BELL, H.C.P. *The Maldive Islands : Monograph on the History, Archaeology and Epigraphy.* Colombo, Ceylon Government Press, 1940.

Notes
1. SLNA 25/16.
2. BELL, H.C.P. 'Excerpta Maldiviana. No. 1. Maldivian Government permit' JRASCB, 29(75), 1922: 99-104.
3. BELL, H.C.P. 'Excerpta Maldiviana. No. 4. A description of the Maldive Islands circa A.C. 1683' JRASCB, 30(78), 1925: 132-42.
4. BELL, H.C.P. 'Excerpta Maldiviana. No. 2. Sultans' Missives : A.C. 1713, 1819' JRASCB, 29(76), 1923: 194-214.
5. BELL, H.C.P. 'Excerpta Maldiviana. No. 13. Some polyglot Missives of Sultan Ibrahim Iskandar II' JRASCB, 33(87), 1934: 47-90.
6. MALONEY, C. *People of the Maldive Islands*. Bombay, Orient Longman, 1980: 28.
7. BELL, H.C.P. 'Excerpta Maldiviana. No. 12. Maldivian proverbs' JRASCB, 32(86), 1933: 372-87.
8. TURNER, J.B. *Report on the Census of Ceylon, 1921*. Vol.I. Part 2. Colombo, Government Printer, 1924: 95, note. 'The leading living authority on the subject of the Maldives is Mr. H.C.P.Bell, C.C.S. (retired)... He was good enough to read this chapter in manuscript and to suggest several important amendments'.
9. BELL, H.C.P. 'Excerpta Maldiviana. No. 5. The Maldive Islands: physical traits and general characteristics' JRASCB, 30(79), 1926: 267, note 5.
10. Ibid.: 259.
11. HEYERDAHL, T. *The Maldive Mystery*. London, Allen & Unwin, 1986; MALONEY, C., op. cit.: 48-70.
12. [BELL, H.C.P. ed.] *Papers relating to the Maldive Islands, 1887-1910*. 3 parts in one volume. Colombo, Secretariat, 1910 : 16.
13. BELL, H.C.P. 'Excerpta Maldiviana. No. 10. The Portuguese at the Maldives' JRASCB, 32(84), 1931: 76-124; 'Excerpta Maldiviana. No. 11. Dutch intercourse with the Maldives: seventeenth century' JRASCB, 32(85), 1932: 226-42.
14. BELL, H.C.P. The Maldive Islands, op. cit.: 27.
15. BELL, H.C.P.'Excerpta Maldiviana. No. 10. The Portuguese at the Maldives' JRASCB. 32(84), 1931: 95-6.
16. YAJIMA, H. ed. *Hasan Taj-ul-Din's The Islamic History of the Maldive Islands, with supplementary chapters by Muhammad Muhibb al-Din and Ibrahim Siraj al-Din. Vol.I. Arabic Text. Vol.II. Annotations and Indices* (Studia Culturae Islamicae 16, 22). Tokyo, Institute for

the Study of Languages and Cultures of Asia and Africa, 1982, 1984. (The second volume contains an account of the authors of the *Tarikh*, a summary of its contents and an estimate of its importance. A third volume is projected, which will contain the text of some official letters which are bound up with one of the Ms. used)
17. YOUNG, I.A. and CHRISTOPHER, W. 'Memoir on the inhabitants of the Maldive Islands' *Transactions of the Bombay Geographical Society,* I, 1836-38: 54-86; CHRISTOPHER, W. 'Notes on customs prevalent among the Maldives' Ibid.: 313-4.
18. ROSSET, C.W. 'On the Maldive Islands, more especially treating of Male Atol' *Journal of the Anthropological Institute of Great Britain and Ireland,* 16, 1887: 171; GARDINER, J.S. 'The natives of the Maldives' *Proceedings of the Cambridge Philosophical Society,* 11, 1900: 20.
19. BELL, H.C.P. *The Maldive Islands,* op. cit.: 107-8.
20. Ibid.: 119-20.
21. Ibid.: 135.
22. Ibid.: 126-7.
23. Ibid.: 131.
24. Ibid.: 134.
25. Ibid.: 132-3.
26. Ibid.: 111.
27. Ibid.: 108.
28. SKJØLSVOLD, A. ed. *Archaeological Test-Excavations on the Maldive Islands* (The Kon-Tiki Museum Occasional Papers Vol.2). Oslo, Kon-Tiki Museum, 1991: 200, 67, 70.(On p.70 the reference to Bell's conclusion on the introduction of Buddhism to the Maldives is given as being on page 180 of his Monograph instead of on p.108)

30. Maldive Studies : Language and Epigraphy

Main Sources
BELL, H.C.P. *The Maldive Islands: an Account of the Physical Features, Climate, History, Inhabitants, Productions and Trade* (SP XLIII, 1881). Colombo, Frank Laker, 1883.
BELL, H.C.P. 'Excerpta Maldiviana. No. 3. "Dives Akuru" gravestone epitaphs' JRASCB, 29 (77), 1924.
BELL, H.C.P. 'Excerpta Maldiviana. No. 9. Lomafanu' JRASCB, 31 (83), 1930.
BELL, H.C.P. *The Maldive Islands: Monograph on the History, Archaeology and Epigraphy.* Colombo, Government Printing Press, 1940.
GEIGER, W. 'Maldivian linguistic studies; translated by Mrs J.C. Willis; edited by H.C.P.Bell.' JRASCB, 27,Extra Number, 1919.

Notes
1. BELL, H.C.P. *The Maldive Islands.* 1883: 21; GEIGER, W., op. cit.: 23.
2. *The Athenaeum*, No. 2975, Nov. 1, 1884: 555.
3. BELL, H.C.P. *The Maldive Islands.* 1883: 69.
4. GEIGER, W., op. cit.: 152; SLNA 25/16/299.
5. GEIGER, W., op. cit.: 20, 131-3; CHRISTOPHER, W. 'Vocabulary of the Maldivian language, communicated to the Bombay Branch of the Royal Asiatic Society by John Wilson' JRAS, 6, 1841: 42-76.
6. BELL, H.C.P. 'Excerpta Maldiviana. No. 3.', op. cit.: 288; GEIGER, W., op. cit.: 149-66.
7. BELL, H.C.P. 'Excerpta Maldiviana. No. 9.', op. cit.: 568-71.
8. BECHERT, H. *Wilhelm Geiger.* Colombo, Gunasera, 1977: 65; GEIGER, W., op. cit.: 61 note, 10.
9. GEIGER, W., op. cit.: 12-9, 127-98, 141-8; BELL, H.C.P. 'Excerpta Maldiviana. No. 3.', op. cit.: 298.

10. GEIGER, W., op. cit.: 12, 145.
11. Ibid.: 59.
12. Ibid.: 138-9, 145.
13. Ibid.: 125, 137.
14. BELL, H.C.P. *The Maldive Islands.* 1883: 68, note, 69, note; GRAY, A. ed. *The Voyage of François Pyrard*, Vol.II. Part 2. London, Hakluyt Society, 1890: 405-22.
15. FERGUSON, D. 'Notes and Queries : Cobily-Mash' *Indian Antiquary*, 8, Nov. 1879: 321; BELL, H.C.P. 'Cobily-Mash' Ibid., 11, Oct. 1882: 294.
16. BELL, H.C.P. *The Maldive Islands.* 1883: 69; GEIGER, W., op. cit.: 160, 164-6.
17. BELL, H.C.P. 'Excerpta Maldiviana. No. 3.', op. cit.: 283-6.
18. Ibid.: 289-90.
19. Ibid.: 289, 291, 292, 299, note 16.
20. Ibid.: 296-8; BELL, H.C.P. *The Maldive Islands.* 1940: 173-7.
21. BELL, H.C.P. 'Excerpta Maldiviana. No. 3.', op. cit.: 283.
22. Ibid.: 300.
23. BELL, H.C.P. *The Maldive Islands.* 1940 : 163, 168.
24. Ibid.: 166, 169.
25. Ibid.: 170-3.
26. Ibid.: 56.
27. Ibid.: 179-82.
28. BELL, H.C.P. 'Excerpta Maldiviana. No. 9.', op. cit.: 541, 549.
29. Ibid.: 541-5, 550-1.
30. Ibid.: 552-7.
31. Ibid.: 560-2, 567, note 6.
32. BELL, H.C.P. *The Maldive Islands.* 1940: 187-198.
33. CO 54/981/2.
34. CO 54/987/8.

31. The Old Man

Main Sources
Family Letters.
BELL, D. *Autobiography*. Unpublished.
BELL, H.C.P. and Maldive correspondents, 1928-31. SLNA 25/16/190.
BELL, H.C.P. and Government publisher, 1927-33. SLNA 25/16/206.
BELL, H.C.P. and Father Vossen, 1932-36. SLNA 25/16/316.
BELL, Z. *Memoir*. Unpublished.

Notes
1. SLNA 25/16/90.
2. BELL, H.C.P. 'Excerpta Maldiviana. No. 14. Maldivian taboo on free English education' JRASCB, 33(88), 1935: 173-9, 185, 187; 183-4; 170-2; 179-80; 191, notes 12 and 13.
3. SLNA 25/16/23.
4. SLNA 25/16/206.
5. Ibid.
6. Ibid.
7. Ibid.
8. BELL, H.C.P. 'Excerpta Maldiviana. No. 11. Dutch intercourse with the Maldives: seventeenth century' JRASCB, 32(85), 1932: 226.
9. SLNA 25/16/316.
10. BELL, H.C.P. 'Excerpta Maldiviana. No. 13. Some polyglot Missives of Sultan Ibrahim Iskandar II' JRASCB, 33(87), 1934: 48.
11. SLNA 25/16/316.
12. Ibid.
13. Ibid.
14. Ibid.
15. *Times of Ceylon*, Sept. 7, 1937.

32. Bell as a Collector

Main Sources
Administration Reports of the Colombo Museum.
DE SARAM, C.J. *The Emergence of the British Official as a Collector of Antiquities in the Colonial Period of Ceylon, with special reference to the role of H.C.P.Bell in the growth of the collection in the Colombo National Museum : a paper presented for the course leading to the Master of Science Degree in Architectural Conservation of Monuments and Sites.* ACOMAS, Faculty of Architecture, University of Moratuwa, 2nd. May, 1983.

Notes
1. SLNA 25/16/41.
2. DE SARAM, C.J., op. cit. Annexure J. Extracted from *Register of Colombo Museum*: 18-21. (Miss Zoë Bell, in 1939, presented to the British Museum four Maldive mats, as described in Chapter 3, and seventeen textiles, including items of male and female clothing, as descibed in Chapter 27. They are held by the Museum of Mankind.)
3. BELL, H.C.P. *The Maldive Islands : an Account of the Physical Features, Climate, History, Inhabitants, Productions and Trade* (SP XLIII, 1881). Colombo, Frank Laker, 1883: 117-9, 121; GRAY, A. ed. *The Voyage of François Pyrard.* Vol.I. London, Hakluyt Society, 1887: 232.
4. SLNA 25/16/41; CO 54/536.
5. SLNA 25/16/41; HALY, A. *First Report on the Exhibited Coins in the Colombo Museum.* Colombo, [1890]: 25.
6. BELL, H.C.P. *The Maldive Islands: Monograph on the History, Archaeology and Epigraphy.* Colombo, Government Printing Press, 1940. Appendix C. 'Maldive Coinage and Currency': 75-91.
7. HALY, A., op. cit.: 1.
8. LOWSLEY, B. 'Coins and tokens of Ceylon' *The Numismatic Chronicle* 3rd series 15, 1895: 211-68.
9. STILL, J. 'Notes on some Roman coins found in Ceylon' JRASCB, 19(58), 1907: 161-90; STILL, J. 'Some early copper coins of Ceylon' JRASCB, 19(58), 1907: 199-214.
10. DE SILVA, P.H.D.H. *A Catalogue of Antiquities and other Cultural Objects from Sri Lanka (Ceylon) Abroad.* Colombo, National Museum, 1975.
11. WIJAYARATNE, D.J. and KULASURIYE, A.S. Catalogue of Sinhalese Manuscripts in the India Office Library; edited by C.H.B. Reynolds. London, 1981.
12. *Fourth Progress Report.* Appendix A 'Ancient beads, glass, etc.' and Appendix B 'Coins and dice': 11-2; ASCAR, 1911-12: 756.
13. ASCAR, 1907: 26, Appendix E: 36-7; ASCAR, 1908, Appendix C: 17-8; ASCAR, 1909: 17, Appendix B: 28-31.
14. BELL, H.C.P. 'Archaeology' JRASCB, 19(57), 1906: 11; STILL, J. *Catalogue of Finds of the Archaeological Survey of Ceylon, 1906-7, Deposited in the Colombo Museum.* Colombo, n.d.
15. BELL, H.C.P. 'Two Buddhist seals' CALR, 3/1, 1917: 55-6.
16. DE SILVA, P.H.D.H. *Colombo Museum Souvenir 1877-1977.* Colombo, 1977.
17. WILLIS, J.C. and GARDINER, J.S. 'The botany of the Maldive Islands' *Annals of the Royal Botanic Gardens, Peradeniya*, 1901: 46; SLNA 25/16/41.
18. DE SARAM, C.J., op. cit.: 36.
19. 'Caste pamphlets' *Kurakshetra (Sri Lanka-Indo Studies)*, (Colombo), 3, 1977: 80-2. List of 26 pamphlets in H.C.P.Bell's Collection in National Museum, Colombo, No. 24/F 2-31. (His notes are reproduced)
20. SLNA 25/16/299.
21. HARWOOD, J. 'Fra Mauro's map' JRASCB, 24(68), 1915-16: 12-15.
22. ASCAR, 1909: 23.
23. DE SARAM, C.J., op. cit.: 31-2.
24. ASCAR, 1901: 14; *Administration Report*, 1895 Part IV: I 11.
25. *Adminstration Report*, 1924 Part IV: E 4.

26. *Administration Report*, 1935 Part IV: F 3.
27. WICKREMARATNE, K.D.L. 'Palm leaf manuscripts of Ceylon' *Ceylon Today*, 16/1, Jan. 1967: 16- 24.
28. *Administration Report*, 1937 Part IV: F 21.
29. Ibid.
30. BELL, H.C.P. *Photographic Views taken in the Kegalla District of Province of Sabaragamuwa, 1889-1890.* (150 Photographs mounted on white card and bound in a volume)
31. ASCAR, 1911-12: 91; *Catalogue of Negatives in the Archaeological Department.* Colombo, Ceylon Government Printer, 1930. (The negatives are grouped in series, which probably reflect the dates at which they were deposited. There is no indication as to which were taken during Bell's career, but it is clear that many are from that period)
32. *Photographs of the Finds of the Archaeological Survey of Ceylon brought to the Colombo Museum in December 1906 and January 1907.* These are the photographs of the finds catalogued by Still. See note 14)
33. DE SARAM, C.J., op. cit.: 35.
34. Ibid.: 38.

33. The Man and his Work

Notes
1. NELL, A. 'H.C.P.Bell: Ceylon's foremost archaeologist' *Ceylon Observer,* Sept. 19, 1937; WIJEYEKOON, A.C.G. *Recollections.* Colombo, Associated Newspapers of Ceylon, 1951: 296.
2. A.N.W. 'A tribute to the late Mr. H.C.P.Bell: Ceylon's pioneer archaeologist' *Times of Ceylon,* Sept. 8, 1937.
3. PERERA, J.A.Will. 'The late Mr. H.C.P.Bell: tribute to a great English pioneer' *Times of Ceylon,* Sept. 9, 1937.

4. WIJEYEKOON, A.C.G. *Recollections,* op.cit.: 296-7.
5. Cutting from *Ceylon Observer,* Sept. 7, 1937.

6. ASCAR, 1922-23: J 2.
7. PHADNIS, U. Private communication.
8. DEVENDRA, D.T. 'H.C.P.Bell, C.C.S. (1851-1937)' JRASCB n.s. 8(1), 1962: 164.
9. CO 54/730.
10. *Ceylon Legislative Council Debates*, Oct. 23, 1901: 9; CO 54/726.
11. SLNA 25/16/206.
12. BELL, H.C.P. 'Anuradhapura : identification of ruins' CLR, 5, 1891: 373; ASCAR, 1910-11: 10, note.
13. MENDIS, J.G.C. 'Dutu Gemunu : a lay of Ancient Lanka' CALR, 2/1, 1916: 29-35.
14. DE SILVA, R.H. 'Archaeology' in *Education in Ceylon : a Centenary Volume.* Vol.III. Colombo, Ministry of Education and Cultural Affairs, 1969: 1164, 1167.
15. SENAVIRATNE, M. 'Were rare treasures pilfered from Sigiriya?' *Weekend*, Sept. 13, 1981: 16.
16. DEVENDRA, D.T., op.cit.: 164.
17. PARANAVITANA, S. *Glimpses of Ceylon's Past.* Colombo, Lake House Investments Ltd., 1972: 6.
18. BOISSELIER, J. *Ceylon, Sri Lanka*; translated from the French by James Hogarth (Archaeologia Mundi). Geneva, Nagel, 1979: 32, 52.
19. HOCART, A.M. 'Archaeology in Ceylon' *Antiquity*, 1, 1927: 480.
20. Unidentified newspaper cutting (? 1912).
21. WOOLF, L. *Growing : an Autobiography 1904-1911*. London, Hogarth Press, 1970: 24.
22. STILL, J. *The Jungle Tide*. Edinburgh and London, Blackwood, 1930: 211.
23. LECLERCQ, J. *Un séjour dans l'île de Ceylan*. Paris, 1900: 286.

H.C.P.Bell Bibliography

This includes writings by Bell and those which he edited or to which he contributed. Some early articles are only signed 'B', but he refers to them as his own in later writings.

In addition to this list it should be noted that Bell submitted an annual account of his excavations to the RASCB and these were published as the section 'Archaeology' in the annual report of the Society. These reports exist for the years 1891 to 1911. The report for 1912 was written by E.R.Ayrton.

Bell edited the *Journal of the Royal Asiatic Society (Ceylon Branch)* from 1881 to 1914; the last issue that he edited being that for 1912. From 1915 to 1916 he was joint editor with John M.Senaveratne of *The Ceylon Antiquary and Literary Register*.

1881   BELL, H.C.P. Illustrations for 'The Maldive Islands' *The Graphic*, June 4: 542, 548.

1882   BELL, H.C.P. 'Fish-curing at the Maldives' *Indian Antiquary*, 11: 196-8.

1882   BELL, H.C.P. 'Cobily Mash' *Indian Antiquary*, 11: 294.
(Reply to D.Ferguson'Notes and Queries : Cobily-Mash' *Indian Antiquary*, 8, 1879: 321)

1882   BELL, H.C.P. 'List of Sinhalese, Pali and Sanskrit books in the Oriental Library, Kandy' *Journal of the Pali Text Society*, 1882: 38-45.

1883   BELL, H.C.P. *The Maldive Islands : an Account of the Physical Features, Climate, History, Inhabitants, Productions and Trade* (Sessional Paper XLIII, 1881). Colombo, Frank Laker.

1883   BELL, H.C.P. 'Sinhalese customs and ceremonies connected with paddy cultivation in the Low Country' *Journal of the Royal Asiatic Society (Ceylon Branch)*, 8(26): 44-93.

1885- BELL, H.C.P. 'Transliteration' *Orientalist*, 2: 208-11. (Remarks by D.Ferguson : 211;
1886   Reply by H.C.P.BELL: 211-3)

1887- GRAY, A. ed. *The Voyage of François Pyrard of Laval to the East Indies, the Maldives, the*
1890   *Moluccas and Brazil; translated into English from the third French edition of 1619, and edited with notes by Albert Gray assisted by H.C.P.BELL*
(Hakluyt Society vols. 76, 77, 80). 3 vols. London, Hakluyt Society.

1888   BELL, H.C.P. 'Sinhalese glossary' JRASCB, 10, Proceedings 1887-8: cv-cix. (A specimen glossary stopping at *Kh*, for consideration for issue by the RASCB)

1888   FYERS, A.B. 'A collection of notes on the attack and defence of Colombo, in the Island of Ceylon, given over to the English on February 16, 1796, translated from the French of Mons. de la Thombé' JRASCB, 10(37): 365-414.
Edited and with Appendices A, B and C by H.C.P.BELL.

1888-   BELL, H.C.P. 'Superstitious ceremonies connected with the cultivation of Alvi or hill paddy'
1889   *Orientalist*, 3: 99-103.

1888-   BELL, H.C.P. 'Treaty of peace between the Dutch and the Sinhalese dated 14 February, 1776'
1889   *Orientalist*, 3: 115-8.

1889   BELL, H.C.P. 'Paddy cultivation ceremonies in the four Korales, Kegalla district' JRASCB, 11(39): 167-71.

1889   BELL, H.C.P. 'Robert Knox and the English captives in "Kandia-Uda"' *Ceylon Literary Register*, 3: 358-60.

1889-   BELL, H.C.P. 'Ehelepola's representations to His Majesty's Commissions of Enquiry: translated'
1890   CLR, 4: 87-8, 95-6, 101-2, 110-2.
            (Reprinted CLR 3rd series 2, 1932: 337-42, 419-25, 469-78)

1890   BELL, H.C.P. *First Report on the Archaeological Survey of Anuradhapura* (SP XLIV, 1890). Colombo, Skeen.

1890   BELL, H.C.P. *Second Report on the Archaeological Survey of Anuradhapura* (SP L, 1890). Colombo, Skeen.

1891   BELL, H.C.P. 'Numismatics : a find of Roman coins in Ceylon' CLR, 6: 133-5.

1891   BELL, H.C.P. 'Anuradhapura : identification of ruins' CLR, 5: 373.
            (Reply to articles by H. Nevill in CLR, 2, 1888: 294; 5, 1891: 356-7, 364-5, 389)

1891   BELL, H.C.P. *Third Progress Report on the Archaeological Survey of Anuradhapura* (SP XXXV, 1891). Colombo, Skeen.

1892   BELL, H.C.P. *Archaeological Survey of Ceylon. Anuradhapura and the North-Central Province. Fourth Progress Report* (SP XVI, 1892). Colombo, Skeen.

1892   BELL, H.C.P. *Archaeological Survey of Ceylon. Report on the Kegalla District of the Province of Sabaragamuwa* (SP XIX, 1892). Colombo, Skeen.
            (Review with many extracts printed in the *Monthly Literary Register and Notes and Queries for Ceylon,* 1/5, 1893: 105-9)

1893   BELL, H.C.P. 'Dewales' *The Buddhist,* 5(13): 103.
            (Reprinted from *Archaeological Survey of Ceylon. Report on the Kegalla District*: 18-9)

1893   BELL, H.C.P. *Archaeological Survey of Ceylon. Anuradhapura. Fifth Progress Report* (SP X, 1893). Colombo, Skeen.
            (Reviewed in MLRC, 2/2, 1894: 46)

Bibliography

1893 FERGUSON, J. *Ceylon in 1893*. London, John Hadden; Colombo, A.M. and J.Ferguson. Appendix VI. 'The excavations at Anuradhapura: depth of ruins under the surface': 371-2, by H.C.P.BELL.

1893 BELL, H.C.P. 'Notes and queries' MLRC, 1/6: 143.(On the transliteration of Sinhalese)

1894 BELL, H.C.P. 'Inscribed pillar at Padaviya' MLRC, 2/4: 75-8.

1894 BELL, H.C.P. *Archaeological Survey of Ceylon. Research on the Kegalla District of the Province of Sabaragamuwa in 1893* (SP XX, 1894, in continuation of SP XIX of 1892). Colombo, Cottle.

1895 BELL, H.C.P. 'Pronunciation of Sinhalese' MLRC, 3/11: 268.

1895 BELL, H.C.P. 'Interim report on the operations of the Archaeological Survey at Sigiriya in 1895' JRASCB, 14(46): 44-56. Discussion: 56-8.

1896 BELL, H.C.P. *Archaeological Survey of Ceylon. Anuradhapura. Sixth Progress Report* (SP XII, 1896). Colombo, Skeen.
(Review with extracts printed in MLRC, 4/9: 197-202)

1896 BELL, H.C.P. *Archaeological Survey of Ceylon. Anuradhapura and the North-Central Province. Seventh Progress Report* (SP XIII, 1896). Colombo, Skeen.
(Review with extracts printed in MLRC, 4/11: 243-59)

1896 BELL, H.C.P. 'Interim report on the operations of the Archaeological Survey at Sigiriya (Second Season), 1896' JRASCB, 14(47): 242-60. Discussion: 260.
(Review with extracts printed in MLRC, 4/12: 278-82)

1897 BELL, H.C.P. 'Interim report on the operations of the Archaeological Survey at Sigiriya, 1897' JRASCB, 15(48): 93-122. Discussion: 122-5. Appendix 'Sigiriya frescoes' by C.M. Fernando: 127-8; Reply by H.C.P.BELL: 128-31. (Appendix reprinted in *The Buddhist* n.s. 1(46), 1898: 2-3)

1898 BELL, H.C.P. 'Letter in reply to one from C.M.Fernando in the *Ceylon Standard*, 20 Jan. 1898' *Tropical Agriculturalist (Literary Register Supplement)*, 17 April: 2-3.

1903 BROHIER, R.L. *Land, Maps and Surveys: a Review of the Evidence of Land Surveys as Practised in Ceylon from Earliest Known Periods and the Story of the Ceylon Survey Department from 1800 to 1950*. Colombo, Government Printing Press, 1950. 'Memorandum on the boundaries of Tamankaduwa, July 28/30, 1903' Appendix I to Vol.I: 115-7, by H.C.P.BELL.

1903 BELL, H.C.P. 'Sannas or royal grants' TA (LR Suppl), 23 Sept.: 108.

1904 BELL, H.C.P. *Archaeological Survey of Ceylon. North-Central Province. Annual Report 1890* (SP XXXV, 1904). Colombo, Skeen.
(Bell's note, p.1, states that this embraces the First, Second and Third Progress Reports)

1904 BELL, H.C.P. *Archaeological Survey of Ceylon. North-Central Province. Annual Report 1891* (SP XXXVI, 1904). Colombo, Skeen.
(Bell's note, p.1, states that this embraces the Fourth, Fifth, Sixth and Seventh Progress Reports)

1904 BELL, H.C.P. *Archaeological Survey of Ceylon. North-Central Province. Annual Report 1892* (SP XXXVII, 1904). Colombo, Skeen.
(Bell's note, p.1, states that this covers the Eighth, Ninth and Tenth Progress Reports, but these were never published. The Plans and Plates for this *Annual Report* were not published until 1914)

1904 BELL, H.C.P. *Archaeological Survey of Ceylon. North-Central and Sabaragamuwa Provinces. Annual Report 1893* (SP XXXVIII, 1904). Colombo, Skeen.
(Bell's note, p.1, states that this covers the Eleventh and Twelfth Progress Reports, but these were never published. The Plans and Plates for this *Annual Report* were not published until 1914)

1904 BELL, H.C.P. *Archaeological Survey of Ceylon. North-Central, Sabaragamuwa, and Central Provinces. Annual Report 1894* (SP XXXIX, 1904). Colombo, Skeen.
(The Plans and Plates for this *Annual Report* were not published until 1914)

1904 BELL, H.C.P. *Archaeological Survey of Ceylon. North-Central, Sabaragamuwa, Central and North-Western Provinces. Annual Report 1895* (SP XL, 1904). Colombo, Skeen.
(The Plans and Plates for this *Annual Report* were not published until 1914)

1904 BELL, H.C.P. *Archaeological Survey of Ceylon. North-Central, Sabaragamuwa and Central Provinces. Annual Report 1896* (SP XLI, 1904). Colombo, Skeen.
(The Plans and Plates for this *Annual Report* were not published until 1914)

1904 BELL, H.C.P. *Archaeological Survey of Ceylon. North-Central, Central and Eastern Provinces. Annual Report 1897* (SP XLII, 1904). Colombo, Skeen.
(The Plans and Plates for this *Annual Report* were not published until 1914)

1904 BELL, H.C.P. *Archaeological Survey of Ceylon. North-Central and Central Provinces. Annual Report 1898* (SP XLIII, 1904). Colombo, Skeen.
(The Plans and Plates for this *Annual Report* were not published until 1914)

1904 BELL, H.C.P. *Archaeological Survey of Ceylon. North-Central and Central Provinces. Annual Report 1899* (SP XLIV, 1904). Colombo, Skeen.
(The Plans and Plates for this *Annual Report* were not published until 1914)

Bibliography

1904 BELL, H.C.P. *Archaeological Survey of Ceylon. North-Central and Central Provinces. Annual Report 1900* (SP XLV, 1904). Colombo, Skeen.
(Some Plates for this *Annual Report* were published with the *Annual Report* for 1902. Extra Plates for 1900, and the Plans, were published in 1914)

1904 BELL, H.C.P. *Archaeological Survey of Ceylon. Summary of Operations 1890-1900* (SP XLVI, 1904). Colombo, Skeen.
(Includes an Index for the *Annual Reports* 1890-1900)

1905 FERNANDO, C.M. 'Two old Sinhalese swords' JRASCB, 18(56): 388-391. Appendix: 447-9 by H.C.P.BELL.

1907 BELL, H.C.P. *Archaeological Survey of Ceylon. North-Central and Central Provinces. Annual Report 1901* (SP LIII, 1907). Colombo, Cottle.
(Some Plates for this *Annual Report* were published with the *Annual Report* for1902. Extra Plates, and the Plans, were published in 1914)

1907 BELL, H.C.P. *Archaeological Survey of Ceylon. North-Central and Central Provinces. Annual Report 1902* (SP LXVIII, 1907). Colombo, Cottle.
(This *Annual Report* included some Plates and a Plan of its own, and some Plates for the *Annual Reports* of 1900 and 1901. Extra Plates and Plans for 1900 and 1902 were published in 1914)

1908 BELL, H.C.P. *Archaeological Survey of Ceylon. North-Central and Central Provinces. Annual Report 1903* (SP LXV, 1908). Colombo, Cottle.
(Supplementary Plates published in 1916)

1908 BELL H.C.P. *Archaeological Survey of Ceylon. North-Central, Central and North-Western Provinces. Annual Report 1904* (SP LXVI, 1908). Colombo, Cottle.

1909 BELL, H.C.P. *Archaeological Survey of Ceylon. North-Central, Central and Northern Provinces. Annual Report 1905* (SP XX, 1909). Colombo, Richards.
(Supplementary Plates published in 1916)

1910 BELL, H.C.P. *Archaeological Survey of Ceylon. North-Central and Central Provinces. Annual Report 1906* (SP XX, 1910). Colombo, Cottle.
(Supplementary Plates published in 1916)

1910 [BELL, H.C.P. ed.] *Papers Relating to the Maldive Islands 1887-1910*. 3 parts in 1 volume. Colombo, Secretariat.

1910 STILL, J. 'Tantri Malai : some archaeological observations and deductions' JRASCB, 22(63): 73-88. Appendix C 'Accounts of Tantri Malai' and Appendix D 'Additional archaeological notes' by H.C.P.BELL: 89-96, 97-101.

1910 FERGUSSON, J. *History of Indian and Eastern Architecture*; revised and edited with additions; Indian Architecture by James Burgess and Eastern Architecture by R. Phene Spiers. 2 vols. London, Murray.
  (In the preface J.Burgess writes 'For Ceylon I am greatly indebted to Lord Stanmore and the Colonial Office, whilst Mr. J.G.Smither, late Government architect, and Mr. H.C.P.BELL, Archaeological Commissioner, very kindly have read the proofs and supplied important advice and material for the chapter on the architecture of the island'.)

1911 BELL, H.C.P. *Archaeological Survey of Ceylon. North-Central, Northern and Central Provinces. Annual Report 1907* (SP V, 1911). Colombo, Cottle.
  (Supplementary Plates published in 1916)

1912 PIERIS, P.E. 'The date of King Bhuwaneka Bahu VII' JRASCB, 22(65): 267-302. Appendix C by H.C.P.BELL: 283-95.

1912 DE SILVA, S. 'Vijaya Bahu VII' JRASCB, 22 (65): 316-81. Appendix D by H.C.P.BELL: 340-66.

1912 DE SILVA, S. 'Inscription at Keragala' JRASCB, 22(65): 404-21. Appendix A by H.C.P.BELL: 410-4.

1913 BELL, H.C.P. *Archaeological Survey of Ceylon. North-Central and Central Provinces. Annual Report 1908* (SP VI, 1913). Colombo, Richards.
  (Supplementary Plates published in 1916)

1914 BELL, H.C.P. 'Kotte : some historical notes' *The Sinhalese*, 2/1: 12-6.

1914 BELL, H.C.P. 'Galapata Vihare inscription' JRASCB (N & Q), Pt.4, No. 29: lxix-lxxvii.

1914 BELL, H.C.P. *Archaeological Survey of Ceylon. North-Central, Central and Western Provinces. Annual Report 1909* (SP VI, 1914). Colombo, Cottle.
  (Supplementary Plates published in 1916)

1914 BELL, H.C.P. *Archaeological Survey of Ceylon. North-Central, Central, North-Western and Western Provinces. Annual Report 1910-11* (SP X, 1914). Colombo, Cottle.
  (Supplementary Plates published in 1916)

1914 BELL, H.C.P. *Archaeological Survey of Ceylon. Plans and Plates for Annual Reports 1892-1902.* Colombo, Cottle.

1915 BELL, H.C.P. 'Kirtti Nissanka and the "Tula-bhara" ceremony' *Ceylon Antiquary and Literary Register*, 1/2: 83-8.

1915 BELL, H.C.P. 'Letter from the Kandyan Court : 1726' CALR, 1/2: 118-23.

Bibliography

1915   BELL, H.C.P. *Archaeological Survey of Ceylon. North-Central, Central and North-Western Provinces. Annual Report 1911-12* (SP III, 1915). Colombo, Cottle.
         (Includes Index to *Annual Reports* 1890-1912)
         (Supplementary Plates published in 1916)

1915-   BELL, H.C.P. ed. 'The Maldive Islands : 1602-1607' CALR, 1/2, 1915: 133-9; 1/3, 1916: 208-12; 1/4, 1916: 266-78; 2/1, 1916: 64-73; 2/2, 1916: 137-42; 2/3, 1917: 196-210; 2/4, 1917:283-6; 3/1, 1917: 64-6; 3/2, 1917: 148-51; 3/3, 1918: 231-4; 3/4, 1918: 299-301; 4/1, 1918:62-3; 4/2, 1918: 120-26.
1918

1916   BELL, H.C.P. and GUNASEKERA, A.M. 'Kelani Vihare and its inscriptions' CALR, 1/3:145-61.

1916   BELL, H.C.P. 'Andreas Amabert : 1764' CALR, 1/4: 243-54.

1916   BELL, H.C.P. 'Some ancient ruins in Uva' CALR, 1/4: 278-81.

1916   BELL, H.C.P. 'Maha Saman Devale and its Sannasa' CALR, 2/1: 36-46.

1916   BELL, H.C.P. 'The "Ahigunthikayo" or Ceylon gypsies' CALR, 2/2: 108-114.

1916   S.G.P. 'Derivation of "Tuppahi"' CALR, 2/2: 124-7. Note A: 126-7 by H.C.P.BELL.

1916   BELL, H.C.P. *Archaeological Survey of Ceylon. Supplementary Plates for Annual Reports 1903, 1905, 1906, 1907, 1908, 1909, 1910-11, 1911-12.* Colombo, Cottle.

1916   BELL, H.C.P. 'Inscription at Embekke Devale' JRASCB (N & Q), Pt. 8, No. 5: cxxi-cxxiv.

1917   BELL, H.C.P. 'Kit-Siri-Mewan Vihare inscription : rejoinder to paper of Simon de Silva' CALR, 2/3: 182-90.

1917   BELL, H.C.P. 'Dimbula-gala : its caves, ruins and inscriptions. I. The Maravidiye caves' CALR, 3/1: 1-12.

1917   BELL, H.C.P. 'Two Buddhist seals' CALR, 3/1: 55-6.

1917   BELL, H.C.P. 'Dimbula-gala : its caves, ruins and inscriptions. II. Other sites' CALR, 3/2: 69-79.

1917   BELL, H.C.P. 'The "Gal Aliya" or "Rock Elephant" at Katupilana, Tamankaduwa' CALR, 3/2: 144-7.

1917   BELL, H.C.P. and IEVERS, R.W. 'The Anuradhapura Anthem' *Times of Ceylon*, Christmas Number: 67.

1917   BELL, H.C.P. 'Bear shooting in Ceylon' *Times of Ceylon*, Christmas Number: 24-7, 76.

1918   BELL, H.C.P. 'Inscribed pillar-slab at Nuwara Eliya' JRASCB, 26(71), Notes and Queries: 61-4.

1918   JOSEPH, G.A. 'The Gal-Vihare and Demala-Maha-Seya paintings at Polonnaruwa' JRASCB, 26(71): 101-6. Appendix 'The "Demala-Maha-Seya" frescoes : Memorandum' by H.C.P.BELL: 106-8.

1918   BELL, H.C.P. '"Demala Maha-Seya" paintings' JRASCB, 26(71), Notes and Queries: 199-201.

1918   BELL, H.C.P. 'Archaeological research in the Egoda Pattuwa, Tamankaduwa' CALR, 3/3: 193-215.

1918   BELL, H.C.P. 'Dutugemunu's Queen' CALR, 3/3: 228.

1918   BELL, H.C.P. and CODRINGTON, H.W. 'Critical notes on the *Epigraphia Zeylanica*. Nos. 1-8' CALR, 4/1: 19-35.

1918   BELL, H.C.P. 'Inscribed pillar at Anuradhapura' CALR, 4/2: 102-8.

1919   BELL, H.C.P. 'Critical notes on the *Epigraphia Zeylanica*. No. 9. Polonnaruwa inscriptions' CALR, 5/1: 20-30.

1919   GEIGER, W. 'Maldivian linguistic studies; translated from the German by Mrs. J.C.Willis, edited by H.C.P.BELL' JRASCB, 27, Extra Volume.
Appendices by H.C.P.BELL: A Pioneers in Maldivian linguistic research; B The Leyden vocabulary; C The old and modern Maldivian alphabets; D Maldivian letters.

1920   BELL, H.C.P. 'Prince Taniyavalla Bahu of Madampe' JRASCB, 28(73): 36-53.

1920   ROBINS, L. *English Lady's Visit to the Maldives*; revised by H.C.P.BELL. Colombo, 'Ceylon Observer' Press.

1921   BELL, H.C.P. *The Maldive Islands : Report on a Visit to Male, January 20 to February 21, 1920* (SP XV, 1921). Colombo, Government Printer.

1922   BELL, H.C.P. 'Excerpta Maldiviana. No. 1. Maldivian government permit' JRASCB, 29(75): 99-104.

1923   BELL, H.C.P. 'Excerpta Maldiviana. No. 2. Sultans' missives : A.C. 1713; 1819' JRASCB, 29(76): 194-214.

1924   BELL, H.C.P. 'Dimbulagala : Maradiviye cave inscription' CALR, 10/1: 1-14.

1924   STOREY, H. 'The temple ruins at Medirigiri : Tamankaduwa' CALR, 10/2: 67-87.
Memorandum 'Medirigiriya pillar-inscription no. 2': 76-87 by H.C.P.BELL.

Bibliography

1924 TURNER, J.B. *Report on the Census of Ceylon, 1921.* Vol.I, Part 2. Colombo, Government Printer. (Note on p. 95 'The leading living authority on the subject of the Maldives is Mr. H.C.P.BELL, C.C.S. (retired)... He was good enough to read this chapter in manuscript and to suggest several important amendments'.)

1924 BELL, H.C.P. 'Excerpta Maldiviana. No. 3. "Dives Akuru" grave-stone epitaphs' JRASCB, 29(77): 283-303.

1925 BELL, H.C.P. 'Excerpta Maldiviana. No. 4. A description of the Maldive Islands : circa A.C. 1683' JRASCB, 30(78): 132-142.

1925 BELL, H.C.P. *Report on the Kuttapitiya Sannasa, Kandy.* Colombo, Millers. (Original Ms. held by Senarath Panawatta, Curator of the Kandy Museum)

1926 BELL, H.C.P. 'Excerpta Maldiviana. No. 5. The Maldive Islands : physical traits and general characteristics' JRASCB, 30(79): 257-70.

1927 BELL, H.C.P. 'Excerpta Maldiviana. No.6. Graves of Captain Overend and PrivateLuckham at the Maldives' JRASCB, 30(80): 436-47.

1928 BELL, H.C.P. 'Excerpta Maldiviana. No. 7. "Lonu Ziyarat" : Male' JRASCB, 31(81): 180-95.

1929 BELL, H.C.P. 'Excerpta Maldiviana. No. 8. Malaku atol : Kolu-Furi Island' JRASCB, 31(82): 400-15.

1930 BELL, H.C.P. 'Excerpta Maldiviana. No. 9. Lomafanu' JRASCB, 31(83): 539-78.

1931 BELL, H.C.P. 'Excerpta Maldiviana. No. 10. The Portuguese at the Maldives' JRASCB, 32(84): 76-124.

1932 BELL, H.C.P. 'Excerpta Maldiviana. No. 11. Dutch intercourse with the Maldives : Seventeenth century' JRASCB, 32(85): 226-42.

1933 BELL, H.C.P. 'Excerpta Maldiviana. No. 12. Maldivian proverbs' JRASCB, 32(86): 372-387.

1934 BELL, H.C.P. 'Excerpta Maldiviana. No. 13. Some polyglot missives of Sultan Ibrahim Iskandar II' JRASCB, 33(87): 47-90.

1935 BELL, H.C.P. 'Excerpta Maldiviana. No. 14. Maldivian taboo of free English education' JRASCB, 33(88): 169-91.

1940 BELL, H.C.P. *The Maldive Islands : Monograph on the History, Archaeology and Epigraphy.* Colombo, Ceylon Government Press. (Reprinted in 1985 by the National Centre for Linguistic and Historical Research, Novelty Press, Male)

Bell Genealogy

ROBERT BELL, 1759-1844, m. 1787 Sarah Sydenham, 1759-1798, and had issue
    3 sons. He m. 1799 Jemima Scott, d. 1813, and had issue
    2 sons and 8 daughters. m. 1820 Margaret Bell, 1784-1851,
    and had issue 1 son.

ALEXANDER BELL, 1794-1853, 2nd. son of Robert Bell and Sarah Sydenham,
    m. 1817 Catherine Baynes, d. 1826, and had issue 3 sons.

HARRY WAINWRIGHT BAX BELL, 1821-1888, 2nd. son of the above, m. 1845
    Harriet Eliza Isabella Croker, d. 1900, and had issue 2 sons and 2 daughters:
   I. Alexander William Croker, 1849-1930, m. 1883 Florence Augusta Clayton,
    d. 1925.
   II. Harry Charles Purvis, 1851-1937. SEE BELOW
   I. Catherine Elizabeth, 1847-1875, m. 1871 John Oliphant Gage, d. 1897, and
    had issue 2 daughters:
      1. Annie Isabel, b. 1871, m. 1stly James Anthony Trail, d. 1901;
        and 2ndly Frank Montgomery.
      2. Kathleen Mary, b. 1872.
   II. Emma Louisa, 1853-1910, m. 1872 Claudius William Bell, d. 1875, and
   had issue 1 daughter:
      1. Henrietta Mary, 1873-1963.

HARRY CHARLES PURVIS BELL, 1851-1937, m. 1876 Renée Sabine Fyers, 1855-1933,
    and had issue 3 sons and 3 daughters:
   I. Harry Amelius, 1879-1915, m. 1909 Ethel Howard.
   II. Cyril Francis, 1883-1957, m. 1916 Phyllis Margaret Aitken, 1885-1978,
   and had issue 1 son and 2 daughters:
      1. Alexander Kenneth, 1917-1917.
      1. Bethia Nancy, 1918-
      2. Heather Margaret, 1920-

Genealogy

III. Malcolm Fyers, 1889-1974, m. 1921 Dorris Murray-Clarke, 1893-1984, and had issue 1 son and 1 daughter:
 1. Kenneth Murray, 1930- , m. 1962 Mary Wallace, 1932- , and had issue 1 son and 1 daughter:
  i) Andrew Wallace, 1963-
  i) Fiona Margaret, 1966- m. 1990 Lee Anthony Davis, 1966- , and had issue 1 son:
   a) Benjamin Guyon, 1992-
 1.Ira Daphne, 1928-
I. Eva Laura, 1877-1900.
II. Renée Isabel, 1878-1967, m. 1903 Arthur Prideaux, 1868-1948, and had issue 1 son and 2 daughters:
 1. Arthur Guyon, 1904-
 1. Iris Renée, 1907-1986.
 2. Laura Sabine, 1910-
III. Zoë Iris, 1886-1985.

HARRY CHARLES PURVIS BELL, 1851-1937, with Saveri Amma had issue 1 daughter:
 I. Lourdanna (Lourdette), 1908-1970, m. 1936 Benedict E.Lambert, 1898-1973, and had issue 2 sons and 3 daughters:
  1. Tony, 1937- , m. 1970 Yvonne Perera, 1950- , and had issue 1 daughter:
   i) Sandra, 1971-
  2. Joe, 1944- , m. 1974 Myrna Ferdinands, 1950- , and had issue 1 son and 1 daughter:
   i) Gerald, 1984-
   i) Rochelle, 1979-

1. Marie, 1939- , m. 1960 Bertie Gomez, 1934- ,
and had issue 1 son and 2 daughters:
    i) Naresh, 1960-
    i) Nedra, 1961- , m. 1985 Eden Forbes, 1955- ,
and had issue 2 sons:
        a) Julian, 1986-
        b) André, 1988-
    ii) Rosanne, 1963- , m. 1990 Manesh Perera, 1956- ,
and had issue 1 son:
        a) Ryan, 1991-
2. Christabel, 1941- , m. 1965 George Ondaatjie, 1934- ,
and had issue 2 sons and 1 daughter:
    i) Gerard, 1966-
    ii) Travis, 1970-
    i) Angeline, 1967-
3. Cecilia, 1947-

HARRY CHARLES PURVIS BELL, 1851-1937, with Perumal Akka had issue 1 son:
    I. John, 1916- , m. 1955 Noeline Marjorie Hieler, 1932- ,
and had issue 3 sons and 1 daughter:
    1. Jerome, 1958- , m. 1985 Udeni Chitra Kumari 1966- ,
and had issue 1 daughter:
    i) Davina, 1988-
    2. Clifford Gerald, 1960- , m. 1992 Bernadine Ursula Vincent, 1969- ,
    3. Anton, 1963-
    1. Rebecca, 1957- , m. 1988 Wilhelm Perera, 1957- ,
and had issue 1 daughter:
    i) Andrea, 1990-

The Anuradhapura Anthem

Anuradhapura! City grand and vast,
Lanka's famous Capital, in ages of the past:
In the 'Mahawansa' the story has been told
Of thy palaces, and temples, and pinnacles of gold. [1]

Chorus
Hail! then hail! to the worth of a bygone day,
Hail! all hail! to the relics of kingly sway,
Hail to thee, Fair City, glorious in decay,
Hail! thrice hail! for ever and for aye!

'Si monumentum quaeris' - cast your gaze around;
Ruined fanes and dagabas everywhere abound.
Alas! for glory faded, for erstwhile beauty sped,
For hierarchs and heroes, long numbered with the dead.

Hail! then hail!......

Great Ruwanveli Seya, once fairest of the fair,
The splendour of thy palmy days has melted into air;
And like 'Imperial Caesar' now 'dead and turned to clay',
Thy sacred bricks 'may stop a hole to keep the wind away'. [2]

See 'Bayagiri' massive - 'Fearless Mount' forsooth -
Centre once of schism rank, from 'Great Vihara' truth. [3]
Patched up by prison labour, anew it flaunts on high
A 'hideous excrescence' athwart a tranquil sky. [4]

Jetawanarama, Great Sena's priestly boon, [5]
Thy comely shape and giddy height will crumble all too soon;
Where forest trees and chequered shade a peaceful picture lend,
From cruel axe and ruthless spade, may gracious Heaven defend! [6]

Thuparama graceful, in outline clear and bold,
Begirt with columns chaste and slim, a gem in ring of gold,
To thee pertains high honour a pious people gave -
The tomb of Sanghamitta, and Prince Mahinda's grave. [7]

With bricks and mortar bolstered up, behold the Sacred Bo;
To some - misguided mortals - 'tis but a '*bo-gas*' show. [8]
Where humble Mirisveti a monarch's fad recalls,
Lo! Royal Siam's silver now builds its futile walls. [9]

What need to tell of sculptures, of 'pokunas' galore,
Of balustrades and Yogi stones and half a hundred more,
Of Brazen Palace spacious, with gilt-roofed storeys dight -
A modern race more 'brazen' would desecrate each site. [10]

For midst these sacred ruins of shrines and cloistered halls,
A reckless generation disports with little balls,
Whilst 'Parliamentary language' and imprecations deep
Disturb the peaceful solitude where saintly Rahats sleep. [11]

Iconoclasts and vandals have had their little day;
No more shall ancient pillars to culverts find their way.
No more a watchful Government such sacrilege condones -
One may not meddle with the gods, nor tamper with the stones. [12]

Anuradhapura! Thy glory shall revive;
Thy sons shall swarm within thee like bees about a hive.
The effort of the present for past neglect atones;
New breath of life resuscitates this vale of driest bones.

Notes
1. 'Mahawansa', the Great Chronicle of Ceylon History, from earliest times to the late 18th century.
2. Ruwanveli Seya, Chetiya, or Dagaba.
3. 'Abhayagiriya', 'Hill without fear', sometimes called Bayagiri. The Abhayagiri Fraternity seceded from that of the Maha Vihara during the reign of Valagam Bahu, B.C. 80.
4. Mr. T.N.Christie, Planting Member, protested in the Legislative Council against the abortive 'restoration' by prison labour of the Abhayagiri Dagaba, rightly dubbing its truncated pinnacle, as half restored, a 'hideous excrescence'.
5. Jetawanarama Dagaba was erected by King Maha Sena in the 4th century A.D.
6. The luckless fate, foreshadowed twenty years before, befell this, most picturesque of all the Anuradhapura Dagabas, in 1910, when an ignorant priest was permitted by the Atamasthana Committee, in whose charge it is as one of the 'Eight Sacred Sites', to work his uncontrolled will on the wooded tumulus. Not a tree remained unfelled, despite assurance to the contrary.
7. The ruins are pointed out, wrongly, as the traditional tombs of Mahinda and Sanghamitta, the apostles of Buddhism to Ceylon.
8. Sinhalese 'Bo-gas' = Bo-Tree.
9. Mirisavetiya Dagaba owed its erection and name, according to the 'Mahawansa', to King Dutugemunu's compunction at forgetting chillies (*miris*) in his almsgiving to monks on one occasion.

The restoration of the Dagaba was undertaken by the Ceylon Government with money provided by the King of Siam. When the pecuniary stream ceased to flow, the work, not half completed, also ceased, to the lasting benefit of myriads of bats!

10. The Loha-maha-paya, or Brazen Palace so called, was once nine storeys high, *teste* the 'Mahawansa'. It is not in reality a 'Palace', or other secular edifice.

11. The ruined area between Ruwanveli and Thuparama Dagabas was, *faute de mieux*, utilised in the nineties and even later by the European residents of Anuradhapura as 'golf links'. Thereby hangs a tale. A certain high official of Colombo (now enjoying his *'otium-cum'* at home), who prided himself upon his golf skill, was invited by certain sly wags at Anuradhapura to 'come along and give us duffers a wrinkle or two'. He came, saw - and was conquered! For, after getting into every possible trouble down the course - where 'bunkers' of all sorts and sizes are as thick as leaves in Vallombrosa owing to ubiquitous ruins - the studied politeness of a peppery soul broke down completely:- 'Call these *links*? They are just a blankety blank *quarry!*' Tableaux!

12. The 'Conservation of Ruins' was entrusted to the Archaeological Survey Department upon its inception in 1890.

The text of the 'Anthem' is taken from the *Times of Ceylon*, Christmas Number, 1917, with some corrections from a manuscript copy. The Notes are by H.C.P.Bell.

Trees of Sri Lanka

From east to west beyond the stretch of eyes
The combers indolently curling, white out of green;
The coral strand, the palm-trees seaward yearning
To the Line, to Antarctica, half a world between.

Homely trees, givers of fuel and oil,
Timber, woven shelter, food and wine;
Lovers of human voices, tenderly shading
Old tombs drifting backward into time.

So they bring to the gods of the trees their fruit and flowers,
Sweet frangipani, lotus opening bright;
To Kataragama, Siva, Skanda, they shatter the nuts,
Propitiatory, bathed and robed in white.

Under the whispering Tree the Enlightened One,
Stronger than kings, learned to loose the hold
Of all desire; his followers, men of thought,
But wearing the lion-colour, cinnamon-gold.

From year to year as far as memories reach
Tamil and trader, conqueror, made their track
Under the spice-trees; raised the mosque, the fortress.
They passed, and the jungle growth came flowing back,

Already veiling dagabas, guardstones of the shrine,
Breaking the bund, draining the life-giving tank.
Minivets call, the jak-tree drops its fruit,
And bear and leopard prowl the crumbling bank;

An Eden indifferent to Man, where the Old Ones, the Aliya
Trod out the paths beneath the blossoming trees.
Only those, and the voices of falling streams
Guide to the peak the pilgrim butterflies.

That is our name, who were drawn to Taprobane
By beauties, ties of faith, by former lives
Under the teak-trees, where in shadowed rooms
Old book or fading photograph survives.

This world so lovely, yet evil - should it pass
In flash or guttering of impermanent flame -
On a greater Rock, some six or seven souls
Under a pine, will seek the Truth again.

Bethia N. Bell

Index

Abdul Hamid Didi, 216, 218, 241, 244, 248, 251
Abdul Majid Didi, 216, 217, 228
Adams, Alexander Young, 85-6
Ahmad Didi, 22, 216, 217, 221, 228, 241, 244, 248, 250
Ali VI, 23, 226
Allan, 222, 254-6
Ambrose, P.Don, 72, 117, 271
Anson, Arthur, 121, 125
Anthonisz, Richard Gerald, 28, 212
Ayrton, Edward Russell, 105, 132-3, 156-7, 199-201

Bailey, John, 85-6, 137-9
Bell, Alexander, grandfather of H.C.P.Bell, 5-6
Bell, Alexander William Croker, brother of H.C.P.Bell, 7, 8
Bell, Bethia Nancy, grand-daughter of H.C.P.Bell, 247
Bell, Cyril Francis, son of H.C.P.Bell, 50, 168-70, 171, 247
Bell, Dorris, née Murray-Clarke, daughter-in-law of H.C.P.Bell, 7-8, 247-8, 254-6
Bell, Daphne Ira, grand-daughter of H.C.P.Bell, 254-5
Bell, Ethel, née Howard, daughter-in-law of H.C.P.Bell, 168
Bell, Eva Laura, daughter of H.C.P.Bell, 42, 167, 256
Bell, Harriet, Eliza Isabella, née Croker, mother of H.C.P.Bell, 6, 19, 167
Bell, Harry Amelius, son of H.C.P.Bell, 14, 42, 167-8
Bell, Harry Charles Purvis: admiration for art, 62-3, 64-5, 66-7, 75-6, 83, 93, 96, 98-9, 127-8, 131, 137-9, 175, 177-80, 184, 185-8, 190, 207, 217-8, 273; appointments and promotions, 10-11, 42-3, 49, 120, 122, 193-4; appreciation of natural beauty, 80, 82, 132, 217, 218, 222, 223, 224-5, 274; archaeological work: at Anuradhapura, 58-9, 60-7, 118, 126-30; at Addu Atoll, 222, 234; at Fua Mulaku, 223, 234-5; at Haddummati Atoll, 223-4, 234, 235-7; at Kegalla, 42-6; at Medigiriya, 135; at Mihintale 130-1; at Nalanda, 75, 103, 135-6; at Polonnaruwa, 173-194; at Sigirya, 83-101, 183-4; at Yapahuwa, 105, 137-9; attitude to his work, 43, 49, 56, 83, 107, 121, 123, 193, 195, 197-8, 250-1, 268-9, 273; attitude to Islam, 8, 217, 243, 249; Buddha figures, 38, 56, 66-7, 67-8, 70, 71, 74, 105, 107, 134-5, 177-8, 186-8, 190-1, 193, 212, 224, 235, 248, 260, 261; circuit work and discoveries, 69-71, 72-6, 134-5; climate and health, 1, 52-3, 55, 69-70, 71, 88-9, 119, 125, 132, 198, 208, 218, 219, 222, 226, 251, 253, 268; collections and museums, 19, 20, 55, 146-7, 205, 226, 228, 257-65; concern for antiquities and records, 25, 28, 96, 99-100, 102-8, 188, 191, 225, 263; controversies, 43, 96-8, 99, 139, 148, 152-4, 155-6, 161-4, 185-6, 208-10, 269; criticism by Bell, 35, 36, 65-6, 108, 109-10, 114, 116, 147-8, 152-3, 162-3, 178, 180, 188, 189-90, 192, 207-8, 241, 269-70; criticism of Bell, 27-8, 43, 66, 106-7, 108, 120-1, 152, 154, 155, 156-7, 159, 163, 196, 199, 200, 211, 272; discovery of inscriptions and documents, 45-6, 70, 73, 81, 99, 116, 142, 144, 145-6, 159, 161, 213, 217-8, 219-20, 226, 243, 246; as editor, 14-5, 22, 119, 205, 213; epigraphy, 34, 99, 142-50, 158-61, 162-4, 209-11, 212-3, 242-6, 250-1; family relationships, 14, 18, 19, 23, 42, 49-50, 87, 167, 169, 201-4, 227, 247-8, 251-2, 254-6 (*see also* references under Bell, Fyers, Lambert *and* Prideaux, *also the* Appendix 'Bell Genealogy'); finds, 64, 65-6, 67, 183-4, 185-6, 224, 225, 234, 235, 236, 260, 261, 273; friends, 8, 10, 49, 54, 57, 100, 120, 123, 155, 214-5, 217, 221, 248-51, 252-4, 267, 270-1; hazards and hardships, 10, 69-70, 71, 72, 79, 80-1, 85-9,

Index

94-6, 108, 142, 143, 182, 218, 225; interest in languages, 12-3, 23, 213, 239-42, 262; jungle peoples, 70, 71, 77-80, 144, 162, 213; numismatics, 20, 38, 139, 184, 257-9; personality, 8, 15, 89-90, 108, 120-1, 167, 169, 202, 205, 210, 227, 241, 243, 247-8, 266-71; as photographer, 19, 43-4, 76, 95, 120, 143, 173, 191, 265; recreations and sports, 8-9, 12, 79-81, 268; relations with Buddhists, 8, 66-7, 105, 106-8, 110, 116, 274; relations with the Ceylon government, 20, 28, 49, 53, 100-1, 102-3, 120, 121, 123, 124-5, 154, 155, 192-3, 195-9, 205, 214, 216, 250, 254, 267 (*see also under* Blake, Douglas, Gordon, Gregory, Havelock, Longden, McCallum, Manning, Noel-Walker, Ridgeway); relations with the Colonial Office, 152, 153, 154, 196, 199, 201, 268-9; restoration of monuments, 63-4, 66-7, 74, 75, 92-5, 102, 114-7, 131, 136, 139, 173, 177-81, 182, 185, 188, 190-4, 207, 208, 272-3; retirement, 132, 156, 161, 193-4, 195, 199-201, 205, 208, 251, 266-7; Royal Asiatic Society (Ceylon Branch), 13, 14-5, 42, 62, 63-4, 83, 96-7, 100-1, 205, 260, 265, 268; sannas and grants, 196-7, 205-7, 244-6, 254; staff, 51-3, 60-1, 87-90, 95-6, 117, 119, 120, 121-2, 125, 182, 188, 195, 198, 207, 268, 270 (*see also under* Ambrose, Dashwood, Fernando, Perera, Siriwadhana, Still *and* Wickremasinghe); Tamil inscriptions, 46, 145, 146, 163, 205; tanks, 49, 70, 71, 73, 82, 272, 274; treasure hunting, 46-7, 103-4, 108, 182-3, 272; tributes to Bell, 20, 43, 47-8, 56, 100-1, 119, 120, 133, 164, 194, 201, 214, 227, 258, 259, 265, 266-8, 271, 272, 274; visits to the Maldives, 16, 18-9, 193, 216-228; working methods, 42-3, 58-9, 60-1, 91-3, 143, 197-8, 223, 268-9, 271-3; writing methods and style, 83, 131-2, 134, 137-9, 147, 187, 273-4; writings on Ceylon: anthropological, 15, 42, 77, 78; epigraphical, 45-6, 64, 162-3, 164, 206, 209-10; historical, 15, 44, 139, 162-1, 209, 211-2; linguistic, 15;

miscellaneous, 78-81; Reports, 43-4, 48, 62, 118, 120, 122-3, 125, 201, 205, 271 (*see also under* archaeological work, individual sites); writings on the Maldives: anthropological, 23, 223, 224, 225-6, 230-1, 241-2; archaeological, 220, 233-8; epigraphical, 242-6; historical, 23, 213, 214, 216-7, 219-20, 225, 226, 229-30, 231-3; linguistic, 23, 239-44; Reports, 16, 18, 19-20, 214, 222, 229-30; youth, 7-10
Bell, Harry Wainwright Bax, father of H.C.P.Bell, 6, 18, 19, 20, 21, 23, 167, 262
Bell, Heather Margaret, grand-daughter of H.C.P.Bell, 247, 262
Bell, John, son of H.C.P.Bell, 203-4
Bell, Kenneth Murray, grandson of H.C.P.Bell, 254-5
Bell, Malcolm Fyers, son of H.C.P.Bell, 14, 50, 87, 168-9, 170, 172, 247-8, 254-6, 266
Bell, Phyllis Margaret, née Aitken, daughter-in-law of H.C.P.Bell, 169-70, 247
Bell, Renée Sabine, née Fyers, wife of H.C.P.Bell, 11, 12, 23, 42, 49-50, 169-70, 171, 227, 247-8, 251-2, 254, 255-6
Bell, General Robert, great-grandfather of H.C.P.Bell, 1-5, 8
Bell, Sarah, née Sydenham, great-grandmother of H.C.P.Bell, 4
Bell, Zoë Iris, daughter of H.C.P.Bell, 49, 50, 169-70, 171, 204, 207, 227, 247-8, 251, 253, 254-5, 259, 261, 267, 270
Bhuwaneka Bahu V, 46, 209
Bhuwaneka Bahu VI, 46
Bhuwaneka Bahu VII, 208-9
Birch, James Wheeler Woodforde, 135, 137
Blake, Sir Henry Arthur, 122, 123, 192-3
Bois, H., 39-40, 110
Booth, Leonard William, 57, 78, 270
Brodie, Alexander Oswald, 141-2
Burgess, James, 143
Burrows, Stephen Montagu, 15, 36, 37-8, 41, 59, 64, 129, 176, 190, 207, 208
Buultjens, Alfred Ernest, 25, 66
Byrde, E.M.D., 12, 55, 270

315

Cameron, Hardinge Hay, 37, 55, 56, 100, 188, 270
Capper, George, 31
Chalmers, Sir Robert, 157
Childers, Robert C., 32
Christopher, Willmott, 17-8, 21, 23, 233, 239, 240, 241
Clark, Alfred, 103, 121
Clifford, Sir Hugh, 43, 171, 198-9, 209
Codrington, Humphrey William, 195, 270
Collins, Sir Charles Henry, 194, 206-7
Cooper, Francis Alford, 111, 112
Corbet, Frederick Hugh Mackenzie, 15, 103, 151
Creasy, Harold Thomas, 116

D'Abbadie, Antoine, 239-40
Dashwood, C.E., 53, 120, 167
Davidson, Sir Walter Edward, 14, 15, 24, 43
De Alwis, James, 27
De Silva, Raja, 208, 271
De Silva, Simon, Mudaliyar, 209-10
De Silva, W.L., 222, 226, 229, 230, 244, 250, 256
De Zoysa, Louis, Mudaliyar, 12-3, 21, 26-7, 31, 242
Dickins, Guy, 196-9
Dickson, Sir John Frederick, 37-8, 55, 102
Douglas, Sir John, 18, 19
Dutugemunu, 37, 76, 110, 159, 271

Eggeling, Julius, 32, 33
Elala (Elara), 76, 108
Ellis, Francis Robert, 12, 113-4

Ferguson, Donald William 209, 211, 229, 241-2
Ferguson, John, 54, 100, 262, 270
Fernando, Charles Matthew, 97, 100
Fernando, W.E., 135
Fernando, W.M., 51-2, 117, 125, 135, 193-4, 198, 207, 271
Fiddes, G.V., 43, 154
Freeman, Herbert Rayner, 270
Fyers, Colonel Amelius Beauclerk, father-in-law of H.C.P.Bell, 13-4, 19, 20, 24, 28-31
Fyers, Henry Francis Clifton, 14, 169

Fyers, Kate Minnie, sister-in-law of H.C.P.Bell, 87

Gaja Bahu II, 46, 145, 161
Gardiner, Stanley, 215, 233, 262
Geiger, Wilhelm, 149, 213, 239, 240-1
Ghazi, Hasan Izz-ud-din, 243, 246
Ghazi Muhammed Bodu Takurufanu, 225, 232-3, 245
Goldschmidt, Paul, 33-4, 141, 155
Gordon, Sir Arthur Hamilton, later Lord Stanmore, 26, 36, 38-41, 42, 43, 49, 51, 54, 58, 87, 109, 111-3, 197
Gray, Albert, 10, 12, 16-7, 18, 20-4, 42, 119, 239, 241, 242, 257-8, 270
Gregory, Sir William Henry, 11, 13, 20, 24, 26, 29-30, 33-4, 35-6, 37, 54, 56, 61, 63, 86, 105, 109, 118, 119
Gunasekera, B., Mudaliyar, 14, 23, 53, 64, 120, 147, 149, 152, 155, 156, 160
Gunasekera, A. Mendis, 209-10
Gunawardhana, W.F., 210

Haly, Amyrald, 258
Harding, A.J., 154
Harischandra, Walisinha, 106
Harris, George, Lord Harris of Seringapatam and Mysore, 2, 4
Harris, George, 112, 113
Hasan, Izz-ud-din, Prince, 218, 222, 223
Hassan Didi, 215
Havelock, Sir Arthur Elibank, 47, 103, 111-2, 119
Hocart, Arthur Maurice, 133, 164, 165, 194, 200, 201, 208, 222, 268, 272
Hockly, T.W. 227, 271
Hogg, Captain J.R., 32, 33
Horsburgh, Benjamin, 194, 216, 217, 227
Hultzsch, Eugen, 143, 145
Hulugalle, S.N.W., 106, 113
Husain Didi, Kazi, 216, 229, 243, 244, 250
Husain Takurufanu, 242-3

Ibn Batuta, 16-7, 22, 216, 227, 241, 244

Index

Ibrahim Didi, 19, 24, 214-6, 217, 221, 228, 240-1, 262
Ibrahim Iskander II, 230, 242, 252-3
Ibrahim Nur-ud-din, 16, 214
Ievers, Robert Wilson, 10, 12, 15, 26, 35, 36, 38, 39-41, 49, 50, 54-5, 57, 66, 69, 100, 120-1, 123, 135, 143, 155, 269, 270, 272
im Thurn, Sir Everard Ferdinand, 123, 215
Iskander Ibrahim I, 242, 258
Ismail Didi, 217, 218, 222, 223, 224, 226, 245

Jaya Bahu I, 145, 161, 163
Joseph, Gerard Abraham, 207

Kasyapa I, 83, 84, 128, 146
Kasyapa IV, 146, 147, 159
Kasyapa V, 45, 130, 147, 156, 159
Keith, Arthur Berriedale 152, 154-5, 156-7, 163-4, 196
Krishna Sastri, 145, 205

Lambert, Lourdette, née Bell, daughter of H.C.P.Bell, 202-4
Lawton, Joseph, 31-2, 36
Liesching, Louis Frederick, 31, 36-7
Longden, Sir James Robert, 19
Longhurst, Arthur Henry, 165, 194
Loutfi, Mohamed Ibrahim, 248

McCallum, Sir Henry Edward, 124-5, 154, 168, 170-1, 195-8
Macdonell, Arthur Anthony, 152, 154, 196
Maha Sena, 73, 148
Mahinda IV 128, 152-3, 156, 158, 159
Manning, Sir William, 163, 216
Marshall, Sir John, 195, 207
Moggallana, 84
Muhammed Didi, 214-5
Muhammad Amin Didi, 9, 12, 221, 244, 248, 249-250, 251
Muhammad Imad-ud-din IV, 16, 18, 249
Muhammad Imad-ud-din VI, 214, 258
Muhammad Mu'in-ud-din, 216, 249
Muhammad Shams-ud-din III, 16, 214, 215, 216, 217, 220-1, 222-4, 226-8, 233

Muhammad-ul-Adil, 216
Muller, Edward, 14, 20, 26, 34-5, 141, 143, 148, 149, 155, 156
Murray, Alexander, 13, 38, 39, 54, 57, 86-7, 96, 113
Muzaffar, Muhammad Imad-ud-din II, 258

Naranwita Sumarasara Unnanse, 35-6, 109
Nell, Andreas, 261, 266
Nevill, Hugh, 55, 142, 148, 269
Nissanka Malla, 29, 134, 159-61, 164, 174, 177, 211
Noel-Walker, Sir Edward, 40-1, 49, 58, 119, 215

Oertel, Frederick Oscar, 112-6, 126

Parakrama Bahu I, 45, 70, 89, 134, 148, 159, 160, 161, 174-5, 184, 189, 211, 258, 259
Parakrama Bahu II, 185, 211, 265
Parakrama Bahu VI, 46, 209
Paranavitana, Senaret, 35, 94, 98, 99-100, 108, 135, 142-3, 147, 164-6, 211, 264-5, 272
Parker, Henry, 14-5, 134, 147-8, 159, 264-5
Perera, A.J.Will, 267
Perera, D.A.L., 51, 86, 89-90, 95-6, 101, 125, 135, 136, 191, 198, 201, 207, 212-3
Perera, P.G., 191, 207
Petrie, W.M.Flinders, 61, 196, 199
Pieris, Paulus Edward, 208-9
Poynter, Henrietta Mary, grand-daughter of Robert Bell, 2-5
Prematilleke, P.Leelananda, 136-7
Price, Ferdinand Hamlin, 27, 42, 43, 47
Prideaux, Arthur Ashburner, son-in-law of H.C.P.Bell, 167, 170, 171, 227
Prideaux, Arthur Guyon, grandson of H.C.P.Bell, 167, 172, 259
Prideaux, Iris Renée, grand-daughter of H.C.P.Bell, 167, 172, 255-6
Prideaux, Laura Sabine, grand-daughter of H.C.P.Bell, 167, 172, 255-6
Prideaux, Renée Isabel, née Bell, daughter of H.C.P.Bell, 42, 87, 167, 171, 227, 248
Purvis, Charles Alexander, godfather of H.C.P.Bell, 6, 167

Pyrard de Laval, François, 10, 17, 22-4, 213, 239, 241-2, 245

Renton, A.V., 86
Rhys Davids, Thomas William, 37, 84, 98, 142
Ridgeway, Sir Joseph West, 54, 100-1, 111-2, 114, 122, 168, 214, 215
Ridout, John Bertram Mais, 57, 67
Robertson, John William, 141
Robins, Mrs Lawson, 218-9, 220
Robinson, Sir Hercules George Robert, 26, 30, 36, 37
Rosset, C.R., 24, 233, 258, 262
Rost, Reinhold, 32, 34, 118
Rothwell, Arthur, 139, 193-4

Senaveratne, Dr. A.F., 251, 259
Senaveratne, John M., 205, 259
Siriwadhana, A.P. 52, 144, 145, 162
Smither, James G., 31, 38, 129, 270
Still, John, career, 53, 121-2, 125, 171-2, 195, 200; work, 99, 105, 122, 123, 124, 128, 143, 145, 175, 260; writings, 59-60, 78-9, 82, 122, 123-4, 134-5, 147, 259, 274-5
Stubbs, R.E., 196, 199, 202
Sundhara, Queen, 145, 157, 161-3, 213
Swettenham, James Alexander, 25, 27-8
Sydenham, Thomas, 3, 4

Tippoo Sultan, 2-3
Trefusis, Robert, 216, 222
Trimen, Henry, 262

Vijaya Bahu I, 141, 145, 161-2
Vijaya Bahu VI, 209
Vikrama Bahu I, 145, 161-3
Vossen, Father, 1, 8, 252-4, 270

Wattagamini Abhaya, 40, 159
Wickramasuriya, A.T.G.A., 72, 202-3, 270-1
Wickremasinghe, Don Martino de Zilva, relations with Bell, 124, 150, 152-3, 156, 163, 164, 196, 269; tributes to him, 53, 151, 153, 156, 164, 165-6; work in Ceylon, 23, 27, 52-3, 64, 65, 69-71, 77, 151; work in Europe, 34, 120, 149, 151-7, 164-5; writings, 14, 62, 144-5, 147, 149, 150, 151-3, 155-7, 158-60, 162-4
Wijeyekoon, Abraham Charles Gerard, 151, 165, 255, 266, 267
Wijeyekoon, G., 85-6
Willey, Arthur, 260
Williams, A.E., 36, 139

Yule, Colonel Sir Henry, 6, 18, 21-3
Yusuf Shams-ud-din, Shaik of Tabriz, 17, 216, 226, 232

MAPS

CEYLON

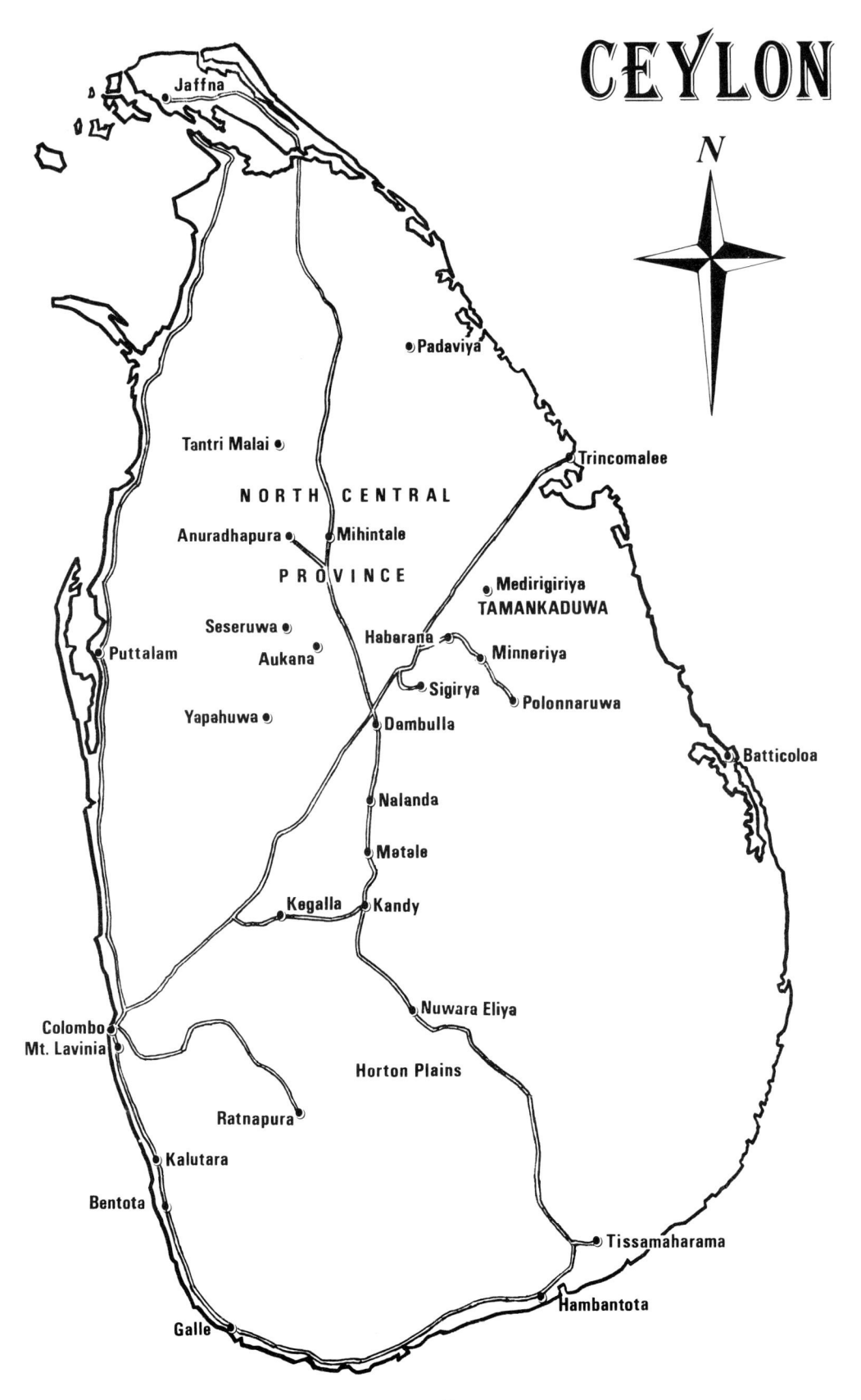

Tisa Wewa

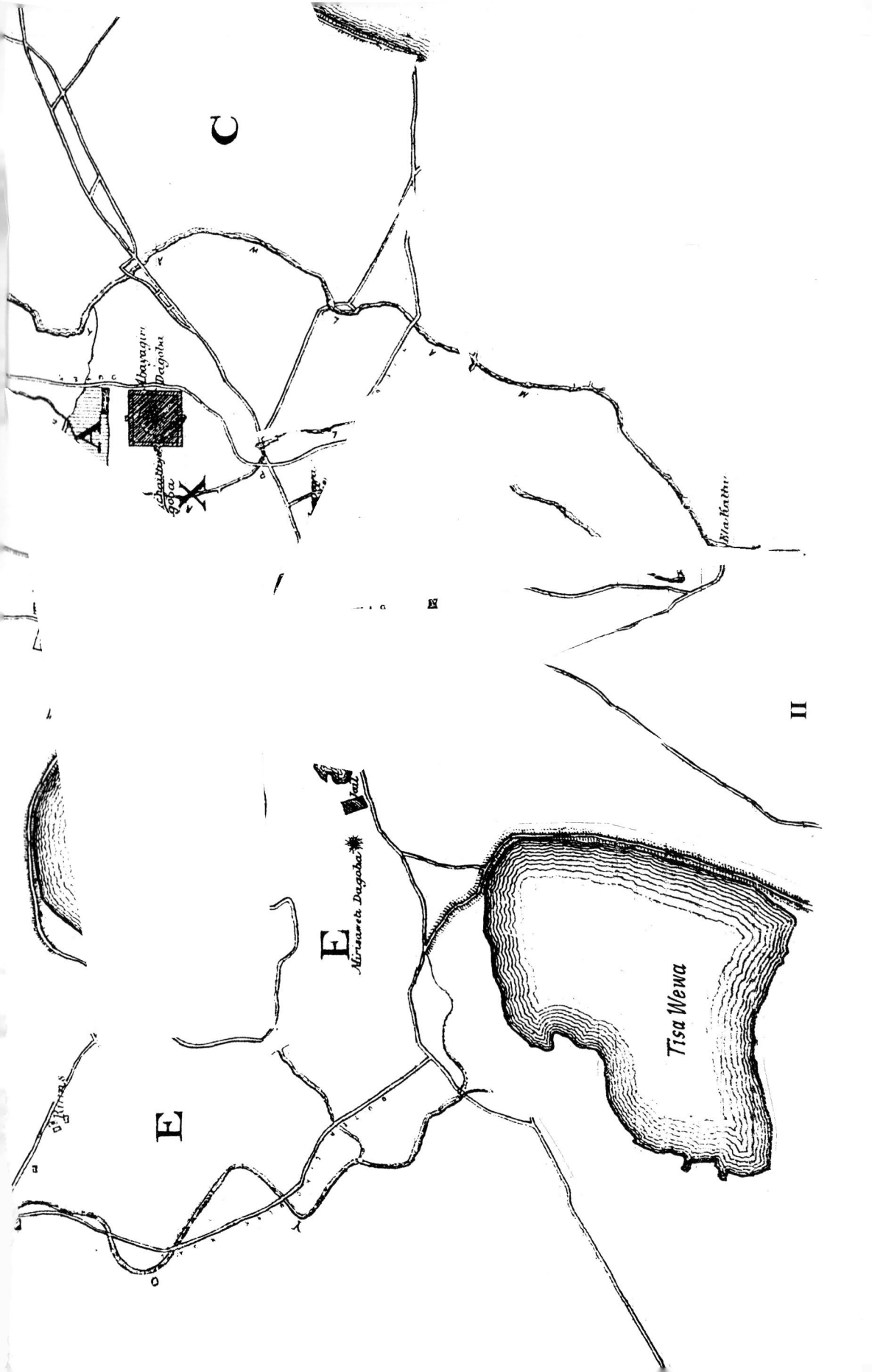

Mirisavti Dagoba

Jayagiri Dagoba

ANURADHAPURA

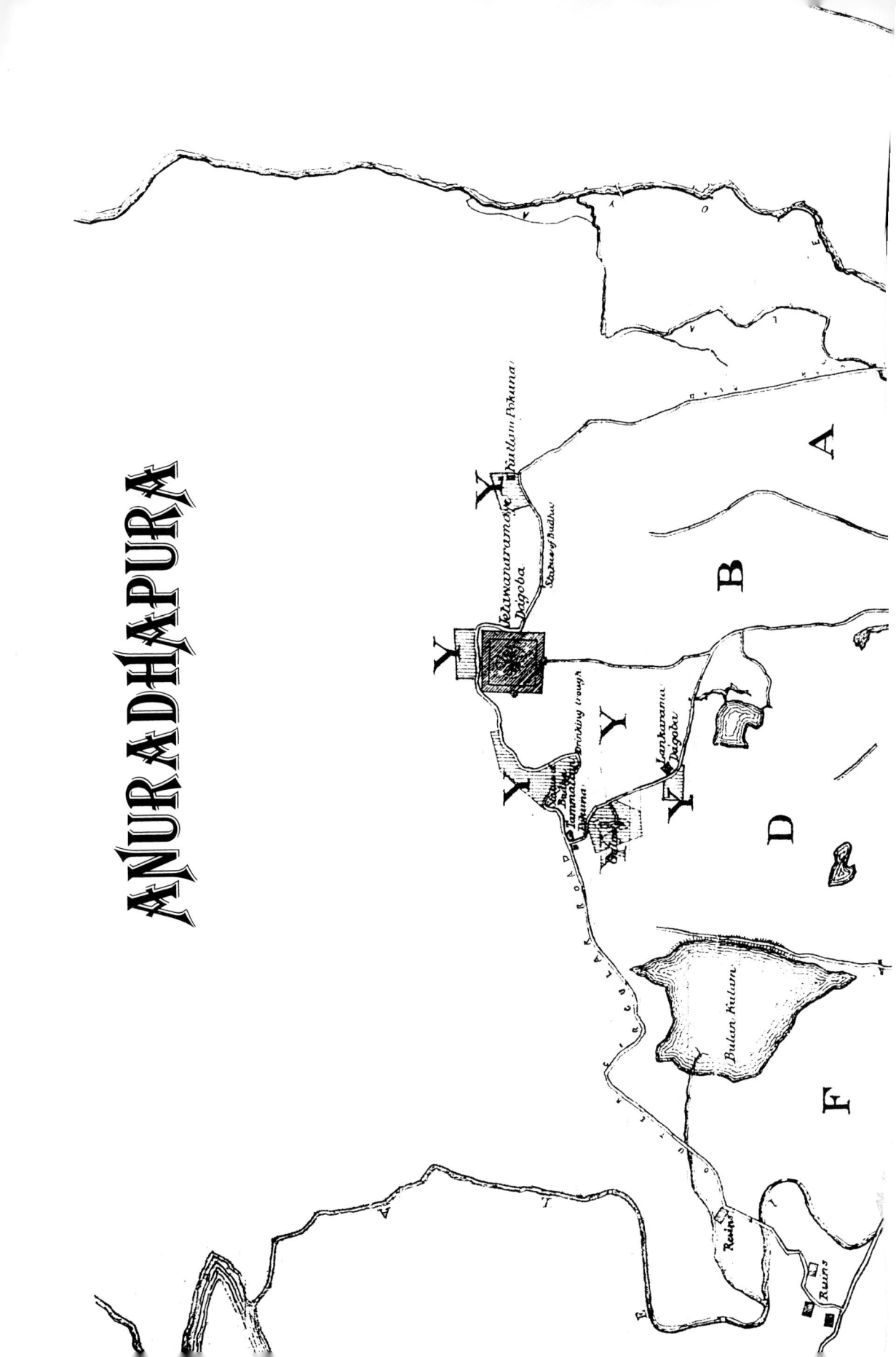

SIGIRIYA

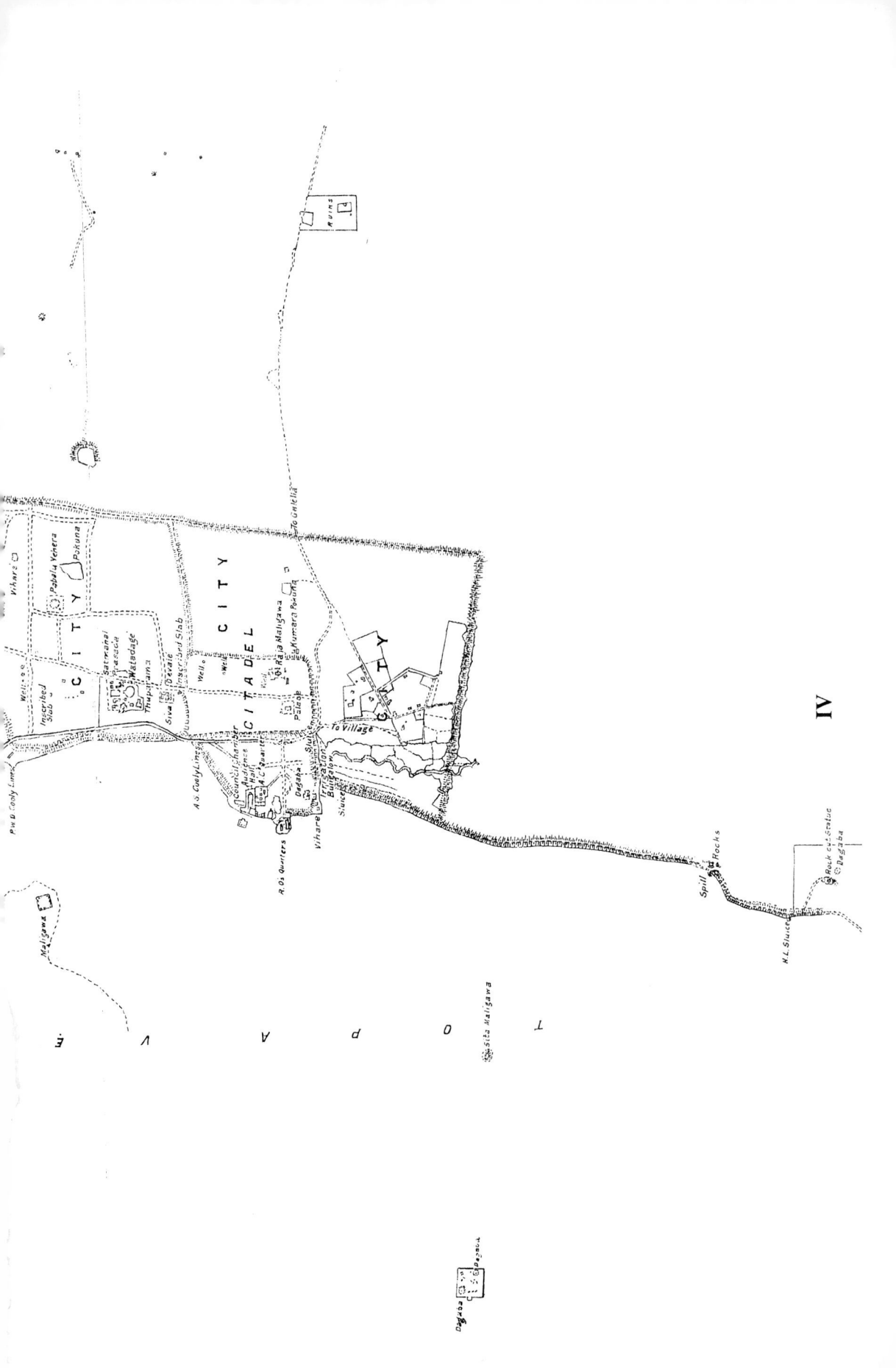

IV

POLONNARUWA

SOUTHERN INDIA & CEYLON WITH THE MALDIVE & LAKKADIVE ISLANDS

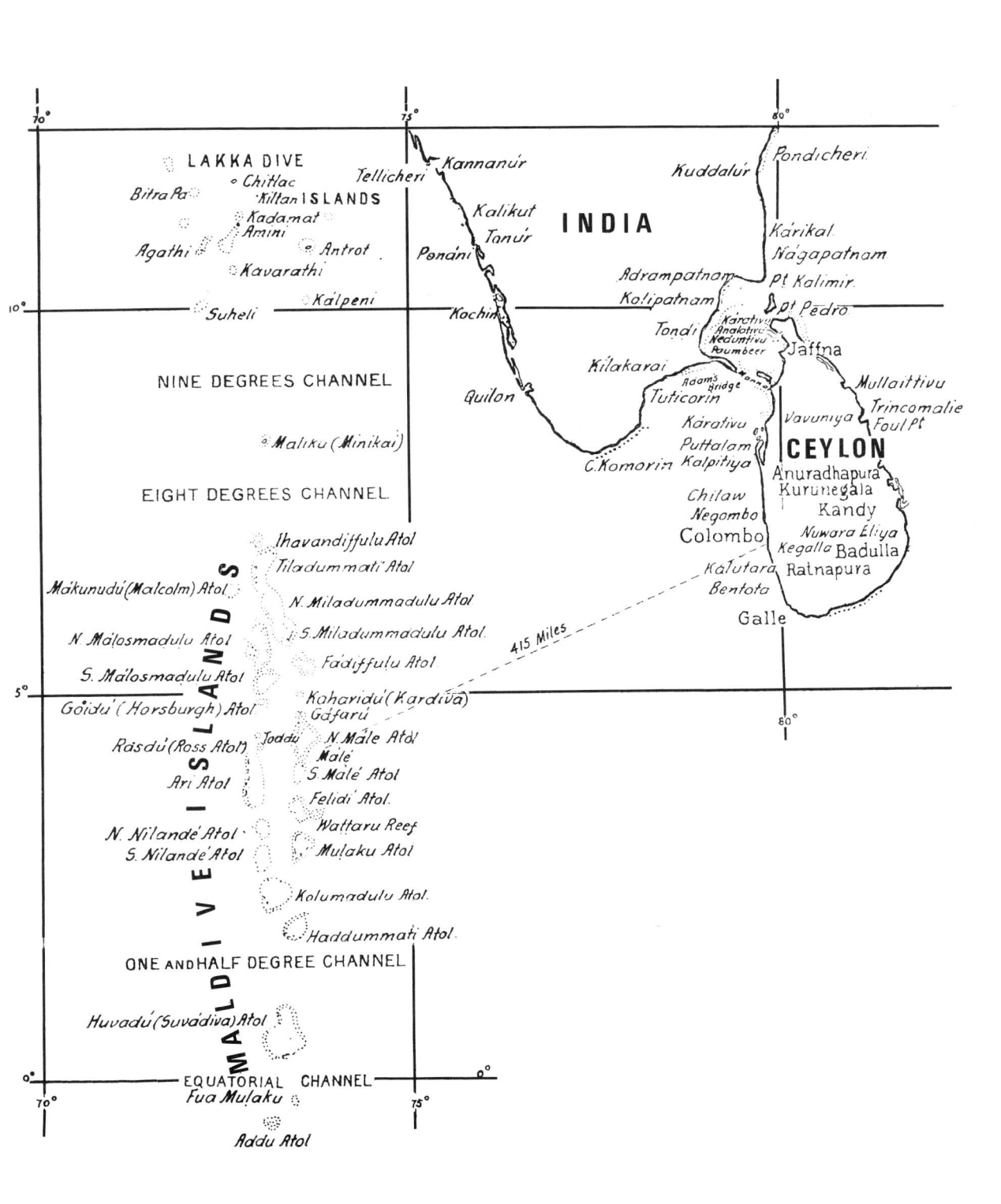